
$\bar{p}$	Average proportion or fraction defective
$100p$	Percent defective
$p_{0.95}, p_{0.05}$	Lot or process quality related to OC curves
R	Range
R_0	Standard or reference value, central line
$\bar{R}$	Average of ranges
Q_u, Q_L	Quality indexes for U and L in variables sampling plan
q	Proportion or fraction good $(1 - p)$
SkSP	Skip-lot sampling plan
$s(\sigma)$	Sample standard deviation (population)
$s^2(\sigma^2)$	Sample variance (population)
s_0	Standard or reference value
s_R	Sample standard deviation of ranges
s_p	Sample standard deviation of proportions
$s_{\bar{x}}$	Sample standard deviation of averages
$\bar{s}$	Average sample standard deviation
U	Upper specification limit
UCL	Upper control limit
URL	Upper reject limit
u	Count per unit
u_0	Standard or reference value, central line
$\bar{u}$	Average count per unit
w	Weight
X_i	Observed value
$\bar{X}(\mu)$	Sample average or average (population mean)
$\bar{X}_0$	Standard or reference value, central line
$\bar{\bar{X}}$	Average of averages or grand average
Z	Standardized normal value
α	Producer's risk, Type I error
β	Consumer's risk, Type II error
λ	Failure rate
μ	See $\bar{X}$
$\sum$	"Sum of"
σ	See s
θ	Mean time to failure

QUALITY CONTROL
Second Edition

Dale H. Besterfield, Ph.D., P.E.
Professor
Department of Technology
College of Engineering and Technology
Southern Illinois University

Prentice-Hall, Englewood Cliffs, New Jersey 07632

Library of Congress Cataloging-in-Publication Data

BESTERFIELD, DALE H.
Quality control.

Bibliography
Includes index.
1. Quality control. I. Title.
TS156.B47 1985 658.5′62 85–25573
ISBN 0–13–745258–6

Editorial/production supervision
and interior design: *Theresa A. Soler*
Cover design: *Joe Curcio*
Manufacturing buyer: *Rhett Conklin*

Printed in the United States of America

10 9 8 7 6

ISBN 0-13-745258-6 025

PRENTICE-HALL INTERNATIONAL (UK) LIMITED, *London*
PRENTICE-HALL OF AUSTRALIA PTY. LIMITED, *Sydney*
PRENTICE-HALL OF CANADA INC., *Toronto*
PRENTICE-HALL HISPANOAMERICANA, S.A., *Mexico*
PRENTICE-HALL OF INDIA PRIVATE LIMITED, *New Delhi*
PRENTICE-HALL OF JAPAN, INC., *Tokyo*
PRENTICE-HALL OF SOUTHEAST ASIA PTE. LTD., *Singapore*
EDITORA PRENTICE-HALL DO BRASIL, LTDA., *Rio de Janeiro*
WHITEHALL BOOKS LIMITED, *Wellington, New Zealand*

To my Parents
and
My Wife, Helen

CONTENTS

9 QUALITY COSTS 299

10 PRODUCT LIABILITY 313

11 COMPUTERS AND QUALITY CONTROL 328

SELECTED BIBLIOGRAPHY 339

APPENDIX 340

ANSWERS TO SELECTED PROBLEMS 351

INDEX 355

PREFACE

This book provides a fundamental, yet comprehensive, coverage of quality control concepts. A practical state-of-the-art approach is stressed throughout. Sufficient theory is presented to ensure that the reader has a sound understanding of the basic principles of quality control. The use of probability and statistical techniques is reduced to simple mathematics or is developed in the form of tables and charts.

The book has served the instructional needs of technology students in technical institutes, community colleges, and universities. It has also been used by undergraduate and graduate business students. Professional organizations and industrial corporations have found the book an excellent training manual for instruction of manufacturing, quality, inspection, marketing, purchasing, and product design personnel.

The book begins with an introductory chapter about quality responsibility. This is followed by a detailed description of the control chart method for variables and attributes. A subsequent group of chapters describes acceptance sampling and standard sampling plans. The final chapters cover the topics of reliability, quality costs, product liability, and computer utilization.

This second edition includes a complete updating of all material and an expanded treatment of most topics. New material includes skewness and kurtosis, tests for normality, process capability, capability index, run charts, charts based on specifications, average sample number, average total inspection, and skip-lot sampling. Simple computer programs, as well as programming exercises, have been included at the end of many chapters.

A major change has been in the use of symbols. The latest change in the standards uses the subscript zero in preference to the prime notation for the standard or reference values. Also, the sample standard deviation is now defined using $n - 1$ in the denominator, which has resulted in changes in Table B and the standard deviation control chart.

More example problems have been added, especially in the chapter on probability. The number of practice problems has also been increased and answers to selected problems have been included. To aid the student and the practitioner, a glossary of symbols has been included on the inside front cover. In addition, a bibliography has been added as a basic reference library to supplement the information in the textbook.

I am indebted to the publishers and authors who have given permission to reproduce their charts, graphs, and tables. Professors, practitioners, and students have been most helpful in pointing out the need for further clarification and additional material in the first edition. Finally, I am indebted to Mrs. Shirley Carlisle, who typed both the original manuscript and the manuscript for this revised edition.

Dale H. Besterfield

1 INTRODUCTION TO QUALITY

INTRODUCTION

Definitions

When the expression "quality product" is used, we usually think in terms of an excellent product or service that fulfills our expectations. These expectations are based on "fitness for use" and the selling price of the product. For example, a customer expects a different performance from a plain steel washer than from a chrome-plated steel washer because the intended use and the selling price are different.

Quality is all of the features and characteristics of a product or service that contribute to the satisfaction of a customer's needs. These needs involve price, safety, availability, maintainability, reliability, and usability. Price is easily defined by some monetary unit such as dollars. The other needs are defined by translating the features and characteristics for the manufacture of a product or the delivery of a service into specifications. Conformance of the product or service to these specifications is measurable and provides a quantifiable definition of quality. Therefore, simply stated, *quality is conformance to specifications and the degree of conformance is the measure of quality.* If the specifications do not satisfy the customer needs (fitness for use), they should be changed. *Quality control* is the use of techniques and activities to achieve, sustain, and improve the quality of a product or service. It involves integrating the following related techniques and activities:

1. *Specifications* of what is needed
2. *Design* of the product or service to meet the specifications
3. *Production* or *installation* to meet the full intent of the specifications
4. *Inspection* to determine conformance to specifications

5. *Review of usage* to provide information for the revision of specifications if needed

Utilization of these activities provides the customer with the best product or service at the lowest cost. The aim should be continued quality improvement.

Statistical quality control is a branch of quality control. It is the collection, analysis, and interpretation of data for use in quality control activities. While much of this textbook emphasizes the statistical approach to quality control, this is only a part of the total picture. A number of different techniques are needed.

All the actions necessary to provide adequate confidence that a product or service will satisfy consumer needs is called *quality assurance*. It involves making sure that quality is what it should be. This includes a continuing evaluation of adequacy and effectiveness with a view to having timely corrective measures and feedback initiated where necessary.

There is a distinct difference between quality control and quality assurance. Quality control is involved with the activities of specification, design, production or installation, inspection, and review of usage. These activities are the responsibility of the functional areas shown in Figure 1-1. Quality assurance is involved with these activities as well as the entire quality system. The generic elements of a quality system are given later in the chapter.

Historical Review

The history of quality control is undoubtedly as old as industry itself. During the Middle Ages the maintenance of quality was to a large extent controlled by the long periods of training required by the guilds. This training instilled in workers pride for the workmanship in a product.

The concept of specialization of labor was introduced during the Industrial Revolution. As a result, a worker no longer made the entire product, only a portion. This change brought about a decline in workmanship. Because most products manufactured during that early period were not complicated, quality was not greatly affected. As products became more complicated and jobs more specialized, it became necessary to inspect products after manufacture.

In 1924, W. A. Shewhart of Bell Telephone Laboratories developed a statistical chart for the control of product variables. This is considered to be the beginning of statistical quality control. Later in the same decade, H. F. Dodge and H. G. Romig, both of Bell Telephone Laboratories, developed the area of acceptance sampling as a substitute for 100% inspection. Recognition of the value of statistical quality control became apparent by 1942. Unfortunately, American managers failed to recognize its value.

In 1946, the American Society for Quality Control was formed. This organization, through its publications, conferences, and training sessions, has promoted the use of quality control for all types of production and service.

In 1950, W. Edwards Deming gave a series of lectures on statistical methods to Japanese engineers and on quality responsibility to top management. Joseph

M. Juran made his first trip to Japan in 1954 and further emphasized management's responsibility to achieve quality. Using these concepts the Japanese set the quality standards for the rest of the world to follow.

In 1960 the first quality control circles were formed for the purpose of quality improvement. Simple statistical techniques were learned and applied by Japanese workers.

By the late 1970s and early 1980s, American managers were making frequent trips to Japan to learn about the Japanese miracle. These trips were really not necessary—they could have read the writings of Deming and Juran. Nevertheless, a quality renaissance began to occur in America's products and services.

One American company, American Telephone and Telegraph, continued to utilize the statistical quality control concepts that were developed in their laboratory. It is the author's opinion that the outstanding quality of the American telephone and telephone service are the result of statistical quality control. These are the concepts emphasized in this textbook.

Metric System

In 1960, the International Committee of Weights and Measures revised the metric system. This revision is the International System of Units (SI),[1] which has the following base units:

Length—meter (m)
Mass—kilogram (kg)
Time—second (s)
Electrical current—ampere (A)
Thermodynamic temperature—kelvin (K)
Amount of matter—mole (mol)
Luminous intensity—candela (cd)

This textbook uses the metric system of units with U. S. units given in parentheses. Commonly used conversion factors are given in Table E of the Appendix.

RESPONSIBILITY FOR QUALITY

Departments Responsible

Quality is not the responsibility of any one person or department; it is everyone's job. It includes the assembly-line worker, the typist, the purchasing agent, and the president of the company. The responsibility for quality begins when

[1]Copies may be purchased from the Superintendent of Documents, Government Printing Office, Washington, D.C. 20402. (Order by SD Catalog No. C13.10: 330/3.)

marketing determines the customer's quality requirements and continues until the product is received by a satisfied customer.

The responsibility for quality is delegated to the various departments with the authority to make quality decisions. In addition, a method of accountability, such as cost, error rate, or number defective, is included with that responsibility and authority. The departments responsible for quality control are shown in Figure 1-1. They are: marketing, product engineering, purchasing, manufacturing engineering, manufacturing, inspection and test, packaging and shipping, and product service. Figure 1-1 is a closed loop with the customer at the top and the departments in the proper sequence in the loop. Since quality assurance does not have direct responsibility for quality, it is not included in the closed loop of the figure.

The information in this section pertains to a manufactured item; however, the concepts can be adapted to a service.

Marketing

Marketing helps to evaluate the level of product quality that the customer wants, needs, and is willing to pay for. In addition, marketing provides the customer with product-quality data and helps to determine quality requirements.

A certain amount of marketing information is readily available to perform this function. Information concerning customer dissatisfaction is provided by customer complaints, sales representative reports, product service, and product

Figure 1-1 Departments responsible for quality

liability cases. The comparison of sales volume with the economy as a whole is a good predictor of customer opinion of product quality. A detailed analysis of spare-part sales can locate potential quality problems. Useful market quality information is also provided by government reports on consumer product safety and independent laboratory reports on quality.

When information is not readily available, there are four methods which can be developed to obtain the desired product quality data:

1. Visit or observe the customer to determine the conditions of product use and the problems of the user.
2. Establish a realistic testing laboratory such as an automotive test track.
3. Conduct a controlled market test.
4. Organize a dealer advisory panel.

Marketing evaluates all the data and determines the customer's quality requirements.

Product Engineering

Product engineering translates the customer's quality requirements into operating characteristics, exact specifications, and appropriate tolerances for a new product or revision of a well-established product. The simplest and least costly design that will meet the customer's requirements is the best design. As the complexity of the product increases, the quality and reliability decreases.

Whenever possible, product engineering should utilize proven designs and standard components. In this regard, industry and government standards are used when applicable.

Tolerance is the permissible variation in the size of the quality characteristic, and the selection of tolerances has a dual effect on quality. As tolerances are tightened, a better product results; however, the manufacturing and quality costs may increase. Ideally, tolerances should be determined scientifically by balancing the precision desired with the cost to achieve that precision. Since there are too many quality characteristics for scientific determination, many tolerances are set using standard dimensioning and tolerancing systems. Critical tolerances should be established based on the process capability as determined by a control chart.

The product designer determines the materials to be used in the product. Material quality is based on written specifications, which include physical characteristics, reliability, acceptance criteria, and packaging.

In addition to the functional aspect, a quality product is one that can be used safely. It is also one that can be repaired or maintained easily.

After the design review team (which includes a manufacturing representative) approves the product for manufacturing, the final quality requirements are distributed. Quality is designed into the product before it is released to manufacturing.

Purchasing

Using the quality requirements established by product engineering, purchasing has the responsibility of procuring quality materials and components. Purchases fall into four categories: standard materials, such as coiled steel and angle iron; standard hardware, such as fasteners and fittings; minor components, such as gears and diodes; and major components, which perform one of the primary functions of the product. The type of inspection will vary depending on the category of the purchase.

A particular raw material or component part may have a single vendor or multiple vendors. Single vendors as a source of supply are usually able to provide better quality at a lower price with better service. The concept of single vendor has been applied quite effectively in breweries, wherein the can or bottle manufacturer was located adjacent to the brewery. Multidivisional companies use the single-vendor technique and can control quality in a manner similar to the control between departments within a plant. The disadvantage of a single vendor is the potential for a material shortage that may result due to natural causes such as fire, earthquake, or flood or due to unnatural causes such as equipment breakdowns, labor problems, or financial difficulties.

To determine if a vendor is capable of supplying quality materials and components, a vendor quality survey is conducted by visiting the vendor's plant. The facilities are observed, the quality control procedures studied, and pertinent data collected. From this information a reasonable decision can be made regarding the ability of the vendor to provide quality materials and components. Once a vendor is a regular supplier, other techniques of evaluation are available.

There are a number of different methods to obtain proof of conformance to quality standards. For small quantities, the purchasing department will frequently rely on the vendor. The inspection of incoming materials and components is one of the most common methods for proof of conformance. Source inspection is identical to incoming inspection except that the inspection is conducted in the vendor's plant. Proof of conformance can also be obtained by inspection of duplicate samples which are received by purchasing prior to the arrival of the shipment. Vendor surveillance is a method of controlling the quality in the vendor's plant by means of an acceptable plan, and proof, such as inspection records, that the plan is followed.

A vendor quality rating system can be used to evaluate the performance of all vendors. Factors such as rejected lots, scrap and rework costs, or complaint information can be used for the evaluation.

To improve the quality of purchased materials and components, two-way communication between the vendor and purchasing is a necessity. Both positive and negative feedback should be given to the vendor.

Purchasing should be concerned with the total cost and not price. For example, vendor A has a lower price than vendor B; however, the cost to utilize vendor A's material is so much greater than vendor B's that the total cost is greater.

Manufacturing Engineering

Manufacturing engineering has the responsibility to develop processes and procedures that will produce a quality product. This responsibility is achieved by specific activities, which include process selection and development, production planning, and support activities.

A product design review is conducted in order to anticipate quality problems. Quality problems are frequently related to specifications. When process capability information indicates that a tolerance is too tight for satisfactory producibility, there are five options: purchase new equipment, revise the tolerance, improve the process, revise the design, or sort out the defective product during manufacturing.

Process selection and development is concerned with cost, quality, implementation time, and efficiency. One of the basic techniques of the manufacturing engineer is the process capability study, which determines the ability of a process to meet specifications. Process capability information provides data for make-or-buy decisions, equipment purchases, and selection of process routes.

The sequence of operations is developed to minimize quality difficulties such as the handling of fragile products and the location of precision operations in the sequence. Methods study is used to determine the best way of performing either a production operation or an inspection operation.

Additional manufacturing engineering responsibilities include the design of equipment, the design of inspection devices, and the maintenance of the production equipment.

Manufacturing

Manufacturing has the responsibility to produce quality products. Quality cannot be inspected into a product; it must be built into the product.

The first-line supervisor is the key to the manufacture of a quality product. Since the first-line supervisor is considered by operating personnel to represent management, his ability to convey quality expectations is critical for good employee relations. A first-line supervisor who is enthusiastic in his commitment to quality can motivate the employees to build quality into each and every part and, thus, into the final unit. It is the supervisor's responsibility to provide the employee with the proper tools for the job, to provide instructions in the method of performing the job and the quality expectations of the job, and to provide information on when expectations are achieved and when they are not achieved.

In order for the operator to know what is expected, training sessions on quality should be given periodically. These training sessions reinforce management's commitment to a quality product. During the training sessions, time can be allocated to presentations by field personnel, to discussions concerning the sources of quality variations, to methods of improving quality, and so on. The primary objective of the sessions is to develop an attitude of "quality mindedness" and an environment where two-way, nonpunitive communications can flourish.

According to Deming, only 15% of the quality problems can be attributed to operating personnel—the balance is due to the rest of the system. Process control charts effectively measure the quality performance of operators and are an invaluable tool for quality improvement.

Inspection and Test

Inspection and test has the responsibility to appraise the quality of purchased and manufactured items and to report the results. The reports are used by other departments to take corrective action when needed. Inspection and test may be a department by itself, part of the manufacturing department, or part of the quality assurance department. It might also be located in both manufacturing and quality assurance.

Although inspection is done by representatives of the inspection and test department, it does not relieve manufacturing of their responsibility to produce a quality product and make their own inspections. In fact, with automated production, workers frequently have time to perform 100% inspection before and after an operation. One of the major problems with the inspection activity is the tendency to view the inspector as a "police person" who has the quality responsibility. This attitude can lead to an ineffective inspection activity and a deterioration of quality.

In order to perform the inspection activity, accurate measuring equipment is needed. Normally, this equipment is purchased; however, it may be necessary to design and build it in cooperation with manufacturing engineering. In either case the equipment must be maintained in a constant state of repair and calibration.

It is necessary to continually monitor the performance of inspectors. Indications are that certain defects are more difficult to find, that inspectors vary in their abilities, and that the defect level affects the number of defects reported. Samples of known composition should be used to evaluate and improve the inspector's performance.

The efficiency of the appraisal activity is a function of the inspection methods and procedures (number inspected, type of sampling, and inspection location). Cooperation from manufacturing engineering, inspection and test, manufacturing, and quality assurance is necessary to maximize the inspector's performance.

Inspection and test should concentrate the majority of their efforts on statistical quality control which will lead to quality improvement. Passing the conforming items and discarding the nonconforming ones is *not* quality control. Quality cannot be inspected into a product or service. Dependency on mass inspection for quality control is in most cases a waste of effort, time, and money.

Packaging and Shipping

The packaging and shipping department has the responsibility to preserve and protect the quality of the product. Control of the product quality must extend beyond manufacturing to the distribution, installation, and use of the product. A dissatisfied customer is not concerned with where the defective condition occurred.

Quality specifications are needed for the protection of the product during transit by all types of common carrier: truck, rail, boat, and air. These specifications are needed for vibration, shock, and environmental conditions such as temperature, moisture, and dust. Additional specifications are needed in regard to the handling of the product during loading, unloading, and warehousing. Occasionally, it is necessary to change the product or process design to correct quality difficulties that occur during transit. In some companies, the responsibility for the design of the package is vested in product engineering rather than packaging and shipping.

Product storage, while awaiting further processing, sale, or use, presents additional quality problems. Specifications and procedures are necessary to ensure that the product is properly stored and promptly used to minimize deterioration and degradation.

Product Service

Product service has the responsibility to provide the customer with the means for fully realizing the intended function of the product during its expected life. This responsibility includes erection, maintenance, repair, and replacement-parts service. Products should be serviced quickly whenever they are improperly installed or fail during the warranty period. Prompt service can change a dissatisfied customer into a satisfied one.

Product service and marketing work closely with each other to determine the quality the customer wants, needs, and obtains.

Quality Assurance

The quality assurance or quality control department (the name is not important) *does not* have direct responsibility for quality. Therefore, it is not shown in Figure 1-1. It assists or supports the other departments as they carry out their quality control responsibilities.

Quality assurance *does* have the direct responsibility to continually evaluate the effectiveness of the total quality system. Generic elements of a total quality system are:

1. Policy, planning, and administration.
2. Design assurance and design change control.
3. Control of purchased material.
4. Production quality control.
5. User contact and field performance.
6. Corrective action.
7. Employee selection, training, and motivation.

Details of these seven elements are given in ANSI/ASQC Standard Z-1.15–1979, which is available from the American Society for Quality Control.

In summary, quality assurance determines the effectiveness of the quality system, appraises the current quality, determines quality problem areas or potential areas, and assists in the correction or minimization of these problem areas. The overall objective is the improvement of the product quality in cooperation with the responsible departments.

CHIEF EXECUTIVE OFFICER

The chief executive officer (CEO) of a plant has responsibility for each of the departments in the closed loop of Figure 1–1 and the quality assurance department. Therefore, the CEO has the ultimate responsibility for quality. The CEO must be involved directly in the quality effort. This activity requires a knowledge of quality control and direct involvement with the quality improvement program. Merely stating that quality is important is not sufficient.

Perhaps the best way for the CEO to be involved is to have some measure of his or her quality performance. Financial information can provide a long-term measure of quality performance. However, in the short term, it is not too difficult to make the financial data look good when in reality the product quality is deteriorating. Quality improvement requires a long-term financial commitment to people, programs, and equipment.

The CEO's quality performance can be effectively measured by a proportion (percent defective) chart which covers his area of responsibility, whether it be a plant or a corporation. If the percent defective is increasing or is constant, then simply stated, the CEO's performance is poor. If the percent defective is decreasing, the CEO's performance is good. This concept—measurement of quality performance—can be adapted for all managers, departments, and operating personnel. In conjunction with quality improvement goals, the proportion chart becomes a very effective technique for quality improvement.

2 FUNDAMENTALS OF STATISTICS

INTRODUCTION

Definition of Statistics

The word *statistics* has two generally accepted meanings:

1. A collection of quantitative data pertaining to any subject or group, especially when the data are systematically gathered and collated. Examples of this meaning are blood pressure statistics, statistics of a football game, employment statistics, and accident statistics, to name a few.
2. The science that deals with the collection, tabulation, analysis, interpretation, and presentation of quantitative data.

It is noted that the second meaning is broader than the first since it, too, is concerned with collection of data. The use of statistics in quality control deals with the second and broader meaning and involves the divisions of collection, tabulating, analyzing, interpreting, and presenting the quantitative data. Each division is dependent on the accuracy and completeness of the preceding one. Data may be collected by an inspector measuring the tensile strength of a plastic part or by a market researcher determining consumer color preferences. It may be tabulated by simple paper-and-pencil techniques or by the use of a computer. Analysis may involve a cursory visual examination or exhaustive calculations. The final results are interpreted and presented to assist in the making of decisions concerning quality.

There are two phases of statistics:

1. *Descriptive* or *deductive statistics*, which endeavors to describe and analyze a subject or group.

2. *Inductive statistics*, which endeavors to determine from a limited amount of data (sample) an important conclusion about a much larger amount of data (population). Since these conclusions or inferences cannot be stated with absolute certainty, the language of *probability* is often used.

This chapter covers the statistical fundamentals necessary to understand the subsequent quality control techniques. Fundamentals of probability are discussed in Chapter 4. An understanding of statistics is vital for an understanding of quality control and, for that matter, many other disciplines.

Collection of Data

Data may be collected by direct observation or indirectly through written or verbal questions. The latter technique is used extensively by market research personnel and public opinion pollsters. Data that are collected for quality control purposes are obtained by direct observation and are classified as either variables or attributes. *Variables* are those quality characteristics which are measurable, such as a weight measured in grams. *Attributes*, on the other hand, are those quality characteristics which are classified as either conforming or not conforming to specifications such as a "go/no go gage."

A variable that is capable of any degree of subdivision is referred to as *continuous*. The weight of a gray iron casting which can be measured as 11 kg, 11.33 kg, or 11.3398 kg (25 lb), depending on the accuracy of the measuring instrument, is an example of a continuous variable. Measurements such as meters (feet), liters (gallons), and pascals (pounds per square inch) are examples of continuous data. Variables that exhibit gaps are called *discrete*. The number of defective rivets in a travel trailer can be any whole number, such as 0, 3, 5, 10, 96, . . . ; however, there cannot be, say, 4.65 defective rivets in a particular trailer. In general, continuous data are measurable, while discrete data are countable.

Sometimes it is convenient for verbal or nonnumerical data to assume the nature of a variable. For example, the quality of the surface finish of a piece of furniture can be classified as poor, average, or good. The poor, average, or good classification can be replaced by the numerical values of 1, 2, or 3, respectively. In a similar manner, educational institutions assign to the letter grades of A, B, C, D, and E the numerical values of 4, 3, 2, 1, and 0, respectively, and use the numerical values as discrete variables for computational purposes.

While many quality characteristics are stated in terms of variables, there are many characteristics which must be stated as attributes. Frequently, those characteristics which are judged by visual observation are classified as attributes. The wire on an electric motor is either attached to the terminal or it is not; the words on this page are correctly spelled or they are incorrectly spelled; the switch is on or it is off; and the answer is right or it is wrong. The examples given in the previous sentence show conformance to a particular specification or nonconformance to that specification.

It is sometimes desirable for variables to be classified as attributes. Factory personnel are frequently interested in knowing if the product they are producing conforms to the specifications. For example, the numerical value for the weight of a package of sugar may not be as important as the information that the weight is within the prescribed limits. Therefore, the data, which are collected on the weight of the package of sugar, are reported as conforming or not conforming to specifications.

In collecting data the degree of accuracy of the figures is a function of the intended use of the data. For example, in collecting data on the life of light bulbs, it is acceptable to record 995.6 h; however, recording a value of 995.632 h is too accurate and unnecessary. Similarly, if a keyway specification has a lower limit of 9.52 mm (0.375 in.) and an upper limit of 9.58 mm (0.377 in.), data would be collected to the nearest 0.001 mm and rounded to the nearest 0.01 mm.

The rounding of data requires that certain conventions be followed. In rounding the numbers 0.9530, 0.9531, 0.9532, 0.9533, and 0.9534 to the nearest thousandth, the answer is 0.953, since all the numbers are closer to 0.953 than they are to 0.954. And in rounding the numbers 0.9535, 0.9536, 0.9537, 0.9538, and 0.9539, the answer is 0.954, since all the numbers are closer to 0.954 than to 0.953.

In working with numerical data, *significant figures* are very important. The significant figures of a number are the accurate digits exclusive of any leading zeros needed to locate the decimal point. For example, the number 3.69 has three significant figures; 36.900 has five significant figures; 2700 has four significant figures; 22.0365 has six significant figures; and 0.00270 has three significant figures. Trailing zeros are counted as being significant, while leading zeros are not. The rule gives some difficulty when working with whole numbers since the number 300 can have one, two, or three significant figures. This difficulty can be eliminated by the use of scientific notation. Therefore, $3. \times 10^2$ has one significant figure, 3.0×10^2 has two significant figures, and 3.00×10^2 has three significant figures. Numbers that are associated with counting have an unlimited number of significant figures, and the counting number 65 can be written as 65 or 65.000. . . .

When performing the mathematical operations of multiplication, division, and exponentiation, the answer has the same number of significant figures as the number with the fewest significant figures. The following examples will help to clarify this rule:

$$\sqrt{81.9} = 9.05$$

$$6.59 \times 2.3 = 15$$

$$32.65 \div 24 = 1.4 \qquad \text{(24 is not a counting number)}$$

$$32.65 \div 24 = 1.360 \qquad \text{(24 is a counting number with a value of 24.00. . .)}$$

When performing the mathematical operations of addition and subtraction, the final answer can have no more significant figures after the decimal point than the number with the fewest significant figures after the decimal point. In cases involving numbers without decimal points, the final answer has no more significant figures than the number with the fewest significant figures. Examples to clarify this rule are as follows:

$$38.26 - 6 = 32 \quad \text{(6 is not a counting number)}$$

$$38.26 - 6 = 32.26 \quad \text{(6 is a counting number)}$$

$$38.26 - 6.1 = 32.2 \quad \text{(answer was rounded from 32.16)}$$

$$8.1 \times 10^3 - 1232 = 6.9 \times 10^3 \quad \text{(fewest significant figures are two)}$$

$$8.100 \times 10^3 - 1232 = 6868 \quad \text{(fewest significant figures are four)}$$

Utilization of the rules above will avoid discrepancies in answers among quality control personnel; however, some judgment may sometimes be required. In any case, the final answer can be no more accurate than the incoming data.

Describing the Data

In industry, business, and government the mass of data that have been collected is voluminous. Even one item, such as the number of defective smoke alarms in 35 lots of 1000 per lot, can represent such a mass of data that it can be more confusing than helpful. Consider the data shown in Table 2-1. Clearly these data, in this form, are difficult to use and are not effective in describing the data's characteristics. Some means of summarizing the data is needed to show what value or values the data tend to cluster about and how the data are dispersed or spread out. Two techniques are available to accomplish this summarization of data—graphical and analytical.

The graphical technique is a plot or picture of a *frequency distribution*, which is a summarization of how the data points (observations) occur within each subdivision of observed values or groups of observed values. Analytical techniques summarize data by computing a *measure of central tendency* and a *measure*

TABLE 2-1 Number of Defective Smoke Alarms in 35 Lots of 1000 per Lot

0	1	3	0	0
0	5	4	1	2
1	0	2	0	0
2	1	1	1	2
0	4	0	3	1
0	3	4	0	0
1	3	0	1	2

of the dispersion. Sometimes both the graphical and analytical techniques are used.

These techniques will be described in the subsequent sections of this chapter.

FREQUENCY DISTRIBUTION

Ungrouped Data

Ungrouped data comprise a listing of the observed values, while grouped data represent a lumping together of the observed values. The data can be discrete, as they are in this section, or continuous, as in the next section.

Because unorganized data are virtually meaningless, a method of processing the data is necessary. Table 2-1 will be used to illustrate the concept. An analyst reviewing the information as given in this table would have difficulty comprehending the meaning of the data. A much better understanding can be obtained by tallying the frequency of each value, as shown in Table 2-2.

TABLE 2-2 Tally of Number of Defective Smoke Alarms

Number Defective	*Tabulation*	*Frequency*
0	~~1111~~ ~~1111~~ 111	13
1	~~1111~~ 1111	9
2	~~1111~~	5
3	1111	4
4	111	3
5	1	1

The first step is to establish an *array*, which is an arrangement of raw numerical data in ascending or descending order of magnitude. An array of ascending order is shown in the first column of Table 2-2. The next step is to tabulate the frequency of each value in Table 2-1 by placing a tally mark under the tabulation column and in the appropriate row of Table 2-2. Start with the numbers 0, 0, 1, 2, . . . of Table 2-1 and continue placing tally marks until all the data have been tabulated. The last column of Table 2-2, "Frequency," is the numerical value for the number of tallies.

Analysis of Table 2-2 shows that one can visualize the distribution of the data. If the "Tabulation" column is eliminated, the resulting table is classified as a *frequency distribution*, which is an arrangement of data to show the frequency of values in each category.

The frequency distribution is a useful method of visualizing data and is a basic statistical concept. To think of a set of numbers as having some type of distribution is fundamental for solving quality control problems. There are different types of frequency distributions, and the type of distribution will indicate the problem-solving approach.

Frequency distributions are presented in graphical form when greater visual clarity is desired. There are a number of different ways to present the frequency distribution.

A *histogram* consists of a set of rectangles that represent the frequency in each category. Figure 2-1a is a histogram for the data in Table 2-2. Since this is a discrete variable, a vertical line in place of a rectangle would have been theoretically correct (see Figure 2-4). However, the rectangle is commonly used.

Another type of graphic representation is the relative frequency distribution. Relative, in this sense, means the proportion or fraction of the total. Relative frequency is calculated by dividing the frequency for each data value (in this case, number defective) by the total, which is the sum of the frequencies for each data value. These calculations are shown in the third column of Table 2-3. Graphical representation is shown in Figure 2-1b. Relative frequency has the advantage of a reference. For example, the proportion that is 2 defective is 0.14 or 14%.

Cumulative frequency is calculated by adding the frequency of each data value to the sum of the frequencies for the previous data values. As shown in the fourth column of Table 2-3, the cumulative frequency for 0 defective is 0 + 13 = 13; for 1 defective, 13 + 9 = 22; for 2 defective, 22 + 5; and so on. Cumulative frequency is the number of data points equal to or less than a data value. For example, the number of lots that have 2 or less defectives is 27. Graphic representation is shown in Figure 2-1c.

Relative cumulative frequency is calculated by dividing the cumulative frequency for each data value by the total. These calculations are shown in the fifth column of Table 2-3, and the graphical representation is shown in Figure 2-1d. The graph shows that the proportion of the smoke alarm lots that have 2 or fewer defectives is 0.77 or 77%.

The foregoing example is limited to a discrete variable with six values. Although this example is sufficient for a basic introduction to the frequency distribution concept, it does not provide a thorough knowledge of the subject.

TABLE 2-3 Different Frequency Distributions of Data Given in Table 2-1

Number Defective	*Frequency*	*Relative Frequency*	*Cumulative Frequency*	*Relative Cumulative Frequency*
0	13	13 ÷ 35 = 0.37	0 + 13 = 13	13 ÷ 35 = 0.37
1	9	9 ÷ 35 = 0.26	13 + 9 = 22	22 ÷ 35 = 0.63
2	5	5 ÷ 35 = 0.14	22 + 5 = 27	27 ÷ 35 = 0.77
3	4	4 ÷ 35 = 0.11	27 + 4 = 31	31 ÷ 35 = 0.89
4	3	3 ÷ 35 = 0.09	31 + 3 = 34	34 ÷ 35 = 0.97
5	1	1 ÷ 35 = 0.03	34 + 1 = 35	35 ÷ 35 = 1.00
Total	35	1.00		

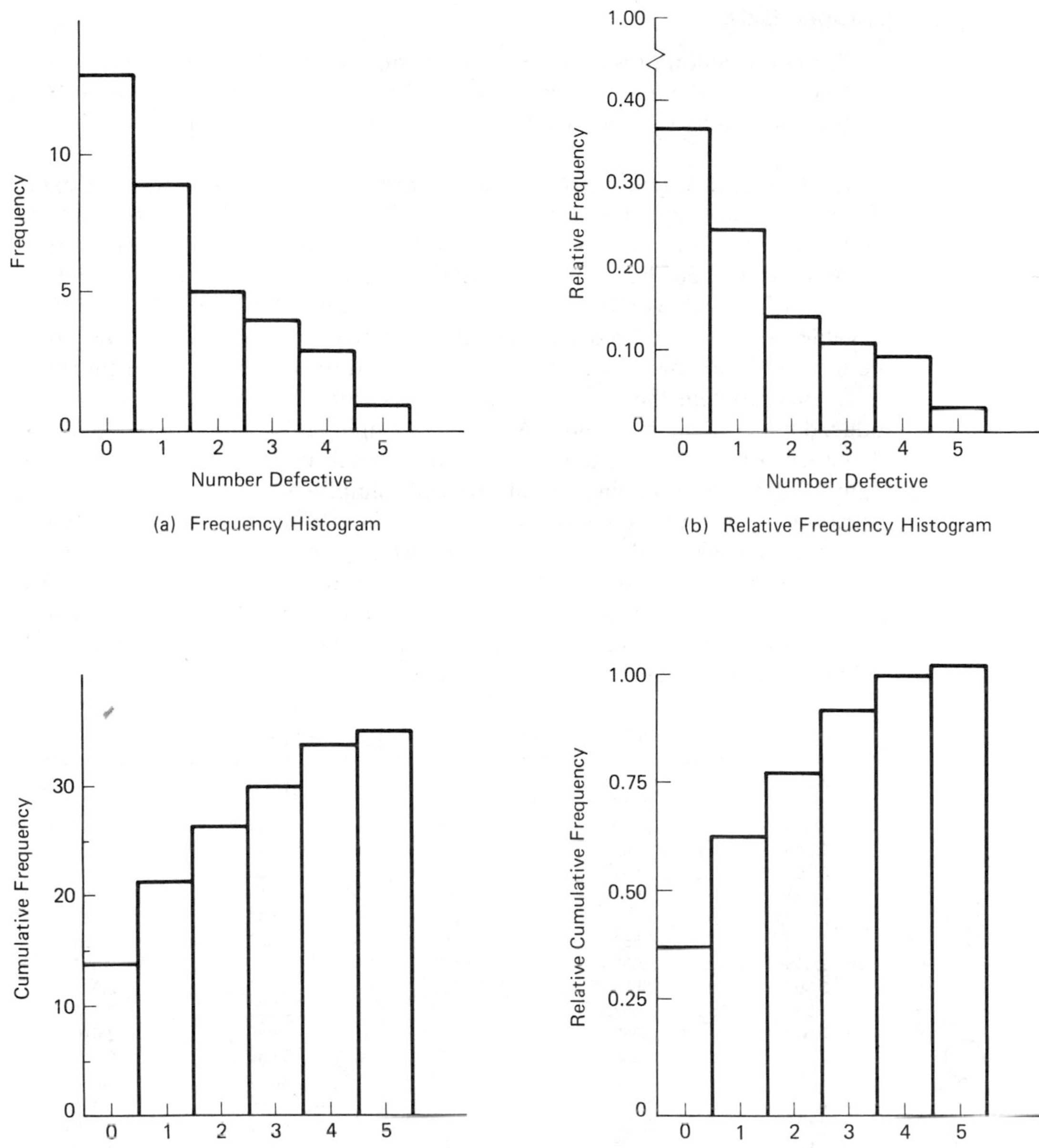

Figure 2-1 Graphic representation of data given in Table 2-2 and Table 2-3.

Grouped Data

The construction of a frequency distribution for grouped data is more complicated because there are a large number of data values. An example problem using a continuous variable will be used to illustrate the concept.

1. *Collect data and construct a tally sheet.* Data collected on the weights of 110 steel shafts are shown in Table 2-4. The first step is to make a tally of the values, as shown in Table 2-5. In order to be more efficient, the weights are coded from 2.500 kg, which is a technique used to simplify data. Therefore, a weight with a value of 31 is equivalent to 2.531 kg (2.500 + 0.031). Analysis of Table 2-5 shows that more information is conveyed to the analyst than from the data of Table 2-4; however, the general picture is still somewhat blurred.

In this problem there are 45 categories, which are too many and must be reduced by grouping into cells.[1] A cell is a grouping within specified boundaries of observed values along the abscissa (horizontal axis) of the histogram (see Figure 2-2). The grouping of data by cells simplifies the presentation of the distribution; however, some of the detail is lost. When the number of cells is large, the true picture of the distribution is distorted by cells having an insufficient number of items or none at all. Or, when the number of cells is small, too many items are concentrated in a few cells and the distribution is also distorted.

The number of cells or groups in a frequency distribution is largely a matter of judgment by the analyst. This judgment is based on the number of obser-

TABLE 2-4 Steel Shaft Weight (kilograms)

2.559	2.556	2.566	2.546	2.561
2.570	2.546	2.565	2.543	2.538
2.560	2.560	2.545	2.551	2.568
2.546	2.555	2.551	2.554	2.574
2.568	2.572	2.550	2.556	2.551
2.561	2.560	2.564	2.567	2.560
2.551	2.562	2.542	2.549	2.561
2.556	2.550	2.561	2.558	2.556
2.559	2.557	2.532	2.575	2.551
2.550	2.559	2.565	2.552	2.560
2.534	2.547	2.569	2.559	2.549
2.544	2.550	2.552	2.536	2.570
2.564	2.553	2.558	2.538	2.564
2.552	2.543	2.562	2.571	2.553
2.539	2.569	2.552	2.536	2.537
2.532	2.552	2.575 (H)	2.545	2.551
2.547	2.537	2.547	2.533	2.538
2.571	2.545	2.545	2.556	2.543
2.551	2.569	2.559	2.534	2.561
2.567	2.572	2.558	2.542	2.574
2.570	2.542	2.552	2.551	2.553
2.546	2.531 (L)	2.563	2.554	2.544

[1]The word "class" is sometimes used in place of the word "cell."

TABLE 2-5 Tally Sheet of Steel Shaft Weight (Coded from 2.500 kg)

Weight	*Tabulation*	*Weight*	*Tabulation*	*Weight*	*Tabulation*
31	I	46	IIII	61	𝍸
32	II	47	III	62	II
33	I	48		63	I
34	II	49	II	64	III
35		50	IIII	65	II
36	II	51	𝍸 III	66	I
37	II	52	𝍸 I	67	II
38	III	53	III	68	II
39	I	54	II	69	III
40		55	I	70	III
41		56	IIII	71	II
42	III	57	I	72	II
43	III	58	III	73	
44	II	59	𝍸	74	II
45	IIII	60	𝍸	75	II

vations and can require trial and error to determine the optimum number of cells. In general, the number of cells should be between 5 and 20. Broad guidelines are as follows: use 5 to 9 cells when the number of observations is less than 100; use 8 to 17 cells when the number of observations is between 100 and 500; and use 15 to 20 cells when the number of observations is greater than 500. To provide flexibility, the number of cells in the guidelines are overlapping. It is emphasized that these guidelines are not rigid and can be adjusted when necessary to present an acceptable frequency distribution.

2. *Determine the range*. It is the difference between the highest number of data and the lowest number of data as shown by the formula

$$R = X_H - X_L$$

where R = range
X_H = highest number
X_L = lowest number

From Table 2-4 the highest number is 2.575 and the lowest number is 2.531. Thus

$$\begin{aligned} R &= X_H - X_L \\ &= 2.575 - 2.531 \\ &= 0.044 \end{aligned}$$

3. *Determine the cell interval.* The *cell interval* is the distance between adjacent cell midpoints as shown in Figure 2-2. Whenever possible, an odd interval such as 0.001, 0.07, 0.5, or 3 is recommended so that the midpoint values

will be to the same degree of accuracy (number of decimal places) as the data values. The cell interval (i) and the number of cells (h) are interrelated by the formula, $h = R/i$. Since h and i are both unknown, a trial-and-error approach is used to find the interval that will meet the guidelines for the number of cells.

$$\text{Assume that } i = 0.003; \quad \text{then} \quad h = \frac{R}{i} = \frac{0.044}{0.003} = 15$$

$$\text{Assume that } i = 0.005; \quad \text{then} \quad h = \frac{R}{i} = \frac{0.044}{0.005} = 9$$

$$\text{Assume that } i = 0.007; \quad \text{then} \quad h = \frac{R}{i} = \frac{0.044}{0.007} = 6$$

A cell interval of 0.005 with nine cells will give the best presentation of the data based on the previously given guidelines.

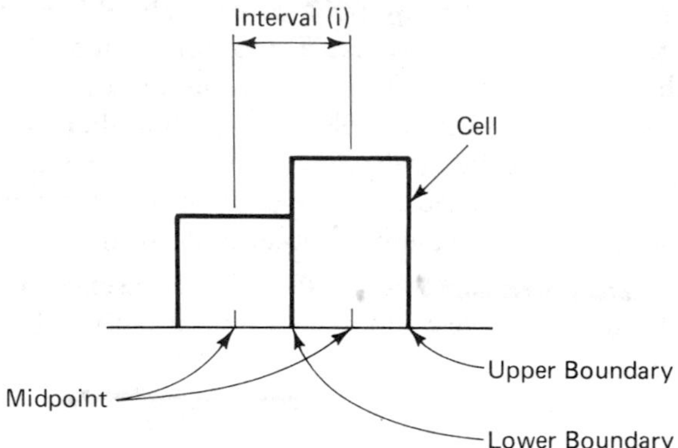

Figure 2-2 Cell nomenclature.

4. *Determine the cell midpoints.* The lowest cell midpoint must be located to include the lowest data value in its cell. The simplest technique is to select the lowest data point (2.531) as the midpoint value for the first cell. This technique is recommended for those readers who are just beginning their statistical career. Since the interval is 0.005, there are five data values in each cell; therefore, a midpoint value of 2.533 can be used for the first cell. This value will have the lowest data value (2.531) in the first cell, which will have data values of 2.531, 2.532, 2.533, 2.534, and 2.535.

Midpoint selection is a matter of judgment, and in this case a midpoint of 2.533 was selected so that the number of cells is 9. Selection of any other midpoint, although not incorrect, would have given 10 cells in the frequency distribution. Selection of different midpoint values will produce different frequency distributions—five are possible. The midpoints for the other eight cells

TABLE 2-6 Frequency Distribution of Steel Shaft Weight (kilograms)

Cell Boundaries	*Cell Midpoint*	*Frequency*
2.531–2.535	2.533	6
2.536–2.540	2.538	8
2.541–2.545	2.543	12
2.546–2.550	2.548	13
2.551–2.555	2.553	20
2.556–2.560	2.558	19
2.561–2.565	2.563	13
2.566–2.570	2.568	11
2.571–2.575	2.573	8
Total		110

are obtained by adding the cell interval to the previous midpoint: 2.533 + 0.005 = 2.538, 2.538 + 0.005 = 2.543, 2.543 + 0.005 = 2.548, . . . , 2.568 + 0.005 = 2.573. These midpoints are shown in Table 2-6.

The midpoint value is the most representative value within a cell provided that the number of observations in a cell is large and the difference in boundaries is not too great. Even if this condition is not met, the number of observations above and below the midpoint of a cell will frequently be equal. And even if the number of observations above and below a cell midpoint is unbalanced in one direction, it will probably be offset by an unbalance in the opposite direction of another cell. Midpoint values should be to the same degree of accuracy as the original observations.

5. *Determine the cell boundaries.* *Cell boundaries* are the extreme or limit values of a cell, referred to as the upper boundary and the lower boundary. All the observations that fall between the upper and lower boundaries are classified into that particular cell. Boundaries are established so there is no question as to the location of an observation. Therefore, the boundary values are an extra decimal place or significant figure in accuracy than the observed values. Since the interval is odd, there will be an equal number of data values on each side of the midpoint. For the first cell with a midpoint of 2.533 and an interval of 0.005, there will be two values on each side. Therefore, that cell will contain the values 2.531, 2.532, 2.533, 2.534, and 2.535. To prevent any gaps, the true boundaries are extended about halfway to the next number, which gives values of 2.5305 and 2.5355. The following number line illustrates this principle:

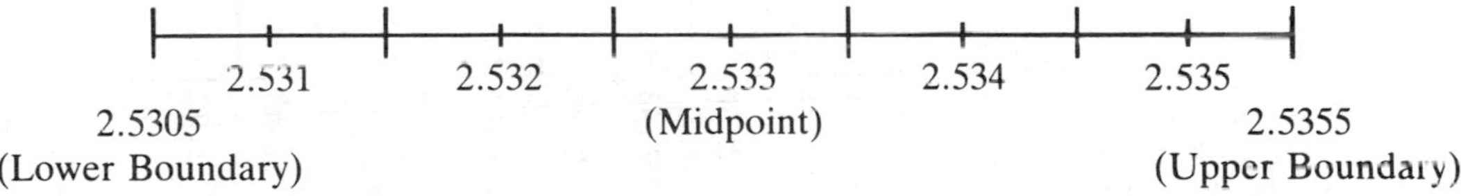

Some analysts prefer to leave the boundaries at the same degree of accuracy as the data. No difficulty is encountered with this practice as long as the cell interval is odd and it is understood that the true boundaries are extended halfway to the next number. Therefore, the lower boundary for the first cell is 2.531.

Once the boundaries are established for one cell, the boundaries for the other cells are obtained by successive additions of the cell interval. Therefore, the lower boundaries are 2.531 + 0.005 = 2.536, 2.536 + 0.005 = 2.541, . . . , 2.566 + 0.005 = 2.571. The upper boundaries are obtained in a similar manner and are shown in the first column of Table 2-6.

6. *Post the cell frequency*. The amount of numbers in each cell is posted to the frequency column of Table 2-6. An analysis of Table 2-5 shows that for the lowest cell there are: one 2.531, two 2.532, one 2.535, two 2.534, and zero 2.535. Therefore, there is a total of six values in the lowest cell, and the cell with a midpoint of 2.533 has a frequency of 6. This amount is posted to Table 2-6. The amounts are determined for the other cells in a similar manner.

The completed frequency distribution is shown in Table 2-6. This frequency distribution gives a better conception of the central value and how the data are dispersed about that value than the unorganized data or a tally sheet. The histogram is shown in Figure 2-3.

Information on the construction of the relative frequency, cumulative frequency, and relative cumulative frequency histograms for grouped data is the same as for ungrouped data but with one exception. With the two cumulative frequency histograms, the true upper cell boundary is the value labeled on the abscissa. Construction of these histograms is left to the reader as an exercise.

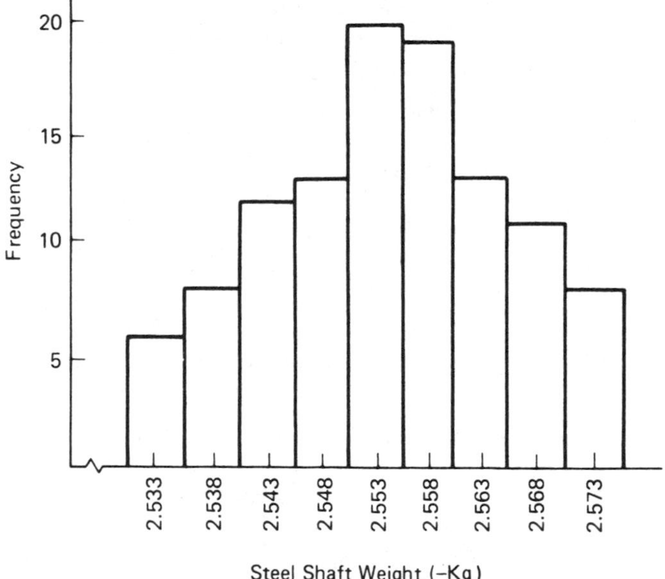

Figure 2-3 Histogram of data given in Table 2-6.

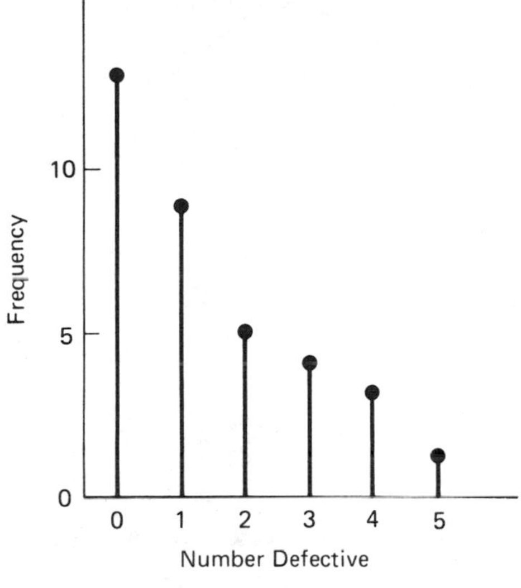

(a) Bar Graph of Data Given in Table 2-1

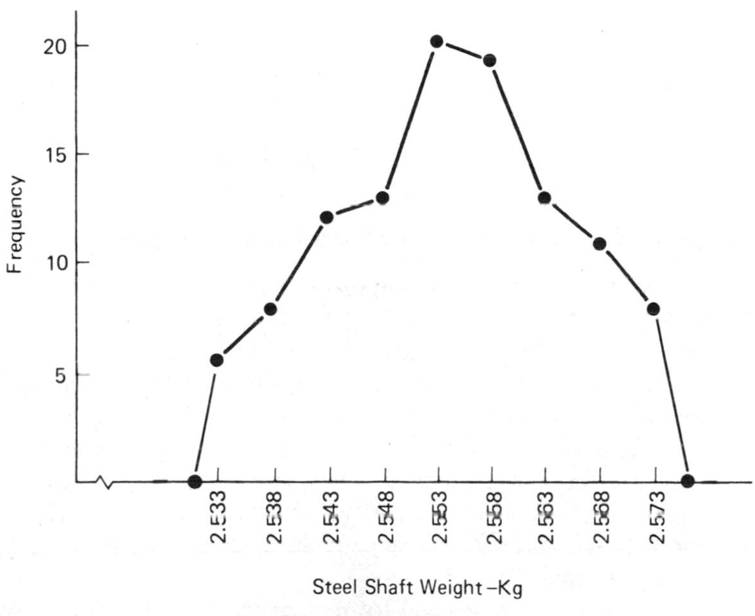

(b) Polygon of Data Given in Table 2-6

Figure 2-4 Other types of frequency distribution graphs.

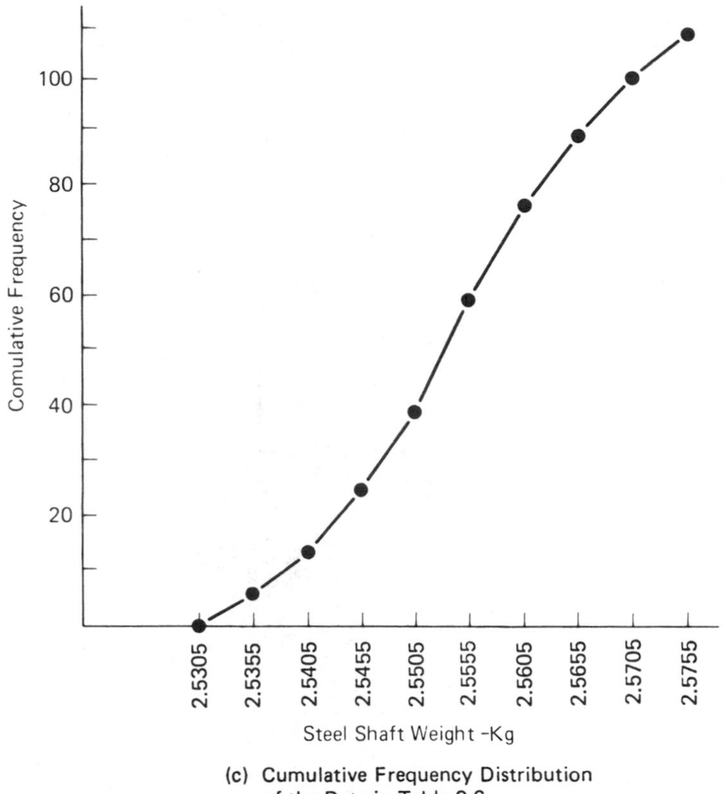

(c) Cumulative Frequency Distribution of the Data in Table 2-6

Figure 2-4 (continued)

Other Types of Frequency Distribution Graphs

The bar chart can also represent frequency distributions, as shown in Figure 2-4a using the data of Table 2-1. As mentioned previously, the bar chart is theoretically correct for discrete data but is not commonly used.

The *polygon* or *frequency polygon* is another graphic way of presenting frequency distributions and is illustrated in Figure 2-4b using the data of Table 2-6. It is constructed by placing a dot over each cell midpoint at the height indicated for each frequency. The curve is extended at each end in order for the figure to be enclosed. Since the histogram shows the area in each cell, it is considered to present a better graphical picture than the polygon and is the one most commonly used.

The graph that is used to present the frequency of all values less than the upper cell boundary of a given cell is called a *cumulative frequency*, or *ogive*. Figure 2-4c shows a cumulative frequency distribution curve for the data in Table 2-6. The cumulative value for each cell is plotted on the graph and joined by a straight line. The true upper cell boundary is labeled on the abscissa.

Characteristics of Frequency Distribution Graphs

The graphs of Figure 2-5 use smooth curves rather than the rectangular associated with the histogram. A smooth curve represents a population frequency distribution, while the histogram represents a sample frequency distribution. The difference between a population and a sample is discussed in another section of this chapter.

Frequency distribution curves have certain identifiable characteristics. One characteristic of the distribution concerns the symmetry or lack of symmetry of the data. Are the data equally distributed on each side of the central value, or are the data skewed to the right or to the left? Another characteristic concerns the number of modes or peaks to the data. There can be one mode, two modes (bimodal), or multiple modes. A final characteristic concerns the peakedness of the data. When the curve is quite peaked, it is referred to as *leptokurtic*, and when it is flatter, it is referred to as *platykurtic*.

Frequency distributions can give sufficient information about a quality control problem to provide a basis for decision making without further analysis.

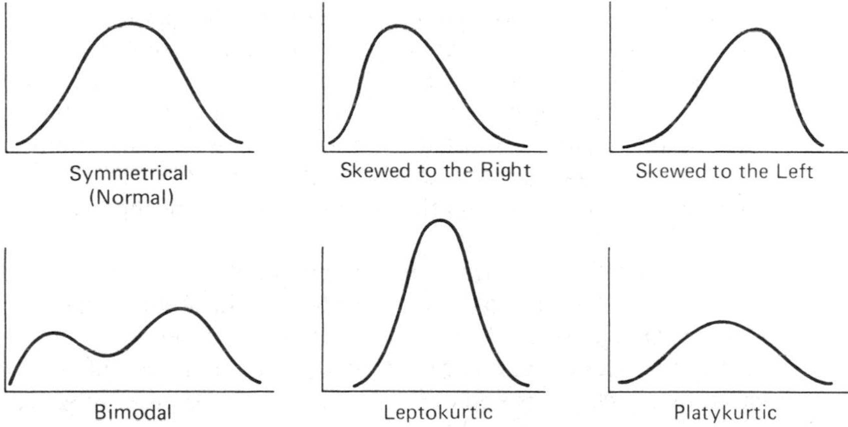

Figure 2-5 Characteristics of frequency distributions.

Analysis of Histograms

Analysis of a histogram can provide information concerning specifications, the shape of the population frequency distribution, and a particular quality control problem. Figure 2-6 shows a histogram for the percentage of wash concentration in a steel tube cleaning operation prior to painting. The ideal concentration is between 1.45 and 1.74%, as shown by the crosshatched rectangle. Concentrations less than 1.45% produce poor quality; concentrations greater than 1.75%, while producing more than adequate quality, are costly and therefore reduce productivity. No complexed statistics are needed to show that corrective measures are needed to bring the spread of the distribution closer to the ideal value of 1.6%.

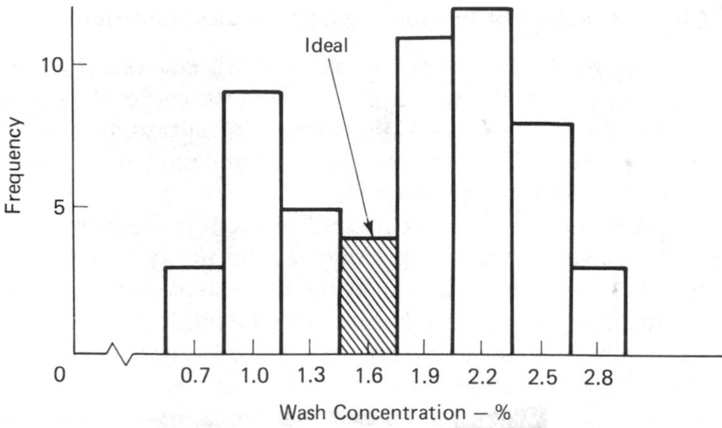

Figure 2-6 Histogram of wash concentration.

Final Comments

Another type of distribution that uses the histogram as a method of presentation is the Pareto distribution. The reader is referred to Chapter 9 for a discussion of this type of distribution. A Pareto analysis is a very effective technique for determining the location of major quality problems. The difference between a Pareto distribution and a frequency distribution are twofold. Categories are used for the abscissa rather than data values and the categories are in desending order from the highest frequency to the lowest one rather than in numerical order.

One limitation of a frequency distribution is the fact that it does not show the order in which the data were produced. In other words, initial data could all be located on one side and later data on the other side. When this situation occurs, the interpretation of the frequency distribution will be different. A run chart, discussed at the end of Chapter 3, shows the order in which the data were produced and can aid in the analysis.

MEASURES OF CENTRAL TENDENCY

A frequency distribution is sufficient for many quality control problems. However, with a broad range of problems a graphical technique is either undesirable or needs the additional information provided by analytical techniques. Analytical methods of describing a collection of data have the advantage of occupying less space than a graph. They also have the advantage of allowing for comparisons between collections of data. And, they also allow for additional calculations and inferences. There are two principal analytical methods of describing a collection of data—measures of central tendency and measures of dispersion. The latter measure is described in the next section, while this section covers measures of central tendency.

A *measure of central tendency* of a distribution is a numerical value that describes the central position of the data or how the data tend to build up in the center. There are three techniques in common use: (1) the average, (2) the median, and (3) the mode.

Average

The average is the sum of the observations divided by the number of observations. It is the most common measure of central tendency. There are three different techniques available for calculating the average: (1) ungrouped data, (2) grouped data, and (3) weighted average.

1. *Ungrouped data*. This technique is used when the data is unorganized. The average is represented by the notation $\overline{X}$, which is read as "X bar" and is given by the formula

$$\overline{X} = \frac{\sum_{i=1}^{n} X_i}{n} = \frac{X_1 + X_2 + \cdots + X_n}{n}$$

where

$\overline{X}$ = average
n = number of observed values
$X_1, X_2, \ldots, X_n$ = observed value identified by the subscript $1, 2, \ldots, n$ or general subscript i
$\sum$ = symbol meaning "sum of"

The first expression is a simplified method of writing the formula whereby $\sum_{i=1}^{n} X_i$ is read as "summation from 1 to n of X sub i" and means to add together the values of the observations.

Example Problem

An inspector checks the resistance value of five coils and records the values in ohms (Ω): $X_1 = 3.35$, $X_2 = 3.37$, $X_3 = 3.28$, $X_4 = 3.34$, and $X_5 = 3.30$. Determine the average.

$$\overline{X} = \frac{\sum_{i=1}^{n} X_i}{n}$$

$$= \frac{3.35 + 3.37 + 3.28 + 3.34 + 3.30}{5}$$

$$= 3.33\ \Omega$$

Most electronic hand calculators have the capability of automatically calculating the average after the data are entered.

2. *Grouped data.* When the data have been grouped into a frequency distribution, the following technique is applicable. The formula for the average of grouped data is

$$\overline{X} = \frac{\sum_{i=1}^{h} f_i X_i}{n} = \frac{f_1X_1 + f_2X_2 + \cdots + f_hX_h}{f_1 + f_2 + \cdots + f_h}$$

where n = sum of the frequencies
f_i = frequency in a cell or frequency of an observed value
X_i = cell midpoint or an observed value
h = number of cells or number of observed values

The formula is applicable when the grouping is by cells with more than one observed value per cell as illustrated by the steel shaft problem (Table 2-6). It is also applicable when each observed value, X_i, has its own frequency, f_i, as illustrated by the smoke alarm problem (Table 2-1). In this situation, h is the number of observed values.

In other words, if the frequency distribution has been grouped into cells, X_i is the cell midpoint and f_i is the number of observations in that cell. If the frequency distribution has been grouped by individual observed values, X_i is the observed value and f_i is the number of times that observed value occurs in the data. This practice holds for both discrete and continuous variables.

Each cell midpoint is used as the representative value of that cell. The midpoint is multiplied by its cell frequency; the products are summed; and they are divided by the total number of observations. In the example problem given below, the first three columns are those of a typical frequency distribution. The fourth column is derived from the product of the second column (midpoint) and third column (frequency) and is labeled "$f\,X$."

Example Problem

Given the frequency distribution of the life of 320 automotive tires in 1000 km (621.37 miles) as shown in Table 2-7, determine the average.

$$\overline{X} = \frac{\sum_{i=1}^{h} f_i X_i}{n}$$

$$= \frac{11{,}549}{320}$$

$$= 36.1 \quad \text{(which is in 1000 km)}$$

Therefore, $\overline{X} = 36.1 \times 10^3$ km.

When comparing an average calculated from this technique with one cal-

TABLE 2-7 Frequency Distributions of the Life of 320 Tires in 1000 km

Boundaries	*Midpoint,* X_i	*Frequency* f_i	f_iX_i
23.6–26.5	25.0	4	100
26.6–29.5	28.0	36	1,008
29.6–32.5	31.0	51	1,581
32.6–35.5	34.0	63	2,142
35.6–38.5	37.0	58	2,146
38.6–41.5	40.0	52	2,080
41.6–44.5	43.0	34	1,462
44.6–47.5	46.0	16	736
47.6–50.5	49.0	6	294
Total		$n = 320$	$\sum f_iX_i = 11{,}549$

culated using the ungrouped technique, there can be a slight difference. This difference is caused by the observations in each cell being unevenly distributed in the cell. In actual practice the difference will not be of sufficient magnitude to affect the accuracy of the problem.

3. *Weighted average*. When a number of averages are combined with different frequencies, a *weighted average* is computed. The formula for the weighted average is given by

$$\overline{X}_w = \frac{\sum_{i=1}^{n} w_i\overline{X}_i}{\sum_{i=1}^{n} w_i}$$

where $\overline{X}_w$ = weighted average
w_i = weight of the ith average

Example Problem

Tensile tests on aluminum alloy rods are conducted at three different times, which results in three different average values in megapascals (MPa). On the first occasion five tests are conducted with a average of 207 MPa (30,000 psi); on the second occasion six tests, with a average of 203 MPa; and on the last occasion three tests, with a average of 206 MPa. Determine the weighted average.

$$\overline{X}_w = \frac{\sum_{i=1}^{n} w_i\overline{X}_i}{\sum_{i=1}^{n} w_i}$$

$$= \frac{(5)(207) + (6)(203) + (3)(206)}{5 + 6 + 3}$$

$$= 205 \text{ MPa}$$

The weighted average technique is a special case of the grouped data technique wherein the data are not organized into a frequency distribution. In the example above, the weights are whole numbers. Another method of solving the same problem is to use proportions. Thus,

$$w_1 = \frac{5}{5 + 6 + 3} = 0.36$$

$$w_2 = \frac{6}{5 + 6 + 3} = 0.43$$

$$w_3 = \frac{3}{5 + 6 + 3} = 0.21$$

and the sum of the weights equals 1.00. The latter technique would be necessary when the weights are given in percent or the decimal equivalent.

Unless otherwise noted, $\overline{X}$ stands for the average of observed values, $\overline{X}_x$. The same equation is used to find

$\overline{X}_{\bar{x}}$ or $\overline{\overline{X}}$ — average of averages

$\overline{R}$ — average of ranges

$\bar{c}$ — average of count of defects

$\bar{s}$ — average of sample standard deviations, etc.

Median

Another measure of central tendency is the *median*, which is defined as the value which divides a series of ordered observations so that the number of items above it is equal to the number below it.

1. *Ungrouped technique*. Two situations are possible in determining the median of a series of raw data—when the number in the series is odd and when the number in the series is even. When the number in the series is odd, the median is the midpoint of the values. Thus, the ordered set of numbers 3, 4, 5, 6, 8, 8, and 10 has a median of 6, and the ordered set of numbers 22, 24, 24, 24, and 30 has a median of 24. When the number in the series is even, the median is the average of the two middle numbers. Thus, the ordered set of numbers 3, 4, 5, 6, 8, and 8 has a median that is the average of 5 and 6, which is (5 + 6)/2 = 5.5. If both middle numbers are the same as in the ordered set of numbers 22, 24, 24, 24, 30, and 30, it is still computed as the average of the two middle numbers, since (24 + 24)/2 = 24. The reader is cautioned to be sure the numbers are ordered before computing the median.

2. *Grouped technique.* When data are grouped into a frequency distribution, the median is obtained by finding the cell that has the middle number and then interpolating within the cell. The interpolation formula for computing the median is given by

$$\text{Md} = L_m + \left(\frac{\frac{n}{2} - cf_m}{f_m} \right) i$$

where Md = median
L_m = lower boundary of the cell with the median
n = total number of observations
cf_m = cumulative frequency of all cells below L_m
f_m = frequency of median cell
i = cell interval

To illustrate the use of the formula, data from Table 2-7 will be used. By counting up from the lowest cell (midpoint 25.0), the halfway point (320/2 = 160) is reached in the cell with a midpoint value of 37.0 and a lower limit of 35.6. The cumulative frequency (cf_m) is 154, the cell interval is 3, and the frequency of the median cell is 58.

$$\begin{aligned} \text{Md} &= L_m + \left(\frac{\frac{n}{2} - cf_m}{f_m} \right) i \\ &= 35.6 + \left(\frac{\frac{320}{2} - 154}{58} \right) 3 \\ &= 35.9 \qquad \text{(which is in 1000 km)} \end{aligned}$$

If the counting is begun at the top of the distribution, the cumulative frequency is counted to the cell upper limit and the interpolated quantity is subtracted from the upper limit. However, it is more common to start counting at the bottom of the distribution.

Mode

The *mode* (Mo) of a set of numbers is that value which occurs with the greatest frequency. It is possible for the mode to be nonexistent in a series of numbers or to have more than one value. To illustrate the series of numbers 3, 3, 4, 5, 5, 5, and 7 has a mode of 5; the series of numbers 22, 23, 25, 30, 32, and 36 does not have a mode; and the series of numbers 105, 105, 105, 107,

108, 109, 109, 109, 110, and 112 has two modes, 105 and 109. A series of numbers is referred to as *unimodal* if it has one mode, *bimodal* if it has two modes, and *multimodal* if there are more than two modes.

When data are grouped into a frequency distribution, the midpoint of the cell with the highest frequency is the mode, since this point represents the highest point (greatest frequency) of the histogram. It is possible to obtain a better estimate of the mode by interpolating in a manner similar to that used for the median. However, this is not necessary, since the mode is employed primarily as an inspection method for determining the central tendency, and greater accuracy than the cell midpoint is not required.

Relationship Among the Measures of Central Tendency

Differences among the three measures of central tendency are shown in the smooth polygons of Figure 2-7. When the distribution is symmetrical, the values for the average, median, and mode are identical; when the distribution is skewed, the values are different.

The average is the most commonly used measure of central tendency. It is used when the distribution is symmetrical or not appreciably skewed to the right or left; when additional statistics, such as measures of dispersion, control charts, and so on, are to be computed based on the average; and when a stable value is needed for inductive statistics.

The median becomes an effective measure of the central tendency when the distribution is positively (to the right) or negatively (to the left) skewed. It is used when an exact midpoint of a distribution is desired. When a distribution has extreme values, the average will be adversely affected while the median will remain unchanged. Thus, in a series of numbers such as 12, 13, 14, 15, 16, the median and average are identical and equal to 14. However, if the first value is changed to a 2, the median remains at 14, but the average becomes 12.

The mode is used when a quick and approximate measure of the central tendency is desired. Thus, the mode of a histogram is easily found by a visual examination. In addition, the mode is used to describe the most typical value of a distribution, such as the modal age of a particular group.

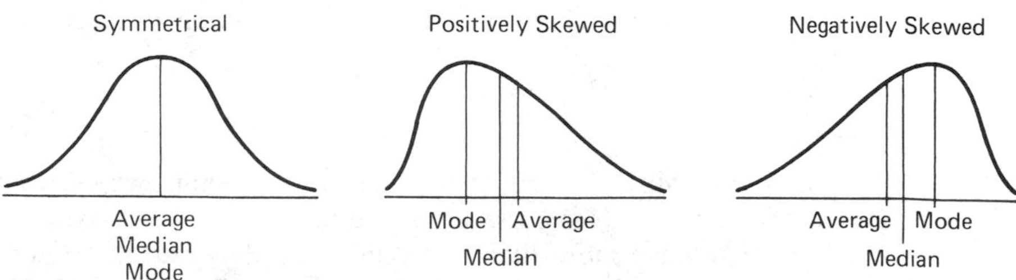

Figure 2-7 Relationship among average, median, and mode.

Other measures of central tendency are the geometric mean, harmonic mean, and quadratic mean. These measures are not used in quality control.

MEASURES OF DISPERSION

Introduction

In the preceding section, techniques for describing the central tendency of data were discussed. A second tool of statistics is composed of the *measures of dispersion*, which describe how the data are spread out or scattered on each side of the central value. Measures of dispersion and measures of central tendency are both needed to describe a collection of data. To illustrate, the employees of the plating and the assembly departments of a factory have identical average weekly wages of \$225.36; however, the plating department has a high of \$230.72 and a low of \$219.43, while the assembly department has a high of \$280.79 and a low of \$173.54. The data for the assembly department are spread out or dispersed farther from the average than are those of the printing department.

Measures of dispersion discussed in this section are range, standard deviation, and variance. Other measures such as mean deviation and quartile deviation are not used in quality control.

Range

The *range* of a series of numbers is the difference between the largest and smallest values or observations. Symbolically, it is given by the formula

$$R = X_{\mathrm{H}} - X_{\mathrm{L}}$$

where R = range
X_{H} = highest observation in a series
X_{L} = lowest observation in a series

Example Problem

If the highest weekly wage in the assembly department is \$280.79 and the lowest weekly wage is \$173.54, determine the range.

$$\begin{aligned} R &= X_{\mathrm{H}} - X_{\mathrm{L}} \\ &= \$280.79 - \$173.54 \\ &= \$107.25 \end{aligned}$$

The range is the simplest and easiest to calculate of the measures of dispersion. A related measure, which is occasionally used, is the *midrange*, which is the range divided by 2, $R/2$.

Standard Deviation

The *standard deviation* is a numerical value in the units of the observed values that measures the spreading tendency of the data. A large standard deviation shows greater variability of the data than does a small standard deviation. In symbolic terms it is given by the formula

$$s = \sqrt{\frac{\sum_{i=1}^{n} (X_i - \overline{X})^2}{n - 1}}$$

where s = sample standard deviation
X_i = observed value
$\overline{X}$ = average
n = number of observed values

Table 2-8 will be used to explain the standard deviation concept. The first column (X_i) gives six observed values in kilograms, and from these values the average, $\overline{X} = 3.0$, is obtained. The second column, $(X_i - \overline{X})$, is the deviation of the individual observed values from the average. If we sum the deviations, the answer will be 0, which is always the case; but it will not lead to a measure of dispersion. However, if the deviations are squared, they will all be positive and their sum will be greater than zero. Calculations are shown in the third column, $(X_i - \overline{X})^2$, with a resultant sum of 0.08, which will vary depending on the observed values. The average of the squared deviations can be found by dividing by n; however, for theoretical reasons we divide by $n - 1$.[2] Thus,

$$\frac{\sum (X_i - \overline{X})^2}{n - 1} = \frac{0.08}{6 - 1} = 0.016 \text{ kg}^2$$

which gives an answer that has the units squared. This result is not acceptable as a measure of the dispersion, but is valuable as a measure of variability for

TABLE 2-8 Standard Deviation Analysis

X_i	$X_i - \overline{X}$	$(X_i - \overline{X})^2$
3.2	+0.2	0.04
2.9	−0.1	0.01
3.0	0.0	0.00
2.9	−0.1	0.01
3.1	+0.1	0.01
2.9	−0.1	0.01
$\overline{X} = 3.0$	$\Sigma = 0$	$\Sigma = 0.08$

[2]The reason for using $n - 1$ is because one degree of freedom is lost due to the use of the sample statistic, $\overline{X}$, rather than the population parameter, μ.

advanced statistics. It is called the *variance* and is given the symbol s^2. If we take the square root, the answer will be in the same units as the observed values. Calculations are

$$s = \sqrt{\frac{\sum (X_i - \overline{X})^2}{n - 1}} = \sqrt{\frac{0.08}{6 - 1}} = 0.13 \text{ kg}$$

This formula is for explanation rather than for the purpose of calculation. Because the form of the data can be either grouped or ungrouped, there are different computing techniques.

1. *Ungrouped technique*. The formula used in the definition of standard deviation can be used for ungrouped data. However, an alternative formula can be more convenient for computation purposes:

$$s = \sqrt{\frac{n \sum_{i=1}^{n} X_i^2 - \left(\sum_{i=1}^{n} X_i\right)^2}{n(n - 1)}}$$

Example Problem

Determine the standard deviation of the moisture content of a roll of kraft paper. The results of six readings across the paper web are 6.7, 6.0, 6.4, 6.4, 5.9, and 5.8%.

$$s = \sqrt{\frac{n \sum_{i=1}^{n} X_i^2 - \left(\sum_{i=1}^{n} X_i\right)^2}{n(n - 1)}}$$

$$= \sqrt{\frac{6(231.26) - (37.2)^2}{6(6 - 1)}}$$

$$= 0.35\%$$

After entry of the data, many hand calculators compute the standard deviation on command.

2. *Grouped technique*. When the data have been grouped into a frequency distribution, the following technique is applicable. The formula for the standard deviation of grouped data is

$$s = \sqrt{\frac{n \sum_{i=1}^{h} (f_i X_i^2) - \left(\sum_{i=1}^{h} f_i X_i\right)^2}{n(n - 1)}}$$

where the symbols f_i, X_i, n, and h have the same meaning as given for the average of grouped data.

To use this technique, two additional columns are added to the frequency distribution. These additional columns are labeled "fX" and "fX^2," as shown in Table 2-9. It will be recalled that the "fX" column is needed for the average computations; therefore, only one additional column is required to compute the standard deviation. The technique is shown by the following example problem.

Example Problem

Given the frequency distribution of Table 2-9 for passenger car speeds during a 15-minute interval on I-57, determine the average and standard deviation.

$$\bar{X} = \frac{\sum_{i=1}^{h} f_i X_i}{n} \qquad s = \sqrt{\frac{n \sum_{i=1}^{h} (f_i X_i^2) - \left(\sum_{i=1}^{h} f_i X_i\right)^2}{n(n-1)}}$$

$$= \frac{9354}{96} \qquad = \sqrt{\frac{96(920{,}742) - (9354)^2}{96(96-1)}}$$

$$= 97.4 \text{ km/h} \qquad = 9.8 \text{ km/h}$$

Do not round $\sum fX$ or $\sum fX^2$, as this action will affect accuracy. Most hand calculators have the capability to enter grouped data and calculate s on command.

Unless otherwise noted, s stands for s_X, the sample standard deviation of observed values. The same formula is used to find

$s_{\bar{X}}$ — sample standard deviation of averages
s_p — sample standard deviation of proportions
s_R — sample standard deviation of ranges
s_s — sample standard deviation of standard deviations, etc.

The standard deviation is a reference value that measures the dispersion in

TABLE 2-9 Passenger Car Speeds (in km/h) During a 15-Minute Interval on I-57 at Location 236

	Midpoint	*Frequency*	*Computations*	
Boundaries	*Xf$_i$*		*f_iX_i*	*$f_iX_i^2$*
73.6–81.5	77.0	5	385	29,645
81.6–90.5	86.0	19	1634	140,524
90.6–99.5	95.0	31	2945	279,775
99.6–108.5	104.0	27	2808	292,032
108.6–117.5	113.0	14	1582	178,766
Total		n = 96	ΣfX = 9354	ΣfX^2 = 920,742

the data. It is best viewed as an index that is defined by the formula. Utilization of the standard deviation later will aid in its understanding.

Relationship Between the Measures of Dispersion

In quality control the range is a very common measure of the dispersion; it is used in one of the principal control charts. The primary advantage of the range is in providing a knowledge of the total spread of the data. It is also valuable when the amount of data is too small or too scattered to justify the calculation of a more precise measure of dispersion. The range is the only measure of dispersion that is not a function of a measure of central tendency. As the number of observations increases, the accuracy of the range decreases, since it becomes easier for an extremely high or low reading to occur. It is suggested that the use of the range be limited to a maximum of 10 observations.

The standard deviation is used when a more precise measure is desired. It is also the most common measure of the dispersion for quality control work and is used when subsequent statistics are to be calculated. When the data have an extreme value for the high or the low, the standard deviation is more desirable than the range.

OTHER MEASURES

There are two other measures that are frequently used to analyze a collection of data—skewness and kurtosis.

Skewness

As indicated previously, *skewness* is a lack of symmetry of the data. The formula is given by[3]

$$a_3 = \frac{\sum_{i=1}^{h} f_i(X_i - \overline{X})^3/n}{s^3}$$

where a_3 represents skewness.

Skewness is a number whose size tells us the extent of the departure from symmetry. If the value of a_3 is 0, the data are symmetrical; if greater than 0 (positive), the data are skewed to the right, which means that the long tail is to the right; and if less than 0 (negative), the data are skewed to the left, which means that the long tail is to the left. See Figure 2-5 for a graphical representation of skewness. Values of $+1$ or -1 imply a strong unsymmetrical distribution.

[3]This formula is an approximation that is good enough for most purposes.

TABLE 2-10 Data for Skewness and Kurtosis Example Problems

X_i	f_i	$X_i - \overline{X}$	$f_i(X_i - \overline{X})^3$	$f_i(X_i - \overline{X})^4$
1	1	$(1 - 7) = -6$	$1(-6)^3 = -216$	$1(-6)^4 = 1296$
4	6	$(4 - 7) = -3$	$6(-3)^3 = -162$	$6(-3)^4 = 486$
7	16	$(7 - 7) = 0$	$16(0)^3 = 0$	$16(0)^4 = 0$
10	8	$(10 - 7) = +3$	$8(+3)^3 = +216$	$8(+3)^4 = 648$
	$\Sigma = 31$		$\Sigma = -162$	$\Sigma = 2430$

Example Problem

Determine the skewness of the frequency distribution of Table 2-10. The average and sample standard deviation are calculated and are 7.0 and 2.32, respectively.

$$a_3 = \frac{\sum_{i=1}^{h} f_i(X_i - \overline{X})^3/n}{s^3}$$

$$= \frac{-162/31}{2.32^3}$$

$$= -0.42$$

The skewness value of -0.42 tells us that the data are quite skewed to the left. Visual examination of the X and f columns or a histogram would have indicated the same information.

In order to use the skewness value, the value of n must be large, say at least 30. Also, the distribution must be unimodal. The skewness value provides information concerning the shape of the population distribution. For example, a normal distribution has a skewness value of zero, $a_3 = 0$.

Kurtosis

As indicated previously, *kurtosis* is the peakedness of the data. The formula is given by[3]

$$a_4 = \frac{\sum_{i=1}^{h} f_i(X_i - \overline{X})^4/n}{s^4}$$

where a_4 represents kurtosis.

Kurtosis is a dimensionless value that is used as a comparative measure of the height of the peak in two distributions. See Figure 2-5 for a graphical representation of kurtosis.

[3]This formula is an approximation that is good enough for most purposes.

Example Problem

Determine the kurtosis of the frequency distribution of Table 2-10, which has $\overline{X} = 7.0$ and $s = 2.32$.

$$a_4 = \frac{\sum_{i=1}^{h} f_i(X_i - \overline{X})^4/n}{s^4}$$

$$= \frac{2430/31}{2.32^4}$$

$$= 2.70$$

The kurtosis value of 2.70 does not provide any information by itself—it must be compared to another distribution. Use of the kurtosis value is the same as skewness—large sample size, n, and unimodal distribution. It provides information concerning the shape of the population distribution. For example, a normal distribution has a kurtosis value of 3, $a_4 = 3$. If $a_4 > 3$, then the height of the distribution is more peaked than normal, and if $a_4 < 3$, the height of the distribution is less peaked than normal.

The concepts of skewness and kurtosis are useful in that they provide some information about the shape of the distribution.

CONCEPT OF A POPULATION AND A SAMPLE

At this point in the chapter, it is desirable to examine the concept of a population and a sample. In order to construct a frequency distribution of the weights of steel shafts, a small portion, or *sample*, is selected to represent all the steel shafts. Similarly, the data collected concerning the passenger car speeds represented only a small portion of all the passenger cars. The population is the whole collection of measurements, and in the examples above, the population would be all the steel shafts and all the passenger cars. When averages, standard deviations, and other measures are computed from samples, they are referred to as *statistics*. Since the composition of samples will fluctuate, the computed statistics will be larger or smaller than their true population values, or *parameters*. Parameters are considered to be fixed reference (standard) values or the best estimate of these values which is available at a particular time.

The population may have a finite number of items, such as a day's production of steel shafts. It may be infinite or almost infinite, such as the number of rivets in a year's production of jet airplanes. The population may be defined differently depending on the particular situation. Thus, a study of a product could involve the population of an hour's production, a week's production, 5000 pieces, and so on.

Since it is rarely possible to measure all of the population, a sample is selected. Sampling is necessary when it may be impossible to measure the entire population when the expense to observe all the data is prohibitive; when the required inspection destroys the product; or when a test of the entire population may be too dangerous, as would be the case with a new medical drug. Actually, an analysis of the entire population may not be as accurate as sampling. It has been shown that 100% manual inspection is not as accurate as sampling. This is probably due to the fact that boredom and fatigue cause inspectors to prejudge each inspected item as being acceptable.

When designating a population, the corresponding Greek letter is used. Thus, the sample average has the symbol $\overline{X}$, and the population mean the symbol μ (mu). Note that the word "average" changes to "mean" when used for the population. The sample standard deviation has the symbol s, and the population standard deviation the symbol σ (sigma). The true population value may never be known; therefore, the symbols $\hat{\mu}$ and $\hat{\sigma}$ are sometimes used to indicate "estimate of." A comparison of sample and population is given in Table 2-11. Additional comparisons will be given as they occur.

The primary objective in selecting a sample is to learn something about the population which will aid in making some type of decision. Therefore, the purpose of sampling is to draw some inference about the population. The sample selected must be of such a nature that it tends to resemble or represent the population. How successfully the sample represents the population is a function of the size of the sample, luck or chance, sampling method, and whether the conditions change or not.

TABLE 2-11 Comparison of Sample and Population

Sample	*Population*
Statistic	Parameter
$\overline{X}$—average	μ—mean
s—sample standard deviation	σ—standard deviation

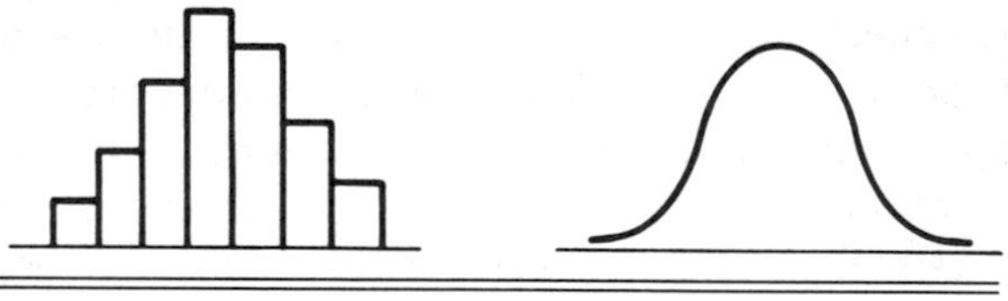

Table 2-12 shows the results of an experiment that illustrates the relationship between samples and the population. A container contain 800 blue and 200 green spheres of 5 mm (approximately 3/16 in.) in diameter. The 1000 spheres are considered to be the population, with 20% being green. Samples of size 10 are selected and posted to the table and then replaced in the container. The table illustrates the differences between the sample results and what should be expected from the known population. Only in samples 2 and 7 are the sample statistics equal to the population parameter. There definitely is a chance factor

TABLE 2-12 Results of Eight Samples of Blue and Green Spheres from a Known Universe

Sample Number	*Sample Size*	*Number of Blue Spheres*	*Number of Green Spheres*	*Percentage of Green Spheres*
1	10	9	1	10
2	10	8	2	20
3	10	5	5	50
4	10	9	1	10
5	10	7	3	30
6	10	10	0	0
7	10	8	2	20
8	10	9	1	10
Total	80	65	15	18.8

which determines the composition of the sample. When the eight individual samples are combined into one large one, the percentage of green spheres is 18.8, which is close to the population value of 20%.

While inferences are made about the population from samples, it is equally true that a knowledge of the population provides information for analysis of the sample. Thus, it is possible to determine whether a sample came from a particular population. This concept is necessary to understand control chart theory. A more detailed discussion is delayed until Chapter 3.

THE NORMAL CURVE

Description

Although there are as many different populations as there are conditions, they can be described by a few general types. One type of population that is quite common is called the *normal curve* or *Gaussian distribution*. The normal curve or normal population distribution is a symmetrical, unimodal, bell-shaped distribution with the mean, median, and mode having the same value.

A population curve or distribution is developed from a frequency histogram. As the sample size of a histogram gets larger and larger, the cell interval gets smaller and smaller. When the sample size is quite large and the cell interval is very small, the histogram will take on the appearance of a smooth polygon or a curve representing the population. A curve of the normal population of 1000 observations of the resistance in ohms of an electrical device with population mean, μ, of 90 ohms and population standard deviation, σ, of 2 ohms is shown in Figure 2-8.

Much of the variation in nature and in industry follows the frequency distribution of the normal curve. Thus, the variations in the weight of elephants, the speed of antelopes, and the height of human beings will follow a normal curve. Also, the variations found in industry, such as the weight of gray iron castings, the life of 60-W light bulbs, and the dimensions of a steel piston ring, will be expected to follow the normal curve. When considering the heights of human beings, we can expect a small percentage of them to be extremely tall and a small percentage to be extremely short, with the majority of human heights clustering about the mean value. The normal curve is such a good description of the variations which occur to most quality characteristics in industry that it is the basis for many quality control techniques.

All normal distributions of continuous variables can be converted to the standardized normal distribution (see Figure 2-9) by using *the standardized normal value*, Z. For example, consider the value of 92 ohms in Figure 2-8, which is one standard deviation above the mean ($\mu + 1\sigma = 90 + 1(2) = 92$). Conversion to the Z value is

$$Z = \frac{X_i - \mu}{\sigma} = \frac{92 - 90}{2} = +1$$

which is also 1σ above μ on the Z scale of Figure 2-9.

The formula for the standardized normal curve is

$$f(Z) = \frac{1}{\sqrt{2\pi}} e^{-Z^2/2} = 0.3989 e^{-Z^2/2}$$

where $\pi = 3.14159$

$e = 2.71828$

$$Z = \frac{X_i - \mu}{\sigma}$$

Figure 2-9 shows the standardized curve with its mean of zero and standard deviation of 1. It is noted that the curve is asymptotic at $Z = -3$ and $Z = +3$.

The area under the curve is equal to 1.00 or 100% and therefore can easily be used for probability calculations. Since the area under the curve between various points is a very useful statistic, a normal area table is provided as Table A in the Appendix.

The normal distribution can be referred to as a normal probability distribution. While it is the most important population distribution, there are a number of other ones for continuous variables. There are also a number of probability distributions for discrete variables. These distributions are discussed in Chapter 4.

Relationship to the Mean and Standard Deviation

As seen by the formula for the standardized normal curve, there is a definite relationship among the mean, the standard deviation and the normal curve. Figure 2-10 shows three normal curves with different mean values; it is noted that the only change is in the location. Figure 2-11 shows three normal curves

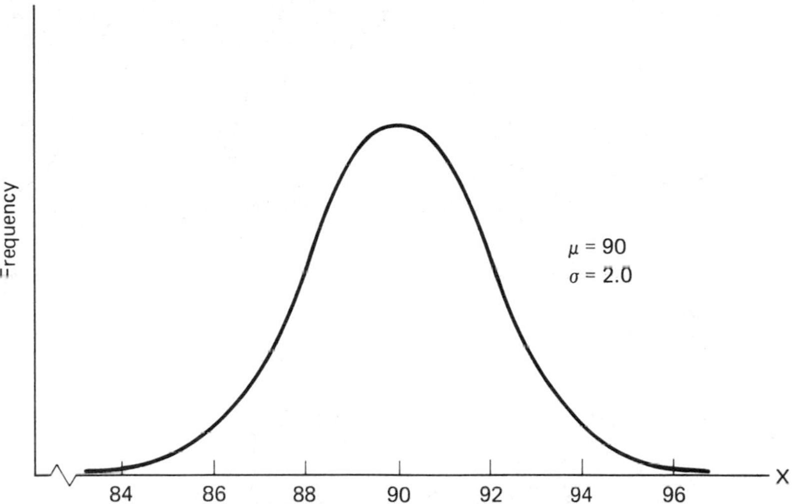

Figure 2-8 Normal distribution for resistance of an electrical device with $\mu = 90$ ohms and $\sigma = 2.0$ ohms.

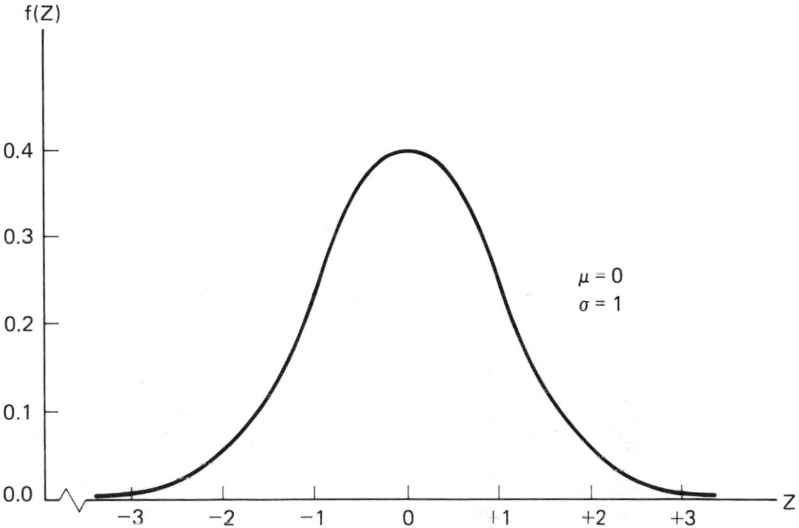

Figure 2-9 Standardized normal distribution with $\mu = 0$ and $\sigma = 1$.

with the same mean but different standard deviations. The figure illustrates the principle that the larger the standard deviation, the flatter the curve (data are widely dispersed), and the smaller the standard deviation, the more peaked the curve (data are narrowly dispersed). If the standard deviation is zero, all values are identical to the mean and there is no curve.

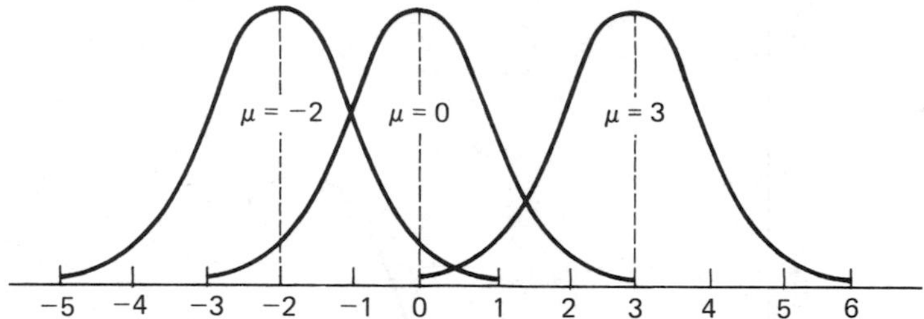

Figure 2-10 Normal curve with different means but identical standard deviations.

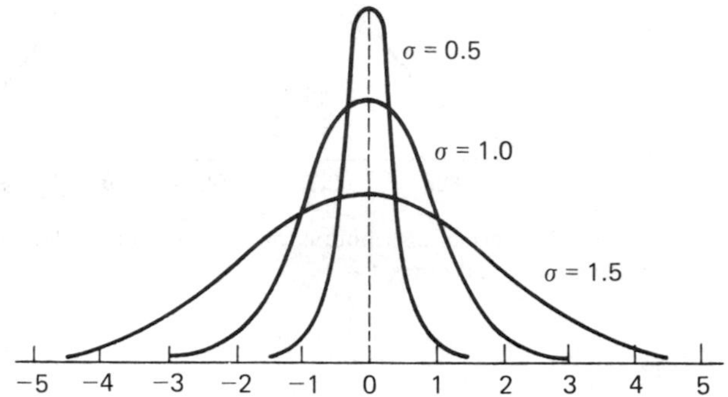

Figure 2-11 Normal curve with different standard deviations but identical means.

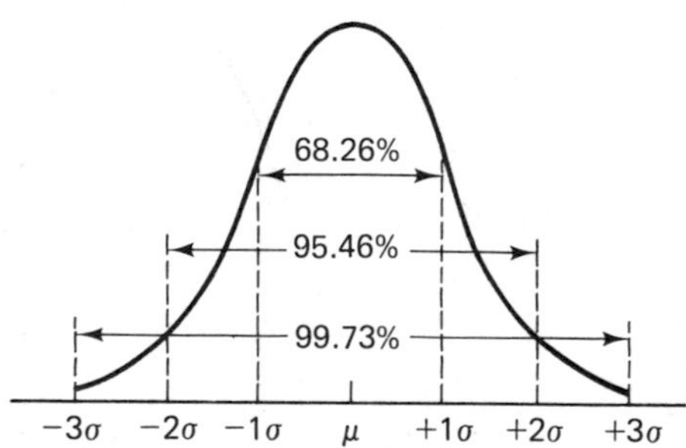

Figure 2-12 Percent of items included between certain values of the standard deviation.

The normal distribution is fully defined by the mean and population standard deviation. Also, as seen by Figures 2-10 and 2-11, these two parameters are independent.

A relationship exists between the standard deviation and the area under the normal curve as shown in Figure 2-12. The figure shows that in a normal distribution 68.26% of the items are included between the limits of $\mu + 1\sigma$ and $\mu - 1\sigma$, 95.46% of the items are included between the limits $\mu + 2\sigma$ and $\mu - 2\sigma$, and 99.73% of the items are included between $\mu + 3\sigma$ and $\mu - 3\sigma$. One hundred percent of the items are included between the limits $+\infty$ and $-\infty$. These percentages hold true regardless of the shape of the normal curve. The fact that 99.73% of the items are included between $\pm 3\sigma$ is the basis for control charts which are discussed in Chapter 3.

Applications

The percentage of items included between any two values can be determined by integration. However, this is not necessary, since the areas under the curve for various Z values are given in Table A in the Appendix. Table A, "Areas Under the Normal Curve," is a left-reading table,[4] which means that the given areas are for that portion of the curve from $-\infty$ to a particular value, X_i.

The first step is to determine the Z value using the formula

$$Z = \frac{X_i - \mu}{\sigma}$$

where Z = standard normal value
X_i = individual value
μ = mean
σ = population standard deviation

Next, using the calculated Z value the area under the curve to the left of X_i is found in Table A. Thus, if a calculated Z value is -1.76, the value for the area is 0.0392. Since the total area under the curve is 1.0000, the 0.0392 value for the area can be changed to a percent of the items under the curve by moving the decimal point two places to the right. Therefore, 3.92% of the items are less than the particular X_i value.

Assuming that the data are normally distributed, it is possible to find the percent of the items in the data which are less than a particular value, greater than a particular value, or between two values. When the values are upper and/or lower specifications, a powerful statistical tool is available. The following example problems will illustrate the technique.

Example Problem

The mean value of the weight of a particular brand of cereal for the past year is 0.297 kg (10.5 oz) with a standard deviation of 0.024 kg. Assuming a normal distribution, find the percent of the data that falls below the lower specification limit of 0.274 kg. (*Note:* Since the mean and standard deviation

[4]In some texts the table for the areas under the normal curve is arranged in a different manner.

were determined from a large number of tests during the year, they are considered to be valid estimates of the population values.)

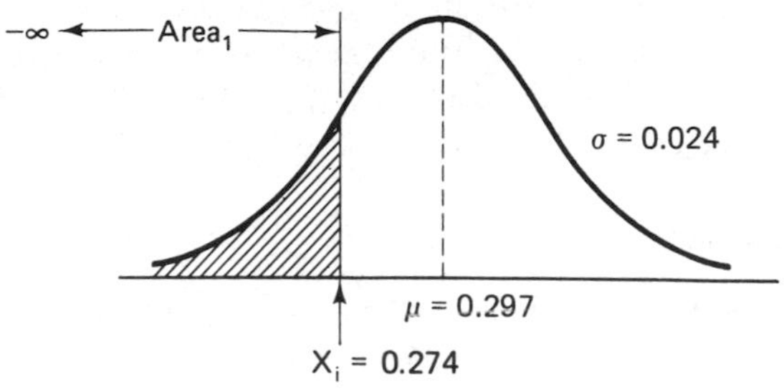

$$Z = \frac{X_i - \mu}{\sigma}$$

$$= \frac{0.274 - 0.297}{0.024}$$

$$= -0.96$$

From Table A it is found that for $Z = -0.96$,

$$\text{Area}_1 = 0.1685 \quad \text{or} \quad 16.85\%$$

Thus, 16.85% of the data are less than 0.274 kg.

Example Problem

Using the data from the preceding problem, determine the percentage of the data that fall above 0.347 kg.

Since Table A is a left-reading table, the solution to this problem requires the use of the relationship: $\text{Area}_1 + \text{Area}_2 = \text{Area}_T = 1.0000$. Therefore, Area_2 is determined and subtracted from 1.0000 to obtain Area_1.

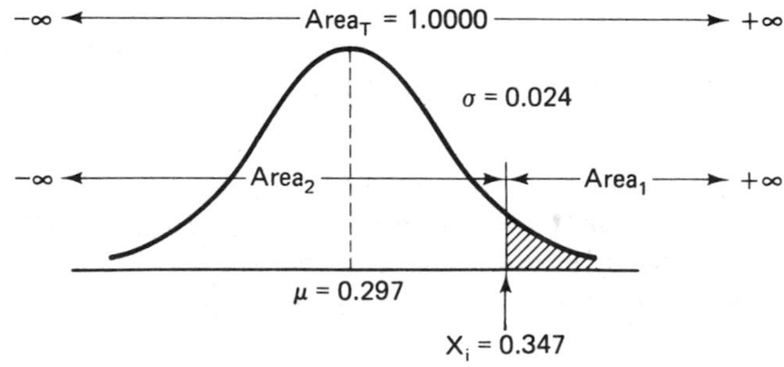

$$Z_2 = \frac{X_i - \mu}{\sigma}$$

$$= \frac{0.347 - 0.297}{0.024}$$

$$= +2.08$$

From Table A it is found that for $Z_2 = +2.08$,

$$\text{Area}_2 = 0.9812$$

$$\text{Area}_1 = \text{Area}_T - \text{Area}_2$$

$$= 1.0000 - 0.9812$$

$$= 0.0188 \quad \text{or} \quad 1.88\%$$

Thus, 1.88% of the data are above 0.347 kg.

Example Problem

A large number of tests of line voltage to home residences show a mean of 118.5 V and a population standard deviation of 1.20 V. Determine the percentage of data between 116 and 120 V.

Since Table A is a left-reading table, the solution requires that the area to the left of 116 V be subtracted from the area to the left of 120 V. The graph and calculations show the technique.

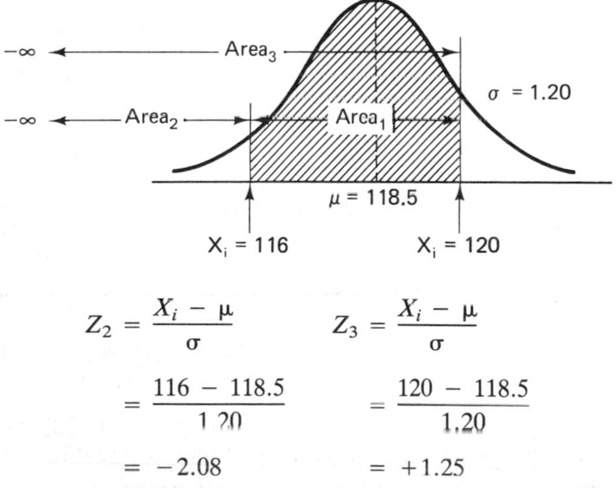

$$Z_2 = \frac{X_i - \mu}{\sigma} \qquad Z_3 = \frac{X_i - \mu}{\sigma}$$

$$= \frac{116 - 118.5}{1.20} \qquad = \frac{120 - 118.5}{1.20}$$

$$= -2.08 \qquad = +1.25$$

From Table A it is found that for $Z_2 = -2.08$, $\text{Area}_2 = 0.0188$; for $Z_3 = +1.25$, $\text{Area}_3 = 0.8944$.

$$
\begin{aligned}
\text{Area}_1 &= \text{Area}_3 - \text{Area}_2 \\
&= 0.8944 - 0.0188 \\
&= 0.8756 \quad \text{or} \quad 87.56\%
\end{aligned}
$$

Thus, 87.56% of the data are between 116 and 120 V.

Example Problem

If it is desired to have 12% of the line voltage below 115 V, how should the mean voltage be adjusted? The dispersion is $\sigma = 1.20$ V.

The solution to this type problem is the reverse of the other problems. First 12%, or 0.1200, is found in the body of Table A. This gives a Z value and using the formula for Z, we can solve for the mean voltage. From Table A with $\text{Area}_1 = 0.1200$, the Z value of -1.175 is obtained by interpolation.

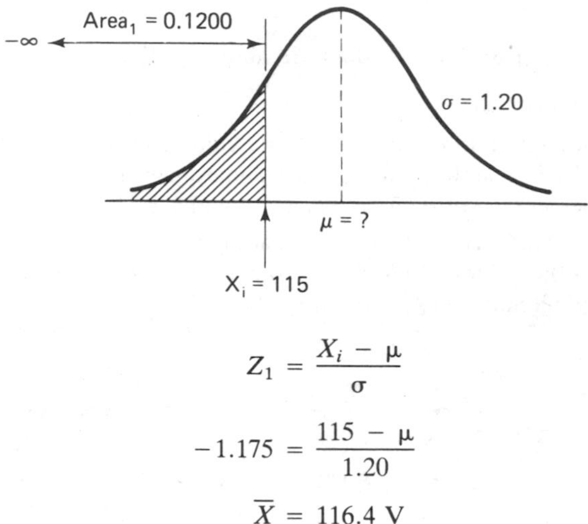

$$
\begin{aligned}
Z_1 &= \frac{X_i - \mu}{\sigma} \\
-1.175 &= \frac{115 - \mu}{1.20} \\
\overline{X} &= 116.4 \text{ V}
\end{aligned}
$$

Thus, the mean voltage should be centered at 116.4 V for 12% of the values to be less than 115 V.

TESTS FOR NORMALITY

Because of the importance of the normal distribution, it is frequently necessary to determine if the data are normal. In using these techniques the reader is cautioned that none are 100% certain. The techniques of histogram, skewness and kurtosis, probability plots, and chi-square test are also applicable with some modification to other population distributions.

Histogram

Visual examination of a histogram developed from a large amount of data will give an indication of the underlining population distribution. If a histogram is unimodal, symmetrical, and tapers off at the tails, normality is a definite possibility and may be sufficient information in many practical situations. The histogram of Figure 2-1 of steel shaft weight is unimodal, tapers off at the tails, and is somewhat symmetrical except for the upper tail. If a sorting operation had discard shafts with weights above 2.575, this would explain the upper tail cutoff.

The larger the sample size, the better the judgment of normality.

Skewness and Kurtosis

Skewness and kurtosis measurements are another test of normality. From the steel shaft data of Table 2-6, we find that $a_3 = -0.11$ and $a_4 = 2.19$. These values indicate that the data are moderately skewed to the left but are close to the normal value of 0; and that the data are not as peaked as the normal distribution, which would have an a_4 value of 3.0.

These measurements tend to give the same information as the histogram. As with the histogram, the larger the sample size, the better the judgment of normality.

Probability Plots

Another test of normality is the plotting of the data on normal probability paper. This type of paper is shown in Figure 2-13. Different probability papers are used for different distributions. To illustrate the procedure we will again use the steel shaft data in its coded form. The step-by-step procedure follows.

1. *Order the data.* The data from the first column of Table 2-4 are used to illustrate the concept. Each observation is recorded as shown in Table 2-13 from the smallest to the largest. Duplicate observations are recorded as shown by the value 46.

2. *Rank the observations.* Starting at 1 for the lowest observation, 2 for the next lowest observation, and so on, rank the observations. The ranks are shown in Column 2 of Table 2-13.

TABLE 2-13 Data on Steel Shaft Weight for Probability Plotting

Observation X_i	Rank i	Plotting Position	Observation X_i	Rank i	Plotting Position
32	1	2.3	56	12	52.3
34	2	6.8	59	13	56.8
39	3	11.4	59	14	61.4
44	4	15.9	60	15	65.9
46	5	20.5	61	16	70.5
46	6	25.0	64	17	75.0
47	7	29.5	67	18	79.5
50	8	34.1	68	19	84.1
51	9	38.6	70	20	88.6
51	10	43.2	70	21	93.2
52	11	47.7	71	22	97.7

3. *Calculate the plotting position.* This step is accomplished using the formula

$$P_i = \frac{100(i - 0.5)}{n}$$

where i = rank
P_i = plotting position
n = sample size

The first plotting position is 100(1 − 0.5)/22, which is 2.3%; the others are calculated similarly and posted to Table 2-13.

4. *Label the data scale.* The coded values range from 32 to 71, so the vertical scale is labeled appropriately and is shown in Figure 2-13.

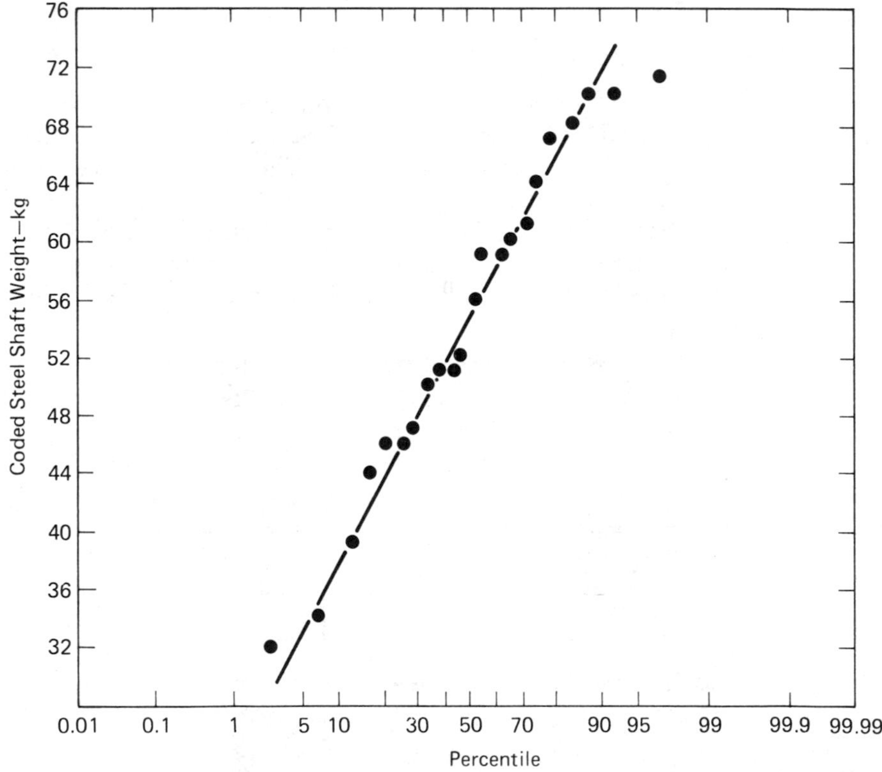

Figure 2-13 Probability plots of data from Table 2-13.

5. *Plot the points.* The plotting position and the observation are plotted on the normal probability paper.

6. *Attempt to fit by eye a "best" line.* A clear plastic straightedge will be most helpful in making this judgment. When fitting this line, greater weight should be given to the center values than to the extreme ones.

7. *Determine normality.* This decision is one of judgment as to how close the points are to the straight line. If we disregard the extreme points at each end of the line, we can reasonably assume that the data are normally distributed.

If normality appears reasonable, additional information can be obtained from the graph. The mean is located at the 50th percentile, which gives a value of approximately 55. Standard deviation is two-fifths the difference between the 90th percentile and the 10th percentile, which would be approximately [(2/5)(72 − 38)] 14. We can also use the graph to determine the percent of data below, above, or between data values. For example, the percent less than 48 is approximately 31%.

Chi-Square

The chi-square test is another technique of determining if the sample data fits a normal distribution or other distribution. This technique is beyond the scope of this book; however, it is available in most statistics textbooks.

It is important for the analyst to understand that none of these techniques prove that the data are normally distributed. We can only conclude that there is no evidence that the data cannot be treated as if they were normally distributed.

COMPUTER PROGRAM

Sample computer programs are given for this chapter and for Chapters 3, 4, 5, 6, and 7. These programs have been designed to run on microcomputers and have been written in microsoft BASIC and tested on a Zenith Z-89. The programs are given in as simple a form as possible and follow the text so that the reader can understand the programming. Provision for storing input data and correcting input data errors is not included in the programs.

The sample program for this chapter computes the seven basic statistics and determines the frequency distribution. It is shown in Figure 2-14. If it is desired to print out the data, an LPRINT statement should be inserted after statement 110. Also, a coding statement can be used after statement 100. Provision is made in the program to change the frequency distribution by changing the cell interval and/or the lowest cell midpoint value. Data used for the program are given in Table 2-4.

```
10 REM                              STAT-PACK
20 REM
30 REM          Average, Median, Range, Standard Deviation
40 REM                  Variance, Kurtosis, Skewness,
50 REM                     Frequency Distribution
60 REM
70 DIM X(600), MP(20), LB(20), UB(20), F(600)
80 PRINT " Enter number of data points." : INPUT N
90 PRINT " Enter data."
100       FOR I = 1 TO N
110       INPUT X(I)
120       NEXT I
130 REM                       Average
140 SX = 0
150       FOR I=1 TO N
160       SX = SX + X(I)
170       NEXT I
180 AVG = SX / N
190 LPRINT TAB(5);" Average = ";AVG
200 REM                       Sample Standard Deviation, Variance,
210 REM                               Skewness, Kurtosis
220 S2 = 0 : S3 = 0 : S4 = 0
230       FOR I = 1 TO N
240       D = X(I) - AVG
250       S2 = S2 + D^2
260       S3 = S3 + D^3
270       S4 = S4 + D^4
280       NEXT I
290 SD = SQR(S2 / (N-1))
300 VA = SD^2
310 A3 = S3 / N / SD^3
320 A4 = S4 / N / SD^4
330 LPRINT TAB(5);" Sample Standard Deviation = ";SD
340 LPRINT TAB(5);" Variance = ";VA
350 LPRINT TAB(5);" Skewness = ";A3
360 LPRINT TAB(5);" Kurtosis = ";A4
370 REM                       Sort Routine
380       FOR J = 1 TO (N - 1)
390       K = N - J
400       FOR I = 1 TO K
410       Q = I + 1
420       IF X(I) < X(Q) GOTO 460
430       A = X(I)
440       X(I) = X(Q)
450       X(Q) = A
460       NEXT I
470       NEXT J
480 REM                       Range
490 R=X(N)-X(1)
500 LPRINT TAB(5);" Range = ";R
510 REM                       Median
520 J = (N + 1) / 2
530 K = (N + 1) / 2
540 MD = (X(J) + X(K)) / 2
550 LPRINT TAB(5);" Median = "; MD
560 REM                    Frequency Distribution
570 PRINT " Enter Interval---odd value preferred.
580 INPUT IN
590 PRINT " Enter 1 if lowest cell midpoint is lowest X(I) value."
600 PRINT " Enter 0 if another lowest cell midpoint is desired."
```

Figure 2-14. Computer program in BASIC to calculate the seven basic statistics and the frequency distribution.

```
610 INPUT M
620 IF M = 1 THEN MP(1) = X(1) : GOTO 650
630 PRINT " Enter midpoint value of lowest cell."
640 INPUT MP(1)
650 LB(1) = MP(1) - IN / 2
660 UB(1) = MP(1) + IN / 2
670 MPS = MP(1) : LBS = LB(1) : UBS = UB(1)
680         FOR K = 2 TO 20
690         MPS = MPS + IN
700         MP(K) = MPS
710         LBS = LBS + IN
720         LB(K) = LBS
730         UBS = UBS + IN
740         UB(K) = UBS
750         IF UB(K) >= X(N) GOTO 810
760         NEXT K
770 IF UB(K - 1) < X(N) GOTO 790
780 GOTO 810
790 PRINT " Cell interval too small select a larger one."
800 GOTO 570
810 H=K
820         FOR J=1 TO H
830         FS = 0
840         FOR I = 1 TO N
850         IF X(I) < LB(J) GOTO 890
860         IF X(I) > UB(J) GOTO 890
870         FS = FS + 1
880         F(J) = FS
890         NEXT I
900         NEXT J
910 LPRINT : LPRINT
920 LPRINT TAB(10);" BOUNDARIES";TAB(29);" MIDPOINT";TAB(45);" FREQUENCY"
930             FOR J = 1 TO H
940             LPRINT TAB(7); LB(J);"/";UB(J);TAB(31); MP(J);TAB(49); F(J)
950             NEXT J
960 PRINT " If the frequency distribution is satisfactory, Enter 1."
970 PRINT " If the frequency distribution is unsatisfactory, Enter 0."
980 PRINT "    and select another interval and/or midpoint."
990 INPUT M
1000 IF M = 1 GOTO 1020
1010 IF M = 0 GOTO 570
1020 END
```

```
Average =  2.554
Sample Standard Deviation =  .0111273
Variance =  1.23817E-04
Skewness = -.0837673
Kurtosis =  2.22477
Range =  .0440002
Median =  2.553
```

BOUNDARIES	MIDPOINT	FREQUENCY
2.5305 / 2.5355	2.533	6
2.5355 / 2.5405	2.538	8
2.5405 / 2.5455	2.543	12
2.5455 / 2.5505	2.548	13
2.5505 / 2.5555	2.553	20
2.5555 / 2.5605	2.558	19
2.5605 / 2.5655	2.563	13
2.5655 / 2.5705	2.568	11
2.5705 / 2.5755	2.573	8

Figure 2-14. Continued.

The program can be enhanced by graphing the frequency distribution in the form of a histogram. This activity is a function of the graphical output device available. Also, relative frequency, cumulative frequency, and relative cumulative frequency can be developed with a few additional statements.

PROBLEMS

1. Round the following numbers to two decimal places.
(a) 0.862 (b) 0.625 (c) 0.149 (d) 0.475

2. Perform the operation indicated and leave the answer in the correct number of significant figures.
(a) (34.6)(8.2) (b) (0.035)(635) (c) 3.8735/6.1 (d) 5.362/6 (6 is a counting number) (e) 5.362/6 (6 is not a counting number)

3. Perform the operation indicated and leave the answer in the correct number of significant figures.
(a) 64.3 + 2.05 (b) 381.0 − 1.95 (c) 8.652 − 4 (4 is not a counting number) (d) 8.652 − 4 (4 is a counting number) (e) $6.4 \times 10^2 - 24.32$

4. In his last 100 games a professional basketball player made the following scores:

10	17	9	17	18	20	16	7	11	15
7	17	19	13	15	14	13	14	13	20
12	13	15	14	13	10	14	12	15	18
11	15	14	11	15	15	16	14	16	10
9	18	15	12	14	13	14	19	17	15
13	14	16	15	16	15	15	16	15	13
14	15	15	16	13	12	16	15	14	15
10	16	14	13	16	14	15	13	16	17
6	15	13	16	15	16	16	17	15	15
12	14	16	15	16	13	15	15	14	12

(a) Make a tally sheet in ascending order.
(b) Using the data above, construct a histogram.

5. A company that fills bottles of shampoo tries to maintain a specific weight of the product. The table gives the weights of 110 bottles which were checked at random intervals. Make a tally of these weights and construct a frequency histogram. (Weight is in kilograms.)

6.00	5.98	6.01	6.01	5.97	5.99	5.98	6.01	5.99	5.98	5.96
5.98	5.99	5.99	6.03	5.99	6.01	5.98	5.99	5.97	6.01	5.98
5.97	6.01	6.00	5.96	6.00	5.97	5.95	5.99	5.99	6.01	6.00
6.01	6.03	6.01	5.99	5.99	6.02	6.00	5.98	6.01	5.98	5.99
6.00	5.98	6.05	6.00	6.00	5.98	5.99	6.00	5.97	6.00	6.00
6.00	5.98	6.00	5.94	5.99	6.02	6.00	5.98	6.02	6.01	6.00
5.97	6.01	6.04	6.02	6.01	5.97	5.99	6.02	5.99	6.02	5.99
6.02	5.99	6.01	5.98	5.99	6.00	6.02	5.99	6.02	5.95	6.02
5.96	5.99	6.00	6.00	6.01	5.99	5.96	6.01	6.00	6.01	5.98
6.00	5.99	5.98	5.99	6.03	5.99	6.02	5.98	6.02	6.02	5.97

6. Listed below are 125 readings obtained by a motion-and-time-study analyst who took five readings each day for 25 days. Construct a tally sheet. Prepare a table showing cell midpoints, cell boundaries, and observed frequencies. Plot a frequency histogram.

Day			*Duration of Operation Time (min)*		
1	1.90	1.93	1.95	2.05	2.20
2	1.76	1.81	1.81	1.83	2.01
3	1.80	1.87	1.95	1.97	2.07
4	1.77	1.83	1.87	1.90	1.93
5	1.93	1.95	2.03	2.05	2.14
6	1.76	1.88	1.95	1.97	2.00
7	1.87	2.00	2.00	2.03	2.10
8	1.91	1.92	1.94	1.97	2.05
9	1.90	1.91	1.95	2.01	2.05
10	1.79	1.91	1.93	1.94	2.10
11	1.90	1.97	2.00	2.06	2.28
12	1.80	1.82	1.89	1.91	1.99
13	1.75	1.83	1.92	1.95	2.04
14	1.87	1.90	1.98	2.00	2.08
15	1.90	1.95	1.95	1.97	2.03
16	1.82	1.99	2.01	2.06	2.06
17	1.90	1.95	1.95	2.00	2.10
18	1.81	1.90	1.94	1.97	1.99
19	1.87	1.89	1.98	2.01	2.15
20	1.72	1.78	1.96	2.00	2.05
21	1.87	1.89	1.91	1.91	2.00
22	1.76	1.80	1.91	2.06	2.12
23	1.95	1.96	1.97	2.00	2.00
24	1.92	1.94	1.97	1.99	2.00
25	1.85	1.90	1.90	1.92	1.92

7. The relative strength of 150 silver solder welds are tested, and the results are given in the table below. Tally these figures and arrange them in a frequency distribution. Determine the cell interval and the approximate number of cells. Make a table showing cell midpoints, cell boundaries, and observed frequencies. Plot a frequency histogram.

1.5	1.2	3.1	1.3	0.7	1.3
0.1	2.9	1.0	1.3	2.6	1.7
0.3	0.7	2.4	1.5	0.7	2.1
3.5	1.1	0.7	0.5	1.6	1.4
1.7	3.2	3.0	1.7	2.8	2.2
1.8	2.3	3.3	3.1	3.3	2.9
2.2	1.2	1.3	1.4	2.3	2.5
3.1	2.1	3.5	1.4	2.8	2.8
1.5	1.9	2.0	3.0	0.9	3.1
1.9	1.7	1.5	3.0	2.6	1.0
2.9	1.8	1.4	1.4	3.3	2.4
1.8	2.1	1.6	0.9	2.1	1.5
0.9	2.9	2.5	1.6	1.2	2.4
3.4	1.3	1.7	2.6	1.1	0.8
1.0	1.5	2.2	3.0	2.0	1.8
2.9	2.5	2.0	3.0	1.5	1.3
2.2	1.0	1.7	3.1	2.7	2.3
0.6	2.0	1.4	3.3	2.2	2.9
1.6	2.3	3.3	2.0	1.6	2.7
1.9	2.1	3.4	1.5	0.8	2.2
1.8	2.4	1.2	3.7	1.3	2.1
2.9	3.0	2.1	1.8	1.1	1.4
2.8	1.8	1.8	2.4	2.3	2.2
2.1	1.2	1.4	1.6	2.4	2.1
2.0	1.1	3.8	1.3	1.3	1.0

8. Using the data of Problem 4, construct:
(a) A relative frequency histogram
(b) A cumulative frequency histogram
(c) A relative cumulative frequency histogram

9. Using the data of Problem 5, construct:
(a) A relative frequency histogram
(b) A cumulative frequency histogram
(c) A relative cumulative frequency histogram

10. Using the data of Problem 6, construct:
(a) A relative frequency histogram
(b) A cumulative frequency histogram
(c) A relative cumulative frequency histogram

11. Using the data of Problem 7, construct:
(a) A relative frequency histogram
(b) A cumulative frequency histogram
(c) A relative cumulative frequency histogram

12. Construct a bar graph of the data in:
(a) Problem 4
(b) Problem 5

13. Using the data of Problem 6, construct:
(a) A polygon
(b) An ogive

14. Using the data of Problem 7, construct:
(a) A polygon
(b) An ogive

15. An electrician testing the incoming line voltage for a residential house obtains five readings: 115, 113, 121, 115, 116. What is the average?

16. An employee makes eight trips to load a trailer. If the trip distances in meters are 25.6, 24.8, 22.6, 21.3, 19.6, 18.5, 16.2, and 15.5, what is the average?

17. Tests of noise ratings at prescribed locations throughout a large stamping mill are given in the frequency distribution below. Noise is measured in decibels. Determine the average.

Cell Midpoint	*Frequency*
148	2
139	3
130	8
121	11
112	27
103	35
94	43
85	33
76	20
67	12
58	6
49	4
40	2

18. The weight of 65 castings in kilograms is distributed as follows:

Cell Midpoint	*Frequency*
3.5	6
3.8	9
4.1	18
4.4	14
4.7	13
5.0	5

Determine the average.

19. Destructive tests on the life of an electronic component were conducted on two different occasions. On the first occasion three tests had a mean of 3320 h; on the second occasion two tests had a mean of 3180 h. What is the weighted average?

20. The average height of 24 students in section 1 of a course in quality control is 1.75 m; the average height of 18 students in section 2 of quality control is 1.79 m; and the average height of 29 students in section 3 of quality control is 1.68 m. What is the average height of the students in the three sections of quality control?

21. Determine the median of the following numbers.
(a) 22, 11, 15, 8, 18
(b) 35, 28, 33, 38, 43 ,36

22. Determine the median for the following:
(a) The frequency distribution of Problem 17
(b) The frequency distribution of Problem 18
(c) The frequency distribution of Problem 28
(d) The frequency distribution of Problem 30
(e) The frequency distribution of Problem 6
(f) The frequency distribution of Problem 7

23. Given the following series of numbers, determine the mode.
(a) 50, 45, 55, 55, 45, 50, 55, 45, 55
(b) 89, 87, 88, 83, 86, 82, 84
(c) 11, 17, 14, 12, 12, 14, 14, 15, 17, 17

24. Determine the modal cell of the data in:
(a) Problem 4
(b) Problem 5
(c) Problem 6
(d) Problem 7
(e) Problem 17
(f) Problem 18

25. Determine the range for each set of numbers.
(a) 16, 25, 18, 17, 16, 21, 14
(b) 45, 39, 42, 42, 43
(c) The data in Problem 4
(d) The data in Problem 5

26. Frequency tests of a brass rod 145 cm long give values of 1200, 1190, 1205, 1185, and 1200 vibrations per second. What is the sample standard deviation?

27. Four readings of the thickness of the paper in this textbook are 0.076 mm, 0.082 mm, 0.073 mm, and 0.077 mm. Determine the sample standard deviation.

28. The frequency distribution given here shows the percent of organic sulfur in Illinois No. 5 coal. Determine the sample standard deviation.

Cell Midpoint (%)	*Frequency (number of samples)*
0.5	1
0.7	16
0.9	12
1.1	10
1.3	3
1.5	12
1.7	20
1.9	12
2.1	14
2.3	6
2.5	4

29. Determine the sample standard deviation for the following.
(a) The data of Problem 7
(b) The data of Problem 17

30. Determine the average and sample standard deviation for the frequency distribution of the number of inspections per day as follows:

Cell Midpoint	*Frequency*
1000	6
1300	13
1600	22
1900	17
2200	11
2500	8

31. Using the data of Problem 17, construct:
(a) A polygon
(b) An ogive

32. Using the data of Problem 18, construct:
(a) A polygon
(b) An ogive

33. Using the data of Problem 28, construct:
(a) A polygon
(b) An ogive

34. Using the data of Problem 30, construct:
(a) A polygon
(b) An ogive

35. Using the data of Problem 17, construct:
(a) A histogram
(b) A relative frequency histogram
(c) A cumulative frequency histogram
(d) A relative cumulative frequency histogram

36. Using the data of Problem 18, construct:
(a) A histogram
(b) A relative frequency histogram
(c) A cumulative frequency histogram
(d) A relative cumulative frequency histogram

37. Using the data of Problem 28, construct:
(a) A histogram
(b) A relative frequency histogram
(c) A cumulative frequency histogram
(d) A relative cumulative frequency histogram

38. Using the data of Problem 30, construct:
(a) A histogram
(b) A relative frequency histogram
(c) A cumulative frequency histogram
(d) A relative cumulative frequency histogram

39. Determine the skewness and kurtosis of:
(a) Problem 4
(b) Problem 5
(c) Problem 6
(d) Problem 7
(e) Problem 18
(f) Problem 30

40. The population mean of a company's racing bicycles is 9.07 kg (20.0 lb) with a population standard deviation of 0.40 kg. If the distribution is approximately normal, determine (a) the percentage of bicycles less than 8.30 kg, (b) the percentage of bicycles greater than 10.00 kg, and (c) the percentage of bicycles between 8.00 and 10.10 kg.

41. If the mean time for a welding operation is 1.60 min and the standard deviation is 0.06 min, what percentage of the parts will take less than 1.48 min to complete? What percentage of the parts will take more than 1.70 min to complete? What percentage of the parts will take between 1.48 and 1.72 min to complete? The data are normally distributed.

42. A cold-cereal manufacturer wants 1.5% of the product to be below the weight specification of 0.567 kg (1.25 lb). If the data are normally distributed and the standard deviation of the cereal filling machine is 0.018 kg, what mean weight is required?

43. In the precision grinding of a complicated part, it is more economical to rework the part than to scrap it. Therefore, it is decided to establish the rework percentage at 12.5%. Assuming normal distribution of the data, a standard deviation of 0.01 mm, and an upper specification limit of 25.38 mm (0.99 in.), determine the process center.

44. Using the information of Problem 39, what is your judgment concerning the normality of the distribution?
(a) Problem 4
(b) Problem 5
(c) Problem 6
(d) Problem 7
(e) Problem 18
(f) Problem 30

45. Using normal probability paper, determine (judgment) the normality of the distribution of the following.
(a) Second column of Table 2-4
(b) First three columns of Problem 5
(c) Second column of Problem 6

46. Test, and if necessary rewrite, the computer program for your computer.

47. Modify the computer program to output a histogram for your graphical output device.

48. Modify the computer program to output a relative frequency histogram, cumulative frequency histogram, and relative cumulative frequency histogram for your graphical output device.

3 CONTROL CHARTS FOR VARIABLES

INTRODUCTION

Variation

One of the axioms or truisms of manufacturing is that no two objects are ever made exactly alike. In fact, the variation concept is a law of nature in that no two natural items in any category are the same. The variation may be quite large and easily noticeable, such as the height of human beings, or the variation may be very small, such as the weight of fiber-tipped pens. When variations are very small, it may appear that items are identical; however, precision instruments will show differences. If two items appear to have the same measurement, it is due to the limits of our measuring instruments. As measuring instruments have become more refined, variation has continued to exist, only the increment of variation has changed. The ability to measure this variation in the product is necessary before it can be controlled.

There are three categories of variations in piece part production.

1. *Within-piece variation.* This type of variation is illustrated by the surface roughness of a piece wherein one portion of the surface is rougher than another portion; or the width of one end of a keyway varies from the other end.
2. *Piece-to-piece variation.* This type of variation occurs among pieces produced at the same time. Thus, the light intensity of four consecutive light bulbs produced from a machine will be different.
3. *Time-to-time variation.* This type of variation is illustrated by the difference in product produced at different times of the day. Thus, product produced in the early morning would be different from that produced later in the day; or as a cutting tool wears, the cutting characteristics change.

Categories of variation for other types of processes will not be exactly the same; however, the concept will be similar.

There are five factors that contribute to these variations, and they are processes, materials, environment, operators, and inspection. The first source of variation is the *process*. This source includes tool wear, machine vibration, workholding-device positioning, and hydraulic and electrical fluctuations. When all these variations are put together; there is a certain capability or accuracy within which the process operates. Even supposedly identical machines will have different capabilities, and this fact becomes a very important consideration when scheduling the manufacture of critical parts.

The second source of variation is the *material*. Since variation occurs in the finished product, it must also occur in the raw material (which was someone else's finished product). Such quality characteristics as tensile strength, ductility, thickness, porosity, and moisture content can be expected to contribute to the variation in the final product.

A third source of variation is the *environment*. Temperature, light, radiation, and humidity can all contribute to variation in the process.

A fourth source is the *operator*. This source of variation includes the method by which the operator performs the operation. Is the instruction sheet being followed, and is it being followed exactly the same each cycle or are there minor variations? The operator's physical and emotional well being also contribute to the variation. A cut finger, a twisted ankle, a personal problem, or a headache can make an operator's quality performance vary. An operator's lack of understanding of process and material variations due to lack of training may lead to frequent machine adjustments, thereby compounding the variability.

The last source is the *inspection* activity. Faulty inspection equipment, or the incorrect application of a quality standard, or too heavy a pressure on a micrometer, can be the cause of the incorrect reporting of variation. In general, variation due to inspection should be one-tenth of the four other sources of variations. It should be noted that three of these sources are present in the inspection activity—an inspector, inspection equipment, and the environment.

As long as these five sources of variation fluctuate in a normal or expected manner, a stable pattern of many *chance causes* of variation develops. Chance causes of variation are inevitable, and because they are very small in magnitude, they are difficult to identify. Those causes of variation which are large in magnitude, and therefore readily identified, are classified as *assignable causes*. When only chance causes are present in a process, the process is considered to be in control. However, when an assignable cause of variation is also present, the variation will be excessive and the process is classified as out of control or beyond the expected normal variation.

The Control Chart Method

In order to indicate when observed variations in quality are greater than could be left to chance, the control chart method of analysis and presentation of data is used. The control chart method for variables is a means of visualizing the variations that occur in the central tendency and dispersion of a set of observations. It is a graphical record of the quality of a particular characteristic.

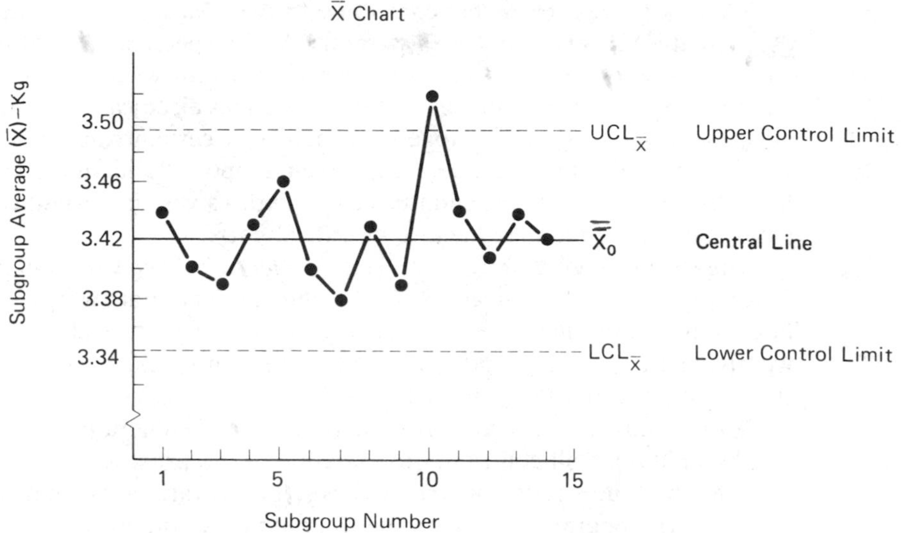

Figure 3-1 Example of a control chart.

An example of a control chart is given in Figure 3-1. This particular chart is referred to as an $\overline{X}$ chart and is used to control the variation in the average value of samples. Another chart, such as the R chart (range), would have also served for explanation purposes. The horizontal axis is labeled "Subgroup Number," which identifies a particular sample consisting of a fixed number of observations. These subgroups are in order, with the first one inspected being 1 and the last one inspected being 14. The vertical axis of the graph is the variable, which in this particular case is weight measured in kilograms.

Each small solid circle represents the average value within a subgroup. Thus, subgroup number 5 consists of, say, four observations: 3.46, 3.49, 3.45, and 3.44, and their average is 3.46 kg. This value is the one posted on the chart for subgroup number 5. Averages are used on control charts rather than individual observations because average values will indicate a change in variation much faster.[1] Also, with two or more observations in a sample, a measure of the dispersion can be obtained for a particular subgroup.

The solid line in the center of the chart can have three different interpretations depending on the available data. First, it can be the average of the plotted points, which in the case of an $\overline{X}$ chart is the average of the averages or "X-double bar," $\overline{\overline{X}}$. Second, it can be a standard or reference value, $\overline{X}_0$, based on representative prior data, an economic value based on production costs or service needs, or an aimed-at value based on specifications. Third, it can be the population mean, μ, if that value is known.

[1]For a proof of this statement, see J. M. Juran, ed., *Quality Control Handbook*, 3rd ed. (New York: McGraw-Hill Book Company, 1974), Sec. 23, p. 13

The two dashed outer lines are the upper and lower control limits. These limits are established to assist in judging the significance of the variation in the quality of the product. Control limits are frequently confused with *specification limits*, which are the permissible limits of a quality characteristic of each *individual* unit of a product. However, *control limits* are used to evaluate the variations in quality from subgroup to subgroup. Therefore, for the $\overline{X}$ chart, the control limits are a function of the subgroup averages. A frequency distribution of the subgroup averages can be determined with its corresponding average and standard deviation. The control limits are then established at ± 3 standard deviations from the central line. One recalls, from the discussion of the normal curve, that the number of items between $+3\sigma$ and -3σ equals 99.73%. Therefore, it is expected that over 997 times out of a 1000, the subgroup values will fall between the upper and lower limits, and when this occurs, the process is considered to be in control. When a subgroup value falls outside the limits, the process is considered to be out of control and an assignable cause for the variation is present. Subgroup number 10 in Figure 3-1 is beyond the upper control limit; therefore, something has gone wrong with the stable nature of the process, causing the out-of-control point.

In practice, control charts are posted at individual machines or work centers to control a particular quality characteristic. Usually, an $\overline{X}$ chart for the central tendency and an R chart for the dispersion are used together. An example of this dual charting is illustrated in Figure 3-2, which shows a method of charting and reporting inspection results for the rubber durometer of printing dies. The inspector stops at work center number 365-2 at 8:30 A.M., selects four printing dies for testing, and records the observations of 55, 52, 51, and 53 in the rows marked X_1, X_2, X_3, and X_4, respectively. A subgroup average value of 52.8 is obtained by summing the observations and dividing by 4, and the range value of 4 is obtained by subtracting the high value, 55, from the low value, 51. The inspector places a small solid circle at 52.8 on the $\overline{X}$ chart and a small solid circle at 4 on the R chart, and then proceeds with his other duties.

An inspector's routine or the frequency that he inspects a product at a particular machine or work center is determined by the quality of the product. When the process is in control and no difficulties are being encountered, fewer inspections may be required, and, conversely, when the process is out of control, more inspections may be needed. The inspection frequency at a machine or work center is also determined by the number of other work centers that must be inspected or the time that must be spent on noninspection duties. In the example problem, the inspection frequency appears to be every 65 or 70 minutes. Inspectors should avoid too fixed a routine, since the operator may influence the reporting of the quality if he knows the exact time the inspector will arrive at the work center.

At 9:30 A.M. the inspector returns and performs the activities for subgroup 2 in the same manner as for subgroup 1. It is noted that the range value of 7 falls right on the upper control limit. Whether to consider this in control or

$\overline{X}$ AND R CHART

Work Center Number 365-2
Quality Characteristic Dies Date 3/6/85

Time	8 30 AM	9 30 AM	10 40 AM	11 50 AM	1 30 PM									
Subgroup	1	2	3	4	5	6	7	8	9	10	11	12	13	14
X_1	55	51	48	45	53									
X_2	52	52	49	43	50									
X_3	51	57	50	45	48									
X_4	53	50	49	43	50									
Sum	211	210	196	176	201									
$\overline{X}$	52.8	52.5	49	44	50.2									
R	4	7	2	2	5									

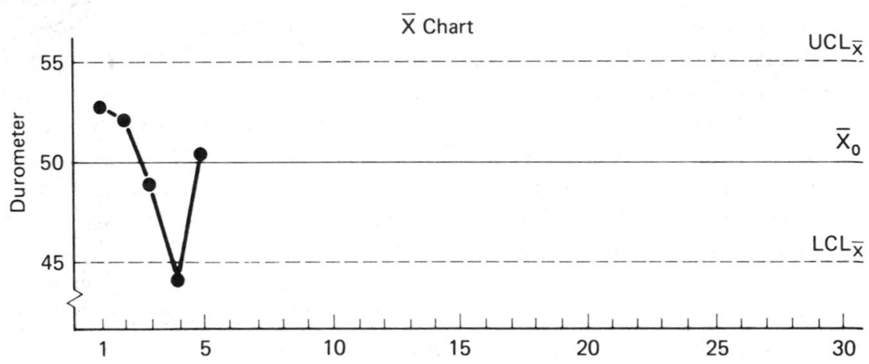

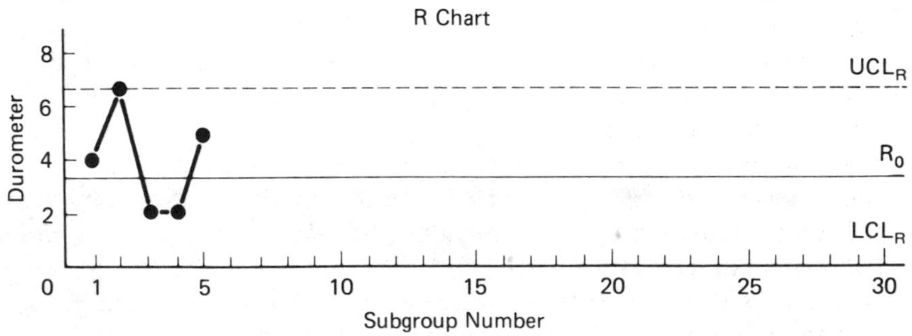

Figure 3-2 Example of a method of reporting inspection results.

out of control would be a matter of company policy. It is suggested that it be classified as in control, and a cursory examination for an assignable cause be conducted by the operator.

The inspection results for subgroup 2 shows that the third observation, X_3, has a value of 57, which exceeds the upper control limit. The reader is cautioned to remember the earlier discussion on control limits and specifications. In other words, the 57 value is an individual observation and does not relate to the control limits. Therefore, the fact that an individual observation is greater than or less than a control limit is meaningless.

Subgroup 4 has an average value of 44, which is less than the lower control limit of 45. Therefore, subgroup 4 is out of control, and the inspector will report this fact to the departmental supervisor. The operator and supervisor will then look for an assignable cause and, if possible, take corrective action. Whatever corrective action is taken will be noted by the inspector on the $\overline{X}$ and R chart or on a separate form. The control chart indicates when and where trouble has occurred; the identification and elimination of the difficulty is a production problem. Ideally, the control chart should be maintained by the operator provided time is available and proper training has been given.

The control chart is used to keep a continuing record of a particular quality characteristic. When the chart is completed, it is replaced by a fresh chart, and the completed chart is stored in an office file. The chart is used to improve the process quality, to determine the process capability, to determine when to leave the process alone and when to make adjustments, and to investigate causes of unacceptable or marginal quality.

Purpose of Variable Control Charts

The use of variable control charts serves the following purposes:

1. To provide information for quality improvement. Having a variables control chart merely because it indicates that there is a quality control program is missing the point. A variable control chart is the most effective technique for achieving quality improvement.

2. To provide information to determine the process capability. The true process capability can be achieved only after substantial quality improvement has been achieved. During the quality improvement cycle, the control chart will indicate that no further improvement is possible without a large dollar expenditure. At that point the true process capability is obtained.

3. To provide information for decisions in regard to product specifications. Once the true process capability is obtained, effective specifications can be determined. If the process capability is ± 0.003, then specifications of ± 0.004 are realistically obtainable by operating personnel.

4. To provide information for current decisions in regard to the production process. Thus, the control chart is used to decide when a normal pattern of

variation occurs and the process should be left alone, and when an unstable pattern of variation is occurring, which requires action to find and eliminate the disturbing or assignable causes.

In this regard, operating personnel are giving a quality performance as long as the plotted points are within the control limits. If this performance is not satisfactory, the solution is the responsibility of the system rather than the operator.

5. To provide information for current decisions in regard to recently produced items. Thus, the control chart is used as one source of information to help decide whether an item or items should be released to the next phase of the sequence or some alternative disposition made, such as sorting and repairing.

These purposes are frequently dependent on each other. For example, quality improvement is needed prior to determining the process capability which is needed prior to determining effective specifications. Control charts for variables should be established to achieve a particular purpose. Their use should be discontinued when the purpose has been achieved or their use continued with the inspection substantially reduced.

CONTROL CHART TECHNIQUES

Introduction

In order to establish a pair of control charts for the average ($\overline{X}$) and the range (R), it is desirable to follow a set procedure. The steps in this procedure are as follows:

1. Select the quality characteristic.
2. Choose the rational subgroup.
3. Collect the data.
4. Determine the trial central line and control limits.
5. Establish the revised central line and control limits.
6. Achieve the purpose.

This procedure is presented in this section as it relates to an $\overline{X}$ and R chart. Information on an s chart is also presented.

Select the Quality Characteristic

The variable that is chosen for an $\overline{X}$ and R chart must be a quality characteristic that is measurable and can be expressed in numbers. Quality characteristics that can be expressed in terms of the seven basic units: length, mass, time, electrical current, temperature, substance, or luminous intensity are appropriate as well as any of the derived units, such as power, velocity, force, energy, density, and pressure.

Those quality characteristics affecting the performance of the product should normally be given first attention. These may be a function of the raw materials, components parts, subassemblies, or finished parts. In other words, give high priority to the selection of those characteristics which are giving difficulty in terms of production problems and/or cost. An excellent opportunity for cost savings is usually selected where spoilage and rework costs are high. A Pareto analysis[2] could also be useful to establish priorities. Another possibility is where destructive testing is being used to inspect a product.

In any manufacturing plant there are an enumerable number of variables which make up a product. It is, therefore, impossible to place $\overline{X}$ and R charts on all variables, and a judicious selection of those quality characteristics for control is required. Since all variables can be treated as attributes, an attribute control chart (see Chapter 5) can also be used to achieve quality improvement.

Choose the Rational Subgroup

As previously mentioned, the data that are plotted on the control chart consists of groups of items that are called rational subgroups. There are two schemes for selecting the subgroup samples:

1. The first method is to select the subgroup samples from product produced at one instant of time or as close to that instant as possible. Four consecutive parts from a machine or four parts from a tray of recently produced parts would be an example of this subgrouping technique. The next subgroup sample would be similar but for product produced at a later time—say, 1 hour later. This method is called the instant-time method.

2. The second method is to select product produced over a period of time so that it is representative of all the product. For example, an inspector makes a visit to a circuit breaker assembling process once every hour. The subgroup sample, of say four, is randomly selected from all the circuit breakers produced in the previous hour. On his next visit, the subgroup is selected from the product produced between visits and so forth. This method is called the period-of-time method.

In comparing the two methods, the instant-time method will have a minimum variation *within* a subgroup and a maximum variation *among* subgroups. The period-of-time method will have a maximum variation *within* a subgroup and a minimum variation *among* subgroups. Some numerical values may help to illustrate this difference. Thus, for the instant-time method, subgroup average values ($\overline{X}$'s) could be from, say, 26 to 34 with subgroup range values (R's) from

[2]An explanation of a Pareto analysis is given in Chapter 9.

0 to 4; while for the period-of-time method, the subgroup average values ($\overline{X}$'s) would be from 28 to 32 with the subgroup range values ($\overline{R}$'s) from 0 to 8.

The instant-time method is the one most commonly used since it provides a particular time reference for determining assignable causes. It also provides a more sensitive measure of changes in the process average. The advantage of the period-of-time method is that it provides better overall results and, therefore, quality reports will present a more accurate picture of the quality. It is also true that because of process limitations the latter method may be the only practical method of obtaining the subgroup samples. In some situations, it may be desirable to use both subgrouping methods. When this occurs, two charts with different control limits are required.

Regardless of the scheme used to obtain the subgroup, the lots from which the subgroups are chosen must be homogeneous. By homogeneous is meant that the pieces in the lot are as alike as possible—same machine, same operator, same mold cavity, and so on. Similarly, a fixed quantity of material, such as that produced by one tool until it wears out and is replaced or resharpened, should be a homogeneous lot. Homogeneous lots can also be designated by equal time intervals, since this technique is easy to organize and administer. No matter how the lots are designated, the items in any one subgroup should have been produced under essentially the same conditions.

Decisions on the size of the sample or subgroup require a certain amount of empirical judgment; however, some helpful guidelines can be given:

1. As the subgroup size increases, the control limits become closer to the central value, which makes the control chart more sensitive to small variations in the process average.
2. As the subgroup size increases, the inspection cost per subgroup increases. Does the increased cost of larger subgroups justify the greater sensitivity?
3. When destructive testing is used and the item is expensive, a small subgroup size of 2 or 3 is necessary, since it will minimize the destruction of expensive product.
4. Because of the ease of computation a sample size of 5 is quite common in industry; however, with the inexpensive electronic hand calculators, this reason is no longer valid.
5. From a statistical basis a distribution of subgroup averages, $\overline{X}$'s, are nearly normal for subgroups of 4 or more even when the samples are taken from a nonnormal population.[3]
6. When the subgroup size exceeds 10, the s chart should be used instead of the R chart for the control of the dispersion.

[3] For proof of this statement, see W. A. Shewhart, *Economic Control of Quality of Manufactured Product* (Princeton, N.J.: Van Nostrand Reinhold Company, Inc., 1931), pp. 180–186.

TABLE 3-1 Sample Sizes (From MIL-STD-414, Normal Inspection, Level IV)

Lot Size	*Sample Size*
66–110	10
111–180	15
181–300	25
301–500	30
501–800	35
801–1,300	40
1,301–3,200	50
3,201–8,000	60
8,001–22,000	85

There is no rule for the frequency of taking subgroups. The inconveniences of the factory layout and the cost of taking subgroups must be balanced with the value of the data obtained. In general, it is best to sample quite often at the beginning and reduce the sampling frequency when the data permit. The use of Table 3-1, which was obtained from MIL-STD 414, can be a valuable aid in making judgments on the amount of sampling required. If a process is expected to produce 4000 pieces per day, then 60 total inspections are required. Therefore, with a subgroup size of four, 15 subgroups would be needed. The frequency of taking a subgroup is expressed in terms of the percent of items produced or in terms of the time interval.

In summary, the selection of the rational subgroup is made in such a manner that no bias exists.

Collect the Data

The next step is to collect the data. This step can be accomplished using the type form shown in Figure 3-2, wherein the data are recorded in a vertical fashion. By recording the measurements one below the other, the summing operation for each subgroup is somewhat easier. An alternative method of recording the data is shown in Table 3-2, wherein the data are recorded in a horizontal fashion. This method permits the summing of the $\overline{X}$ values in an easier fashion; however, the particular method makes no difference when an electronic hand calculator is available. For illustrative purposes, the latter method will be used.

Assuming that the quality characteristic and the plan for the rational subgroup have been selected, an inspector can be assigned the task of collecting the data as part of his normal duties. The first-line supervisor and the operator should be informed of the inspector's activities; however, no charts or data are posted at the work center at this time.

Because of difficulty in the assembly of a gear hub to a shaft using a key and keyway, an investigation using an $\overline{X}$ and R chart is initiated. The quality characteristic chosen is the shaft keyway depth of 6.35 mm (0.250 in.). Using a rational subgroup of four, an inspector obtains five subgroups per day for 5

TABLE 3-2 Data on the Depth of the Keyway (millimeters)[a]

Subgroup Number	Date	Time	Measurements X_1	X_2	X_3	X_4	Average $\overline{X}$	Range R	Comment
1	12/23	8:50	35	40	32	33	6.35	0.08	
2		11:30	46	37	36	41	6.40	0.10	
3		1:45	34	40	34	36	6.36	0.06	
4		3:45	69	64	68	59	6.65	0.10	New, temporary operator
5		4:20	38	34	44	40	6.39	0.10	
6	12/27	8:35	42	41	43	34	6.40	0.09	
7		9:00	44	41	41	46	6.43	0.05	
8		9:40	33	41	38	36	6.37	0.08	
9		1:30	48	52	49	51	6.50	0.04	
10		2:50	47	43	36	42	6:42	0.11	
11	12/28	8:30	38	41	39	38	6.39	0.03	
12		1:35	37	37	41	37	6.38	0.04	
13		2:25	40	38	47	35	6.40	0.12	
14		2:35	38	39	45	42	6.41	0.07	
15		3:55	50	42	43	45	6.45	0.08	
16	12/29	8:25	33	35	29	39	6.34	0.10	
17		9:25	41	40	29	34	6.36	0.12	
18		11:00	38	44	28	58	6.42	0.30	Damaged oil line
19		2:35	33	32	37	38	6.35	0.06	
20		3:15	56	55	45	48	6.51	0.11	Bad material
21	12/30	9:35	38	40	45	37	6.40	0.08	
22		10:20	39	42	35	40	6.39	0.07	
23		11:35	42	39	39	36	6.39	0.06	
24		2:00	43	36	35	38	6.38	0.08	
25		4:25	39	38	43	44	6.41	0.06	
Sum							160.25	2.19	

[a]For simplicity in recording, the individual measurements are coded from 6.00 mm.

days using the instant-time method. The samples are measured, the subgroup average ($\overline{X}$) and range R are calculated, and the results are recorded on the form. Additional recorded information includes the date, time, and any comments pertaining to the process.

It is necessary to collect a minimum of 20 subgroups of data; however, since some observations may be discarded, 25 subgroups are used. A fewer number of subgroups would not provide a sufficient amount of data for the accurate computation of the control limits; and a larger number of subgroups would delay the introduction of the control chart.

Determine the Trial Control Limits

The central lines for the $\overline{X}$ and R charts are obtained using the formulas

$$\overline{\overline{X}} = \frac{\sum_{i=1}^{g} \overline{X}_i}{g} \quad \text{and} \quad \overline{R} = \frac{\sum_{i=1}^{g} R_i}{g}$$

where $\overline{\overline{X}}$ = average of the subgroup averages (read "X double bar")
$\overline{X}_i$ = average of the ith subgroup
g = number of subgroups
$\overline{R}$ = average of the subgroup ranges
R_i = range of the ith subgroup

Trial control limits for the charts are established at ±3 standard deviations from the central value, as shown by the formulas

$$UCL_{\overline{X}} = \overline{\overline{X}} + 3\sigma_{\overline{X}} \qquad UCL_R = \overline{R} + 3\sigma_R$$

$$LCL_{\overline{X}} = \overline{\overline{X}} - 3\sigma_{\overline{X}} \qquad LCL_R = \overline{R} - 3\sigma_R$$

where UCL = upper control limit
LCL = lower control limit
$\sigma_{\overline{X}}$ = population standard deviation of the subgroup averages ($\overline{X}$'s)
σ_R = population standard deviation of the range

In practice, the calculations are simplified by using the product of the range ($\overline{R}$) and a factor (A_2) to replace the three standard deviations ($A_2\overline{R} = 3\sigma_{\overline{X}}$)[4] in the formulas for the $\overline{X}$ chart. For the R chart, the range $\overline{R}$ is used to estimate the standard deviation of the range (σ_R).[5] Therefore, the derived formulas are

$$UCL_{\overline{X}} = \overline{\overline{X}} + A_2\overline{R} \qquad UCL_R = D_4\overline{R}$$

$$LCL_{\overline{X}} = \overline{\overline{X}} - A_2\overline{R} \qquad LCL_R = D_3\overline{R}$$

where A_2, D_3, and D_4 are factors that vary with the subgroup size and are found in Table B of the Appendix. For the $\overline{X}$ chart the upper and lower control limits are symmetrical about the central line. Theoretically, the control limits for an R chart should also be symmetrical about the central line. But, for this situation to occur, with subgroup sizes of 6 or less, the lower control limit would need to

[4]The derivation of $3\sigma_{\overline{X}} = A_2\overline{R}$ is based on the substitution of $\sigma_{\overline{X}} = \sigma/\sqrt{n}$ and an estimate of $\sigma = \overline{R}/d_2$, where d_2 is a factor for the subgroup size.

$$3\sigma_{\overline{X}} = \frac{3\sigma}{\sqrt{n}} = \frac{3}{d_2\sqrt{n}}\overline{R}; \qquad \text{therefore,} \quad A_2 = \frac{3}{d_2\sqrt{n}}$$

[5]The derivation of the simplified formula is based on the substitution of $d_3\sigma = \sigma_R$ and $\sigma = \overline{R}/d_2$, which gives

$$\left(1 + \frac{3d_3}{d_2}\right)\overline{R} \quad \text{and} \quad \left(1 - \frac{3d_3}{d_2}\right)\overline{R}$$

for the control limits. Thus, D_4 and D_3 are set equal to the coefficients of $\overline{R}$.

have a negative value. Since a negative range is impossible, the lower control limit is located at zero by assigning to D_3 the value of zero for subgroup sizes of 6 or less.

When the subgroup size is 7 or more, the lower control limit is greater than zero and symmetrical about the central line. However, when the R chart is posted at the work center, it may be more practical to keep the lower control limit at zero. This provides the operator with an extra incentive to keep the variation in the dispersion at a minimum. And this eliminates the difficulty of explaining to the operator that points below the lower control limit on the R chart are the result of exceptionally good performance rather than poor performance. However, quality personnel should keep their own charts with the lower control limit in its proper location, and any out-of-control low points investigated to determine the reason for the exceptionally good performance. Since subgroup sizes of seven or more are uncommon, the situation occurs infrequently.

Example Problem

In order to illustrate the calculations necessary to obtain the trial control limits and the central line, the data in Table 3-2 concerning the depth of the shaft keyway will be used. From Table 3-2, the $\sum \overline{X} = 160.25$, $\sum R = 2.19$, and $g = 25$; thus, the central lines are

$$\overline{\overline{X}} = \frac{\sum_{i=1}^{g} \overline{X}_i}{g} = \frac{160.25}{25} = 6.41 \text{ mm} \qquad \overline{R} = \frac{\sum_{i=1}^{g} R_i}{g} = \frac{2.19}{25} = 0.0876 \text{ mm}$$

From Table B in the Appendix, the values for the factors for a subgroup size (n) of four are $A_2 = 0.729$, $D_3 = 0$, and $D_4 = 2.282$. Trial control limits for the $\overline{X}$ chart are:

$$\text{UCL}_{\overline{X}} = \overline{\overline{X}} + A_2\overline{R} = 6.41 + (0.729)(0.0876) = 6.47 \text{ mm} \qquad \text{LCL}_{\overline{X}} = \overline{\overline{X}} - A_2\overline{R} = 6.41 - (0.729)(0.0876) = 6.35 \text{ mm}$$

Trial control limits for the R chart are

$$\text{UCL}_R = D_4\overline{R} = (2.282)(0.0876) = 0.20 \text{ mm} \qquad \text{LCL}_R = D_3\overline{R} = (0)(0.0876) = 0 \text{ mm}$$

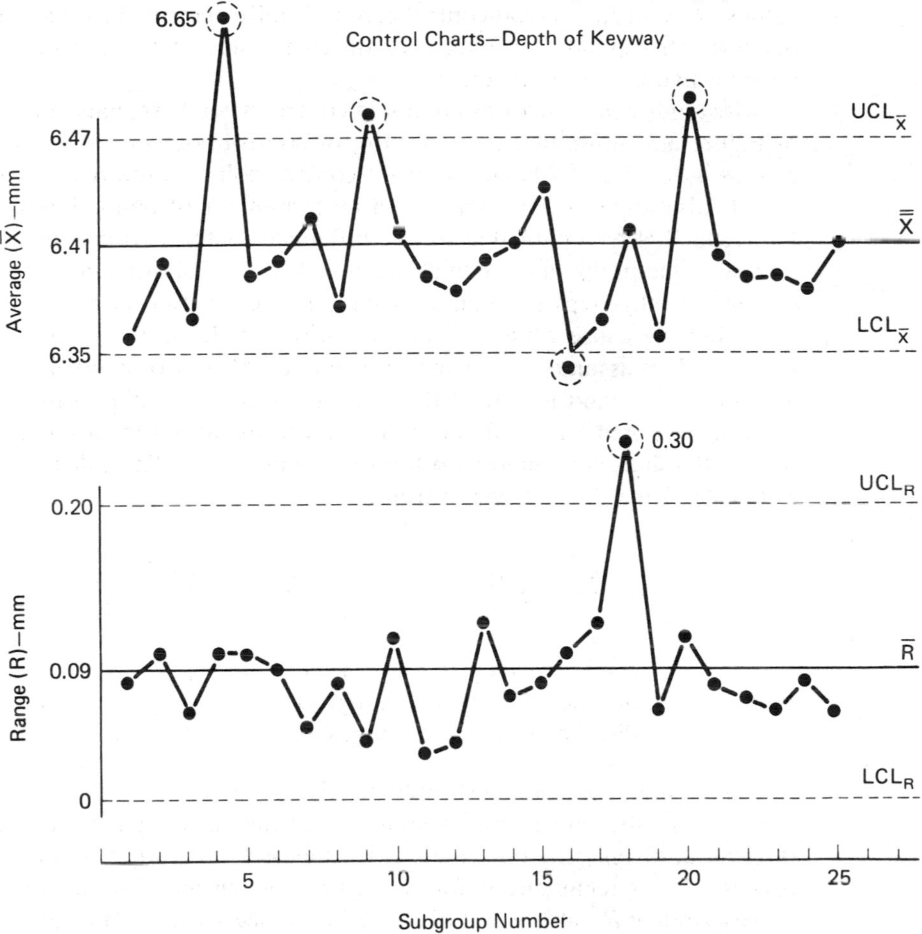

Figure 3-3 $\overline{X}$ and R chart for preliminary data with trial control limits.

Figure 3-3 shows the central lines and the trial control limits for the $\overline{X}$ and R charts for the preliminary data.

Establish the Revised Control Limits

The first step is to post the preliminary data to the chart along with the control limits and central lines. This has been accomplished and is shown in Figure 3-3.

The next step is to adopt standard values for the central lines, or, more appropriately stated, the best estimate of the standard values with the available data. If an analysis of the preliminary data shows good control, then $\overline{\overline{X}}$ and $\overline{R}$ can be considered as representative of the process and these become the standard values, $\overline{X}_0$ and R_0. Good control can be briefly described as that which has no out-of-control points, no long runs on either side of the central line, and no unusual patterns of variation.

Most industrial processes are not in control when first analyzed. An analysis of Figure 3-3 shows that there are out-of-control points on the $\overline{X}$ chart at subgroups 4, 9, 16 and 20 and an out-of-control point on the R chart at subgroup 18. It also appears that there are a large number of points below the central line, which is no doubt due to the influence of the extreme high points. A review of the preliminary data as given in Table 3-2 shows that some of the out-of-control subgroups have an assignable cause. Subgroups 4, 18, and 20 had an assignable cause while the out-of-control condition for subgroups 9 and 16 do not. It is assumed that subgroups 9 and 16's out-of-control state is due to a chance cause and is part of the normal variation. Subgroups 4, 18, and 20 are not part of the normal variation and are discarded from the data and new $\overline{\overline{X}}$ and $\overline{R}$ values computed with the remaining data. The calculations are simplified by using the following formulas:

$$\overline{\overline{X}}_{\text{new}} = \frac{\sum \overline{X} - \overline{X}_d}{g - g_d} \qquad \overline{R}_{\text{new}} = \frac{\sum R - R_d}{g - g_d}$$

where $\overline{X}_d$ = discarded subgroup averages
g_d = number of discarded subgroups
R_d = discarded subgroup ranges

There are two techniques used to discard data. If either the $\overline{X}$ or the R value of a subgroup is out of control and has an assignable cause, both are discarded, or only the out-of-control value of a subgroup is discarded. In this text the latter technique is followed; thus, when an $\overline{X}$ value is discarded, its corresponding R value is not discarded and vice versa. Calculations for a new $\overline{X}$ are based on discarding the $\overline{X}$ values of 6.65 and 6.51 for subgroups 4 and 20, respectively. Calculations for a new $\overline{R}$ are based on discarding the R value of 0.30 for subgroup 18.

$$\overline{\overline{X}}_{\text{new}} = \frac{\sum \overline{X} - \overline{X}_d}{g - g_d} \qquad \overline{R}_{\text{new}} = \frac{\sum R - R_d}{g - g_d}$$

$$= \frac{160.25 - 6.65 - 6.51}{25 - 2} \qquad = \frac{2.19 - 0.30}{25 - 1}$$

$$= 6.40 \text{ mm} \qquad = 0.079 \text{ mm}$$

These new values of $\overline{\overline{X}}$ and $\overline{R}$ are used to establish the standard values of $\overline{X}_0$, R_0, and σ_0. Thus,

$$\overline{X}_0 = \overline{\overline{X}}_{\text{new}}, \quad R_0 = \overline{R}_{\text{new}}, \quad \text{and} \quad \sigma_0 = \frac{R_0}{d_2}$$

where d_2 = a factor from Table B for estimating σ_0 from R_0. The standard or reference values can be considered to be the best estimate with the data available. As more data become available, better estimates or more confidence in the existing standard values are obtained.

Using the standard values, the central lines and the 3σ control limits for actual operations are obtained using the formulas

$$\text{UCL}_{\overline{X}} = \overline{X}_0 + A\sigma_0 \qquad \text{LCL}_{\overline{X}} = \overline{X}_0 - A\sigma_0$$

$$\text{UCL}_R = D_2\sigma_0 \qquad \text{LCL}_R = D_1\sigma_0$$

where A, D_1, and D_2 are factors from Table B for obtaining the 3σ control limits from $\overline{X}_0$ and σ_0. From Table B in the Appendix and for a subgroup size of 4, the factors and A = 1.500, d_2 = 2.059, D_1 = 0, and D_2 = 4.698. Calculations to determine $\overline{X}_0$ and σ_0 using the data previously given are:

$$\overline{X}_0 = \overline{\overline{X}}_{\text{new}} = 6.40 \text{ mm}$$

$$R_0 = \overline{R}_{\text{new}} = 0.08$$

$$\sigma_0 = \frac{R_0}{d_2} = \frac{0.079}{2.059} = 0.038 \text{ mm}$$

Thus, the control limits are:

$$\text{UCL}_{\overline{X}} = \overline{X}_0 + A\sigma_0 = 6.40 + (1.500)(0.038) = 6.46 \text{ mm}$$

$$\text{LCL}_{\overline{X}} = \overline{X}_0 - A\sigma_0 = 6.40 - (1.500)(0.038) = 6.34 \text{ mm}$$

$$\text{UCL}_R = D_2\sigma_0 = (4.698)(0.038) = 0.18 \text{ mm}$$

$$\text{LCL}_R = D_1\sigma_0 = (0)(0.038) = 0 \text{ mm}$$

The central lines and control limits are drawn on the $\overline{X}$ and R charts for the next period and are shown in Figure 3-4. For illustrative purposes the trial control limits and the revised control limits are shown on the same chart. The limits for both the $\overline{X}$ and R charts became narrower, as was expected. No change occurred in LCL_R because the subgroup size is less than 7. Figure 3-4 also illustrates a simpler charting technique in that lines are not drawn between the points.

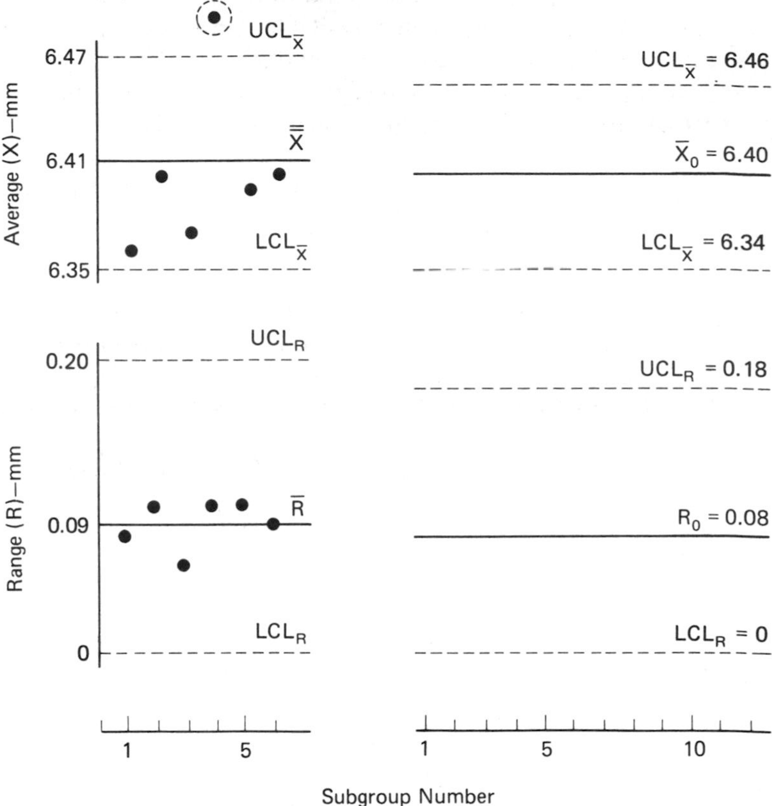

Figure 3-4 Trial control limits and revised control limits for $\overline{X}$ and R charts.

The preliminary data for the initial 25 subgroups are not plotted with the revised control limits. These revised control limits are for reporting the results of future subgroups. To make effective use of the control chart during production, it should be displayed in a conspicuous place where it can be seen by operators and supervisors.

Before proceeding to the action step, some final comments are appropriate. First, many analysts eliminate this step in the procedure because it appears to be somewhat redundant. However, by discarding out-of-control points with assignable causes, the central line and control limits are more representative of the population. Also, the parameter σ_0 is now available to obtain the initial process capability, which is $6\sigma_0$.

Second, the central line $\overline{X}_0$ for the $\overline{X}$ chart is frequently based on the specifications. In such a case, the procedure is used only to obtain R_0 and σ_0.

Finally, when population values are known (μ and σ) the central lines and control limits may be calculated immediately, saving time and work.

Thus $\overline{X}_0 = \mu$; $\sigma_0 = \sigma$; and $R_0 = d_2\sigma$ and the limits are obtained using the appropriate formulas.

Achieving the Purpose

When control charts are first introduced at a work center, an improvement in the process performance usually occurs. This initial improvement is especially noticeable when the process is dependent on the skill of the operator. The posting of a quality control chart appears to be a psychological signal to the operator to improve his performance. Most workers want to produce a quality product; therefore, when management shows an interest in the quality, the operator responds.

Figure 3-5 illustrates the initial improvement which occurred after the introduction of the $\overline{X}$ and R charts in January. Owing to space limitations, only a representative number of subgroups for each month are shown in the figure. During January the subgroup averages had less variation and tended to be centered at a slightly higher point. A reduction in the range variation occurred also.

Not all of the improved performance in January was the result of operator effort. The first-line supervisor initiated a program of tool wear control which was a contributing factor. This program was responsible for the apparent shift of the process center.

At the end of January new central lines and control limits were calculated using the data from subgroups obtained during the month. It is a good idea,

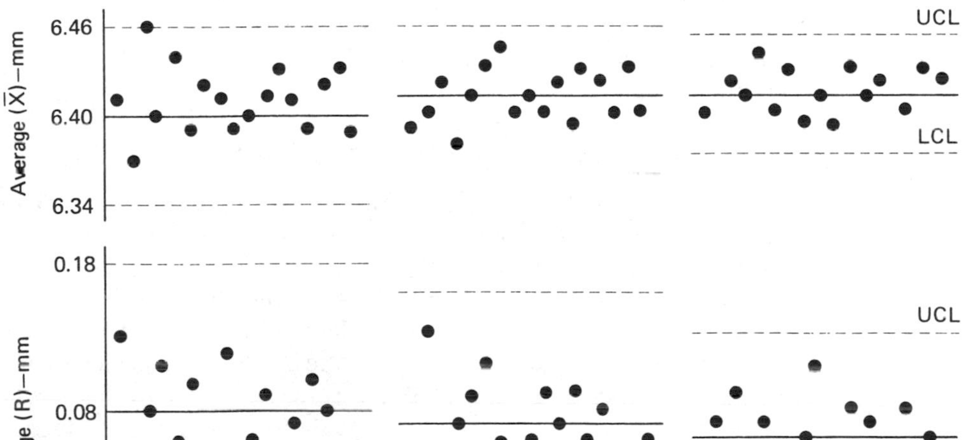

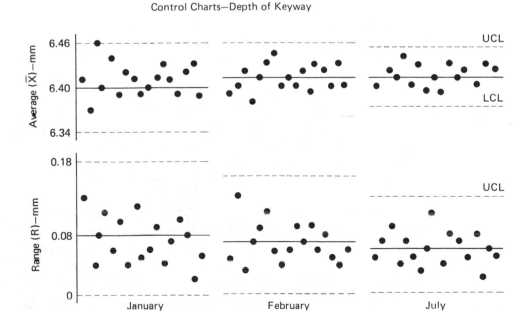

Figure 3-5 Continuing use of control charts, showing improved quality.

especially when a chart is being initiated, to calculate standard values periodically to see if any changes have occurred. This reevaluation can be done for every 20 to 25 subgroups, and the results compared to the previous values.[6]

New central lines and control limits were established for the $\overline{X}$ and R chart for the month of February. During the ensuing months the maintenance department replaced a pair of worn gears; purchasing changed the material supplier; and tooling modified a workholding device. All these improvements were the result of investigations that tracked down the causes for out-of-control conditions or were proposed ideas that might lead to quality improvement. The generation of ideas by many different personnel is the most essential ingredient for quality improvement. Ideas by the operator, first-line supervisor, quality assurance, maintenance, manufacturing engineering, and industrial engineering should be evaluated. This evaluation or testing of an idea requires from 20 to 25 subgroups. The control chart will tell if the idea is a good one. Only one idea should be tested at a time; otherwise, the results will be confounded.

At the end of June, the periodic evaluation of the past performance showed the need to revise the central lines and the control limits. The performance for the month of July and subsequent months showed a normal pattern of variation with no quality improvement. At this point no further quality improvement is possible without a substantial investment in new equipment or equipment modification.

W. Edward Deming has stated "that if he were a banker, he would not lend any money to a company unless statistical methods were used to prove that the money was necessary." This is precisely what the control chart can achieve, provided that all personnel use the chart as a method of quality improvement.

When the purpose for initiating the charts has been achieved, its use should be discontinued or the frequency of inspection be substantially reduced to a monitoring action. Efforts should then be directed toward the improvement of some other quality characteristic.

The Sample Standard Deviation Control Chart

While the $\overline{X}$ and R charts are the most common charts for variables, some companies prefer the sample standard deviation, s, as the measure of the subgroup dispersion. In comparing an R chart with an s chart, an R chart is easier to compute and easier to explain. On the other hand, the subgroup sample standard deviation for the s chart is calculated using all the data rather than just the high and the low value as done for the R chart. An s chart is therefore more accurate than an R chart. When subgroup sizes are less than 10, both charts will graphically portray the same variation;[7] however, as subgroups sizes

[6]These values are usually compared without the use of formal tests. An exact evaluation can be obtained by mathematically comparing the central lines to see if they are from the same population.

[7]A proof of this statement can be observed by comparing the R chart of Figure 3-3 with the s chart of Figure 3-6.

TABLE 3-3 Data on the Depth of the Keyway (millimeters)[a]

Subgroup Number	Date	Time	Measurement X_1	X_2	X_3	X_4	Average $\overline{X}$	Sample Standard Deviation, s	Comment
1	12/23	8:50	35	40	32	33	6.35	0.036	
2		11:30	46	37	36	41	6.40	0.045	
3		1:45	34	40	34	36	6.36	0.028	
4		3:45	69	64	68	59	6.65	0.045	New, temporary operator
5		4:20	38	34	44	40	6.39	0.042	
6	12/27	8:35	42	41	43	34	6.40	0.040	
7		9:00	44	41	41	46	6.43	0.024	
8		9:40	33	41	38	36	6.37	0.034	
9		1:30	48	52	49	51	6.50	0.018	
10		2:50	47	43	36	42	6.42	0.045	
11	12/28	8:30	38	41	39	38	6.39	0.014	
12		1:35	37	37	41	37	6.38	0.020	
13		2:25	40	38	47	35	6.40	0.051	
14		2:35	38	39	45	42	6.41	0.032	
15		3:55	50	42	43	45	6.45	0.036	
16	12/29	8:25	33	35	29	39	6.34	0.042	
17		9:25	41	40	29	34	6.36	0.067	
18		11:00	38	44	28	58	6.42	0.125	Damaged oil line
19		2:35	33	32	37	38	6.35	0.029	
20		3:15	56	55	45	48	6.51	0.054	Bad material
21	12/30	9:35	38	40	45	37	6.40	0.036	
22		10:20	39	42	35	40	6.39	0.029	
23		11:35	42	39	39	36	6.39	0.024	
24		2:00	43	36	35	38	6.38	0.036	
25		4:25	39	38	43	44	6.41	0.029	
Sum							160.25	0.981	

[a]For simplicity in recording, the individual measurements are coded from 6.00 mm.

increase to 10 or more, extreme values have an undue influence on the R chart. Therefore, at larger subgroup sizes the s chart is used.

The steps necessary to obtain the $\overline{X}$ and s trial control and revised control limits are the same as those used for the $\overline{X}$ and R chart except for different formulas. In order to illustrate the method, the same data will be used. They are reproduced in Table 3-3 with the addition of an s column and the elimination of the R column. The appropriate formulas used in the computation of the trial control limits are

$$\bar{s} = \frac{\sum_{i=1}^{g} s_i}{g} \qquad \overline{\overline{X}} = \frac{\sum_{i=1}^{g} \overline{X}_i}{g}$$

$$UCL_{\overline{X}} = \overline{\overline{X}} + A_3\bar{s} \qquad UCL_s = B_4\bar{s}$$

$$LCL_{\overline{X}} = \overline{\overline{X}} - A_3\bar{s} \qquad LCL_s = B_3\bar{s}$$

where s_i = sample standard deviation of the subgroup values
$\bar{s}$ = average of the subgroup sample standard deviations
A_3, B_3, B_4 = factors found in Table B of the Appendix for obtaining the 3σ control limits for $\overline{X}$ and s charts from $\bar{s}$

Formulas for the computation of the revised control limits using the standard values of $\overline{X}_0$ and σ_0 are

$$\overline{X}_0 = \overline{\overline{X}}_{\text{new}} = \frac{\sum \overline{X} - \overline{X}_d}{g - g_d}$$

$$s_0 = \bar{s}_{\text{new}} = \frac{\sum s - s_d}{g - g_d} \qquad \sigma_0 = \frac{s_0}{c_4}$$

$$\text{UCL}_{\overline{X}} = \overline{X}_0 + A\sigma_0 \qquad \text{UCL}_s = B_6\sigma_0$$
$$\text{LCL}_{\overline{X}} = \overline{X}_0 - A\sigma_0 \qquad \text{LCL}_s = B_5\sigma_0$$

where s_d = sample standard deviation of the discarded subgroup
c_4 = factor found in Table B for computing σ_0 from $\bar{s}$
A, B_5, B_6 = factors found in Table B for computing 3σ process control limits for $\overline{X}$ and s charts

The first step is to determine the standard deviation for each subgroup from the preliminary data. For subgroup 1, with values of 6.35, 6.40, 6.32, and 6.33, the standard deviation is

$$s = \sqrt{\frac{n \sum_{i=1}^{n} X_i^2 - \left(\sum_{i=1}^{n} X_i\right)^2}{n(n-1)}}$$

$$= \sqrt{\frac{4(6.35^2 + 6.40^2 + 6.32^2 + 6.33^2) - (6.35 + 6.40 + 6.32 + 6.33)^2}{4\,(4 - 1)}}$$

$$= 0.036 \text{ mm}$$

The standard deviation for subgroup 1 is posted to the s column as shown in Table 3-3, and the process is repeated for the remaining 24 subgroups.

The next step is to obtain $\bar{s}$ and $\overline{\overline{X}}$, which are computed from $\sum s$ and $\sum \overline{X}$, whose values are found in Table 3-3.

$$\bar{s} = \frac{\sum_{i=1}^{g} s}{g} \qquad \overline{\overline{X}} = \frac{\sum_{i=1}^{g} \overline{X}_i}{g}$$

$$= \frac{0.981}{25} \qquad = \frac{160.25}{25}$$

$$= 0.039 \text{ mm} \qquad = 6.41 \text{ mm}$$

From Table B the values of the factors—$A_3 = 1.628$, $B_3 = 0$, and $B_4 = 2.266$—are obtained, and the trial control limits are

$$\begin{aligned} UCL_{\bar{X}} &= \bar{\bar{X}} + A_3\bar{s} & LCL_{\bar{X}} &= \bar{\bar{X}} - A_3\bar{s} \\ &= 6.41 + (1.628)(0.039) & &= 6.41 - (1.628)(0.039) \\ &= 6.47 \text{ mm} & &= 6.35 \text{ mm} \\ UCL_s &= B_4\bar{s} & LCL_s &= B_3\bar{s} \\ &= (2.266)(0.039) & &= (0)(0.039) \\ &= 0.088 \text{ mm} & &= 0 \text{ mm} \end{aligned}$$

The next step is to plot the subgroup $\bar{X}$ and s on graph paper with the central lines and control limits. This step is shown in Figure 3-6. Subgroups 4, 9, 16, and 20 are out of control on the $\bar{X}$ chart, and since subgroup 4 and 20 have assignable causes, they are discarded. Subgroup 18 is out of control on the s

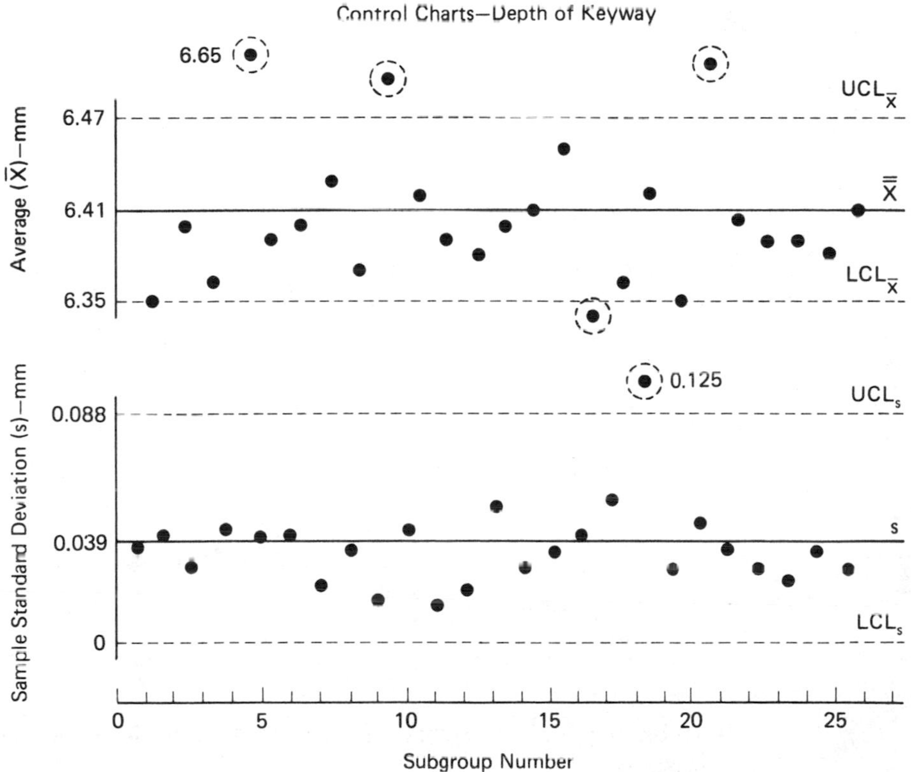

Figure 3-6 $\bar{X}$ and s chart for preliminary data with trial control limits.

chart, and since it has an assignable cause, it is discarded. Computation to obtain the standard values of $\overline{X}_0$, s_0, and σ_0 are as follows:

$$\overline{\overline{X}}_{\text{new}} = \frac{\sum \overline{X} - \overline{X}_d}{g - g_d}$$

$$= \frac{160.25 - 6.65 - 6.51}{25 - 2}$$

$$= 6.40 \text{ mm}$$

$$\overline{X}_0 = \overline{\overline{X}}_{\text{new}} = 6.40 \text{ mm}$$

$$s_0 = \bar{s}_{\text{new}} = \frac{\sum s - s_d}{g - g_d}$$

$$= \frac{0.981 - 0.125}{25 - 1}$$

$$= 0.036 \text{ mm}$$

$$\sigma_0 = \frac{s_0}{c_4} \qquad \text{from Table B,} \quad c_4 = 0.9400$$

$$= \frac{0.036}{0.9400}$$

$$= 0.038 \text{ mm}$$

The reader should note that the standard deviation, σ_0, is the same as the value obtained from the range in the preceding section. Using the standard values of $\overline{X}_0 = 6.40$ and $\sigma_0 = 0.038$, the revised control limits are computed.

$$\text{UCL}_{\overline{X}} = \overline{X}_0 + A\sigma_0 \qquad \text{LCL}_{\overline{X}} = \overline{X}_0 - A\sigma_0$$

$$= 6.40 + (1.500)(0.038) \qquad = 6.40 - (1.500)(0.038)$$

$$= 6.46 \text{ mm} \qquad = 6.34 \text{ mm}$$

$$\text{UCL}_s = B_6\sigma_0 \qquad \text{LCL}_s = B_5\sigma_0$$

$$= (2.088)(0.038) \qquad = (0)(0.038)$$

$$= 0.079 \text{ mm} \qquad = 0 \text{ mm}$$

Continuation of the $\overline{X}$ and s charts is accomplished in the same manner as the $\overline{X}$ and R charts.

STATE OF CONTROL

Process in Control

When the assignable causes have been eliminated from the process to the extent that the points plotted on the control chart remain within the control limits, the process is in a state of control. No higher degree of uniformity can be attained with the existing process. Greater uniformity can, however, be attained through a change in the basic process through quality improvement ideas.

When a process is in control, there occurs a normal pattern of variation which is illustrated in Figure 3-7. This natural pattern of variation has (1) about two-thirds of the points near the central line, (2) a few points closer to the control limits, (3) points located back and forth across the central line, (4) points balanced on both sides of the central line, and (5) no points beyond the control limits. The natural pattern of the points or subgroup values forms its own frequency distribution, which follows a normal curve. As the number of plotted points increases, the frequency distribution will take on the appearance of a smooth polygon. The dashed normal curve at the left end of Figure 3-7 represents the distribution of the points when a process is in control.

Control limits are usually established at three standard deviations from the central line. They are used as a basis to judge whether there is evidence of lack of control. The choice of 3σ limits is an economic one with respect to two types of errors that can occur. One error, called Type I by statisticians, occurs when looking for an assignable cause of variation when in reality a chance cause is present. When the limits are set at three standard deviations, a Type I error will occur 0.27% (3 out of 1,000) of the time. In other words, when a point is outside the control limits, it is assumed to be due to an assignable cause even though it would be due to a chance cause 0.27% of the time. The other type error, called Type II, occurs when assuming that a chance cause of variation is present when in reality there is an assignable cause. In other words, when a point is inside the control limits, it is assumed to be due to a chance cause even though it might be an assignable cause. Abundant experience since 1930 in all types of industry indicates that 3σ limits provide an economic balance between the costs resulting from the two types of errors. Unless there are strong practical reasons for doing otherwise, the ± 3 standard deviation limits should be used.

When a process is in control, only chance causes of variation are present.

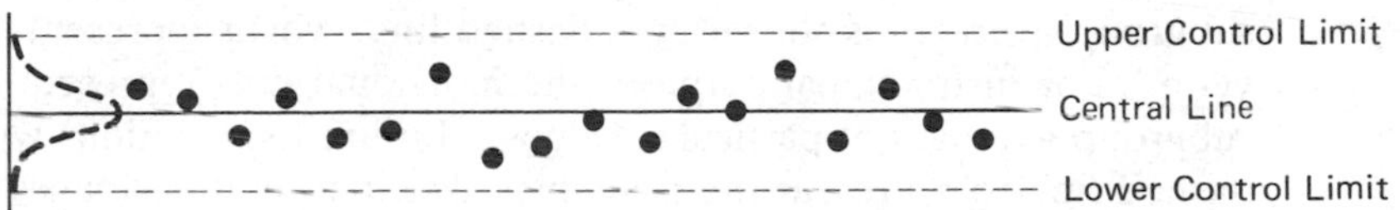

Figure 3-7 Natural pattern of variation of a control chart.

Small variations in machine performance, operator performance, and material characteristics are expected and are considered to be part of a stable process.

When a process is in control, certain practical advantages accrue to the producer and consumer.

1. Individual units of the product will be more uniform—or, stated another way, there will be less variation.

2. Since the product is more uniform, fewer samples are needed to judge the quality. Therefore, the cost of inspection can be reduced to a minimum. This advantage is extremely important when 100% conformance to specifications is not essential.

3. The process capability or spread of the process is easily attained from 6σ. With a knowledge of the process capability, a number of reliable decisions relative to specifications can be made, such as:
   (a) To decide the product specifications.
   (b) To decide the amount of rework or scrap when there is insufficient tolerance.
   (c) To decide whether to produce the product to tight specifications and permit interchangeability of components or to produce the product to loose specifications and use selective matching of components.

4. The percentage of product that falls within any pair of values may be predicted with the highest degree of assurance. For example, this advantage can be very important when adjusting filling machines to obtain different percentage of items below, between, or above particular values.

5. It permits the consumer to use the producer's data and, therefore, to test only a few subgroups as a check on the producer's records.

6. The operator is performing satisfactorily from a quality viewpoint.

Process Out of Control

When a point (subgroup value) falls outside its control limits, the process is out of control. This means that an assignable cause of variation is present. Another way of viewing the out-of-control point is to think of the subgroup value as coming from a different population than the one from which the control limits were obtained. Figure 3-8 shows a frequency distribution of subgroup averages for cereal boxes which was developed from a large number of subgroups and, therefore, represents the population mean, $\mu = 450$ g, and the population standard deviation for the averages, $\sigma_{\bar{x}} = 8$ g. The frequency distribution for subgroup averages is shown by a dashed line, which represents a smooth polygon. For instructional purposes the individual dots represent the number of subgroup averages at particular values. Future explanations will use only the dashed line to represent the frequency distribution of averages and will use a solid line for the frequency distribution of individual values. The out-of-control point has a value of 483 g. This point is so far away from the 3σ limits (99.73%)

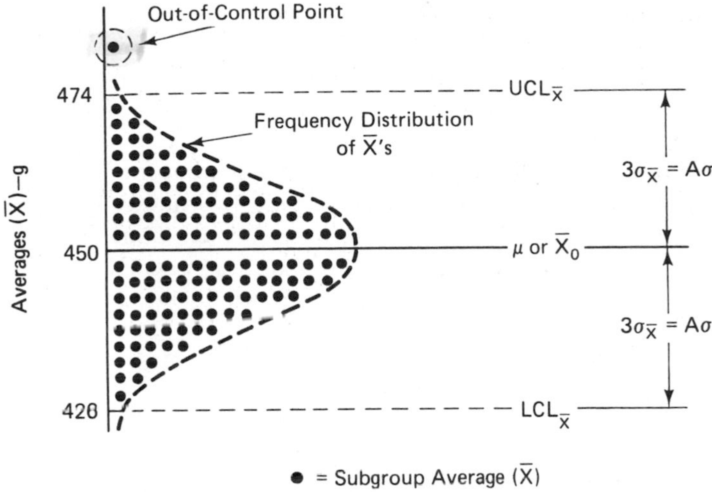

Figure 3-8 Frequency distribution of subgroup averages with control limits.

that it can only be considered to have come from another population. In other words, the process that produced the subgroup average of 483 g is a different process than the stable process from which the 3σ control limits were developed. Therefore, something has gone wrong with the process; some assignable cause of variation is present. This assignable cause must be found and corrected before a normal, stable process can continue.

A process can also be considered out of control even when the points fall inside the 3σ limits. This situation occurs when unnatural patterns of variation are present in the process. It is not normal for seven or more consecutive points to be above or below the central line. Also when 10 out of 11 points or 12 out of 14 points, etc., are located on one side of the central line, it is an unnatural pattern. These unnatural patterns are shown in Figure 3-9. The chance that these unnatural patterns or runs will occur is the same chance that a point will fall outside the 3σ control limits. Proof of this fact is based on the binomial probability distribution, which is given in Chapter 4.

There are many other unnatural patterns, and it is important to remember

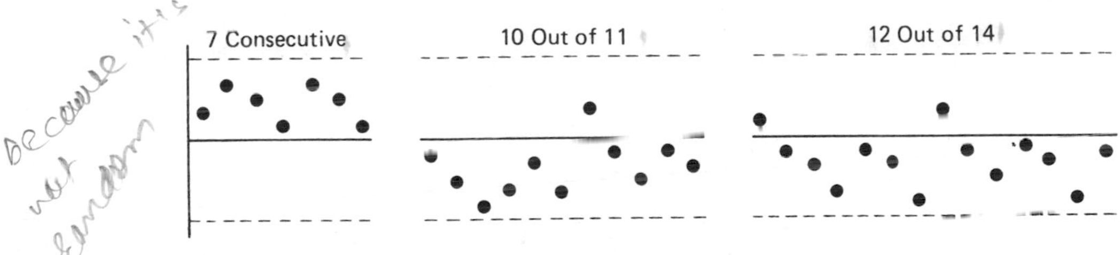

Figure 3-9 Some unnatural patterns of variation—process out of control.

the conditions of normality described in the preceding section. One technique for recognizing unnatural patterns is to divide the control chart into six equal imaginary bands. Three equals bands are between the central line, and the lower control limit and three equal bands are between the central line and the upper control limit. A normal pattern of variation occurs when (1) about 34% of the points fall in each of the two bands adjacent to the center value, (2) about $13\frac{1}{2}$% of the points fall in each of the two middle bands, and (3) $2\frac{1}{2}$% of the points fall in each of the three outer bands. Any significant divergence from the normal pattern, such as 2 out of 3 consecutive points in the outer band, would be an unnatural pattern and would be classified as an out-of-control condition.

Analysis of Out-of-Control Condition

When a process is out of control, the assignable cause responsible for the condition must be found. The detective work necessary to locate the cause of the out-of-control condition can be minimized by a knowledge of the types of out-of-control patterns and their assignable causes. Types of out-of-control $\overline{X}$ and R patterns are (1) change or jump in level, (2) trend or steady change in level, (3) recurring cycles, (4) two populations, and (5) mistakes.

1. *Change or jump in level.* This type is concerned with a sudden change in level to the $\overline{X}$ chart, to the R chart, or to both charts. Figure 3-10 illustrates the change in level. For an X chart, the change in the process average can be due to:

   (a) An intentional or unintentional change in the process setting
   (b) A new or inexperienced operator
   (c) A different raw material
   (d) A minor failure of a machine part

Some causes for a sudden change in the process spread or variability as shown on the R chart are:

   (a) Inexperienced operator
   (b) Sudden increase in gear play
   (c) Greater variation in incoming material

Sudden changes in level can occur on both the $\overline{X}$ and the R charts. This situation

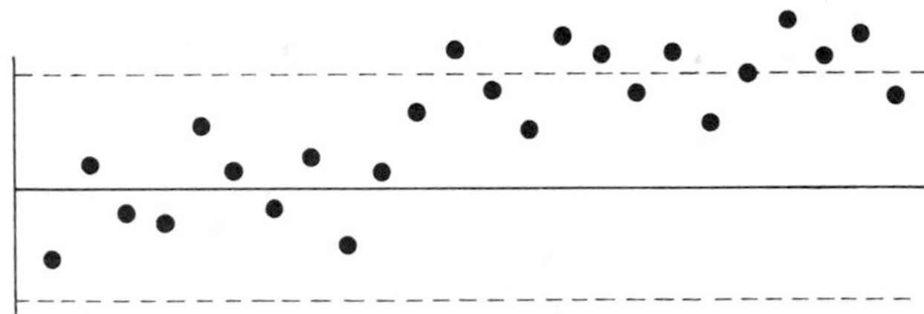

Figure 3-10 Out-of-control pattern: change or jump in level.

is common during the beginning of control chart activity prior to the attainment of a state of control. There may be more than one assignable cause, or it may be a cause that could affect both charts, such as an inexperienced operator.

2. *Trend or steady change in level.* Steady changes in control chart level are a very common industrial phenomena. Figure 3-11 illustrates a trend or steady change that is occurring in the upward direction; the trend could have been illustrated in the downward direction. Some causes of steady progressive changes on an $\overline{X}$ chart are:

(a) Tool or die wear
(b) Gradual deterioration of equipment
(c) Gradual change in temperature or humidity
(d) Viscosity in a chemical process
(e) Buildup of chips in a work-holding device

A steady change in level or trend on the R chart is not as common as the $\overline{X}$ chart. It does, however, occur and some possible causes are:

(a) An improvement in worker skill (downward trend)
(b) A decrease in worker skill due to fatigue, boredom, inattention, and so on
(c) A gradual improvement in the homogeneity of incoming material

3. *Recurring cycles.* When the plotted points on an $\overline{X}$ or R chart show a wave or periodic high and low points, it is called a *cycle.* A typical recurring out-of-control pattern is shown in Figure 3-12. For an $\overline{X}$ chart, some of the causes of recurring cycles are:

(a) The seasonal effects of incoming material.

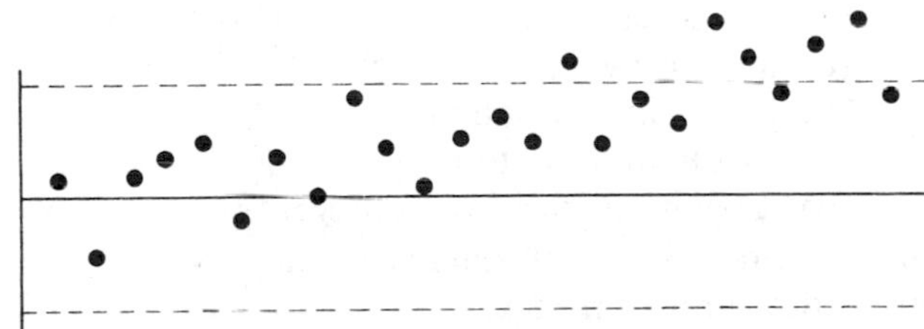

Figure 3-11 Out-of-control pattern: trend or steady change in level.

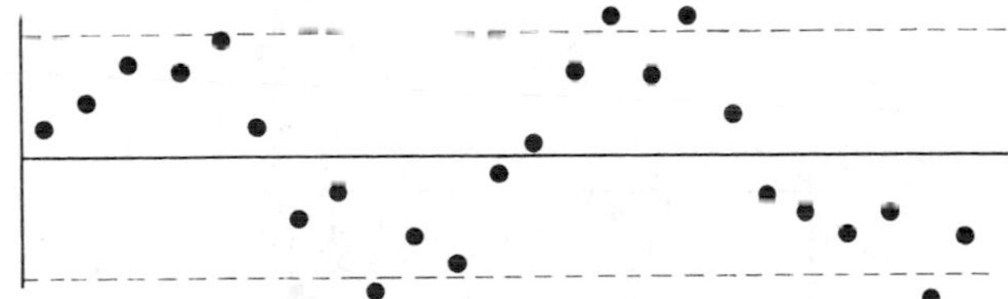

Figure 3-12 Out-of-control pattern: recurring cycles.

(b) The recurring effects of temperature and humidity (cold morning start up)
(c) Any daily or weekly chemical, mechanical, or psychological event
(d) The periodic rotation of operators

Periodic cycles on an R chart are not as common as for an $\overline{X}$ chart. Some affecting the R chart are due to:

(a) Operator fatigue and rejuvenation resulting from morning, noon, and afternoon breaks
(b) Lubrication cycles

The out-of-control pattern of a recurring cycle sometimes goes unreported because of the inspection cycle. Thus, a cyclic pattern of a variation that occurs approximately every 2 hours could coincide with the inspection frequency. Therefore, only the low points on the cycle are reported, and there is no evidence that a cyclic event is present.

4. *Two populations.* When there are a large number of points near or outside the control limits, a two-population situation may be present. This type of out-of-control pattern is illustrated in Figure 3-13. For an $\overline{X}$ chart the out-of-control pattern can be due to:

(a) Large differences in material quality
(b) Two or more machines on the same chart
(c) Large differences in test method or equipment

Some causes for an out-of-control pattern on an R chart are due to:

(a) Different workers using the same chart
(b) Materials from different suppliers

5. *Mistakes.* Mistakes can be very embarrassing to the quality assurance operation. Some causes of out-of-control patterns resulting from mistakes are:

(a) Measuring equipment out of calibration
(b) Errors in calculations
(c) Errors in using test equipment
(d) Taking samples from different populations

Many of the out-of-control patterns that have been described can also be attributed to inspection error or mistakes.

The causes given for the different types of out-of-control patterns are suggested possibilities and are not meant to be all-inclusive. These causes will give

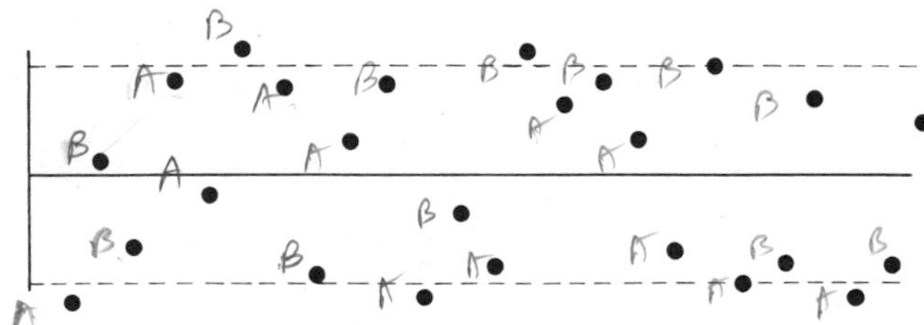

Figure 3-13 Out-of-control pattern: two populations.

production and quality personnel ideas for the solution of particular industrial problems. They can be a start toward the development of an assignable cause checklist which is applicable to a particular manufacturing entity.

When out-of-control patterns occur in relation to the lower control limit of the *R* chart, it is the result of outstanding performance. The cause should be determined so that the outstanding performance can continue.

The preceding discussion has used the *R* chart as the measure of the dispersion. Information on patterns and causes also pertains to an *s* chart.

SPECIFICATIONS

Individual Values Compared to Averages

Before discussing specifications and their relationship with control charts, it appears desirable, at this time, to obtain a better understanding of individual values and average values. Figure 3-14 shows a tally of the subgroup values or individual values (*X*'s) and a tally of the subgroup averages ($\bar{X}$'s) for the data on keyway depths given in Table 3-2. The four out-of-control subgroups were not used in the two tallys; therefore, there are 84 individual values and 21 averages. It is observed that the averages are grouped much closer to the center

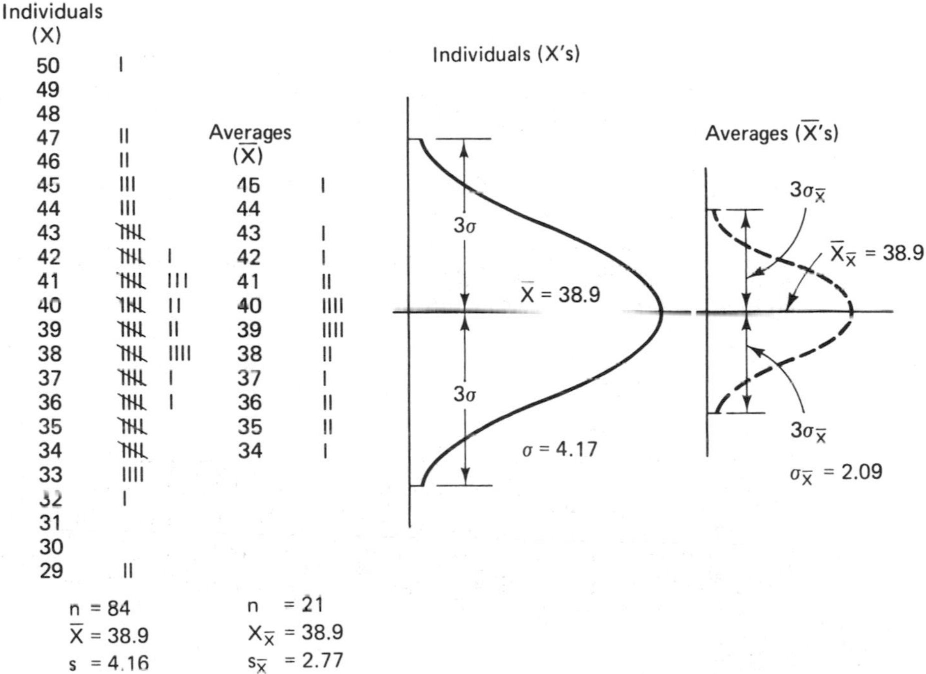

Figure 3-14 Comparison of individual values and averages using the same data.

than the individual values. This is true because when we average four values, the affect of an extreme value is minimized, since the chance of four extremely high or four extremely low values in one subgroup is slight.

Calculations of the average for both the individual values and for the subgroup averages are the same, $\overline{X} = 38.9$. However, the sample standard deviation of the individual values (s) Is 4.16, while the sample standard deviation of the subgroup average ($s_{\overline{X}}$) is 2.77.

If there are a large number of individual values and subgroup averages, the smooth polygons of Figure 3-14 would represent their frequency distributions if the distribution is normal. The curve for the frequency distribution of the averages has a dashed line while the curve for the frequency distribution of individual values has a solid line; this convention will be followed throughout the text. In comparing the two distributions it is observed that both distributions are normal in shape; in fact, even if the curve for individual values was not quite normal, the curve for averages would be close to a normal shape. The base of the curve for individual values is about twice as large as the base of the curve for averages. When population values are available for the standard deviation for individual values (σ) and for the standard deviation for averages ($\sigma_{\overline{X}}$), there is a definite relationship between them, as given by the formula

$$\sigma_{\overline{X}} = \frac{\sigma}{\sqrt{n}}$$

where $\sigma_{\overline{X}}$ = population standard deviation of subgroup averages ($\overline{X}$'s)
σ = population standard deviation of individual values
n = subgroup size

Thus, for a subgroup of size 5, $\sigma_{\overline{X}} = 0.45\sigma$, and for a subgroup of size 4, $\sigma_{\overline{X}} = 0.50\sigma$.

If we assume normality (which may or may not be true), the population standard deviation can be estimated from

$$\hat{\sigma} = \frac{s}{c_4}$$

where $\hat{\sigma}$ is the "estimate" of the population standard deviation[8] and c_4 is "approximately equal to ($\doteq$) 0.996997 for $n = 84$. Thus, $\sigma = s/c_4 = 4.16/0.996997 = 4.17$ and $\sigma_{\overline{X}} = \sigma/\sqrt{n} = 4.17/\sqrt{4} = 2.09$. Note that $s_{\overline{X}}$, which was calculated from sample data, and $\sigma_{\overline{X}}$ which was calculated above, are different. This difference is due to sample variation or the small number of samples, which was

[8]Values of c_4 are given in Table B of the Appendix up to $n = 25$. For values greater than 25, $c_4 \doteq \frac{4(n-1)}{4n-3}$.

only 21, or some combination thereof. The difference would not be caused by a nonnormal population of X's.

Since the height of the curve is a function of the frequency, the curve for individual values is higher. This is easily verified by comparing the tally sheet in Figure 3-14 and is a true relationship when making comparisons using frequencies from the sample data. However, if the curves represent relative or percentage frequency distributions, then the area under the curve must be equal to 100%. Therefore, the percentage frequency distribution curve for averages, with its smaller base, would need to be much higher to enclose the same area as the percentage frequency distribution curve for individual values.

Central Limit Theorem

Now that you are aware of the difference between the frequency distribution of individual values, X's, and the frequency distribution of averages, $\overline{X}$'s, the central limit theorem can be discussed. In simple terms it is:

> If the population from which samples are taken is *not* normal, the distribution of sample averages will tend toward normality provided that the sample size, n, is at least 4. This tendency gets better and better as the sample size gets larger. Furthermore, the standardized normal can be used for the distribution of averages with the modification,

$$Z = \frac{\overline{X} - \mu}{\sigma_{\overline{X}}} = \frac{\overline{X} - \mu}{\sigma/\sqrt{n}}$$

This theorem was illustrated by Shewhardt[9] for a uniform population distribution and a triangular population distribution of individual values as shown in Figure 3-15. Obviously, the distribution of X's are considerably different than a normal distribution; however, the distribution of $\overline{X}$'s is approximately normal.

The central limit theorem is one of the reasons the $\overline{X}$ chart works, in that we do not need to be concerned if the distribution of X's is not normal provided that the sample size is 4 or more.

Control Limits and Specifications

Control limits are established as a function of the averages; in other words, control limits are for averages. Specifications, on the other hand, are the permissible variation in the size of the part and are, therefore, for individual values. The specification or tolerance limits are established by product engineers to meet a particular function. Figure 3-16 shows that the location of the specifications is optional and is not related to any of the other features in the figure. The control limits, process spread, distribution of averages, and distribution of individual values are interdependent, since $\sigma_{\overline{X}} = \sigma/\sqrt{n}$.

[9] W. A. Shewhart, *Economic Control of Quality of Manufactured Product* (Princeton, N.J.: Van Nostrand Reinhold Company, Inc., 1931), pp. 180–186.

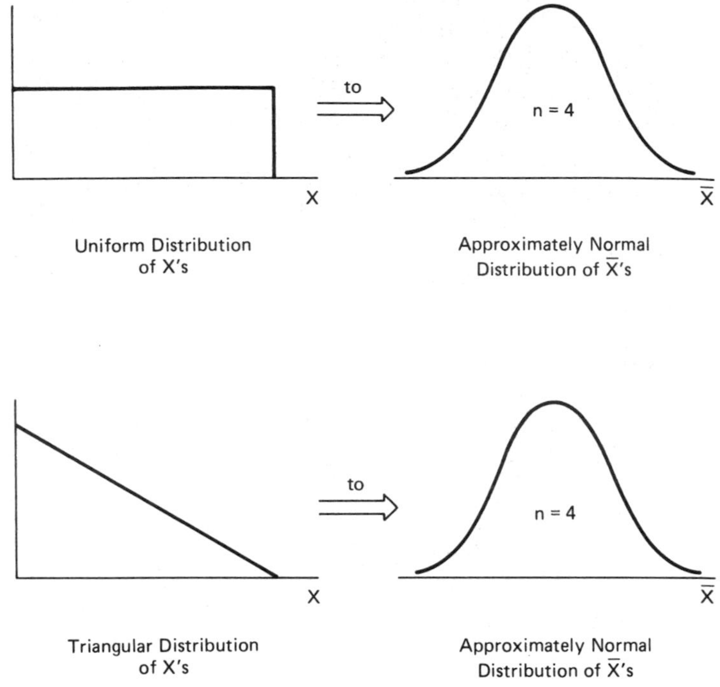

Figure 3-15 Illustration of central limit theorem.

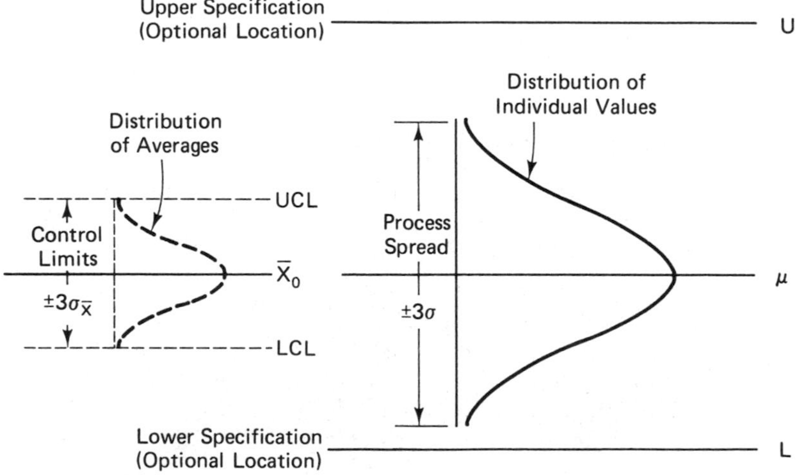

Figure 3-16 Relationship of limits, specifications, and distributions.

Process Spread and Specifications

While specifications can be established by the product engineer without regard for the spread of the process, serious situations can result when this type of action is adopted. There are three situations: (1) when the process spread is less than the difference between specifications, (2) when the process spread is equal to the difference between specifications, (3) and when the process spread is greater than the difference between specifications.

Case I: $6\sigma < U - L$. This situation, where the spread of the process (6σ) is less than the difference between specifications ($U - L$), is the most desirable case. Figure 3-17 illustrates this ideal relationship by the distribution of individual values labeled A. Since the specifications are appreciably greater than the process spread, no difficulty is encountered even when there is a substantial shift in the process average, as shown by the distributions at B. At C a shift in the dispersion is illustrated, and all the individual values are between specifications. Case I is economically advantageous since an out-of-control condition, as illustrated at B and C, does not produce defective product. Therefore, frequent machine adjustments or searches for assignable causes are not necessary. In fact, this satisfactory state of affairs suggests that the control chart may be discontinued.

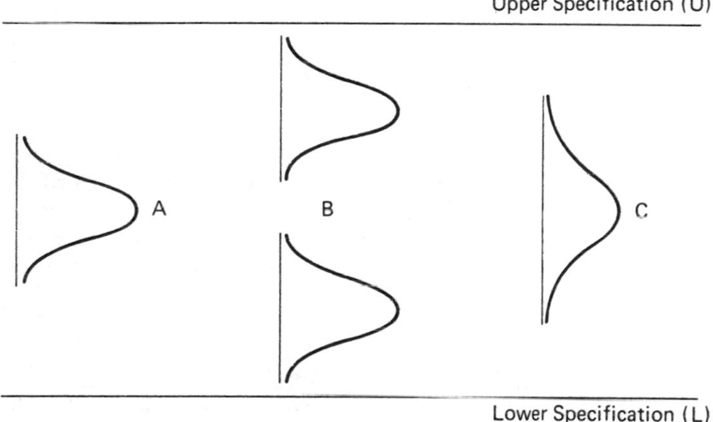

Figure 3-17 Changes in the process average and dispersion when $6\sigma < U - L$.

Case II: $6\sigma = U - L$. Figure 3-18 illustrates this case where the spread of the process, or process capability, is equal to the difference between specifications. The frequency distribution at A represents a natural pattern of variation. However, when there is a shift in the process average, as indicated at B, or a change in the dispersion, as indicated at C, the individual values exceed the specifications. As long as the process remains in control as indicated at A, no defective product is produced; however, when the process is out of control as indicated at B and C, defective product is being produced.

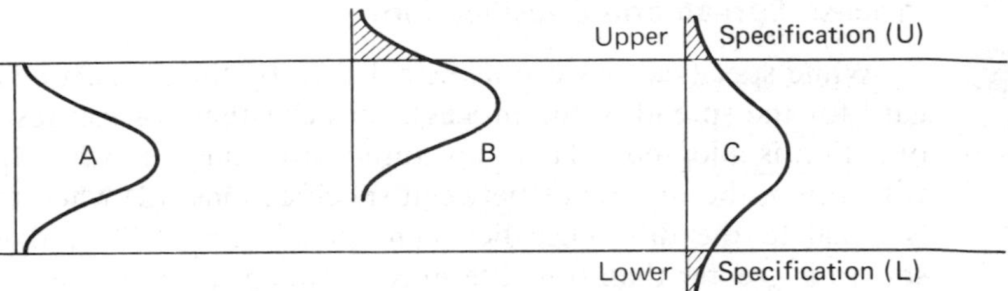

Figure 3-18 Changes in the process average and dispersion when $6\sigma = U - L$.

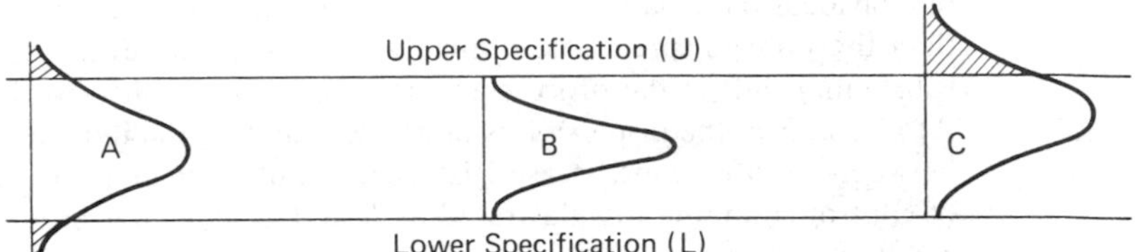

Figure 3-19 Changes in the process average and dispersion when $6\sigma > U - L$.

Therefore, assignable causes of variation must be corrected as soon as they occur.

Case III: $6\sigma > U - L$. When the spread of the process or process capability is greater than the difference between specifications, an undesirable situation exists. Figure 3-19 illustrates this case. Even though a natural pattern of variation is occurring, as shown by the frequency distribution at A, some of the individual values are greater than the upper specification and are less than the lower specification. This case presents the unique situation where the process is in control, but defective product is produced. In other words, the process is not capable of manufacturing a product that will meet the specifications.

One solution is to discuss with the product engineer the possibility of increasing the difference between the upper and lower specifications. This solution may require reliability studies with mating parts to determine if the product can function with increased specification differences.

Another solution is to leave the process and the specifications alone and perform 100% inspection to eliminate the defective parts. This is not an attractive solution, but it may be the most economical or only one.

A third possibility to change the process dispersion so that a more peaked distribution occurs, as illustrated by frequency distribution B. To obtain such a substantial shift in the standard deviation might require new material, a more experienced operator or retraining, a new or overhauled machine, or possibly automatic in-process control.

Another solution is to shift the process average so that all of the defective product occurs at one tail of the frequency distribution as indicated at C of

Figure 3-19. To illustrate this solution, assume that a shaft is being ground to tight specifications. If too much metal is removed, the part is scrapped; if too little is removed, the part must be reworked. By shifting the process average the amount of scrap is eliminated and the amount of rework is increased. A similar situation exists for an internal member such as a hole or keyway except that scrap occurs above the upper specification and rework occurs below the lower specification. This type of solution is feasible when the cost of the part is sufficient economically to justify the reworking operation. Note that the crosshatched area at C is much more than that at A.

Example Problem

Location pins for workholding devices are ground to a diameter of 12.50 mm (approximately $\frac{1}{2}$ in.), with a tolerance of 0.05 mm. If the process is centered at 12.50 mm (μ) and the dispersion is 0.02 mm (σ), what percent of the product must be scrapped and what percent can be reworked? How can the process center be changed to eliminate the scrap? What is the rework percentage?

The techniques for solving this problem were given in Chapter 2 and are shown below.

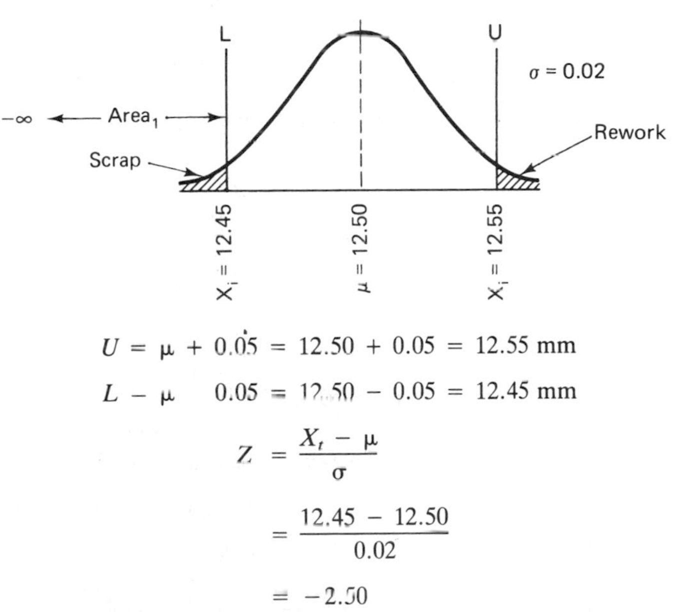

$$U = \mu + 0.05 = 12.50 + 0.05 = 12.55 \text{ mm}$$

$$L = \mu - 0.05 = 12.50 - 0.05 = 12.45 \text{ mm}$$

$$Z = \frac{X_i - \mu}{\sigma}$$

$$= \frac{12.45 - 12.50}{0.02}$$

$$= -2.50$$

From Table A of the Appendix for a Z value of -2.50:

$$\text{Area}_1 = 0.0062 \text{ or } 0.62\% \text{ scrap}$$

Since the process is centered between the specifications and a symmetrical distribution is assumed, the rework percentage will be equal to the scrap percentage of 0.62%. The second part of the problem is solved using the following sketch:

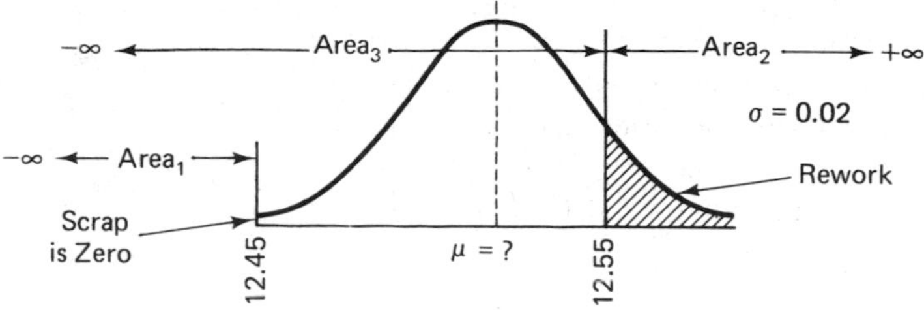

If the amount of scrap is to be zero, then $\text{Area}_1 = 0$. From Table A, the closest value to an Area_1 value of zero is 0.00017, which has a Z value of −3.59. Thus,

$$Z = \frac{X_i - \mu}{\sigma}$$

$$-3.59 = \frac{12.45 - \mu}{0.02}$$

$$\mu = 12.52 \text{ mm}$$

The percentage of rework is obtained by first determining Area_3.

$$Z = \frac{X_i - \mu}{\sigma}$$

$$= \frac{12.55 - 12.52}{0.02}$$

$$= +1.50$$

From Table A, $\text{Area}_3 = 0.9332$ and

$$\text{Area}_2 = \text{Area}_T - \text{Area}_3$$

$$= 1.0000 - 0.9332$$

$$= 0.0668 \quad \text{or} \quad 6.68\%$$

The amount of rework is 6.68%, which, incidentally, is considerably more than the combined rework and scrap percentage (1.24%) when the process is centered.

The preceding analysis of the process spread and the specifications was made utilizing an upper and a lower specification. Many times there is only one specification and it may be either upper or lower. A similar and much simpler analysis could be for a single specification limit.

PROCESS CAPABILITY

The true process capability cannot be determined until the $\overline{X}$ and R charts have achieved the optimal quality improvement without a substantial investment for new equipment or equipment modification. Process capability or spread of the process is equal to 6 standard deviations, which is $6\sigma_0$ or 6σ if the population standard deviation is known.

In the example problem for the X and R charts, the quality improvement process began in January with $\sigma_0 = 0.038$. The process capability is $6\sigma = (6)(0.038) = 0.228$ mm or ± 0.114 mm. By July, $\sigma_0 = 0.030$, which gives a process capability of 0.180 mm or ± 0.090 mm. This is a 20% improvement in the process capability, which in most situations would be sufficient to solve a quality problem.

It is frequently necessary to obtain the process capability by a quick method rather than by using the $\overline{X}$ and R charts. The procedure is:

1. Take 20 subgroups of size 4 for a total of 80 measurements. These subgroups should be selected at random to minimize any bias.
2. Calculate the sample standard deviation, s, for each subgroup.
3. Calculate the average sample standard deviation, $\bar{s} = \sum s/g = \sum s/20$.
4. Calculate the estimate of the population standard deviation.

$$\hat{\sigma}_0 = \bar{s}/c_4.$$

5. Process capability will equal $6\sigma_0$.

Remember that this technique does not give the true process capability and should be used only if circumstances require its use.

Process capability and the tolerance are combined to form a *capability index*, defined as

$$\text{Cp} = \frac{U - L}{6\sigma_0}$$

where Cp = capability index
$U - L$ = upper specification − lower specification, or tolerance
$6\sigma_0$ = process capability

If the capability index is 1.00, we have the case II situation discussed in the preceding section; if the ratio is greater than 1.00, we have the case I situation, which is desirable; and if the ratio is less than 1.00, we have the case III situation, which is undesirable.

Example Problem

Assume that the specifications are 6.50 and 6.30 in the depth of keyway problem. Determine the capability index before and after improvement.

$$Cp = \frac{U - L}{6\sigma_0} = \frac{6.50 - 6.30}{6(0.038)} = 0.88$$

$$Cp = \frac{U - L}{6\sigma_0} = \frac{6.50 - 6.30}{6(0.030)} = 1.11$$

In the example problem the improvement in quality resulted in a desirable capability index. The minimum capability index is frequently established at 1.33. Below this value, design engineers have to seek approval from manufacturing before the product can be released for production.

In Chapter 1, quality was defined as conformance to specifications. Using the capability index concept, we can measure quality provided the process is centered correctly. The larger the capability index, the better the quality. We should strive to make the capability index as large as possible. This is accomplished by having realistic specifications and continual striving to improve the process capability.

DIFFERENT CONTROL CHARTS

The basic control charts for variables were discussed in previous sections. While most of the quality control activity for variables is concerned with the $\overline{X}$ and R chart or the $\overline{X}$ and s chart, there are other charts which find application in some situations. These charts are discussed briefly in this section.

Charts for Better Operator Understanding

Since production personnel have difficulty understanding the relationships between averages, individual values, control limits, and specifications, various charts have been developed to overcome this difficulty.

1. *Placing individual values on the chart.* This technique plots both the individual values and the subgroup average and is illustrated in Figure 3-20. A small dot represents an individual value and a larger circle represents the subgroup average. In some cases, an individual value and a subgroup average are identical, in which case the small dot is located inside the circle. When two individual values are identical, the two dots are placed side by side. A further refinement of the chart can be made by the addition of upper and lower specification lines; however, this practice is not recommended.

2. *Chart for subgroup sums.* This technique plots the subgroup sum, $\sum X$, rather than the subgroup average, $\overline{X}$. Since the values on the chart are of a

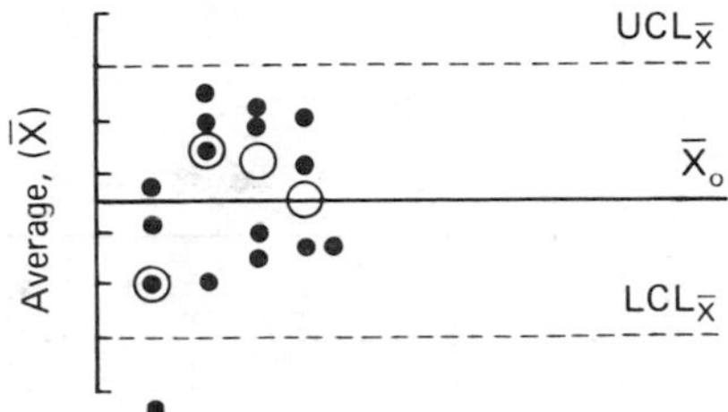

Figure 3-20 Chart showing a technique for plotting individual values and subgroup averages.

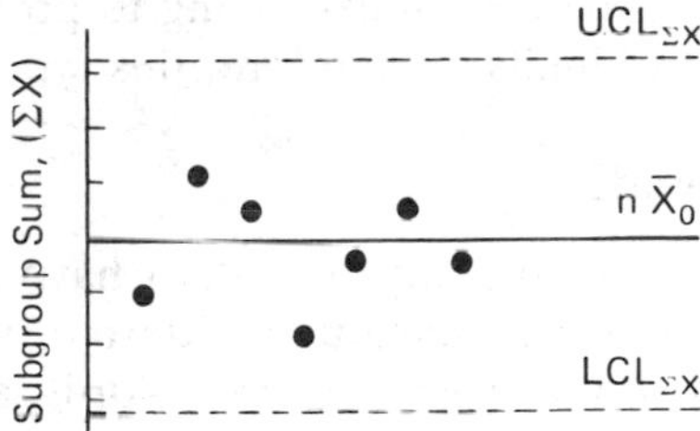

Figure 3-21 Subgroup sum chart.

different magnitude than the specifications, there is no chance for confusion. Figure 3-21 shows a subgroup sums chart, which is an $\bar{X}$ chart with the scale magnified by the subgroup size, n. The central line is $n\bar{X}_0$ and the control limits are obtained by the formulas

$$\mathrm{UCL}_{\Sigma X} = n(\mathrm{UCL}_{\bar{X}})$$

$$\mathrm{LCL}_{\Sigma X} = n(\mathrm{LCL}_{\bar{X}})$$

Chart for Variable Subgroup Size

Every effort should be made to keep the subgroup size constant. Occasionally, however, because of lost material, laboratory tests, production problems, or inspection mistakes, the subgroup size varies. When this situation occurs, the control limits will vary with the subgroup size. As the subgroup size, n, increases, the control limits become narrower; as the subgroup size decreases, the control limits become wider apart (Figure 3-22). This fact is confirmed by an analysis of the control limit factors A, D_1, and D_2, which are a function of the subgroup size and which are part of the control limit formulas. Control limits will also vary for the R chart.

One of the difficulties associated with a chart for variable subgroup size is

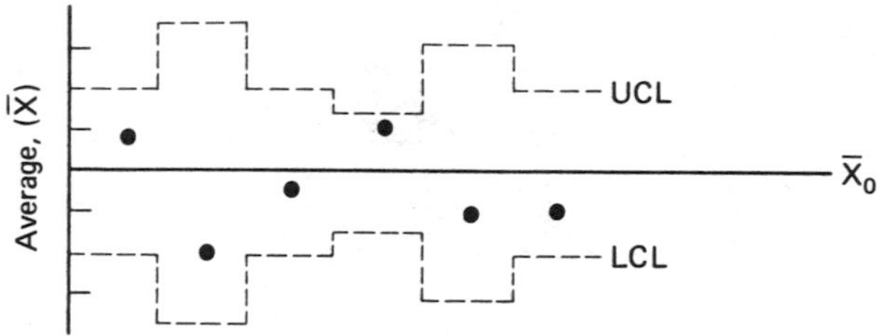

Figure 3-22 Chart for variable subgroup size.

the need to make a number of control limit calculations. A more serious difficulty involves the task of explaining to production people the reason for the different control limits. Therefore, this type of chart should be avoided.

Chart for Trends

When the plotted points of a chart have an upward or downward trend, it can be attributed to an unnatural pattern of variation or to a normal pattern of variation such as tool wear. In other words, as the tool wears, a gradual change in the average is expected and considered to be normal. Figure 3-23 illustrates a chart for a trend that reflects die wear. As the die wears, the measurement gradually increases until it reaches the upper reject limit. The die is then replaced or reworked.

Since the central line is on a slope, its equation must be determined. This is best accomplished using the least-squares method of fitting a line to a set of points. The equation for the trend line, using the slope-intercept form, is

$$\overline{X} = a + bW$$

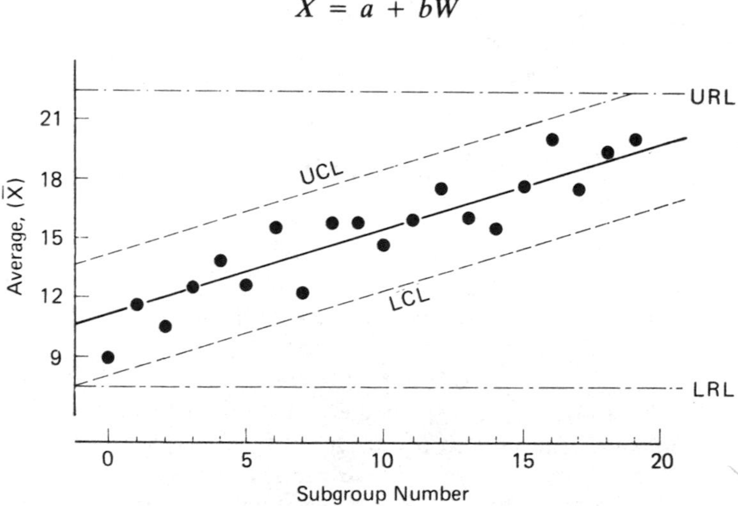

Figure 3-23 Chart for trend.

where $\overline{X}$ = subgroup average and represents the vertical axis
W = subgroup number and represents the horizontal axis
a = point on the vertical axis where the line intercepts the vertical axis

$$a = \frac{\left(\sum \overline{X}\right)\left(\sum W^2\right) - \left(\sum W\right)\left(\sum W\overline{X}\right)}{g \sum W^2 - \left(\sum W\right)^2}$$

b = the slope of the line

$$b = \frac{g \sum W\overline{X} - \left(\sum W\right)\left(\sum \overline{X}\right)}{g \sum W^2 - \left(\sum W\right)^2}$$

g = number of subgroups

The coefficients of a and b are obtained by establishing columns for W, X, $W\overline{X}$, and W^2, as illustrated in Table 3-4, determining their sums, and inserting the sums in the equation.

TABLE 3-4 Least-Squares Calculations for Trend Line

Subgroup Number, W	*Subgroup Average,* $\overline{X}$	*Product of W and* $\overline{X}$, $W\overline{X}$	W^2
1	9	9	1
2	11	22	4
3	10	30	9
·	·	·	·
·	·	·	·
·	·	·	·
g	·	·	·
$\sum W$	$\sum \overline{X}$	$\sum W\overline{X}$	$\sum W^2$

Once the trend-line equation is known, it can be plotted on the chart by assuming values of W and calculating $\overline{X}$. When two points are plotted, the trend line is drawn between them. The control limits are drawn on each side of the trend line a distance (in the vertical direction) equal to $A_2\overline{R}_x$ or $A\sigma_0$.

The R chart will generally have the typical appearance shown in Figure 3-5. However, the dispersion may also be increasing. In such a case the central line would still be horizontal, but the control limits would diverge.

Chart for Moving Average and Moving Range

In some situations a chart is used to combine a number of individual values and plot them on a control chart. This type is referred to as a moving-average and moving range chart and is quite common in the chemical industry, where a moving average and moving range is plotted rather than a daily value. Table 3-5 illustrates the technique. In the development of Table 3-5, no calculations

TABLE 3-5 Calculations of Moving Average and Moving Range

Daily Value	*Three-Day Moving Sum*	$\overline{X}$	*R*
35	—	—	—
26	—	—	—
28	89	29.6	9
32	86	28.6	6
36	96	32.0	8
⋮	⋮	⋮	⋮
		$\sum \overline{X} =$	$\sum R =$

are made until the third day when the sum of the three values is posted to the three-day moving-sum column (35 + 26 + 28 = 89). The average and range are calculated ($\overline{X}$ = 89/3 = 29.6) (R = 35 − 26 = 9) and posted to the $\overline{X}$ and R columns. Subsequent calculations are accomplished by adding a new daily value and dropping the earliest one; therefore, 32 is added and 35 is dropped, making the sum 26 + 28 + 32 = 86. The average and range calculations are $\overline{X}$ = 86/3 = 28.6 and R = 32 − 26 = 6. Once the columns for $\overline{X}$ and R are completed, the charts are developed and used in the same manner as regular $\overline{X}$ and R charts.

The discussion above used a time period of 3 days; the time period could have been 2 days, 5 days, 3 shifts, and so on.

In comparing the moving-average and moving-range charts with conventional charts, it is observed that an extreme reading has a greater effect on the former charts. This is true because an extreme value is used a number of times in the calculations.

Chart for Median and Range

A simplified variable control chart which minimizes calculations is the median and range. The data are collected in the conventional manner and the median, Md, and range, R, of each subgroup are found. These are arranged in ascending order and the median of the subgroup medians or grand median, Md_{Md}, and the median of the subgroup range, R_{Md}, are found by counting to the midpoint value. The median control limits are determined from the formulas

$$\text{UCL}_{\text{Md}} = \text{Md}_{\text{Md}} + A_5 R_{\text{Md}}$$

$$\text{LCL}_{\text{Md}} = \text{Md}_{\text{Md}} - A_5 R_{\text{Md}}$$

where Md_{Md} = grand median (median of the medians); Md_0 can be substituted in the formula

A_5 = factor for determining the 3σ control limits (see Table 3-6)

R_{Md} = median of subgroup ranges

TABLE 3-6 Factors for Computing 3σ Control Limits for Median and Range Charts from the Median Range

Subgroup Size	A_5	D_5	D_6	d_3
2	2.224	0	3.865	0.954
3	1.265	0	2.745	1.588
4	0.829	0	2.375	1.978
5	0.712	0	2.179	2.257
6	0.562	0	2.055	2.472
7	0.520	0.078	1.967	2.645
8	0.441	0.139	1.901	2.791
9	0.419	0.187	1.850	2.916
10	0.369	0.227	1.809	3.024

Source: Extracted by permission from P. C. Clifford, "Control Charts Without Calculations," *Industrial Quality Control*, 15, No. 6 (May 1959), 44.

The range control limits are determined from the formulas

$$\text{UCL}_R = D_6 R_{\text{Md}}$$

$$\text{LCL}_R = D_5 R_{\text{Md}}$$

where D_5 and D_6 are factors for determining the 3σ control limits based on R_{Md} and are found in Table 3-6. An estimate of the population standard deviation can be obtained from $\sigma = R_{\text{Md}}/d_3$.

The principal benefits of the median chart are (1) less arithmetic, (2) easier to understand, and (3) can be maintained by the operators. However, the median chart fails to grant any weight to extreme values in a subgroup.

When these charts are maintained by operating personnel a subgroup size of 3 is recommended. For example, consider the three values 36, 38, and 35. The Md is 36 and R is 3—all three values are used. While these charts are not as sensitive to variation as the $\overline{X}$ and R, they can be quite effective, especially after quality improvement has been obtained and the process is in a monitoring phase.

Chart for Individual Values

In many situations only one measurement is taken on a quality characteristic. This may be due to the fact that it is too expensive, too time consuming, or there are few items to inspect. In such cases an X chart will provide some information from limited data, whereas an $\overline{X}$ chart would provide no information or information only after considerable delay to obtain sufficient data. Figure 3-24 illustrates an X chart.

Formulas for the trial central line and control limits are

$$\overline{X} = \frac{\sum X}{g} \qquad \overline{R} = \frac{\sum R}{g}$$

$$\text{UCL}_x = \overline{X} + 2.660\overline{R} \qquad \text{UCL}_R = 3.276\overline{R}$$

$$\text{LCL}_x = \overline{X} - 2.660\overline{R} \qquad \text{LCL}_R = (0)\overline{R}$$

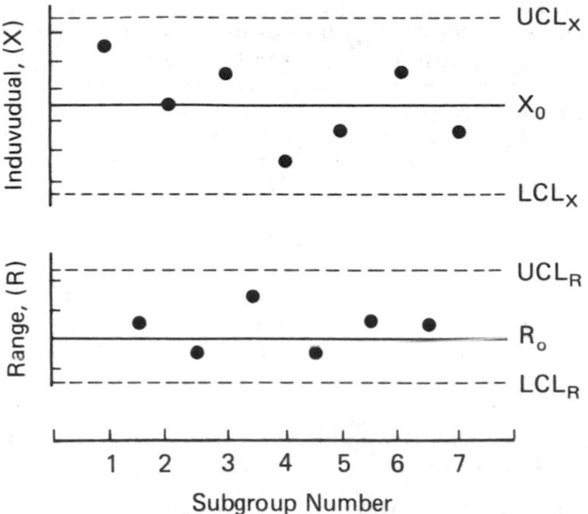

Figure 3-24 Control charts for individual values and moving range.

These formulas require the moving range technique with a subgroup size of 2.[10] To obtain the first range point, the value of X_1 is subtracted from X_2; to obtain the second point, X_2 is subtracted from X_3; and so forth. Each individual value is used for two different points except for the first and last: therefore, the name "moving" range. The range points are placed between the subgroup number on the R chart since they are obtained from both values.

These range points are averaged to obtain $\overline{R}$. Note that g for obtaining $\overline{R}$ will be one less than g for obtaining $\overline{X}$.

Formulas for the revised central line and control limits are

$$X_0 = \overline{X}_{new} \qquad R_0 = \overline{R}_{new}$$

$$UCL_x = X_0 + 3\sigma_0 \qquad UCL_R = (3.686)\sigma_0$$

$$LCL_x = X_0 - 3\sigma_0 \qquad LCL_R = (0)\sigma_0$$

where $\sigma_0 = 0.8865R_0$.

The X chart has the advantage of being easier for production personnel to understand and of providing a direct comparison with specifications. It does have the disadvantages of (1) requiring too many subgroups to indicate an out-of-control condition, (2) not summarizing the data as well as $\overline{X}$, and (3) distorting the control limits when the distribution is not normal. To correct for the last disadvantage, tests for normality should be used since the central limit theorem will not be applicable. Unless there is an insufficient amount of data, the $\overline{X}$ chart is recommended.

[10]This technique is the simplest approach to $\overline{X}$ and R charts. Other techniques are given on pages 23–15 to 23–17 of Juran, *Quality Control Handbook*, 3rd ed.

OTHER CHARTS

There are other charts that may assist quality personnel in the attainment of quality improvement.

Charts with Reject Limits

Reject limits have the same relationship to averages as specifications have to individual values. Figure 3-25 shows the relationship of reject limits, control limits, and specifications for the three cases discussed in the section on specifications. The upper, U, and lower, L, specifications are shown in Figure 3-25 to illustrate the technique and are not included in actual practice.

In case I the reject limits are greater than the control limits, which is a desirable situation, since an out-of-control condition will not result in defective product. Case II shows the situation where the reject limits are equal to the control limits; therefore, any out-of-control situations will result in defective product being manufactured. Case III illustrates the situation where the reject limits are inside the control limits, and therefore some defective product will be manufactured even when the process is in control.

The figure shows that the reject limits are a prescribed distance from the specifications. This distance is equal to $V\sigma$, where V varies with the subgroup size and is equal to the value $3 - 3/\sqrt{n}$. The formula for V was derived from case II, because in that situation the control limits are equal to the reject limits.

Control limits tell what the process is capable of doing and reject limits tell when the product is conforming to specifications. This can be a valuable tool

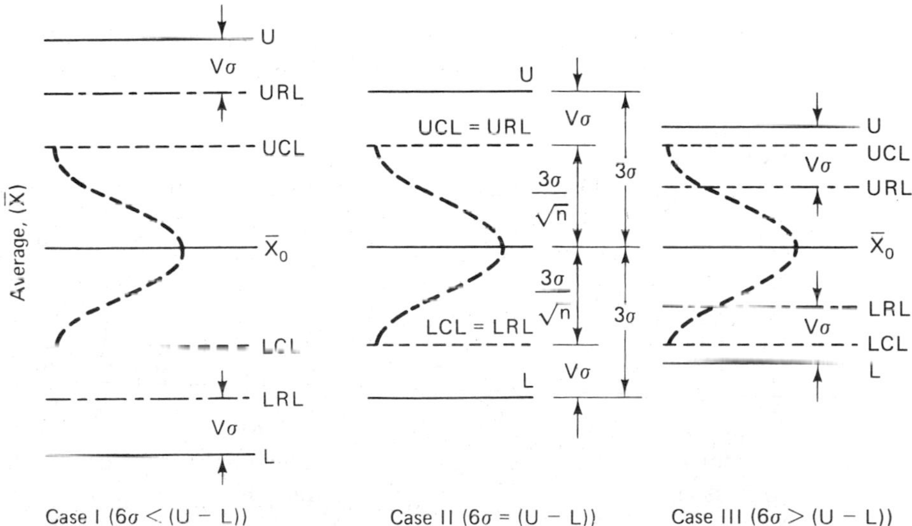

Figure 3-25 Relationship of reject limits, control limits, and specifications.

for the quality professional and perhaps the first-line supervisor. Posting of reject limits for operating personnel should be avoided since they will be confusing and may lead to unnecessary adjustment. Also, the operator is only responsible to maintain the process between the control limits.

Chart for Short Production Runs

Short production runs present a problem in that the run may be completed before the control chart can be implemented. For this situation a chart can be designed that will give some measure of control and a method for quality improvement. The central line and the control limits for this type of chart are established using the specifications.

Assume that the specifications call for 25.00 ± 0.12 mm. Then the central line, $\overline{X}_0$, = 25.00. The difference between the upper specification and the lower specification ($U - L$) is 0.24 mm, which is the spread of the process under the case II situation. Therefore, $6\sigma = U - L = 0.24$ and $\sigma = 0.04$. It follows that $\sigma_{\overline{X}} = \sigma/\sqrt{n}$ and for a subgroup size of 4, $\sigma_{\overline{X}} = 0.04/\sqrt{4} = 0.02$. Thus,

$$\begin{aligned} \text{URL}_{\overline{X}} &= \overline{X}_0 + 3\sigma_{\overline{X}} & \text{LRL}_{\overline{X}} &= \overline{X} - 3\sigma_{\overline{X}} \\ &= 25.00 + 3(0.02) & &= 25.00 - 3(0.02) \\ &= 25.06 & &= 24.94 \\ \text{URL}_R &= D_2\sigma_0 & \text{LRL}_R &= D_1\sigma_0 \\ &= (4.698)(0.04) & &= (0)(0.04) \\ &= 0.19 & &= 0 \end{aligned}$$

These limits, which are reject limits, represent what we would like the process to do (as a maximum condition) rather than what it is capable of doing.

Run Chart

A run chart does not have control limits and can be used to analyze the data especially in the development stage of a product or prior to a state of statistical control. The data points are plotted by order of production, as shown in Figure 3-26. It is obvious from the chart that the hardness resulting from a heat-treating operation is declining. Plotting the data points are a very effective way of finding out about the process. This should be done as the first step in data analysis. Without a run chart other data analysis tools, such as the average, sample standard deviation, and histogram, can lead to erroneous conclusions.

Many chemical processing plants are designed to produce a few basic products to customer specifications. While the ingredients and process are essentially the same, the specifications will change with each customer's batch. Figure 3-27 shows a run chart for batch viscosity. The solid point represents the vis-

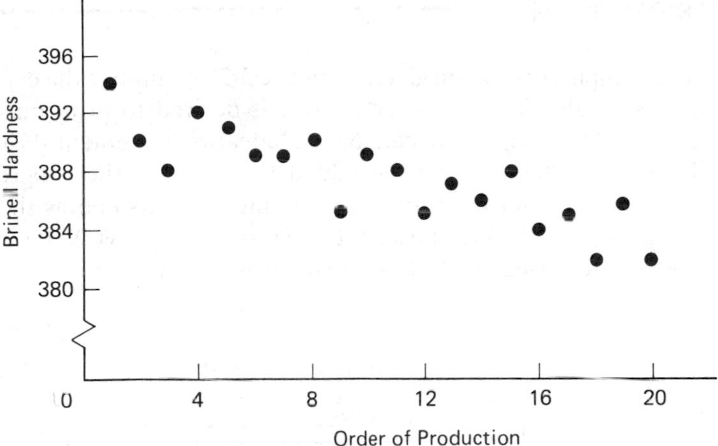

Figure 3-26 Run chart for heat treatment operation.

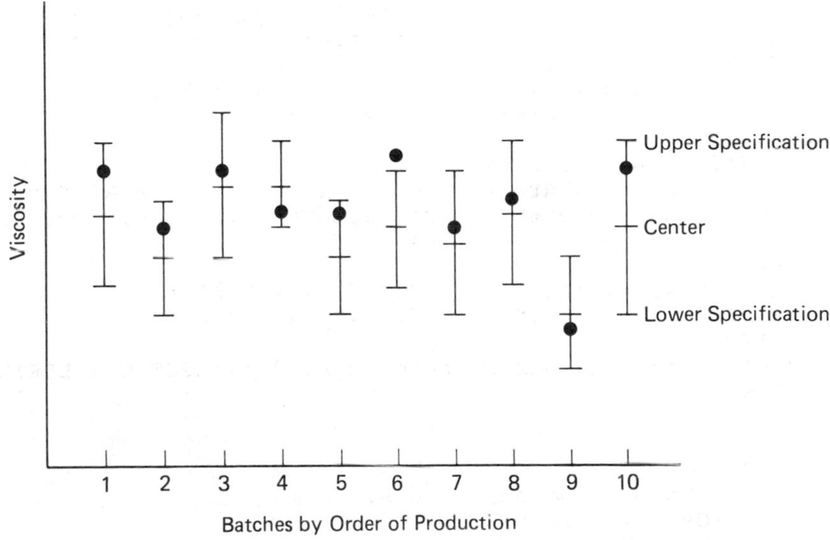

Figure 3-27 Run chart for different batches with different specifications.

cosity value and the vertical line represents the specification range. A cursory analysis of the batches shows that eight of the 10 plotted points are on the high end of the specification. This information may lead to a minor adjustment so that the viscosity of future batches will be closer to the center of each batch specification. Run charts such as this for the other quality characteristics can be an effective technique for quality improvement.

COMPUTER PROGRAM

The computer program given in Figure 3-28 computes the central line and control limits for the $\bar{X}$ and R charts. If it is desired to print out the incoming data, an LPRINT statement can be added after statement 170. Also, additional LPRINT statements can be added to print out the subgroup values that are discarded. Data used for the program are the same as the example problem. By using the coding statement $X(I) = 6.00 + X(I)/100$ after statement 300, coded data using the last two digits was entered.

```
10 REM                          XBAR and R CHARTS
20 REM
30 REM                          N = Subgroup Size
40 REM                          G = Number of Subgroups
50 REM                       X(I) = Observed Values
60 REM                  A(J)/R(J) = Subgroups Average/Range
70 REM                  ABAR/RBAR = Average of Averages/Ranges
80 REM                    UCL/LCL = Central Limits(A & R)
90 REM                      AO/RO = Standard Value and Central Line
100 REM                               of Average/Range
110 REM                         SO = Standard value of Standard
120 REM                               Deviation
130 REM       A2,D,D1,D2,D3,D4 = Control Chart Factors
140 REM                Note:   A = 3 / SQR(N)
150 REM
155 DIM X(25), A(30), R(30)
160 PRINT " Enter subgroup size." : INPUT N : LPRINT " n = ";N
170 PRINT " Enter control chart factors A2, d2, D1, D2, D3, D4."
180 INPUT A2, D, D1, D2, D3, D4
190 LPRINT
200 LPRINT " A2 = ";A2," d2 = ";D," D1 = ";D1
210 LPRINT " D2 = ";D2," D3 = ";D3," D4 = ";D4
220 LPRINT
230 PRINT " Enter number of subgroups. " : INPUT G : LPRINT " g = ";G
240 LPRINT
250 J = 0
260 SX = 0
270 J = J + 1
280 PRINT " Enter subgroup values. "
290       FOR I = 1 TO N
300       INPUT X(I)
310       SX = SX + X(I)
320       NEXT I
330 REM                       Sort Routine
340       FOR K = 1 TO (N - 1)
350       L = N - K
360             FOR M = 1 TO L
370             Q = M + 1
380             IF X(M) < X(Q) GOTO 420
390             A = X(M)
```

Figure 3-28 Computer program in BASIC to calculate the central line and control limits for $\bar{X}$ and R charts.

```
400              X(M) = X(Q)
410              X(Q) = A
420              NEXT M
430        NEXT K
440 REM          Subgroup Average & Range
450 R(J) = X(N) - X(1)
460 A(J) = SX / N
480 IF J < G GOTO 260
490 REM                          Trial Central Lines(A Bar & R Bar)
500 SA = 0 : SR = 0
510        FOR K = 1 TO G
520        SA = SA + A(K)
530        SR = SR + R(K)
540        NEXT K
550 ABAR = SA / G
560 RBAR = SR / G
580 REM                          Trial Control Limits
590 UCLA = ABAR + A2 * RBAR
600 LCLA = ABAR - A2 * RBAR
610 UCLR = D4 * RBAR
620 LCLR = D3 * RBAR
630 REM                          Discard Out-of-Control
640 DA = G : DR = G
650        FOR J = 1 TO G
660        IF A(J) < LCLA GOTO 710
670        IF A(J) > UCLA GOTO 770
680        IF R(J) < LCLR GOTO 800
690        IF R(J) > UCLR GOTO 860
700        GOTO 890
710        PRINT " Subgroup number = ";J
720        PRINT " A < LCL; Enter 0 to discard, else 1."
730        INPUT K
740        IF K = 1 GOTO 890
750        IF K = 0 THEN SA = SA - A(J) : DA = DA - 1
760        GOTO 890
770        PRINT " Subgroup number = ";J
780        PRINT " A > UCL; Enter 0 to discard, else 1."
790        INPUT K : GOTO 740
800        PRINT " Subgroup number = ";J
810        PRINT " R < LCL; Enter 0 to discard, else 1."
820        INPUT L
830        IF L = 1 GOTO 890
840        IF L = 0 THEN SR = SR - R(J) : DR = DR - 1
850        GOTO 890
860        PRINT " Subgroup number = ";J
870        PRINT " R > UCL; Enter 0 to discard, else 1."
880        INPUT L : GOTO 830
890        NEXT J
900 REM                         Standard Values and Central Line
910 XO = SA / DA
920 RO = SR / DR
930 SO = RO / D
940 REM                         Control Limits
950 UCLA = XO + (3 / SQR(N)) * SO
960 LCLA = XO - (3 / SQR(N)) * SO
```

Figure 3-28 Continued.

```
970 UCLR = D2 * SO
980 LCLR = D1 * SO
990 LPRINT " XO = ";XO," RO = ";RO," SO = ";SO
1000 LPRINT " UCLA = ";UCLA,"    LCLA = ";LCLA
1010 LPRINT " UCLR = ";UCLR,"    LCLR = ";LCLR
1020 END

n =  4

A2 =  .729          d2 = 2.059          D1 = 0
D2 = 4.698          D3 = 0              D4 = 2.282

g = 25

XO =    6.39522          RO = .0787499           SO = .0382467
UCLA = 6.45259           LCLA = 6.33785
UCLR = .179683           LCLR = 0
```

Figure 3-28 Continued.

The program can be enhanced by graphing the chart and plotting the actual points. This activity is a function of the available graphical output device.

PROBLEMS

1. Control charts for $\overline{X}$ and R are to be established on a certain dimension part, measured in millimeters. Data were collected in subgroup sizes of 6 and are given below. Determine the trial central line and control limits. Assume assignable causes and revise the central line and limits.

Subgroup Number	$\overline{X}$	*R*	*Subgroup Number*	$\overline{X}$	*R*
1	20.35	0.34	14	20.41	0.36
2	20.40	0.36	15	20.45	0.34
3	20.36	0.32	16	20.34	0.36
4	20.65	0.36	17	20.36	0.37
5	20.20	0.36	18	20.42	0.73
6	20.40	0.35	19	20.50	0.38
7	20.43	0.31	20	20.31	0.35
8	20.37	0.34	21	20.39	0.38
9	20.48	0.30	22	20.39	0.33
10	20.42	0.37	23	20.40	0.32
11	20.39	0.29	24	20.41	0.34
12	20.38	0.30	25	20.40	0.30
13	20.40	0.33			

2. The table below gives the average and range in kilograms for tensile tests on an improved plastic cord. The subgroup size is 4. Determine the trial central line and control limits. If any points are out of control, assume assignable causes and calculate revised limits and central line.

Subgroup Number	$\overline{X}$	R	Subgroup Number	$\overline{X}$	R
1	476	32	14	482	22
2	466	24	15	506	23
3	484	32	16	496	23
4	466	26	17	478	25
5	470	24	18	484	24
6	494	24	19	506	23
7	486	28	20	476	25
8	496	23	21	485	29
9	488	24	22	490	25
10	482	26	23	463	22
11	498	25	24	469	27
12	464	24	25	474	22
13	484	24			

3. Rework Problem 1 assuming a subgroup size of 3.

4. Rework Problem 2 assuming a subgroup size of 5.

5. Control charts for $\overline{X}$ and R are kept on the weight in kilograms of a color pigment for a batch process. After 25 subgroups with a subgroup size of 4, $\sum \overline{X} = 52.08$ kg (114.8 lb), $\sum R = 11.82$ kg (26.1 lb). Assuming the process is in a state of control, compute the $\overline{X}$ and R chart central line and control limits for the next production period.

6. Control charts for $\overline{X}$ and s are to be established on the Brinell hardness of hardened tool steel in kilograms per square millimeter. Data for subgroup sizes of 8 are shown below. Determine the trial central line and control limits for the $\overline{X}$ and s charts. Assume that the out-of-control points have assignable causes. Calculate the revised limits and central line.

Subgroup Number	$\overline{X}$	s	Subgroup Number	$\overline{X}$	s
1	540	26	14	551	24
2	534	23	15	522	29
3	545	24	16	579	26
4	561	27	17	549	28
5	576	25	18	508	23
6	523	50	19	569	22
7	571	29	20	574	28
8	547	29	21	563	33
9	584	23	22	561	23
10	552	24	23	548	25
11	541	28	24	556	27
12	545	25	25	553	23
13	546	26			

7. Control charts for $\overline{X}$ and s are maintained on the resistance in ohms of an electrical part. The subgroup size is 6. After 25 subgroups, $\sum \overline{X} = 2046.5$ and $\sum s = 17.4$. If the process is in statistical control, what are the control limits and central line?

8. Rework Problem 6 assuming a subgroup size of 3.

9. Copy the s chart of Figure 3-6 on transparent paper. Place this copy on top of the R chart of Figure 3-3 and compare the pattern of variation.

10. In filling bags of nitrogen fertilizer, it is desired to hold the average overfill to as low a value as possible. The lower specification limit is 22.00 kg (48.50 lb), the population mean weight of the bags is 22.73 kg (50.11 lb), and the population standard deviation is 0.80 kg (1.76 lb). What percent of the bags contain less than 22 kg? If it is permissible for 5% of the bags to be below 22 kg, what would be the average weight? Assume a normal distribution.

11. Plastic strips that are used in a sensitive electronic device are manufactured to a maximum specification of 305.70 mm (approximately 12 in.) and a minimum specification of 304.55 mm. If the strips are less than the minimum specification, they are scrapped; if greater than the maximum specification, they are reworked. The part dimensions are normally distributed with a population mean of 305.20 mm and a population standard deviation of 0.25 mm. What percentage of the product is scrap? What percentage is rework? How can the process be centered to eliminate all but 0.1% of the scrap? What is the rework percentage now?

12. A company that manufactures oil seals found the population mean to be 49.15 mm (1.935 in.), the population standard deviation to be 0.51 mm (0.020 in.), and the data to be normally distributed. If the ID of the seal is below the lower specification limit of 47.80 mm, the part is reworked. However, if above the upper specification limit of 49.80 mm, the seal is scrapped. (a) What percentage of the seals are reworked? What percentage are scrapped? (b) For various reasons the process average is changed to 48.50 mm. With this new mean or process center, what percentage of the seals is reworked? What percentage is scrapped? If rework is economically feasible, is the change in the process center a wise decision?

13. Determine the process capability of the data on Table 3-3. Use the first 20 subgroups.

14. Repeat Problem 13 using the last 20 subgroups and compare the results.

15. Determine the capability index before and after improvement for the chapter example problem using specifications of 6.40 ± 0.15 mm.

16. A new process is started and the sum of the sample standard deviations for

20 subgroups of size 4 is 600. If the specifications are 700 ± 80, what is the process capability index? What action would you recommend?

17. Determine the revised central line and control limits for a subgroup sum chart using the data of:

a. Problem 1
b. Problem 2

18. Determine the trial central line and control limits for moving average and moving range charts using a time period of 3. Data in liters are as follows: 4.56, 4.65, 4.66, 4.34, 4.65, 4.40, 4.50, 4.55, 4.69, 4.29, 4.58, 4.71, 4.61, 4.66, 4.46, 4.70, 4.65, 4.61, 4.54, 4.55, 4.54, 4.54, 4.47, 4.64, 4.72, 4.47, 4.66, 4.51, 4.43, 4.34. Are there any out of control points?

19. Repeat Problem 18 using a time period of 4. What is the difference in the central line and control limits? Are there any out-of-control points?

20. The Get-Well Hospital has completed a quality improvement project on the time to admit a patient using $\overline{X}$ and R charts. They now wish to monitor the activity using median and range charts. Determine the central line and control limits with the latest data in minutes as given below.

Subgroup Number	Observation			Subgroup Number	Observation		
	X_1	X_2	X_3		X_1	X_2	X_3
1	6.0	5.8	6.1	13	6.1	6.9	7.4
2	5.2	6.4	6.9	14	6.2	5.2	6.8
3	5.5	5.8	6.2	15	4.9	6.6	6.6
4	5.0	5.7	6.5	16	7.0	6.4	6.1
5	6.7	6.5	5.5	17	5.4	6.5	6.7
6	5.8	5.2	5.0	18	6.6	7.0	6.8
7	5.6	5.1	5.2	19	4.7	6.2	7.1
8	6.0	5.8	6.0	20	6.7	5.4	6.7
9	5.5	4.9	5.7	21	6.8	6.5	5.2
10	4.3	6.4	6.3	22	5.9	6.4	6.0
11	6.2	6.9	5.0	23	6.7	6.3	4.6
12	6.7	7.1	6.2	24	7.4	6.8	6.3

21. Determine the trial central line and control limits for median and range charts for the data of Table 3-2. Assume assignable causes for any out-of-control points and determine the revised central line and control limits. Compare the pattern of variation with the $\overline{X}$ and R charts in Figure 3-3.

22. Determine upper and lower reject limits for the $\overline{X}$ chart of Problem 1. The specifications are 20.40 ± 0.25. Compare these limits to the revised control limits.

23. Determine the central line and control limits for a short production run that will be completed in 3 h. The specifications are 25.0 ± 0.3 ohms. Use n = 4.

24. A new process is starting and there is the possibility that the process temperature will give problems. Eight readings are taken each day at 8:00 A.M., 10:00 A.M., 12:00 noon, 2:00 P.M., 4:00 P.M., 6:00 P.M., 8:00 P.M., and 10:00 P.M. Prepare a run chart and evaluate the results.

Day	*Temperature (0°C)*							
Monday	78.9	80.0	79.6	79.9	78.6	80.2	78.9	78.5
Tuesday	80.7	80.5	79.6	80.2	79.2	79.3	79.7	80.3
Wednesday	79.0	80.6	79.9	79.6	80.0	80.0	78.6	79.3
Thursday	79.7	79.9	80.2	79.2	79.5	80.3	79.0	79.4
Friday	79.3	80.2	79.1	79.5	78.8	78.9	80.0	78.8

25. The viscosity of a liquid is checked every half-hour during one three-shift day. Prepare a histogram with five cells and the midpoint value of the first cell equal to 29 and evaluate the distribution. Prepare a run chart and evaluate the distribution again. What does the run chart indicate? Data are: 39, 42, 38, 37, 41, 40, 38, 36, 40, 36, 35, 38, 34, 35, 37, 36, 39, 34, 38, 36, 32, 37, 35, 34, 33, 35, 32, 32, 38, 34, 37, 35, 35, 34, 31, 33, 35, 32, 36, 31, 29, 33, 32, 31, 30, 32, 32, and 29.

26. Test, and if necessary rewrite, the computer program for the $\overline{X}$ and R charts for your computer.

27. Modify the computer program to output the central line and control limits for your graphical output device. Also, write the program to plot the subgroup $\overline{X}$ and R values.

28. Write a computer program for:
(a) $\overline{X}$ and s charts
(b) Short production run chart
(c) Moving average and moving range charts
(d) Median and range charts
(e) Upper and lower reject limits
(f) Process capability (quick method)
(g) Capability ratio

4 FUNDAMENTALS OF PROBABILITY

BASIC CONCEPTS

Definition of Probability

The term *probability* has a number of synonyms, such as likelihood, chance, tendency, and trend. To the layman, probability is a well-known term which refers to the chance that something will happen. "I will probably play golf tomorrow" or "I will probably receive an A in this course" are typical examples. When the commentator on the evening news states that, "The probability of rain tomorrow is 25%," the definition has been quantified. It is possible to define probability with extreme mathematical rigor; however, in this text we will define probability from a practical viewpoint as it applies to quality control.

If a nickel is tossed, the probability of a head is $\frac{1}{2}$ and the probability of a tail is $\frac{1}{2}$. A die, which is used in games of chance, is a cube with six sides and spots on each side from one to six. When the die is tossed on the table, the likelihood or probability of a one is $\frac{1}{6}$, the probability of a two is $\frac{1}{6}$, . . . , the probability of a six is $\frac{1}{6}$. Another example of probability is illustrated by the drawing of a card from a deck of cards. The probability of a spade is $\frac{13}{52}$, since there are 13 spades in a deck of cards which contains 52 total cards. For hearts, diamonds, and clubs, the other three suits in the deck, the probability is also $\frac{13}{52}$.

Figure 4-1 shows the probability distributions for the examples above. It is noted that the area of each distribution is equal to 1.000 ($\frac{1}{2} + \frac{1}{2} = 1.00$; $\frac{1}{6} + \frac{1}{6} + \frac{1}{6} + \frac{1}{6} + \frac{1}{6} + \frac{1}{6} = 1.00$; and $\frac{13}{52} + \frac{13}{52} + \frac{13}{52} + \frac{13}{52} = 1.00$). It is recalled that the area under the normal distribution curve, which is a probability distribution, is also equal to 1.000. Therefore, the total probability of any situation will be equal to 1.000. The probability is expressed as a decimal such as (1) the probability of heads is 0.500 [which is expressed in symbols as [$P(h) = 0.500$], (2)

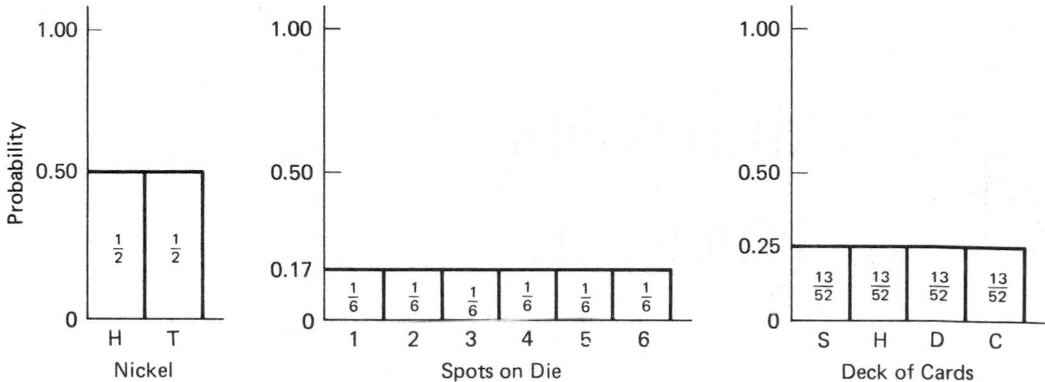

Figure 4-1 Probability distributions.

the probability of a 3 on a die is 0.167[$P(3) = 0.167$], and (3) the probability of a spade is 0.250 [$P(s) = 0.250$].

The probabilities given in the examples above will occur provided sufficient trials are made and provided there is an equal likelihood of the events occurring. In other words, the probability of a head (the event) will be 0.500 provided that the chance of a head or a tail is equal (equally likely). In most coins the equally likely condition is met; however, the addition of a little extra metal on one side would produce a biased coin and the equally likely condition could not be met. Similarly, an unscrupulous person might fix a die so that a three appears more often than one out of six times, or he might stack a deck of cards so that all the aces were at the top.

Returning to the example of a six-sided die, there are six possible outcomes (1, 2, 3, 4, 5, and 6). An *event* is a collection of outcomes. Thus, the event of a 2 or 4, occurring on a throw of the die has two outcomes and the total number of outcomes is 6. The probability is obviously $\frac{2}{6}$ or 0.333.

From the discussion above, a definition based on a frequency interpretation can be given. If an event A can occur in N_A outcomes out of a total of N possible and equally likely outcomes, then the probability that the event will occur is

$$P(A) = \frac{N_A}{N}$$

where $P(A)$ = probability of an event occurring
N_A = number of successful outcomes
N = total number of possible outcomes

This definition can be used when the number of outcomes is known or when the number of outcomes is found by experimentation.

Example Problem

A part is selected at random from a container of 50 parts that are known to have 10 defective. The part is returned to the container and a record of the number of trials and the number defective maintained. After 90 trials, 16 defective were recorded. What is the probability based on known outcomes and on experimental outcomes?

Known outcomes:

$$P(A) = \frac{N_A}{N} = \frac{10}{50} = 0.200$$

Experimental outcomes:

$$P(A) = \frac{N_A}{N} = \frac{16}{90} = 0.178$$

The probability calculated using known outcomes is the true probability and the one calculated using experimental outcomes is different due to the chance factor. If, say, 900 trials were taken, the probability using experimental outcomes would be much closer since the chance factor would be minimized.

In most cases, the number defective in the container would not be known; therefore, the probability with known outcomes cannot be determined. If we consider the probability using experimental outcomes to represent the sample and known outcomes to represent the population, there is the same relationship between sample and population that was discussed in Chapter 2.

The definition above is useful for finite situations where N_A, the number of successful outcomes, and N, total number of outcomes, are known or must be found experimentally. For an infinite situation, where $N = \infty$, the definition would always lead to a probability of zero. Therefore, in the infinite situation the probability of an event occurring is proportional to the population distribution. A discussion of this is given under the discussion of continuous and discrete probability distributions.

Theorems of Probability

Theorem 1. Probability is expressed as a number between 1.00 and 0, where a value of 1.00 is a certainty that an event will occur and a value of 0 is a certainty that an event will not occur.

Theorem 2. If $P(A)$ is the probability that event A will occur, then the probability that A will not occur, $P(\not{A})$, is $1.00 - P(A)$.

Example Problem

If the probability of obtaining a defective electrical outlet is 0.04, what is the probability of obtaining an acceptable electrical outlet?

$$\begin{aligned} P(\not{A}) &= 1.00 - P(A) \\ &= 1.00 - 0.04 \\ &= 0.96 \end{aligned}$$

Therefore, the probability of obtaining an acceptable electrical outlet is 0.96.

Theorem 3. If A and B are two mutually exclusive events, then the probability that either event A or event B will occur is the sum of their respective probabilities.

$$P(A \text{ or } B) = P(A) + P(B)$$

Mutually exclusive means that the occurrence of one event makes the other event impossible. Thus, if on one throw of a die a 3 occurred (event A), then event B, say a 5, could not possibly occur.

Whenever an "or" is verbalized, the mathematical operation is addition, or as we shall see in Theorem 4, it can be subtraction. Theorem 3 was illustrated with two events—it is equally applicable for more than two $[P(A \text{ or } B \text{ or} \cdots \text{ or } F) = P(A) + P(B) + \cdots + P(F)]$.

Example Problem

If the 261 parts described in Table 4-1 are contained in a box, what is the probability of selecting a random part produced by supplier X or by supplier Z?

$$\begin{aligned} P(X \text{ or } Z) &= P(X) + P(Z) \\ &= \frac{53}{261} + \frac{77}{261} \\ &= 0.498 \end{aligned}$$

What is the probability of selecting a defective part from supplier X or an acceptable part from supplier Z?

$$\begin{aligned} P(\text{def. } X \text{ or ac. } Z) &= P(\text{def. } X) + P(\text{ac. } Z) \\ &= \frac{3}{261} + \frac{75}{261} \\ &= 0.299 \end{aligned}$$

TABLE 4-1 Inspection Results by Supplier

Supplier	*Number Acceptable*	*Number Defective*	*Total*
X	50	3	53
Y	125	6	131
Z	75	2	77
Total	250	11	261

Example Problem

If the 261 parts described in Table 4-1 are contained in a box, what is the probability that a randomly selected part will be from supplier Z, a defective from supplier X, or an acceptable from supplier Y?

$$\begin{aligned} P(Z \text{ or def. } X \text{ or ac. } Y) &= P(Z) + P(\text{def. } X) + P(\text{ac. } Y) \\ &= \frac{77}{261} + \frac{3}{261} + \frac{125}{261} \\ &= 0.785 \end{aligned}$$

Theorem 3 is frequently referred to as the *additive law of probability*.

Theorem 4. If event A and event B are not mutually exclusive events, then the probability of either event A or event B or both is given by

$$P(A \text{ or } B) = P(A) + P(B) - P(\text{both})$$

Events that are not mutually exclusive have some outcomes in common.

Example Problem

If the 261 parts described in Table 4-1 are contained in a box, what is the probability that a randomly selected part will be from supplier X or a defective?

$$\begin{aligned} P(X \text{ or def.}) &= P(X) + P(\text{def.}) - P(X \text{ and def.}) \\ &= \frac{53}{261} + \frac{11}{261} - \frac{3}{261} \\ &= 0.234 \end{aligned}$$

In the example problem, there are three outcomes common to both events. The 3 defectives of supplier X are counted twice as outcomes of $P(X)$ and of $P(\text{def.})$; therefore, one set of three is subtracted out. This theorem is also applicable to more than two events.

Theorem 5. The sum of the probabilities of the events of a situation is equal to 1.000.

$$P(A) + P(B) + \cdots + P(N) = 1.000$$

This theorem was illustrated in Figure 4-1 for the coin-tossing, die-rolling, and card-drawing situations wherein the sum of the events equaled 1.000.

Example Problem

An inspector examines three products in a subgroup to determine if they are defective. From past experience it is known that the probability of finding no defectives in the sample of 3 is 0.89, the probability of 1 defective in the sample of 3 is 0.06, and the probability of finding 2 defectives in the sample of 3 is 0.03. What is the probability of finding 3 defectives in the sample of 3?

There are four, and only four, events to this situation: 0 defective, 1 defective, 2 defectives, and 3 defectives.

$$P(0) + P(1) + P(2) + P(3) = 1.000$$

$$0.89 + 0.06 + 0.03 + P(3) = 1.000$$

$$P(3) = 0.02$$

Thus, the probability of 3 defectives in the sample of 3 is 0.02.

Theorem 6. If A and B are independent events, then the probability of both A and B occurring is the product of their respective probabilities.

$$P(A \text{ and } B) = P(A) \times P(B)$$

An independent event is one where its occurrence has no influence on the probability of the other event or events. This theorem is referred to as the *multiplicative law of probabilities.*

Example Problem

If the 261 parts described in Table 4-1 are contained in a box, what is the probability that two randomly selected parts will be from supplier X and supplier Y? Assume that the first part is returned to the box before the second part is selected (called with replacement).

$$P(X \text{ and } Y) = P(X) \times P(Y)$$

$$= \left(\frac{53}{261}\right)\left(\frac{131}{261}\right)$$

$$= 0.102$$

At first thought, the result of the example problem seems too low, but there are five other possibilities: XX, YY, ZZ, XZ, and YZ. This theorem is applicable to more than two events.

Theorem 7. If A and B are *dependent* events, the probability of both A and B occurring is the product of the probability of A and the probability that if A occurred, then B will occur also.

$$P(A \text{ and } B) = P(A) \times P(B|A)$$

The symbol $P(B|A)$ is defined as the probability of event B provided that event A has occurred. A dependent event is one whose occurrence influences the probability of the other event or events. This theorem is sometimes referred to as the *conditional theorem*, since the probability of the second event depends on the result of the first event.

Example Problem

Assume that in the preceding example problem the first part was not returned to the box before the second part is selected. What is the probability?

$$\begin{aligned} P(X \text{ and } Y) &= P(X) \times P(Y|X) \\ &= \left(\frac{53}{261}\right)\left(\frac{131}{260}\right) \\ &= 0.102 \end{aligned}$$

What is the probability of both parts from supplier Z?

$$\begin{aligned} P(Z \text{ and } Z) &= P(Z) \times P(Z|Z) \\ &= \left(\frac{77}{261}\right)\left(\frac{76}{260}\right) \\ &= 0.086 \end{aligned}$$

This theorem is applicable to more than two events.

To solve many probability problems it is necessary to combine the theorems.

Example Problem

If the 261 parts described in Table 4-1 are contained in a box, what is the probability that two randomly selected parts (with replacement) has one acceptable from supplier X and one acceptable from supplier Y or supplier Z?

$$\begin{aligned} P[\text{ac. } X \text{ and } (\text{ac. } Y \text{ or ac. } Z)] &= P(\text{ac. } X)\,[P(\text{ac. } Y) + P(\text{ac. } Z)] \\ &= \left(\frac{50}{261}\right)\left(\frac{125}{261} + \frac{75}{261}\right) \\ &= 0.147 \end{aligned}$$

Counting of Events

Many probability problems, such as those where the events are uniform probability distributions, can be solved using counting techniques. There are three counting techniques which are quite often used in the computation of probabilities.

1. *Simple multiplication.* If an event A can happen in any of a ways or outcomes, and after it has occurred another, event B can happen in b ways or outcomes, the number of ways that both events can happen is ab.

Example Problem

A witness to a hit-and-run accident remembered the first three digits of the license plate out of five and noted the fact that the last two were numerals. How many owners of automobiles would the police have to investigate?

$$\begin{aligned} ab &= (10)(10) \\ &= 100 \end{aligned}$$

If the last two were letters, how many would need to be investigated?

$$\begin{aligned} ab &= (26)(26) \\ &= 676 \end{aligned}$$

2. *Permutations.* A *permutation* is an ordered arrangement of a set of objects. The permutations of the word "cup" are cup, cpu, upc, ucp, puc, and pcu. In this case there are 3 objects in the set and we arranged them in groups of 3 to obtain six permutations. This is referred to as a permutation of n objects taking r at a time where $n = 3$ and $r = 3$. How many permutations would there be for 4 objects taken 2 at a time? Using the word "fork" to represent the four objects, the permutations are fo, of, fr, rf, fk, kf, or, ro, ok, ko, rk, and kr. As the number of objects, n, and the number that are taken at one time, r become larger, it becomes a tedious task to list all the permutations. The formula to find the number of permutations more easily is

$$P_r^n = \frac{n!}{(n - r)!}$$

where P_r^n = number of permutations of n objects taken r of them at a time
n = total number of objects
r = number of objects selected out of the total number

The expression $n!$ is read "n factorial" and means $n(n - 1)(n - 2) \cdots (1)$. Thus, $6! = 6 \cdot 5 \cdot 4 \cdot 3 \cdot 2 \cdot 1 = 720$. By definition, $0! = 1$.

Example Problem.

How many permutations are there of 5 objects taken 3 at a time?

$$P_r^n = \frac{n!}{(n - r)!}$$

$$P_3^5 = \frac{5!}{(5 - 3)!} = \frac{5 \cdot 4 \cdot 3 \cdot 2 \cdot 1}{2 \cdot 1}$$

$$= 60$$

Example Problem

In the license plate example, suppose the witness further remembers that the numerals were not the same.

$$P_r^n = \frac{n!}{(n - r)!}$$

$$P_2^{10} = \frac{10!}{(10 - 2)!} = \frac{10 \cdot 9 \cdot 8 \cdot 7 \cdots 1}{8 \cdot 7 \cdots 1}$$

$$= 90$$

This problem could also have been solved by simple multiplication where $a = 10$ and $b = 9$. In other words, there are 10 ways for the first digit but only 9 ways for the second since duplicates are not permitted.

The symbol P is used for both permutation and probability. No confusion should result from this dual usage, since for permutations the superscript n and subscript r are used.

3. *Combinations*. If the way the objects are ordered is unimportant, then we have a *combination*. The word "cup" has *six* permutations when the 3 objects are taken 3 at a time. However, there is only *one* combination, since the same three letters are in a different order. The word "fork" has 12 permutations when the 4 letters are taken 2 at a time; but the number of combinations is fo, fr, fk, or ok, and rk, which gives a total of six. The formula for the number of combinations is

$$C_r^n = \frac{n!}{r!(n - r)!}$$

where C_r^n = number of combinations of n objects taken r at a time
n = total number of objects
r = number of objects selected out of the total number

Example Problem

If there are 5 balls in a bowl, how many different combinations are possible if 3 are selected at a time?

$$C_r^n = \frac{n!}{r!(n - r)!}$$

$$C_3^5 = \frac{5!}{3!(5 - 3)!} = \frac{5 \cdot 4 \cdot 3 \cdot 2 \cdot 1}{3 \cdot 2 \cdot 1 \cdot 2 \cdot 1}$$

$$= 10$$

There is a symmetry associated with combinations such that $C_3^5 = C_2^5$, $C_1^4 = C_3^4$, $C_2^{10} = C_8^{10}$, and so on. Proof of this symmetry is left as an exercise.

The probability definition, the seven theorems, and the three counting techniques are all used to solve probability problems. Many hand calculators have permutation and combination functional keys which eliminate calculation errors provided that the correct keys are punched.

DISCRETE PROBABILITY DISTRIBUTIONS

When specific values such as the integers 0, 1, 2, 3 are used, then the probability distribution is discrete. Typical discrete probability distributions are hypergeometric, binomial, and Poisson.

Hypergeometric Probability Distribution

The *hypergeometric* probability distribution occurs when the population is finite and the random sample is taken without replacement. Figure 4-2 illustrates probability distributions for different number defective in the lot D, when the lot size, N, is 20 and the sample size, n, is 4. The formula for the hypergeometric is constructed of three combinations (total combinations, defective combinations, and good combinations) and is given by

$$P(d) = \frac{C_d^D C_{n-d}^{N-D}}{C_n^N}$$

where $P(d)$ = probability of d defectives in a sample of size n
C_n^N = combinations of all objects
C_d^D = combinations of defective objects
C_{n-d}^{N-D} = combinations of good objects
N = number of objects in the lot (population)
n = number of objects in the sample
$N - D$ = number of good objects in the lot
$n - d$ = number of good objects in the sample

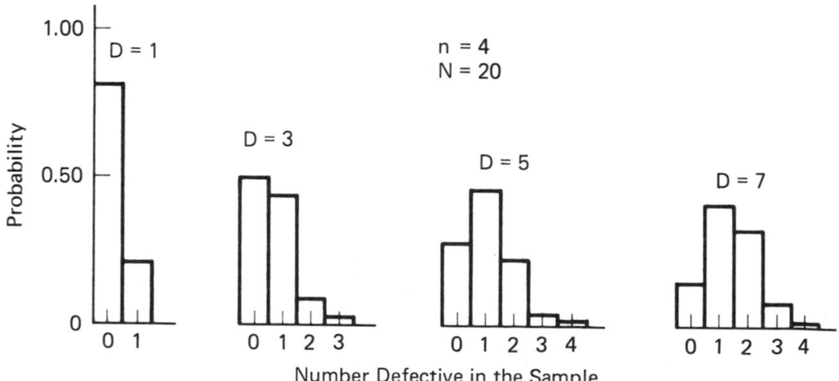

Figure 4-2 Comparison of hypergeometric distributions with different fraction defective in lot.

D = number of defective objects in the lot
d = number of defective objects in the sample

The formula is obtained from the application of the probability definition, simple multiplication, and combinations. In other words, the numerator is the ways or outcomes of obtaining defectives times the ways or outcomes of obtaining good product and the denominator is the total possible ways or outcomes. Note that symbols in the combination formula have been changed to make them more appropriate for quality control.

An example will make the application of this distribution more meaningful.

Example Problem

A lot of 9 balls located in a container has 3 defectives. What is the probability of drawing one defective in a random sample of 4?

For instructional purposes a graphical illustration of the problem is shown below.

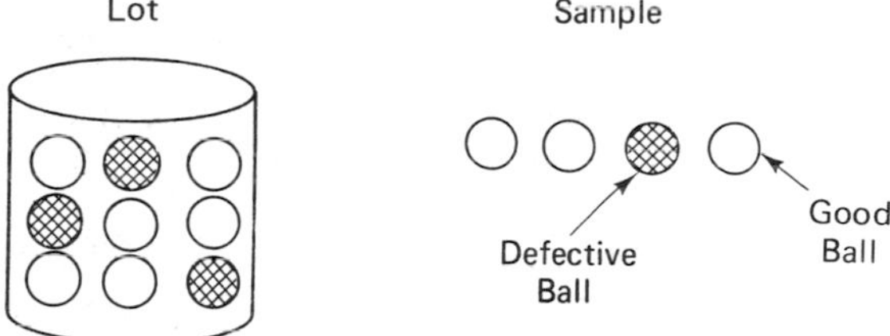

From the picture or from the statement of the problem, $N = 9$, $D = 3$, $n = 4$ and $d = 1$.

$$P(d) = \frac{C_d^D C_{n-d}^{N-D}}{C_n^N}$$

$$P(1) = \frac{C_1^3 C_{4-1}^{9-3}}{C_4^9}$$

$$= \frac{\dfrac{3!}{1!(3-1)!} \cdot \dfrac{6!}{3!(6-3)!}}{\dfrac{9!}{4!(9-4)!}}$$

$$= 0.476$$

Similarly, $P(0) = 0.119$, $P(2) = 0.357$, and $P(3) = 0.048$. Since there are only 3 defectives in the lot, $P(4)$ is impossible. The sum of the probabilities must equal 1.000, and this is verified as follows:

$$P(T) = P(0) + P(1) + P(2) + P(3)$$

$$= 0.119 + 0.476 + 0.357 + 0.048$$

$$= 1.000$$

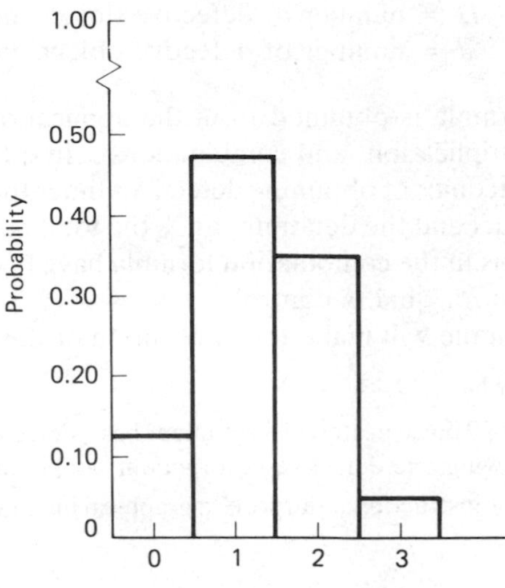

Figure 4-3 Hypergeometric distribution for $N = 9$, $n = 4$, and $D = 3$.

The complete probability distribution is given in Figure 4-3. As the parameters of the hypergeometric distribution change, the shape of the distribution changes as illustrated by Figures 4-2 and 4-3. Therefore, each hypergeometric distribution has a unique shape based on N, n, and D. Hypergeometric tables are available; however, since four variables (including d) are involved, they are quite large. With hand calculators and microcomputers, these tables are no longer necessary for the efficient calculation of the distribution.

Some solutions require an "or less" probability. In such cases the method is to add up the respective probabilities. Thus,

$$P(2 \text{ or less}) = P(2) + P(1) + P(0)$$

Similarly, some solutions require an "or more" probability and use the formulas

$$\begin{aligned} P(2 \text{ or more}) &= P(T) - P(1 \text{ or less}) \\ &= P(2) + P(3) + \cdots \end{aligned}$$

In the latter series, the number of terms to calculate is determined by the sample size, the number defective in the lot, or when the value is less than 0.001.

Binomial Probability Distribution

The *binomial* probability distribution is applicable to discrete probability problems which have an infinite number of items or which have a steady stream of items coming from a work center. The binomial is applied to problems which are attributes such as good or defective, success or failure, pass or fail, and heads or tails. It corresponds to successive terms in the binomial expansion, which is

$$(p + q)^n = p^n + np^{n-1}q + \frac{n(n-1)}{2}p^{n-2}q^2 + \cdots + q^n$$

where p = probability of an event such as a defective product (the probability of a single article being defective is the same as the fraction defective)
$q = 1 - p$ = probability of a nonevent such as a good product (fraction good)
n = number of trials or the sample size

Applying the expansions to the distribution of tails ($p = \frac{1}{2}$, $q = \frac{1}{2}$) resulting from an infinite number of throws of 11 coins at once, the expansion is

$$\begin{aligned}(\tfrac{1}{2} + \tfrac{1}{2})^{11} &= (\tfrac{1}{2})^{11} + 11(\tfrac{1}{2})^{10}(\tfrac{1}{2}) + 55(\tfrac{1}{2})^{9}(\tfrac{1}{2})^{2} + \cdots + (\tfrac{1}{2})^{11} \\ &= 0.001 + 0.005 + 0.027 + 0.080 + 0.161 + \cdots + 0.001\end{aligned}$$

The probability distribution of the number of tails is shown in Figure 4-4. Since $p = q$, the distribution is symmetrical regardless of the value of n; however, when $p \neq q$, the distribution is asymmetrical. In quality control work p is the fraction defective and is usually less than 0.15. Figure 4-5 illustrates the change in the distribution as the sample size increases for the fraction defective of $p = 0.10$, and Figure 4-6 illustrates the change for $p = 0.05$. As the sample size gets larger, the shape of the curve will become symmetrical even though $p \neq q$. Comparing the distribution for $p = 0.10$ and $n = 15$ in Figure 4-5 with the distribution of $p = 0.05$, $n = 15$ in Figure 4-6, it is noted that for the same value of n, the larger the value of the fraction defective p, the greater the symmetry of the distribution.

The shape of the distribution is always a function of the sample size, n, and the fraction defective, p. Change either of these values and a different distribution results.

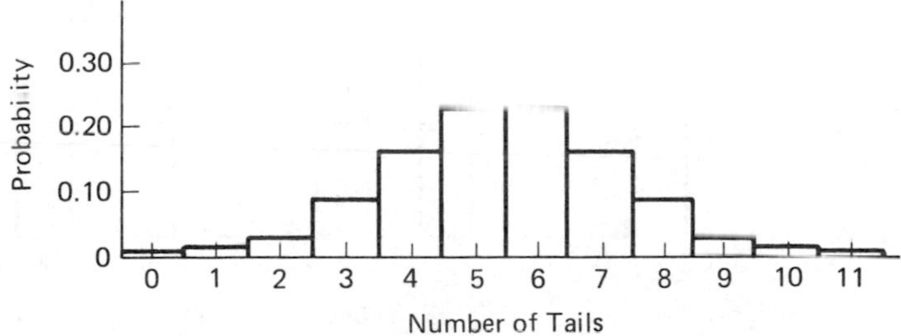

Figure 4-4 Distribution of the number of tails for an infinite number of tosses of 11 coins.

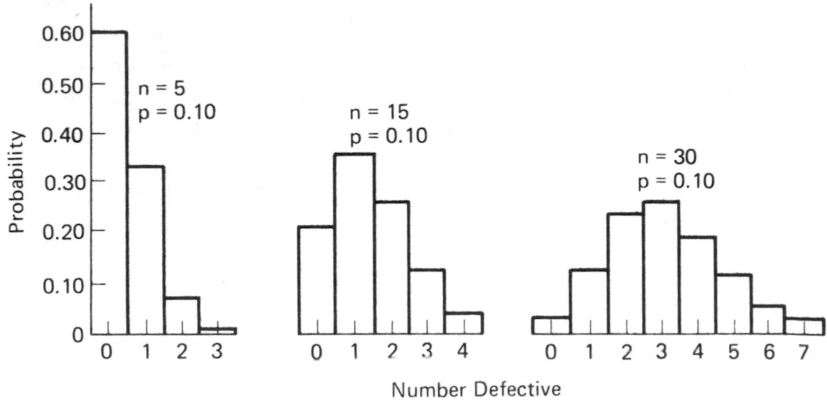

Figure 4-5 Binomial distribution for various sample sizes when $p = 0.10$.

In most cases in quality control work, we are not interested in the entire distribution, only in one or two terms of the binomial expansion. The binomial formula for a single term is

$$P(d) = \frac{n!}{d!(n-d)!} p_0^d q_0^{n-d}$$

where $P(d)$ = probability of d defectives
n = number in the sample
d = number of defectives in the sample
p_0 = fraction defective in the population[1]
q_0 = fraction good $(1 - p_0)$ in the population

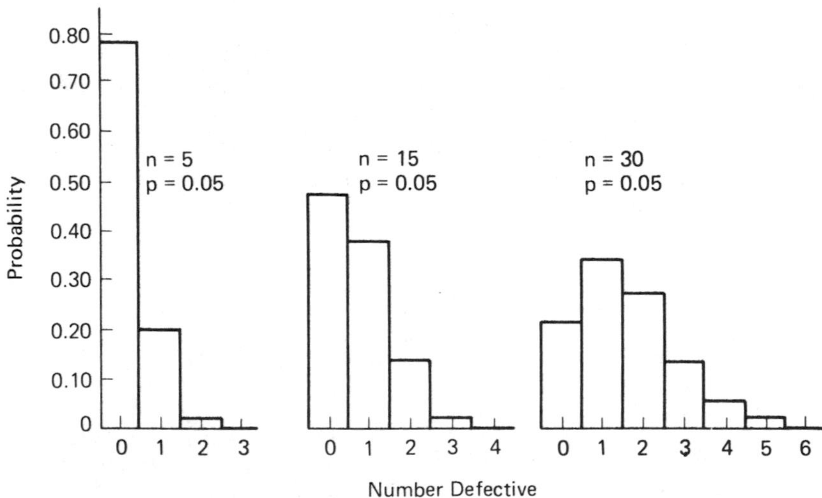

Figure 4-6 Binomial distributions for various sample sizes when $p = 0.05$.

Since the binomial is for the infinite situation, there is no lot size, N, in the formula.

Example Problem

A random sample of 5 is selected from a steady stream of product from a punch press and the fraction defective is 0.10. What is the probability of 1 defective in the sample? What is the probability of 1 or less? What is the probability of 2 or more?

$$q_0 = 1 - p_0 = 1.00 - 0.10 = 0.90$$

$$P(d) = \frac{n!}{d!(n-d)!} p_0^d q_0^{n-d}$$

$$P(1) = \frac{5!}{1!(5-1)!} (0.10^1)(0.90^{5-1})$$

$$= 0.328$$

What is the probability of 1 or less defectives? To solve, we need to use the addition theorem and add $P(1)$ and $P(0)$.

$$P(d) = \frac{n!}{d!(n-d)!} p_0^d q_0^{n-d}$$

$$P(0) = \frac{5!}{0!(5-0)!} (0.10^0)(0.90^{5-0})$$

$$= 0.590$$

Thus,

$$P(1 \text{ or less}) = P(0) + P(1)$$

$$= 0.590 + 0.328$$

$$= 0.918$$

What is the probability of 2 or more defectives? Solution can be accomplished using the addition theorem and adding the probabilities of 2, 3, 4 and 5 defectives.

$$P(2 \text{ or more}) = P(2) + P(3) + P(4) + P(5)$$

[1]Also standard or reference value; see Chapter 5.

Or it can be accomplished by using the theorem that the sum of the probabilities is 1.

$$P(2 \text{ or more}) = P(T) - P(1 \text{ or less})$$
$$= 1.000 - 0.918$$
$$= 0.082$$

Calculations for two defectives and three defectives for the data in the example problem give $P(2) = 0.073$ and $P(3) = 0.008$. The complete distribution is shown as the graph on the left of Figure 4-5. Calculations for $P(4)$ and $P(5)$ give values less than 0.001 so they are not included in the graph.

Tables are available for the binomial distribution. However, since three variables (n, p, and d) are needed, they require a considerable amount of space. The hand calculator and microcomputer can make the required calculations quite efficiently; therefore, there is no longer any need for the tables.

The binomial is used for the infinite situation but will approximate the hypergeometric under certain conditions which are discussed later in the chapter. It requires that there be two and only two possible outcomes (a defective or a good unit), and that the probability of each outcome does not change. In addition, the use of the binomial requires that the trials are independent; that is, if a defective unit occurs, then the chance of the next one being defective neither increases nor decreases.

In addition, the binomial distribution is the basis for the defective control charts discussed in Chapter 5.

Poisson Probability Distribution

A third discrete probability distribution is referred to as the Poisson, named after Simeon Poisson, who described it in 1837. The distribution is applicable to many situations that involve observations per unit of time. For example, the count of cars arriving at a highway toll booth in 1-minute intervals; the count of machine breakdowns in 1 day, and the count of shoppers entering a grocery store in 5-minute intervals. The distribution is also applicable to situations involving observations per unit of amount. For example, the count of weaving defects in 1000 square meters of cloth, the count of defects per lot of product, and the count of rivet defects in a mobile home.

In each of the preceding situations, there are many equal opportunities for the occurrence of an event. Each rivet in a recreational vehicle has an equal opportunity to be defective; however, there will only be a few defective out of the hundreds of rivets. The Poisson is applicable when n is quite large and p_0 is small.

The formula for the Poisson distribution is

$$P(c) = \frac{(np_0)^c}{c!} e^{-np_0}$$

where c = count of occurrences per unit time or amount, such as count of defects, cars, customers, or machine breakdowns

np_0 = average count of occurrences per unit time or amount

e = 2.718281

When the Poisson is used as an approximation to the binomial (to be discussed later in the chapter), the symbol c has the same meaning as d has in the binomial and hypergeometric formulas. Since c and np_0 have similar definitions, there is some confusion. This can be corrected by thinking of c as an individual value or sample and np_0 as an average or population value.

Using the formula, a probability distribution can be determined. Suppose that the average count of cars which arrive at a highway toll booth in a 1-minute interval is 2; then the calculations are

$$P(c) = \frac{(np_0)^c}{c!} e^{-np_0}$$

$$P(0) = \frac{(2)^0}{0!} e^{-2} = 0.135$$

$$P(1) = \frac{(2)^1}{1!} e^{-2} = 0.271$$

$$P(2) = \frac{(2)^2}{2!} e^{-2} = 0.271$$

$$P(3) = \frac{(2)^3}{3!} e^{-2} = 0.180$$

$$P(4) = \frac{(2)^4}{4!} e^{-2} = 0.090$$

$$P(5) = \frac{(2)^5}{5!} e^{-2} = 0.036$$

$$P(6) = \frac{(2)^6}{6!} e^{-2} = 0.012$$

$$P(7) = \frac{(2)^7}{7!} e^{-2} = 0.003$$

The resulting probability distribution is the one on the right in Figure 4-7. This distribution indicates the probability that a certain count of cars will arrive in any 1-minute time interval. Thus, the probability of zero cars in any 1-minute interval is 0.135, the probability of one car in any 1-minute interval is 0.271, . . . , and the probability of seven cars in any 1-minute interval is 0.003.

Figure 4-7 also illustrates the property that as np_0 gets larger, the distribution

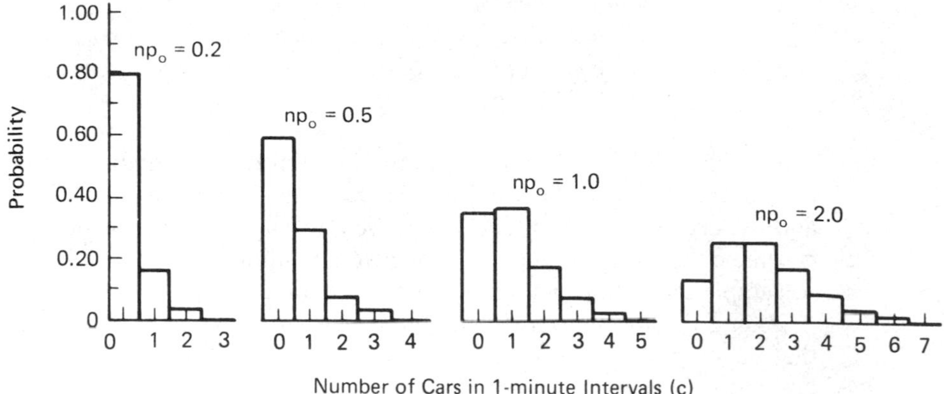

Figure 4-7 Poisson probability distributions for various np_0 values.

approaches symmetry. Other properties of the Poisson distribution are that the mean equals np_0, and the standard deviation equals $\sqrt{np_0}$.

Probabilities for the Poisson distribution for np_0 values of from 0.1 to 5.0 in intervals of 0.1 and from 6.0 to 15.0 in intervals of 1.0 are given in Table C. Values in parentheses in the table are cumulative probabilities for obtaining "or less" answers. The use of this table simplifies the calculations as illustrated in the following problem.

Example Problem

If the probability that a heat-treating batch will be defective is 0.01, what is the probability of two bad batches out of 250? What is the probability of 2 or less?

$$np_0 = (250)(0.01) = 2.5$$

From Table C, the intersection of the column with an np_0 value of 2.5 and the row with a c value of 2 gives

$$P(2) = 0.256 \qquad P(2 \text{ or less}) = 0.543$$

Example Problem

The average count of billing errors per 8-h shift is 1.0. What is the probability of two billing errors? The probability of one or less? The probability of two or more?

From Table C for an np_0 value of 1.0:

$$P(2) = 0.184$$

$$P(1 \text{ or less}) = 0.736$$

$$\begin{aligned} P(2 \text{ or more}) &= 1.000 - P(1 \text{ or less}) \\ &= 1.000 - 0.736 \\ &= 0.264 \end{aligned}$$

The Poisson probability distribution is the basis for the defect control chart for attributes and for acceptance sampling, which are discussed in subsequent chapters. It is also applicable as an approximation to the binomial, which is discussed later in this chapter. In addition to the quality control applications, the Poisson distribution is used in other industrial situations, such as accident frequencies, computer simulation, operations research, and work sampling.

From a theoretical viewpoint a discrete probability distribution should use a bar graph. However, it is a common practice to use the histogram.

Other discrete probability distributions are the uniform, geometric, and negative binomial. The uniform distribution was illustrated in Figure 4-1. From an application viewpoint it is the one we would hope to generate from a random digit-generating program. The geometric and negative binomial are used in reliability studies for discrete data.

CONTINUOUS PROBABILITY DISTRIBUTIONS

When measurable data such as meters, kilograms, and ohms are used, the probability distribution is continuous. While there are many continuous probability distributions, only the normal is of sufficient importance in quality control to warrant a detailed discussion in an introductory text.

Normal Probability Distribution

The *normal curve* is a continuous probability distribution. Solutions to probability problems that involve continuous data can be solved using the normal probability distribution. In Chapter 2 techniques were learned to determine the percentage of the data that were above a certain value, below a certain value, or between two values. These same techniques are applicable to probability problems, as illustrated in the following example problem.

Example Problem

If the operating life of an electric mixer, which is normally distributed, has a mean of 2200 h and standard deviation of 120 h, what is the probability that a single electric mixer will fail to operate at 1900 h or less?

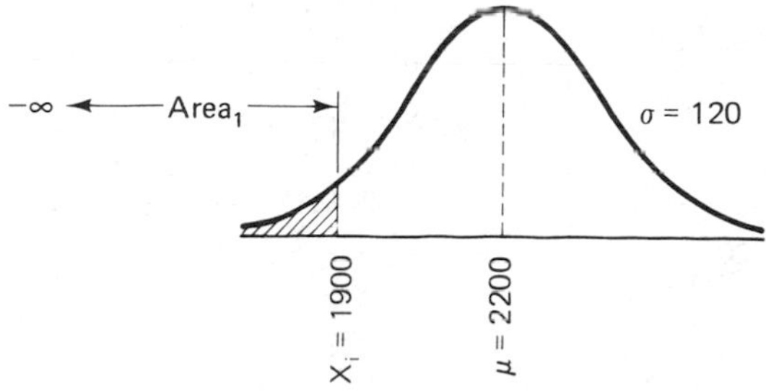

$$Z = \frac{X_i - \mu}{\sigma}$$

$$= \frac{1900 - 2200}{120}$$

$$= -2.5$$

From Table A of the Appendix, for a Z value of -2.5, $\text{area}_1 = 0.0062$. Therefore, the probability of an electric mixer failing is

$$P(\text{failure at 1900 h or less}) = 0.0062$$

The answer in the problem could have been stated as "The percent of items less than 1900 h is 0.62%." Therefore, the areas under the normal curve can be treated as either a probability value or a relative frequency value.

Under certain conditions the normal probability distribution will approximate the binomial probability distribution. These conditions will be discussed later in the chapter. For the present, we are concerned with the problem-solving technique which is illustrated in the next example problem.

Example Problem

Find the probability of getting 2, 3, or 4 tails in 12 tosses of a coin by the normal approximation to the binomial. The problem is shown graphically here. The required probability area is crosshatched and can be approximated by the normal curve, which is shown as a dashed line. Since the data must be continuous for the normal curve, the probability of obtaining 2 to 4 tails is considered to be from 1.5 to 4.5.

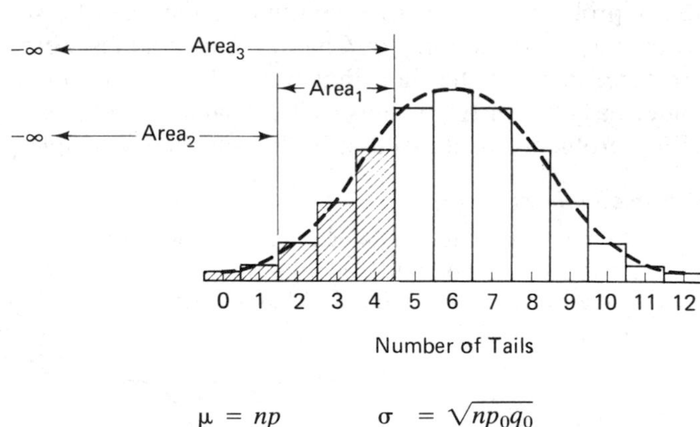

$$\mu = np \qquad \sigma = \sqrt{np_0q_0}$$

$$= 12(\tfrac{1}{2}) \qquad = \sqrt{12(\tfrac{1}{2})(\tfrac{1}{2})}$$

$$= 6 \qquad = 1.73$$

$$Z_2 = \frac{X_i - \mu}{\sigma} \qquad Z_3 = \frac{X_i - \mu}{\sigma}$$

$$= \frac{1.5 - 6}{1.73} \qquad = \frac{4.5 - 6}{1.73}$$

$$= -2.60 \qquad = -0.87$$

From Table A, For $Z_2 = -2.60$, $\text{area}_2 = 0.0047$, and for $Z_3 = -0.87$, $\text{area}_3 = 0.1922$.

$$\text{Area}_1 - \text{Area}_3 \quad \text{Area}_2$$

$$= 0.1922 - 0.0047$$

$$= 0.1875$$

Thus, the required probability is

$$P(2, 3, \text{ or } 4 \text{ tails}) = 0.1875$$

Other Continuous Probability Distributions

Of the many other continuous probability distributions only two are of significant importance to mention their practical applications. The exponential probability distribution is used in reliability studies when there is a constant failure rate and the Weibull is used when the time to failure is not constant. These two distributions are discussed in Chapter 8.

DISTRIBUTION INTERRELATIONSHIP

With so many distributions, it is sometimes difficult to know when they are applicable. Certainly, since the Poisson can be easily calculated using Table C, it should be used whenever possible.

The hypergeometric is used for finite lots of stated size N. It can be approximated by the binomial when $n/N \leqq 0.10$; or by the Poisson when $n/N \leqq 0.10$, $p_0 \leqq 0.10$, and $np_0 \leqq 5$; or by the normal when $n/N \leqq 0.10$ and the normal approximates the binomial.

The binomial is used for infinite situations or when there is a steady stream of product so that an infinite situation is assumed. It can be approximated by the Poisson when $p_0 \leqq 0.10$ and $np_0 \leqq 5$. The normal curve is an excellent approximation when p_0 is close to 0.5 and $n \geqq 10$. As np_0 deviates from 0.5, the approximation is still good as long as $np_0 \geqq 5$ and n increases to 50 or more for values of p_0 as low as 0.10 and as high as 0.90. Since the binomial calculation time is not too much different than the normal calculation time, there is little advantage to using the normal as an approximation.

The information given above can be considered to provide approximation guidelines rather than absolute laws. Approximations are better the farther the data are from the limiting values. For the most part the efficiency of the calculator and microcomputer have made the use of approximations obsolete.

COMPUTER PROGRAM

The computer program given in Figure 4-8 calculates the hypergeometric probability distribution for a lot of size, N, number defective in the lot, D, and sample size, n. Since three combinations must be calculated, a combination routine is established in the program. Provision is made for 0! and the special cases where $R = 0$ and $R = 1$. Also, the combination numerator and denominator operate together to eliminate the possibility of any overflow problems. This is the same distribution that is shown in Figure 4-2.

```
10 REM                    HYPERGEOMETRIC DISTRIBUTION
20 REM
30 REM              NL = Lot Size(N)
40 REM              NS = Sample Size(n)
50 REM              DL = Number Defective in Lot(D)
60 REM              DS = Number Defective in Sample(d)
70 REM              P  = Probability
80 REM              C  = Combination
90 REM              CG = Combination Good
100 REM             CD = Combination Defective
110 REM             CT = Combination Total
120 REM
130 DIM P(100)
140 PRINT " Enter the Lot Size." : INPUT NL
150 LPRINT TAB(5);" N = ";NL
160 PRINT " Enter the number defective in the Lot." : INPUT DL
170 LPRINT TAB(5);" D = ";DL
180 PRINT " Enter the Sample Size." : INPUT NS
190 LPRINT TAB(5);" n = ";NS : LPRINT
200 LPRINT TAB(5);" Number Defective";TAB(30);" Probability"
210 DS = 0
220 K=0
230 K = K + 1
240 IF K = 1 GOTO 270
250 IF K = 2 GOTO 280
260 N = NL : R = NS : GOTO 300
270 N = NL - DL : R = NS - DS : GOTO 300
280 N = DL : R = DS
290 REM                Combination Routine
300 IF R = 0 THEN C = 1
310 IF R = 1 THEN C = N
320 IF R < 2 GOTO 400
330 CS = 1
340         FOR I = N TO (N - R + 1) STEP -1
350         J = I - (N - R)
360         CS = CS * (I / J)
```

Figure 4-8 Computer program in BASIC to calculate the hypergeometric distribution.

```
37Ø         NEXT I
38Ø C = CS
39Ø REM                 Hypergeometric Calculation
4ØØ IF K = 1 THEN CG = C
41Ø IF K = 2 THEN CD = C
42Ø IF K < 3 GOTO 23Ø
43Ø CT = C
44Ø P(DS) = CG * (CD / CT)
45Ø LPRINT TAB(12); DS; TAB(32) ; P(DS)
46Ø IF DS = NS GOTO 51Ø
47Ø IF DS = DL GOTO 51Ø
48Ø IF P(DS) < .ØØ5 GOTO 51Ø
49Ø DS = DS + 1
5ØØ GOTO 22Ø
51Ø SP = Ø
52Ø         FOR I = Ø TO DS
53Ø         SP = SP + P(I)
54Ø         NEXT I
55Ø LPRINT
56Ø LPRINT TAB(5);" Sum of Probabilities = ";SP
57Ø END

N =  2Ø
D =  5
n =  4

Number Defective          Probability
       Ø                    .281734
       1                    .469556
       2                    .216718
       3                    .Ø3Ø9598
       4                    1.Ø3199E-Ø3

Sum of Probabilities =  1
```

Figure 4-8 Continued.

PROBLEMS

1. If an event is certain to occur, what is its probability? If an event will not occur, what is its probability?
2. If the probability of obtaining a 3 on a 6-sided die is 0.167, what is the probability of obtaining any number but a 3?
3. The probability of drawing a pink chip from a bowl of different-colored chips is 0.35, the probability of a blue chip is 0.46, the probability of a green chip is 0.15, and the probability of a purple chip is 0.04. What is the

probability of a blue or a purple chip? What is the probability of a pink or a blue chip?

4. A ball is drawn at random from a container that holds 8 yellow balls numbered 1 to 8, 6 orange balls numbered 1 to 6, and 10 gray balls numbered 1 to 10. What is the probability of obtaining an orange ball or a ball numbered 5 or an orange ball numbered 5 in a draw of one ball? What is the probability of a gray ball or a ball numbered 8 or a gray ball numbered 8 in a draw of one ball?

5. If the probability of obtaining 1 defective in a sample of 2 from a large lot of neoprene gaskets is 0.18 and the probability of 2 defectives 0.25, what is the probability of 0 defectives?

6. Using the information of Problem 5, find the probability of obtaining 2 defectives on the first sample of 2 and 1 defective on the second sample of 2. What is the probability of 0 defectives on the first sample and 2 defectives on the second?

7. A tray contains 34 die-cast parts, 5 of which are defective. If a sample of 2 is drawn and not replaced, what is the probability that both will be defective?

8. If a sample of 1 can be drawn from three different storage racks and 6 different trays in each rack, what is the number of different ways of obtaining the sample of one?

9. A sample of 3 is selected from a lot of 10 door locks. How many permutations are possible?

10. From a lot of 90 alarm clocks a sample of 8 is selected. How many permutations are possible?

11. A sample of 4 is selected from a lot of 20 piston rings. How many different sample combinations are possible?

12. From a lot of 100, a sample of 3 is selected. How many different sample combinations are possible?

13. A sample of 2 is selected from a tray of 20 bolts. How many different sample combinations are possible?

14. Compare the answers of C_3^5 with C_2^5, C_1^4 with C_3^4, and C_2^{10} with C_8^{10}. What conclusion can you draw?

15. Calculate C_0^6, C_0^{10}, and C_0^{25}. What conclusion can you draw?

16. Calculate C_3^3, C_9^9, and C_{35}^{35}. What conclusion can you draw?

17. Calculate C_1^7, C_1^{12}, and C_1^{18}. What conclusion can you draw?

18. A random sample of 4 baseball bats is selected from a lot of 12 that has 3 defectives. Using the hypergeometric distribution, what is the probability that the sample will contain exactly 0 defectives? I defective? 2 defectives? 3 defectives? 4 defectives?

19. A finite lot of 20 digital watches is 20% defective. Using the hypergeometric distribution, what is the probability that a sample of 3 will contain 2 defective watches?

20. In Problem 19 what is the probability of obtaining 2 or more defectives? What is the probability of 2 or less defectives?

21. A steady stream of product has a fraction defective of 0.03. What is the probability of obtaining 2 defectives from a sample of 20? Use the binomial distribution.

22. Find the probability, using the binomial distribution, of obtaining 2 or more defectives when sampling 5 typewriters from a batch known to be 6% defective.

23. Using the binomial distribution, find the probability of obtaining 2 or less defectives in a sample of 9 when the lot is 15% defective.

24. What is the probability of guessing correctly exactly 4 answers on a true-false examination that has 9 questions? Use the binomial distribution.

25. An injection molder produces golf tees that are 15.0% defective. Using the normal distribution as an approximation to the binomial, find the probability that, in a random sample of 300 golf tees, 34 or less are defective.

26. A random sample of 10 automotive bumpers is taken from a stream of product that is 5% defective. Using the Poisson as an approximation to the binomial distribution, determine the probability of 2 defective automotive bumpers. Compare the result with the binomial distribution.

27. If the probability is 0.08 that a single article is defective, what is the probability that a sample of 20 will contain 2 or less defective? Use the Poisson as an approximation to the binomial distribution.

28. Using the data from Problem 27, determine the probability of 2 or more defectives.

Solve Problems 29, 30, 31, and 32 by the easiest applicable distribution (Poisson, binomial, hypergeometric). Using quantifiable criteria, state the reasons for using a particular distribution.

29. A sample of 10 washing machines is selected from a finite lot of 100. If $p_0 = 0.08$, what is the probability of 1 defective washing machine in the sample?

30. A lot of 15 has 3 defectives. What is the probability that a sample of 3 will have 1 defective?

31. A sample of 3 medicine bottles is taken from a tray of 30 bottles. If the tray is 10% defective, what is the probability of 1 defective medicine bottle in the sample?

32. A steady flow of light bulbs has a fraction defective of 0.09. If 67 are sampled, what is the probability of 3 defectives?

33. Test, and if necessary rewrite, the computer program for your computer.

34. Modify the computer program to output the information for your graphical output devise.

35. Write a computer program for:
(a) The binomial probability distribution
(b) The Poisson probability distribution

5 CONTROL CHARTS FOR ATTRIBUTES

INTRODUCTION

Attribute

An attribute was defined in Chapter 2 and is repeated to refresh the reader's memory. The term *attribute*, as used in quality control, refers to those quality characteristics that conform to specifications or do not conform to specifications. For simplicity the terms "good" and "defective" are used rather than the more appropriate conforming and nonconforming terms.

There are two types of attributes:

1. Where measurements are not possible, for example visually inspected items such as color, missing parts, scratches, and damage.
2. Where measurements can be made but are not made because of time, cost, or need. In other words, while the diameter of a hole can be measured with an inside micrometer, it may be more convenient to use a "go–no go" gage and determine if it conforms or does not conform to specifications.

Some confusion occurs between the terms "defect" and "defective." A defect refers to a quality characteristic, and since there are many quality characteristics, there are many opportunities for a defect in a unit. A defective refers to the entire unit; therefore, a defective unit can have many defects.

Limitations of Variable Charts

Variable control charts are excellent means for controlling quality and subsequently improving it; however, they do have limitations. One obvious limitation is that these charts cannot be used for quality characteristics which are attributes. The converse is not true, since a variable can be changed to an attribute by stating that it conforms or does not conform to specifications. In other words, defects such as missing parts, incorrect color, and so on, are not measureable and a variable control chart is not applicable.

Another limitation concerns the fact that there are many variables in a manufacturing entity. Even a small manufacturing plant could have as many as 10,000 variable quality characteristics. Since an $\overline{X}$ and R chart is needed for each characteristic, 10,000 charts would be required. Clearly, this would be too expensive and impractical. A control chart for attributes can minimize this limitation by providing overall quality information at a fraction of the cost.

Types of Attribute Charts

There are two different groups of control charts for attributes. One group of charts is for defectives. It is based on the binomial distribution. A proportion, p, chart shows the fraction defective in a sample or subgroup. In addition to the p chart for fraction defective, other charts in the group are a $100p$ chart, which is for percent defective, and an np chart, which is for the number defective.

Another group of charts is for defects. It is based on the Poisson distribution. A c chart shows the count of defects in an inspected unit such as an automobile, bolt of cloth, or roll of paper. Another closely related chart is the u chart, which is for the count of defects per unit.

Much of the information on control charts for attributes is similar to that given in Chapter 3. The reader is referred to the sections on "State of Control" and "Analysis of Out-of-Control Condition."

CONTROL CHARTS FOR PROPORTION OR FRACTION DEFECTIVE

Introduction

The p chart is used for data that consist of the proportion of the number of occurrences of an event to the total number of occurrences. It is used in quality control to report the fraction defective in a product, quality characteristic, or group of quality characteristics. As such, the *fraction defective* is the proportion of the number defective in a sample or subgroup to the total number in the sample or subgroup. In symbolic terms the formula is

$$p = \frac{np}{n}$$

where p = proportion or fraction defective in the sample or subgroup
n = number in the sample or subgroup
np = number defective in the sample or subgroup

Example Problem

During the first shift, 450 inspections are made and 5 defective units are found. Production during the shift was 15,000 units. What is the fraction defective?

$$p = \frac{np}{n} = \frac{5}{450} = 0.011$$

The fraction defective, p, is usually quite small, say 0.15 or less. Except in unusual circumstances values greater than 0.15 would indicate that the company is in serious difficulty and that measures more drastic than a control chart are required. Since the fraction defective is very small, the subgroup sizes must be quite large to produce a meaningful chart.

The p chart is an extremely versatile control chart. It can be used to control one quality characteristic, as is done with the $\overline{X}$ and R chart; to control a group of quality characteristics of the same type or of the same part; or to control the entire product. The p chart can be established to measure the quality produced by a work center, by a department, by a shift, or by an entire plant. It is frequently used to report the performance of an operator or group of operators as a means of evaluating their quality performance in a manner similar to that practiced for production performance.

Data for p charts which are used for a work center, department, shift, or plant can be obtained by inspecting parts and products for that particular objective. In such a case the subgroup size can be kept constant. Data can also be obtained from other p charts and from $\overline{X}$ and R charts. In this case the subgroup size will vary from one subgroup to the next, depending on the number inspected for those charts.

Objectives

The objectives or purposes of defective charts are:

1. To determine the average quality level. Knowledge of the quality average is essential as a benchmark.

2. To bring to the attention of management any changes in the average. Once the average quality level (fraction defective) is known, changes, either increasing or decreasing, become significant.

3. To improve the product quality. In this regard a p chart can motivate operating and management personnel to initiate ideas for quality improvement. The chart will tell whether the idea is an appropriate or unappropriate one. A continual and relentless effort must be made to improve the quality.

4. To evaluate the quality performance of operating and management personnel. Supervisors of manufacturing activities and especially the chief executive officer (CEO) should be evaluated by a defective chart. Other functional

areas, such as engineering, sales, finance, and so on, may find a defect chart more applicable for evaluation purposes.

5. To suggest places to use $\overline{X}$ and R charts. Even though the cost of computing and charting $\overline{X}$ and R charts is more than the defective chart, the $\overline{X}$ and R charts are much more sensitive to variations and are more helpful in diagnosing causes. In other words, the defective chart suggests the source of difficulty and the $\overline{X}$ and R chart finds the cause.

6. To determine acceptance criteria of a product before shipment to the customer. Knowledge of the fraction defective provides management with information on whether or not to release an order.

These objectives indicate the scope and value of a defective chart.

p-Chart Construction for Constant Subgroup Size

The general procedures that apply to variable control charts also apply to the p chart.

1. *Select the purpose.* The first step in the procedure is to determine the use of the control chart. A p chart can be established to control the fraction defective of (a) a single quality characteristic, (b) a group of quality characteristics, (c) a part, (d) an entire product, or (e) a number of products. This establishes a hierarchy of utilization so that any inspections applicable for a single quality characteristic also provide data for other p charts, which represent larger groups of characteristics, parts, or products.

A p chart can also be established for performance control of an (a) operator, (b) work center, (c) department, (d) shift, (e) plant, or (f) corporation. Using the chart in this manner, comparisons may be made between like units. It is also possible to evaluate the quality performance of a unit. A hierarchy of utilization exists so that data collected for one chart can also be used on a more all-inclusive chart.

The purpose or use for the chart or charts will be based on securing the greatest benefit for a minimum of cost. One chart should measure the CEO's quality performance.

2. *Determine the subgroup size.* The size of the subgroup is a function of the fraction defective. If a part has a fraction defective, p, of 0.001 and a subgroup size, n, of 1000, then the average number defective, np, would be one per subgroup. This would *not* make a good chart, since a large number of values, posted to the chart, would be zero. If a part has a fraction defective of 0.15 and a subgroup size of 50, the average number defective would be 7.5, which would make a good chart.

Therefore, the selection of the subgroup size requires some preliminary observations to obtain a rough idea of the fraction defective and some judgment as to the average number of defectives that will make an adequate graphical chart. Inspection can either be by audit or on-line. Audits are usually done in a laboratory under optimal conditions. On-line provides immediate feedback for corrective action.

3. *Collect the data.* The inspector will need to collect sufficient data for at least 25 subgroups, or the data may be obtained from historical records. Table 5-1 gives the inspection results for the blower motor in an electric hair dryer for the second shift of the motor department. For each subgroup the fraction defective is calculated by the formula $p = np/n$. The inspector reported that subgroup 19 had an abnormally large number of defectives, owing to faulty contacts.

4. *Calculate the trial central line and control limits.* The formula for the trial control limits is given by

$$\text{UCL} = \bar{p} + 3\sqrt{\frac{\bar{p}(1 - \bar{p})}{n}}$$

$$\text{LCL} = \bar{p} - 3\sqrt{\frac{\bar{p}(1 - \bar{p})}{n}}$$

where $\bar{p}$ = average fraction defective for many subgroups
n = number inspected in a subgroup

The average fraction defective, $\bar{p}$, is the central line and is obtained by the

TABLE 5-1 Inspection Results of Electric Hair Dryer Blower Motor, Second Shift, Motor Department, May

Subgroup Number	*Number Inspected, n*	*Number Defective, np*	*Fraction Defective, p*	*Subgroup Number*	*Number Inspected, n*	*Number Defective, np*	*Fraction Defective, p*
1	300	12	0.040	14	300	3	0.010
2	300	3	0.010	15	300	0	0.0
3	300	9	0.030	16	300	5	0.017
4	300	4	0.013	17	300	7	0.023
5	300	0	0.0	18	300	8	0.027
6	300	6	0.020	19	300	16	0.053
7	300	6	0.020	20	300	2	0.007
8	300	1	0.003	21	300	5	0.017
9	300	8	0.027	22	300	6	0.020
10	300	11	0.037	23	300	0	0.0
11	300	2	0.007	24	300	3	0.010
12	300	10	0.033	25	300	2	0.007
13	300	9	0.030	Total	7500	138	

formula $\bar{p} = \sum np / \sum n$. Calculations for the 3σ trial control limits using the data on the electric hair dryer are as follows:

$$\bar{p} = \frac{\sum np}{\sum n}$$
$$= \frac{138}{7500}$$
$$= 0.018$$

$$\text{UCL} = \bar{p} + 3\sqrt{\frac{\bar{p}(1 - \bar{p})}{n}} \qquad \text{LCL} = \bar{p} - 3\sqrt{\frac{\bar{p}(1 - \bar{p})}{n}}$$

$$= 0.018 + 3\sqrt{\frac{0.018(1 - 0.018)}{300}} \qquad = 0.018 - 3\sqrt{\frac{0.018(1 - 0.018)}{300}}$$

$$= 0.041 \qquad = -0.005 \text{ or } 0.0$$

Calculations for the lower control limit resulted in a *negative* value, which is a theoretical result. In practice, a negative fraction defective would be impossible. Therefore, the lower control limit value of -0.005 is changed to zero.

When the lower control limit is positive, it may in some cases be changed to zero. If the p chart is to be viewed by operating personnel, it would be difficult to explain why a fraction defective that is below the lower control limit is out of control. In other words, performance of exceptionally good quality would be classified as out of control. To avoid the need to explain this situation to operating personnel, the lower control limit is changed from a positive value to zero. When the p chart is to be used by quality control personnel and by management, a positive lower control limit is left unchanged. In this manner exceptionally good performance (below the lower control limit) will be treated as an out-of-control situaton and investigated for an assignable cause. Hopefully, the assignable cause will indicate how the situation can be repeated.

The central line, $\bar{p}$, and the control limits are shown in Figure 5-1; the fraction defective, p, from Table 5-1 is also posted to that chart. This chart is for instructional purposes and is only used to determine the revised control limits.

5. *Establish the revised central line and control limits.* In order to determine the revised 3σ control limits, the standard or reference value for the fraction defective, p_0, needs to be determined. If an analysis of the preliminary data shows good control (a stable process), then $\bar{p}$ can be considered to be representative of that process. Therefore, the best estimate of p_0 at this time, is $\bar{p}$, and $p_0 = \bar{p}$.

Most industrial processes, however, are not in control when first analyzed, and this fact is illustrated in Figure 5-1 by subgroup 19, which is above the upper

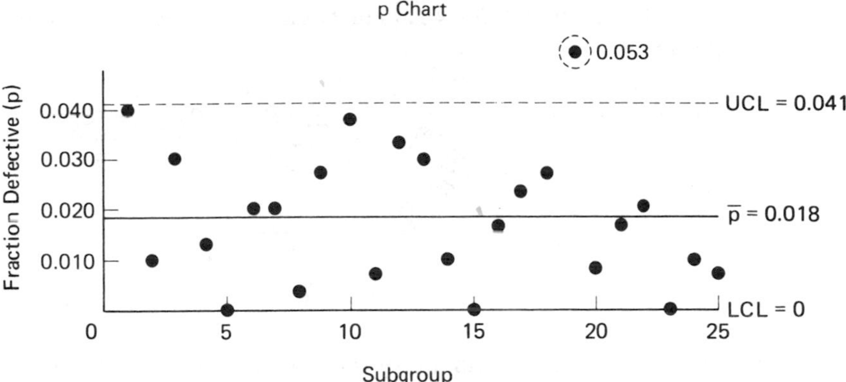

Figure 5-1 *p* Chart to illustrate the trial central line and control limits using the data from Table 5-1.

control limit and, therefore, out of control. Since subgroup 19 has an assignable cause, it can be discarded from the data and a new $\bar{p}$ computed with all of the subgroups except 19. The calculations can be simplified by using the formula

$$\bar{p}_{\text{new}} = \frac{\sum np - np_d}{\sum n - n_d}$$

where np_d = number defective in the discarded subgroups
n_d = number inspected in the discarded subgroups

In discarding data it must be remembered that only those subgroups with assignable causes are discarded. Those subgroups without assignable causes are left in the data. Also, out-of-control points below the lower control limit are not discarded, since they represent exceptionally good quality. If the out-of-control point is due to an inspection error, it should be discarded.

With an adopted standard or reference value for the fraction defective, p_0, the revised control limits are given by

$$p_0 = \bar{p}_{\text{new}}$$

$$\text{UCL} = p_0 + 3\sqrt{\frac{p_0(1 - p_0)}{n}}$$

$$\text{LCL} = p_0 - 3\sqrt{\frac{p_0(1 - p_0)}{n}}$$

where p_0, the central line, represents the reference or standard value for the fraction defective. These formulas are for the control limits for three standard deviations from the central line p_0.

Thus, for the preliminary data in Table 5-1, a new $\overline{p}$ is obtained by discarding subgroup 19.

$$\overline{p}_{\text{new}} = \frac{\sum np - np_d}{\sum n - n_d}$$

$$= \frac{138 - 16}{7500 - 300}$$

$$= 0.017$$

Since $\overline{p}_{\text{new}}$ is the best estimate of the standard or reference value, $p_0 = 0.017$. The revised control limits for the p chart are obtained as follows:

$$\text{UCL} = p_0 + 3\sqrt{\frac{p_0(1 - p_0)}{\text{n}}} \qquad \text{LCL} = p_0 - 3\sqrt{\frac{p_0(1 - p_0)}{n}}$$

$$= 0.017 + 3\sqrt{\frac{0.017(1 - 0.017)}{300}} \qquad = 0.017 - 3\sqrt{\frac{0.017(1 - 0.017)}{300}}$$

$$= 0.039 \qquad = -0.005 \quad \text{or} \quad 0.0$$

The revised control limits and the central line, p_0, are shown in Figure 5-2.

Continuing the Use of the *p* Chart

The first five steps are planning—this is the action step.

The revised control limits were based on data collected in May. These control limits are applicable to the inspection results for the next month. Some representative values of inspection results for the month of June are shown in Figure 5-2. Analysis of the June results for the subgroup fraction defective shows that the quality improved. This improvement is expected, since the

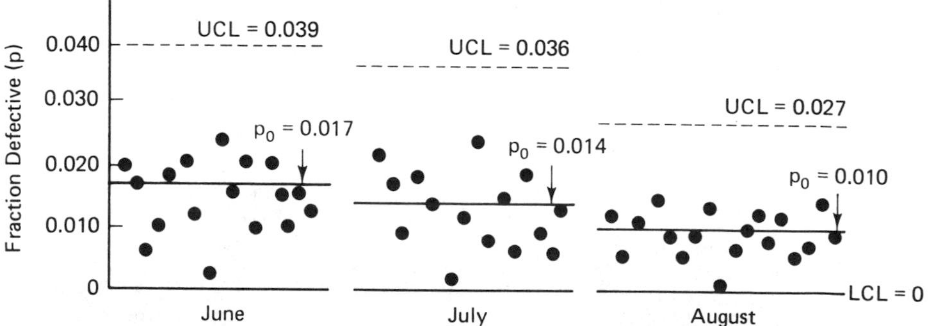

Figure 5-2 Continuing use of the *p* chart for representative values of the fraction defective, *p*.

posting of a quality control chart usually results in improved quality. Using the June data, a better estimate of the fraction defective is obtained. The new value (p_0 = 0.014) is used to obtain the UCL of 0.036.

During the latter part of June and the entire month of July, various quality improvement ideas are tested. These ideas are new shellac, change in wire size, stronger spring, $\overline{X}$ and R charts on the armature, and so on. In testing ideas there are three criteria; a minimum of 20 subgroups are required, the 20 subgroups can be compressed in time as long as no sampling bias occurs, and only one idea can be tested at one time. The control chart will tell whether the idea is a good one, a poor one, or has no effect.

Data from July are used to determine the central line and control limits for August. The pattern of variation for August indicates that no further improvement resulted. However, a 41% improvement occurred from June (0.017) to August (0.010). At this point, we have obtained considerable improvement testing the ideas of operating, supervisory, and quality personnel. While this improvement is very good, we must continue our relentless pursuit of quality improvement—1 out of every 100 is still defective. Perhaps a detailed failure analysis or technical assistance from product engineering will lead to additional ideas that can be evaluated.

Quality improvement is never terminated. Efforts may be redirected to other areas based on need and/or resources available.

Some Comments on *p* Charts

Like the $\overline{X}$ and R chart, the p chart is most effective if it is posted where operating and quality control personnel can view it. Also, like the $\overline{X}$ and R chart, the control limits are three standard deviations from the central value. Therefore, 99.73% of the points for the subgroup fraction defective, p, will fall between the upper and lower control limits.

A state of control for a p chart is treated in a manner similar to that described in Chapter 3. The reader may wish to briefly review that section. A control chart for subgroup values of p will aid in disclosing the occasional presence of assignable causes of variation in the manufacturing process. The elimination of these assignable causes will lower p_0 and, therefore, have a positive effect on spoilage, production efficiency, and cost per unit. A p chart will also indicate long-range trends in the quality, which will help to evaluate changes in personnel, methods, equipment, tooling, materials, and inspection techniques.

If the population fraction defective, ϕ, is known, it is not necessary to calculate the trial control limits. This is a considerable time saver, since $p_0 = \phi$ which allows the p chart to be introduced immediately. Also, p_0 may be assigned a desired value—in which case the trial control limits are not necessary.

Since the p chart is based on the binomial distribution, there must be a constant chance of selecting a defective product. In some manufacturing operations, if one defective occurs, all product that follows will be defective until the condition is corrected. This type of condition also occurs in batch processes where the entire batch is defective or when an error is made in dimensions, color, and so on. In such cases a constant chance of obtaining a defective does not occur, and therefore the p chart is not suitable.

p-Chart Construction for Variable Subgroup Size

Whenever possible, p charts should be developed and used with a constant subgroup size. This situation is not possible when the p chart is used for 100% inspection of output that varies from day to day. Also, data for p-chart use are frequently collected from other sources, such as $\overline{X}$ and R charts or other p charts, and therefore the subgroup size varies. Since the control limits are a function of the subgroup size, n, the control limits will vary with the subgroup size. They need to be calculated for each subgroup.

While a variable subgroup size is undesirable, it does exist and must be handled. The procedures of data collection, trial central line and control limits, and revised central line and control limits are the same as that used for a p chart with constant subgroup size. An example will be used to illustrate the procedure.

1. *Data collection.* A wheelbarrow manufacturer has collected data on the quality of his product for the end of March and all of April. Subgroup size was 1 day's inspection results, which is usually the case. The inspection results for 25 subgroups are shown in the first three columns of Table 5-2: subgroup designation, number inspected, and number defective. A fourth column for the fraction defective is calculated by the inspector using the formula $p = np/n$. The last two columns are for the upper and lower control limit calculations, which are discussed in the next section.

The variation in the number inspected per day can be due to a number of reasons. Inspectors may be assigned other duties during a particular day, or they may be absent or sick. Machines may have breakdowns or not be scheduled. Product models may have different production requirements, which will cause day-to-day variations. For the data in Table 5-2 there was a low on April 9 of 1238 inspections because the second shift did not work, and a high on April 22 of 2678 inspections because of overtime in one work center.

2. *Trial central line and control limits.* Control limits are calculated using the same procedures and formulas as for a constant subgroup. However, since the subgroup size changes each day, limits must be calculated for each day. First the average fraction defective, which is the central line, must be determined, and it is

$$\overline{p} = \frac{\sum np}{\sum n} = \frac{1035}{50{,}515} = 0.020$$

TABLE 5-2 Preliminary Data of Wheelbarrow Inspections and Control Limits for Each Subgroup

Subgroup	*Number Inspected, n*	*Number Defective, np*	*Fraction Defective, p*	*Limit*	
				UCL	*LCL*
March 29	2,385	47	0.020	0.029	0.011
30	1,451	18	0.012	0.031	0.009
31	1,935	74	0.038	0.030	0.010
April 1	2,450	42	0.017	0.028	0.012
2	1,997	39	0.020	0.029	0.011
5	2,168	52	0.024	0.029	0.011
6	1,941	47	0.024	0.030	0.010
7	1,962	34	0.017	0.030	0.010
8	2,244	29	0.013	0.029	0.011
9	1,238	39	0.032	0.032	0.008
12	2,289	45	0.020	0.029	0.011
13	1,464	26	0.018	0.031	0.009
14	2,061	47	0.023	0.029	0.011
15	1,667	34	0.020	0.030	0.010
16	2,350	31	0.013	0.029	0.011
19	2,354	38	0.016	0.029	0.011
20	1,509	28	0.018	0.031	0.009
21	2,190	30	0.014	0.029	0.011
22	2,678	113	0.042	0.028	0.012
23	2,252	58	0.026	0.029	0.011
26	1,641	52	0.032	0.030	0.010
27	1,782	19	0.011	0.030	0.010
28	1,993	30	0.015	0.030	0.010
29	2,382	17	0.007	0.029	0.011
30	2,132	46	0.022	0.029	0.011
	50,515	1,035			

Using $\overline{p}$, the control limits for each day can be obtained; for March 29 the limits are

$$\text{UCL}_{29} = \overline{p} + 3\sqrt{\frac{\overline{p}(1-\overline{p})}{n_{29}}} \qquad \text{LCL}_{29} = \overline{p} - 3\sqrt{\frac{\overline{p}(1-\overline{p})}{n_{29}}}$$

$$= 0.020 + 3\sqrt{\frac{0.020(1-0.020)}{2385}} \qquad = 0.020 - 3\sqrt{\frac{0.020(1-0.020)}{2385}}$$

$$= 0.029 \qquad = 0.011$$

For March 30 the control limits are

$$\text{UCL}_{30} = \overline{p} + 3\sqrt{\frac{\overline{p}(1-\overline{p})}{n_{30}}} \qquad \text{LCL}_{30} = \overline{p} - 3\sqrt{\frac{\overline{p}(1-\overline{p})}{n_{30}}}$$

$$= 0.020 + 3\sqrt{\frac{0.020(1-0.020)}{1451}} \qquad = 0.020 - 3\sqrt{\frac{0.020(1-0.020)}{1451}}$$

$$= 0.031 \qquad = 0.009$$

The control limit calculations above are repeated for the remaining 23 subgroups. Since n is the only variable that is changing, it is possible to simplify the calculations as follows:

$$\text{CL's} = \bar{p} \pm \frac{3\sqrt{\bar{p}(1 - \bar{p})}}{\sqrt{n}}$$

$$= 0.020 \pm \frac{3\sqrt{0.020(1 - 0.020)}}{\sqrt{n}}$$

$$= 0.020 \pm \frac{0.42}{\sqrt{n}}$$

Using this technique the calculations are much quicker. The control limits for all 25 subgroups are shown in columns four and five of Table 5-2. A graphical illustration of the trial control limits, central line, and subgroup values are shown in Figure 5-3.

Note that as the subgroup size gets larger, the control limits are closer together; as the subgroup size gets smaller, the control limits become wider apart. This fact is apparent from the formula and by comparing the subgroup size, n, with its UCL and LCL.

3. *Revised central line and control limits.* A review of Figure 5-3 shows that an out-of-control situation is present on March 31, April 22, April 26, and

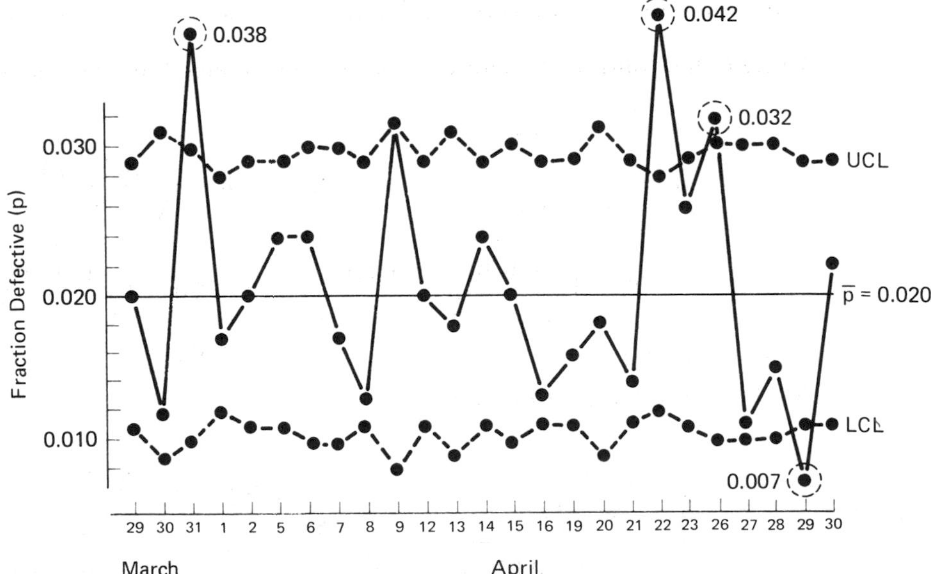

Figure 5-3 Preliminary data, central line, and trial control limits.

April 29. Assuming the March 31 and April 22 points have assignable causes, they are discarded from the data. The April 26 point does not have a reason for being out of control; it is assumed to be due to a chance cause and is not discarded. For April 29 the quality is exceptionally good, and it, too, is not discarded. A new $\overline{p}$ is obtained as follows:

$$\overline{p}_{\text{new}} = \frac{\sum np - np_d}{\sum n - n_d}$$

$$= \frac{1035 - 74 - 113}{50{,}515 - 1935 - 2678}$$

$$= 0.018$$

Since this value represents the best estimate of the standard or reference value of the fraction defective, $p_0 = 0.018$.

The fraction defective, p_0, is used to calculate upper and lower control limits for the next period, which is the month of May. However, the limits cannot be calculated until the end of each day, when the subgroup size, n, is known. This means that the control limits are never known ahead of time. Table 5-3 shows the inspection results for the first three working days in May. Control limits and the fraction defective for May 3 are as follows:

$$p_{\text{May 3}} = \frac{np}{n} = \frac{31}{1535} = 0.020$$

$$\text{UCL}_{\text{May 3}} = p_0 + 3\sqrt{\frac{p_0(1 - p_0)}{n_{\text{May 3}}}}$$

$$= 0.018 + 3\sqrt{\frac{0.018(1 - 0.018)}{1535}}$$

$$= 0.028$$

$$\text{LCL}_{\text{May 3}} = p_0 - 3\sqrt{\frac{p_0(1 - p_0)}{n_{\text{May 3}}}}$$

$$= 0.018 - 3\sqrt{\frac{0.018(1 - 0.018)}{1535}}$$

$$= 0.008$$

The upper and lower control limits and the fraction defective for May 3 are

TABLE 5-3 Inspection Results for May 3, 4, and 5

Subgroup	*Number Inspected*	*Number Defective*
May 3	1535	31
4	2262	28
5	1872	45

posted to the p chart as illustrated in Figure 5-4. In a similar manner, calculations are made for May 4 and 5 and the results posted to the chart.

The chart is continued until the end of May, using $p_0 = 0.018$. Since an improvement usually occurs after introduction of a chart, a better estimate of p_0 will probably be obtained at the end of May using that month's data. In the future the value of p_0 should be evaluated periodically.

If p_0 is known, the process of data collection and trial control limits is not necessary. This saves considerable time and effort.

Since some confusion occurs among p_0, $\bar{p}$, and p, their definitions will be repeated:

1. p is the fraction defective in a single subgroup. It is posted to the chart but is *not* used to calculate the control limits.
2. $\bar{p}$ is the average fraction defective of many subgroups. It is the sum of the number defective divided by the sum of the number inspected and is used to calculate the trial control limits.
3. p_0 is the standard or reference value of the fraction defective based on the

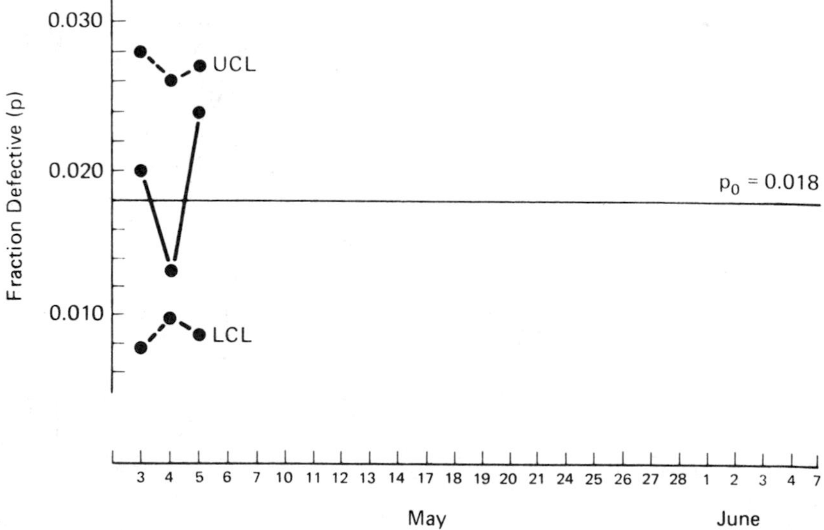

Figure 5-4 Control limits and fraction defective for first three working days in May.

best estimate of $\overline{p}$. It is used to calculate the revised control limits. It can be specified as a desired value.

4. ϕ is the population fraction defective. When this value is known, it can be used to calculate the limits since $p_0 = \phi$.

Minimizing the Effect of Variable Subgroup Size

When the control limits vary from subgroup to subgroup, it presents an unattractive chart that is difficult to explain to operating personnel. It is also difficult to explain that control limits are calculated at the end of each day or time period rather than ahead of time. There are two techniques that minimize the effect of thc variable subgroup size.

1. *Control limits for an average subgroup size.* By using an average subgroup size, one limit can be calculated and placed on the control chart. The average group size can be based on the anticipated production for the month or the previous month's inspections. As an example, the average number inspected for the preliminary data in Table 5-2 would be

$$n_{av} = \frac{\sum n}{g} = \frac{50{,}515}{25} = 2020.5, \quad \text{say } 2000$$

Using a value of 2000 for the subgroup size, n, and $p_0 = 0.018$, the upper and lower control limits become

$$\text{UCL} = p_0 + 3\sqrt{\frac{p_0(1-p_0)}{n_{av}}} \qquad \text{LCL} = p_0 - 3\sqrt{\frac{p_0(1-p_0)}{n_{av}}}$$

$$= 0.018 + 3\sqrt{\frac{0.018(1-0.018)}{2000}} \qquad = 0.018 - 3\sqrt{\frac{0.018(1-0.018)}{2000}}$$

$$= 0.027 \qquad = 0.009$$

These control limits are shown in the p chart of Figure 5-5 along with the fraction defective, p, for each day in May.

When an average subgroup size is used, there are four situations which occur between the control limits and the individual fraction defective values.

Case I. This case occurs when a point (subgroup fraction defective) falls inside the limits and its subgroup size is smaller than thc average subgroup size. The data for May 3, $p = 0.020$ and $n = 1535$, represent this case. Since the May 3 subgroup size (1535) is less than the average of 2000, the control limits for May 3 will be wider apart than the control limits for the average subgroup size. Therefore, in this case individual control limits are

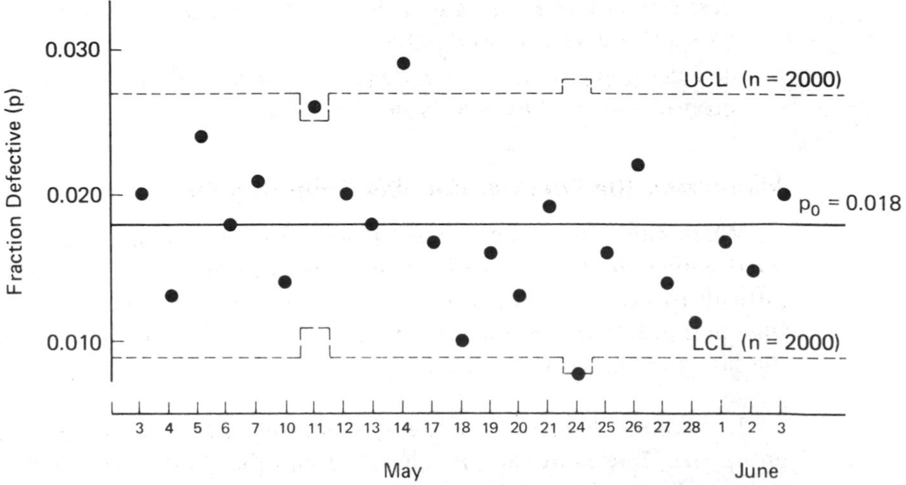

Figure 5-5 Chart for May data illustrating use of an average subgroup size.

not needed. If p is in control when $n = 2000$, it must also be in control when $n = 1535$.

Case II. This case occurs when a point (subgroup fraction defective) falls inside the average limits and its subgroup size is larger than the average subgroup size. The data for May 11, $p = 0.026$ and $n = 2900$, illustrate this case. Since the May 11 subgroup size is greater than the average subgroup size, the control limits for May 11 will be closer together than the control limits for the average subgroup size. Therefore, when there is a substantial difference in the subgroup size, individual control limits are calculated. For May 11 the values for the upper and lower control limits are 0.025 and 0.011, respectively. These individual control limits are shown in Figure 5-5. It is seen that the point is beyond the individual control limit and so we have an out-of-control situation.

Case III. This case occurs when a point (subgroup fraction defective) falls outside the limits and its subgroup size is larger than the average subgroup size. The data for May 14, $p = 0.029$ and $n = 2300$, illustrate this case. Since the May 14 subgroup size (2365) is greater than the average of 2000, the control limits for May 14 will be narrower than the control limits for the average subgroup size. Therefore, in this case individual control limits are not needed. If p is out of control when $n = 2000$, it must also be out of control when $n = 2365$.

Case IV. This case occurs when a point (subgroup fraction defective) falls outside the limits and its subgroup size is less than the average subgroup size. The data for May 24, $p = 0.008$ and $n = 1590$, illustrate this case. Since the May 24 subgroup size (1590) is less than the average of 2000, the control limits for May 24 will be wider apart than the control limits for the average subgroup size. Therefore, when there is a substantial difference in the subgroup size, individual control limits are calculated. For May 24 the values for the upper and lower control limits are 0.028 and 0.008, respectively. These individual control limits are shown in Figure 5-5. It is seen that the point is on the individual control limit and is assumed to be in control.

It is not always necessary to calculate the individual control limits in cases II and IV. Only when the value of p is close to the control limits is it necessary to determine the individual limits. For this example problem p values within, say, ± 0.002 of the original limits should be checked. Since approximately 95% of the p values will be close to the central line, few p values will need to be evaluated.

In addition, it is not necessary to calculate individual control limits as long as the subgroup size does not deviate substantially from the average, say 15%. For this example, subgroup sizes of from 1700 to 2300 would be satisfactory and not need to have individual limit calculations.

Actually, when the average subgroup size is used, individual control limits are determined infrequently—about once every 3 months.

2. *Control limits for different subgroup sizes.* Another technique, which has been found to be effective, is to establish control limits for different subgroup sizes. Figure 5-6 illustrates such a chart. Using the different control limits and the four cases described previously, the need to calculate individual control limits would be rare. For example, the subgroup for July 16 with 1150 inspections is in control, and the subgroup for July 22 with 3500 inspections is out of control.

An analysis of Figure 5-6 shows that the relationship of the control limits to the subgroup size, n, is exponential rather than linear. In other words, the

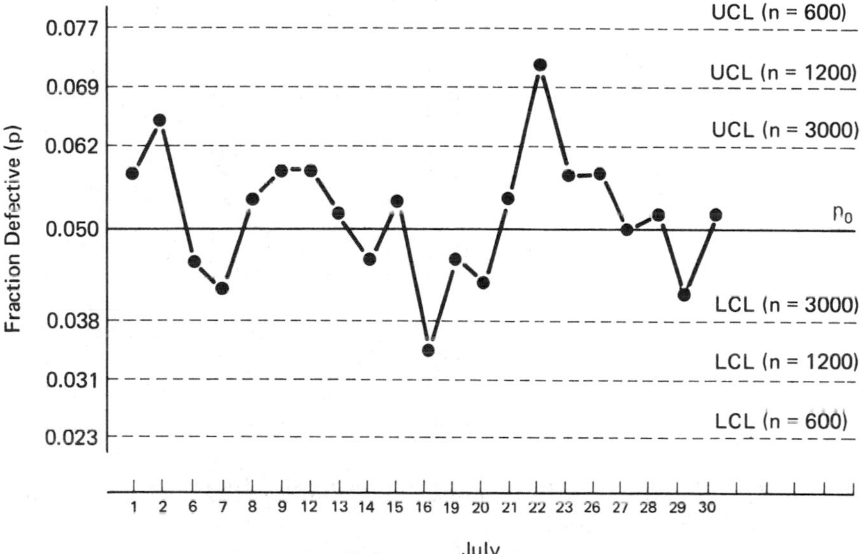

Figure 5-6 p Chart illustrating central line and control limits for different subgroup sizes.

control limit lines are not equally spaced for equal subdivisions of the subgroup size, n.

Adaptations to the Basic *p* Chart

There are two other p charts which are frequently used in place of the basic p chart. They are the percent defective and the number defective charts.

1. *Percent defective chart.* The percent defective chart is used because it is easier for operating personnel to understand than the fraction defective. Values are the same as the fraction defective chart except that the scale is changed by a factor of 100. Therefore, the values for the central line and control limits are

$$\text{central line} = 100p_0 \text{ (percent defective)}$$

$$\text{CL's} = 100\left[p_0 \pm 3\sqrt{\frac{p_0(1 - p_0)}{n}}\right]$$

The formula for the trial control limits is obtained by substitution of $\bar{p}$ for p_0. Figure 5-7 shows a $100p$ chart with a population percent defective of 2.40% and control limits based on a subgroup size of 1200. Calculations are:

$$\begin{aligned}\text{UCL} &= 100\left[p_0 + 3\sqrt{\frac{p_0(1 - p_0)}{n}}\right]\\ &= 100\left[0.024 + 3\sqrt{\frac{0.024(1 - 0.024)}{1200}}\right]\\ &= 3.73\end{aligned}$$

$$\begin{aligned}\text{LCL} &= 100\left[p_0 - 3\sqrt{\frac{p(1 - p_0)}{n}}\right]\\ &= 100\left[0.024 - 3\sqrt{\frac{0.024(1 - 0.024)}{1200}}\right]\\ &= 1.06\end{aligned}$$

The procedures for obtaining and using the $100p$ chart are identical with those of the basic p chart.

2. *Number defective chart.* While the percent defective chart is almost the same as the fraction defective chart, the number defective chart has a few differences. The number defective chart (np chart) is easier for operating per-

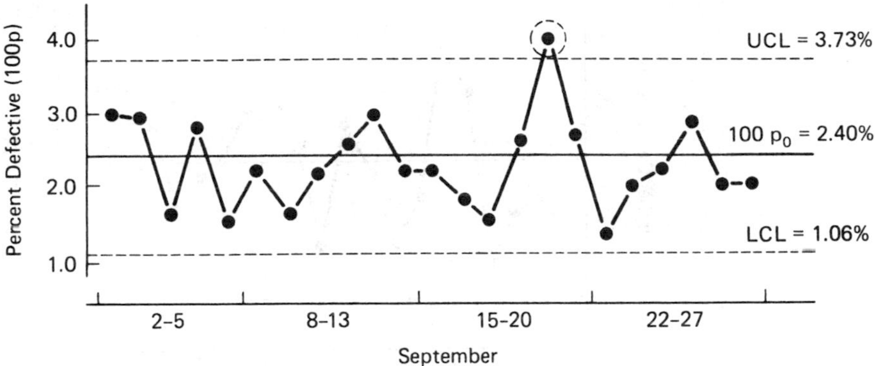

Figure 5-7 Percent defective chart (100*p* chart).

sonnel to understand, and inspection results are posted directly to the chart without any calculations. Since the number defective chart is mathematically equivalent to the fraction defective chart, the central line and control limits are changed by a factor of n. Formulas are

$$\text{central line} = np_0$$

$$\text{CL's} = np_0 \pm 3\sqrt{np_0(1 - p_0)}$$

If the fraction defective p_0 is unknown, then it must be determined by collecting data, calculating trial control limits, and obtaining the best estimate of p_0. The trial control limit formulas are obtained by substituting $\bar{p}$ for p_0 in the formulas above.

Figure 5-8 illustrates a typical number defective chart (np chart) for $p_0 = 0.025$ and $n = 600$. Central line and control limit calculations are:

$$np_0 = 600(0.025) = 15.0$$

$$\begin{aligned} \text{UCL} &= np_0 + 3\sqrt{np_0(1 - p_0)} & \text{LCL} &= np_0 - 3\sqrt{np_0(1 - p_0)} \\ &= 15 + 3\sqrt{15(1 - 0.025)} & &= 15 - 3\sqrt{15(1 - 0.025)} \\ &= 26.4, \quad \text{say } 26 & &= 3.6, \quad \text{say } 4 \end{aligned}$$

Since the number defective is a whole number, the limit values must be whole numbers; however, the central line can be a fraction.

If the subgroup size is allowed to vary, the central line and the width of the control limits will vary, which presents a chart that is almost meaningless. Therefore, one limitation of an np chart is the requirement that the subgroup size be constant.

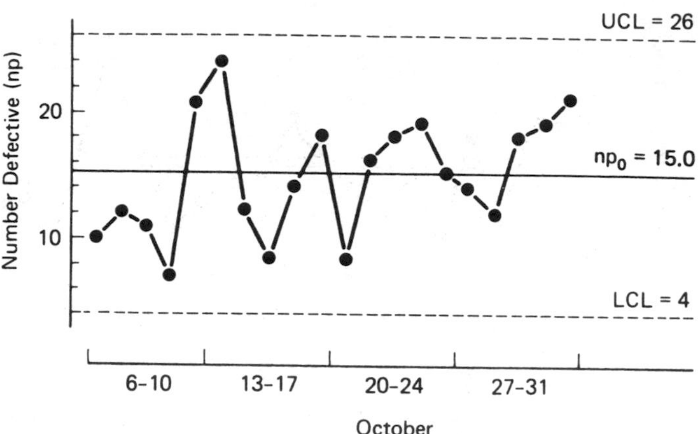

Figure 5-8 Number defective chart (*np* chart).

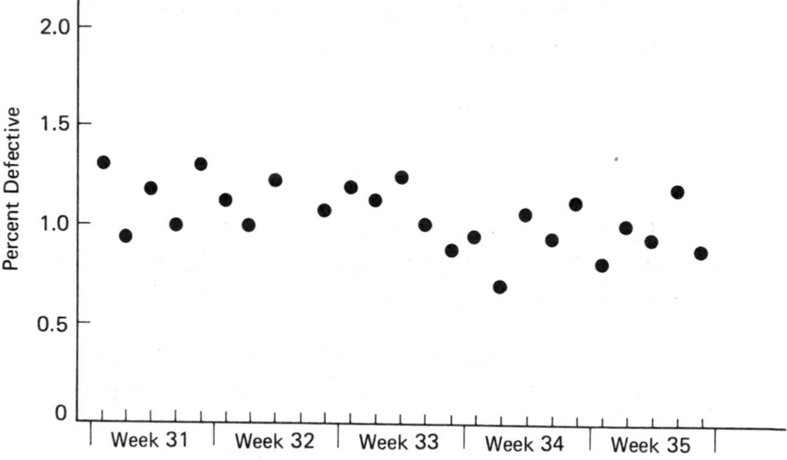

Figure 5-9 Run chart for percent defective.

3. *Run chart.* A run chart for variables was described in Chapter 3. The same type of chart can be used for attributes. Figure 5-9 shows a run chart for percent defective covering a 5-week period. The results of each day's inspections are posted to the chart.

This type of chart is very effective during the startup phase of a new item or process when the process is very erratic. Also, many companies prefer to use this type of chart to measure quality performance rather than a control chart. Since zero percent defective is the goal, the central line and control limits may convey to operating personnel that a defective percentage less than zero is acceptable. This type of approach is satisfactory as long as management recognizes that system constraints may be limiting the quality rather than operating personnel. An analysis of Figure 5-9 indicates that the process is relatively stable; therefore, better quality can only result in improvements to the system.

Since the run chart does not have limits, it is not a control chart. This fact does not limit its effectiveness in many situations.

One final comment is appropriate for defective charts. Some companies prefer to take a positive approach and use fraction good, percent good, and number good charts. The transformation is quite easy and is left as an exercise.

CONTROL CHARTS FOR COUNT OF DEFECTS

Introduction

The other group of attribute charts is the defect charts. While a p chart controls the fraction defective in the product, the defect chart controls the count of defects in the product. Remember an item is classified as defective whether it has one or many defects. There are two types of charts: count of defects (c) chart and count of defects per unit (u) chart.

Since these charts are based on the Poisson distribution, two conditions must be met. First, the average count of defects must be much less than the total possible count of defects. In other words, the opportunity for defects is large, while the chance of a defect at any one location is very small. This situation is typified by the rivets on a commercial airplane, where there are a large number of rivets but a small chance of any one rivet being a defect. The second condition specifies that the occurrences are independent. In other words, the occurrence of one defect does not increase or decrease the chance of the next occurrence being a defect. For example, if a typist types an incorrect letter there is an equal likelihood of the next letter being incorrect. Any beginning typist knows that this is not always the case because if the hands are not on the home keys the chance of the second letter being incorrect is almost a certainty.

Other places where a defect chart meets the two conditions are: imperfections in a large roll of paper, typographical errors on a printed page, rust spots on steel sheets, seeds or air pockets in glassware, adhesion defects per 1000 square feet of corrugated board, and mold marks on fiberglass canoes.

Like defective charts, the control limits for defect charts are based on three standard deviations from the central line. Therefore, 99.73% of the subgroup values will fall within the limits. It is suggested that the reader review the section "State of Control" in Chapter 3, since much of that information is applicable to the defect charts.

Purpose or Objectives

While the defect charts are not as inclusive as the $\overline{X}$ and R charts or the p charts, they still have a number of applications, some of which have been mentioned. Like the p chart, the defect chart can be established for a single quality characteristic or a group of quality characteristics, a single machine or a group of machines, or for the entire product.

The purpose or objectives of defect charts are:

1. To determine the average quality level as a benchmark or starting point.
2. To bring to the attention of management any changes in the average. Once the average quality is known, any change becomes significant.
3. To improve the product quality. In this regard a defect chart can motivate operating and management personnel to initiate ideas for quality improvement. The chart will tell whether the idea is an appropriate or inappropriate one. A continual and relentless effort must be made to improve the quality.
4. To evaluate the quality performance of operating and management personnel. As long as the chart is in control operating personnel are performing satisfactorily. Since the defect charts are usually applicable to errors, they are very effective in quality evaluation of the functional areas of finance, sales, customer service, and so on.
5. To suggest places to use the $\overline{X}$ and R charts. Some applications of the defect charts lend themselves to more detailed analysis by the $\overline{X}$ and R charts.
6. To provide information concerning the acceptability of the product prior to shipment.

These objectives are almost identical to those for defective charts. Therefore, the reader is cautioned to be sure that the appropriate group of charts is being used.

Because of the limitations of the defect chart, many plants and industries do not have occasion to use it in quality control.

c-Chart Construction

The procedures for the construction of a c chart are the same as those for the p chart. If the count of defects, c_0, is unknown, it must be found by collecting data, calculating trial control limits, and obtaining the best estimate.

1. *Data collection.* Data were collected on the count of defects of a blemish nature for plastic canoes by an experienced inspector. These data were collected during the first and second weeks of May by inspecting random production samples. Data are shown in Table 5-4 for 25 canoes, which is the minimum number of subgroups needed for trial control limit calculations. Note that canoes MY132 and MY278 both had production difficulties.

2. *Trial central line and control limits.* The formulas for the trial control limits are

$$\text{UCL} = \bar{c} + 3\sqrt{\bar{c}}$$

$$\text{LCL} = \bar{c} - 3\sqrt{\bar{c}}$$

TABLE 5-4 Count of Blemish Defects (c) by Canoe Serial Number

Serial Number	*Count of Defects*	*Comment*	*Serial Number*	*Count of Defects*	*Comment*
MY102	7		MY198	3	
MY113	6		MY208	2	
MY121	6		MY222	7	
MY126	3		MY235	5	
MY132	22	Mold Sticking	MY241	7	
MY143	8		MY258	2	
MY150	6		MY259	8	
MY152	1		MY264	0	
MY164	0		MY267	4	
MY166	5		MY278	14	Fell off skid
MY172	14		MY281	4	
MY184	3		MY288	3	
MY185	1				
			Total	$\Sigma c = 141$	

where $\bar{c}$ is the average count of defects for a number of subgroups. The value of $\bar{c}$ is obtained from the formula $c = \sum c/g$, where g is the number of subgroups and c is the count of defects. For the data in Table 5-4, the calculations are:

$$\bar{c} = \frac{\sum c}{g} = \frac{141}{25} = 5.64$$

$$\begin{aligned} \text{UCL} &= \bar{c} + 3\sqrt{\bar{c}} & \text{LCL} &= \bar{c} - 3\sqrt{\bar{c}} \\ &= 5.64 + 3\sqrt{5.64} & &= 5.64 - 3\sqrt{5.64} \\ &= 12.76 \quad \text{or} \quad 13 & &= -1.48 \quad \text{or} \quad 0 \end{aligned}$$

Since a lower control limit of a -1.48 is impossible, it is changed to zero. The upper control limit of 12.76 is rounded to the whole number 13 since a fraction count of defects is impossible. Figure 5-10 illustrates the central line, $\bar{c}$, the control limits, and the count of defects, c, for each canoe of the preliminary data. This chart is only used to determine the revised central line and control limits.

3. *Revised central line and control limits.* In order to determine the revised 3σ control limits, the standard or reference value for the count of defects, c_0, is needed. If an analysis of the preliminary data shows good control, then $\bar{c}$ can be considered to be representative of that process $c_0 = \bar{c}$. Usually, however, an analysis of the preliminary data does not show good control, as illustrated in Figure 5-10. A better estimate of $\bar{c}$ (one that can be adopted for c_0 can be obtained by discarding out-of-control high values with assignable causes. Low

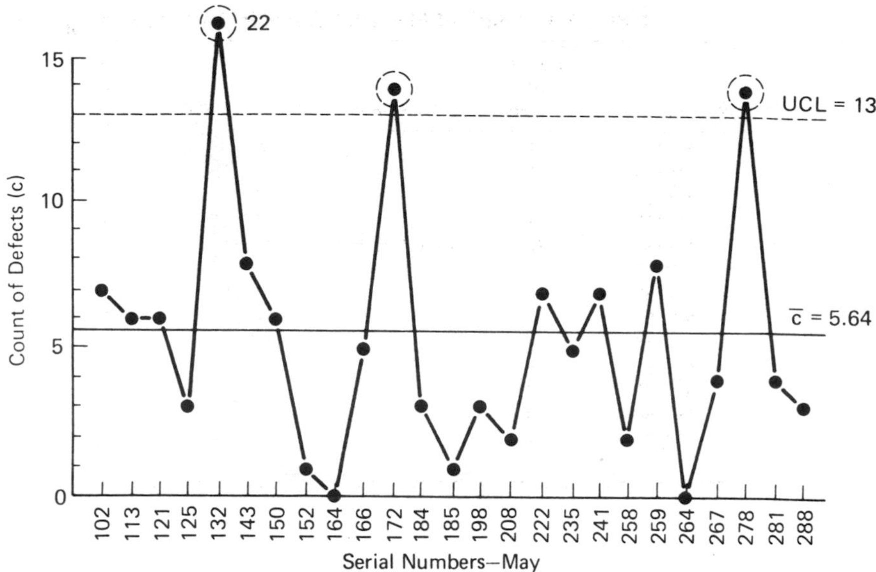

Figure 5-10 Control chart for count of defects (c chart), using preliminary data.

values do not need to be discarded, since they represent exceptionally good quality. The calculations can be simplified by using the formula

$$\bar{c}_{\text{new}} = \frac{\sum c - c_d}{g - g_d}$$

where c_d = count of defects in the discarded subgroups
g_d = number of discarded subgroups

Once an adopted standard or reference value is obtained, the revised 3σ control limits are found using the formulas

$$\text{UCL} = c_0 + 3\sqrt{c_0}$$

$$\text{LCL} = c_0 - 3\sqrt{c_0}$$

where c_0 is the reference or standard value for the count of defects. The count of defects, c_0, is the central line of the chart; it is the best estimate using the available data and equals $\bar{c}_{\text{new}}$.

Using the information from Figure 5-10 and Table 5-4, revised limits can be obtained. An analysis of Figure 5-10 shows that canoe numbers 132, 172, and 278 are out of control. Since canoes 132 and 278 have an assignable cause (see

Table 5-4), they are discarded; however, canoe 172 is evidently due to a chance cause and is not discarded. Therefore, $\bar{c}_{new}$ is obtained as follows:

$$\bar{c}_{new} = \frac{\sum c - c_d}{g - g_d}$$

$$= \frac{141 - 22 - 14}{25 - 2}$$

$$= 4.56$$

Since $\bar{c}_{new}$ is the best estimate of the central line, $c_0 = 4.56$. The revised control limits for the c chart are:

$$\text{UCL} = c_0 + 3\sqrt{c_0} \qquad \text{LCL} = c_0 - 3\sqrt{c_0}$$

$$= 4.56 + 3\sqrt{4.56} \qquad = 4.56 - 3\sqrt{4.56}$$

$$= 10.97 \text{ or } 11 \qquad = -1.85 \text{ or } 0$$

These control limits are used to start the chart beginning with canoes produced during the third week of May and are shown in Figure 5-11. It is noted that the lower control limit will be negative as long as c_0 is less than 9; therefore, it can be given the value of zero without the necessity of performing the calculations.

If c_0 had been known, the data collection and trial control limit phase would have been unnecessary.

Continuing to use the *c* Chart

As with the other types of control charts, an improvement in the quality is expected after the introduction of a chart. At the end of the initial period of use a better estimate of the population number of defects can be obtained. Figure 5-11 illustrates the change in c_0 and in the control limits for August as the chart is continued in use. Quality improvement resulted from the evaluation of ideas such as attaching small pieces of carpet to the skids, faster drying ink, worker training programs, and so on. The control chart shows whether the idea improves the quality, reduces the quality, or does not change the quality. A minimum of 20 subgroups is needed to evaluate each idea.

Figure 5-11 also illustrates a technique for reporting the number of defects of individual quality characteristics, while the graph reports the total. This is an excellent technique for presenting the total picture and one that is accomplished with little additional time or cost. It is interesting to note that the serial numbers of the canoes that were selected for inspection were obtained from a random-number table.

Chart for Canoe Blemish Defects
Model—17S

Type of Defect																														
Scratches	1		2		2		3			1						2					1	2	1		1			1		
Paint Imperfections						1	2	1						1			3				1				1					3
Indentations	1		2						2					1					1		1	2							1	
Scuff Marks	1	1	5		3	4	3	5	2	2				4	1	2		1	2		1	3	1	5	2	1	2	2		3
Total	3	1	9	0	5	5	8	6	4	3			0	6	1	4	3	1	3	0	4	7	2	5	4	1	2	3	1	6
Serial Number	305	310	321	354	373	409	441	469	485	487			129	150	178	185	209	230	260	283	303	321	347	359	407	471	485	493	564	589

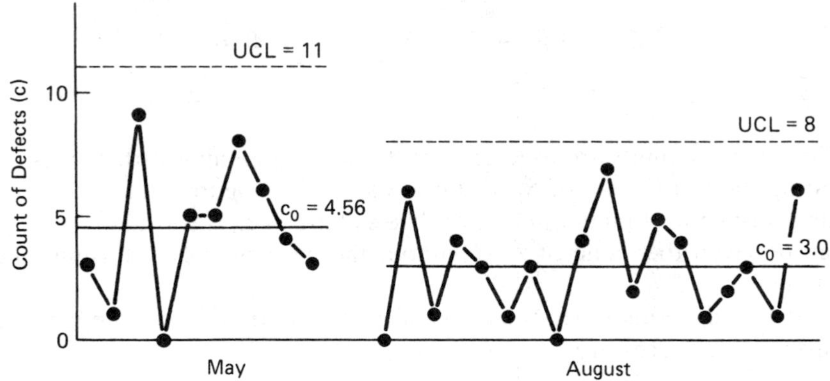

Figure 5-11 *c* Chart for canoe blemish defects.

The control chart should be placed in a conspicuous place where it can be viewed by manufacturing and quality personnel.

Adaptation to the *c* Chart

The *c* chart is applicable where the subgroup size is a single unit of product such as a canoe, an airplane, 1000 square feet of cloth, a ream of paper, or a keg of nails. At times it is desirable to have a larger subgroup size in order for the chart to present a clearer picture. this would certainly be the case if after a period of time the count of blemish defects for each canoe was 0.5. With such a low c_0, the individual c values on the chart would be 0 or 1, with an occasional 2 or 3. A much better chart for such a situation is obtained by having a larger subgroup size. This type of chart is called a u chart, or count of defects-per-unit chart, and is mathematically equivalent to the c chart.

The u chart is developed in the same manner as the c chart, with the collection of 25 subgroups, calculation of trial central line and control limits, obtaining an estimate of the standard or reference count of defects per unit, and calculation of the revised limits. Formulas used for the procedure are:

$$u = \frac{c}{n} \qquad \bar{u} = \frac{\sum c}{\sum n}$$

$$\text{UCL} = \bar{u} + 3\sqrt{\frac{\bar{u}}{n}} \qquad \text{LCL} = \bar{u} - 3\sqrt{\frac{\bar{u}}{n}}$$

where c = count of defects in a subgroup
n = number inspected in a subgroup
u = count of defects/unit in a subgroup
$\bar{u}$ = average count of defects/unit for many subgroups

Revised control limits are obtained by substituting u_0 in the trial-control limit formula. The u chart will be illustrated by an example.

A plant that produces stereo phonographs randomly inspects 45 each day at a final inspection station. Data are collected as shown in Table 5-5. The date, number inspected, and count of defects are obtained and posted to the table. Count of defects per unit, u, is calculated from the formula $u = c/n$ and posted in its column. For September 13,

$$u_{\text{Sept. 13}} = \frac{c}{n} = \frac{36}{45} = 0.80$$

TABLE 5-5 Count of Defects per Unit for Stereo Phonographs, Preliminary Data

Date	Number Inspected, *n*	Count of Defects, *c*	Defects per Unit, *u*	Date	Number Inspected, *n*	Count of Defects, *c*	Defects per Unit, *u*
Sept. 13	45	36	0.80	Sept. 30	45	52	1.16
14	45	48	1.07	Oct. 1	45	42	0.93
15	45	45	1.00	4	45	47	1.04
16	45	68	1.51	5	45	64	1.42
17	45	77	1.71	6	45	61	1.36
20	45	56	1.24	7	45	66	1.47
21	45	58	1.29	8	45	37	0.82
22	45	67	1.49	11	45	59	1.31
23	45	38	0.04	12	45	38	0.84
24	45	74	1.64	13	45	41	0.91
27	45	69	1.53	14	45	68	1.51
28	45	54	1.20	15	45	78	1.73
29	45	56	1.24				
				Total	1125	1399	

For each of the 25 subgroups, the defects per unit are calculated and posted to the table. The average number of defects per unit is

$$\bar{u} = \frac{\sum c}{\sum n} = \frac{1399}{1125} = 1.24$$

and the trial control limits are:

$$\text{UCL} = \bar{u} + 3\sqrt{\frac{\bar{u}}{n}} \qquad \text{LCL} = \bar{u} - 3\sqrt{\frac{\bar{u}}{\text{n}}}$$

$$= 1.24 + 3\sqrt{\frac{1.24}{45}} \qquad = 1.24 - 3\sqrt{\frac{1.24}{45}}$$

$$= 1.74 \qquad = 0.74$$

A comparison of the subgroup values with the upper and lower control limits shows that there are no out-of-control values. Therefore, $\bar{u}$ can be considered the best estimate of u_0 and $u_0 = 1.24$. Since $u_0 = \bar{u}$, there is no difference between the trial control limits and the revised control limits. A u chart is illustrated in Figure 5-12 for u_0, revised control limits, and new data that start with October 18.

The u chart is identical to the c chart in all aspects except two. One difference is the scale, which is continuous for a u chart but discrete for the c chart. This difference provides more flexibiilty for the u chart. The other difference is the subgroup size which is one for the c chart. The u chart is limited in that we do not know the location of the defects. For example, in Table 5-5, October 8

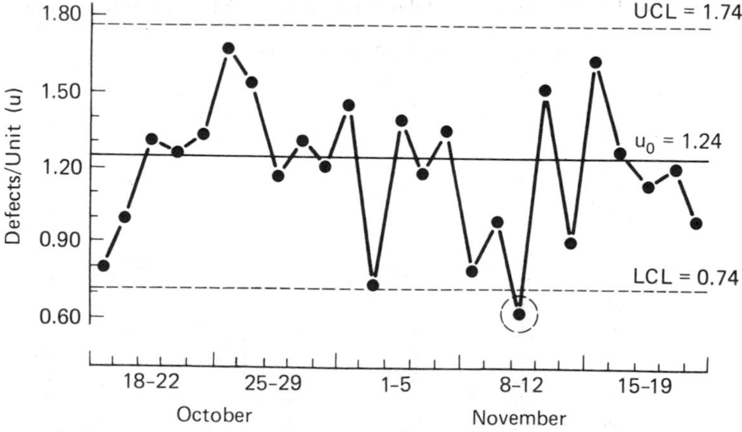

Figure 5-12 *u* Chart for count of defects per unit for stereo phonographs.

has 37 defects out of 45 inspected for an average of 0.82. All 37 defects could have been counted on one unit or it is possible that 37 units had one defect each.

The subgroup size of the u chart must be kept constant. If not, both the central line and the control limits will vary, which will result in a meaningless chart.

A QUALITY RATING SYSTEM

Introduction

In the c charts of the preceding section, all defects had the same weight, regardless of their seriousness. For example, in the inspection of desk chairs, one chair might have 5 defects, all related to the surface finish, while another chair might have 1 defect, a broken leg. The usable chair with 5 trivial defects has five times the influence on the c chart as the unusable chair with 1 serious defect. This situation presents an incorrect evaluation of the product quality. A quality rating system will correct this deficiency.

There are industrial and nonindustrial situations where it is desirable to compare the performance of operators, shifts, plants, or vendors. In order to compare quality performance, a quality rating system is needed to classify, weigh, and evaluate defects.

Defect Classification

Defects are classified according to their severity. The defects are normally grouped into three classes:

1. *Critical defects*. A critical defect is a defect that judgment and experience indicate is likely to result in hazardous or unsafe conditions for individuals using, maintaining, or depending upon the product; or a defect which judgment and experience indicate is likely to prevent performance of the function of the product.
2. *Major defects*. A major defect is a defect, other than critical, which is likely to result in failure, or to reduce materially the usability of the product for its intended purpose.
3. *Minor defects*. A minor defect is a defect that is not likely to reduce materially the usability of the product for its intended purpose. Minor defects are usually associated with appearance.

To summarize, a critical defect *will* affect usability; a major defect *might* affect usability; and a minor defect *will not* affect usability of the piece.

Other classification systems use four classes or two classes, depending on the complexity of the product.

Once the defect classifications are determined, the weights to assign to each defect class can be established. While any weights can be assigned to the classifications, 9 points for a critical, 3 points for a major, and 1 point for a minor are usually considered to be satisfactory since a major is three times as important as a minor and a critical is three times as important as a major.

Control Chart

Control charts are established and plotted for count of demerits per unit. A demerit per unit is given by the formula

$$D = w_c u_c + w_{ma} u_{ma} + w_{mi} u_{mi}$$

where D = demerits per unit

w_c, w_{ma}, w_{mi} = weights for the three classes—critical, major, and minor

u_c, u_{ma}, u_{mi} = count of defects per unit in each of the three classes—critical, major, minor

When w_c, w_{ma}, and w_{mi} are 9, 3 and 1, respectively, the formula is

$$D = 9u_c + 3u_{ma} + 1u_{mi}$$

The D values calculated from the formula are posted to the chart for each subgroup.

The central line and the 3σ control limits are obtained from the formulas

$$D_0 = 9u_{0c} + 3u_{0ma} + 1u_{0mi}$$

$$\sigma_{0u} = \sqrt{\frac{9^2 u_{0c} + 3^2 u_{0ma} + 1^2 u_{0mi}}{n}}$$

$$\text{UCL} = D_0 + 3\sigma_{0u} \qquad \text{LCL} = D_0 - 3\sigma_{0u}$$

where u_{0c}, u_{0ma}, and u_{0mi} represent the population defects per unit for the critical, major, and minor classifications, respectively. The population defects per unit for the critical, major, and minor classifications are obtained by separating the defects into the three classifications and treating each as a separate u chart.

Example Problem

Assuming that a 9:3:1 three-class weighting system is used, determine the central line and control limits when $u_{0c} = 0.08$, $u_{0ma} = 0.5$, $u_{0mi} = 3.0$, and $n = 40$. Also calculate the demerits per unit for May 25 when critical defects are 2, major defects are 26, and minor defects are 160 for the 40 units inspected on that day. Is the May 25 subgroup in control or out of control?

$$D_0 = 9u_{0c} + 3u_{0ma} + 1u_{0mi}$$
$$= 9(0.08) + 3(0.5) + 1(3.0)$$
$$= 5.2$$

$$\sigma_{0u} = \sqrt{\frac{9^2u_{0c} + 3^2u_{0ma} + 1^2u_{0mi}}{n}}$$
$$= \sqrt{\frac{81(0.08) + 9(0.5) + 1(3.0)}{40}}$$
$$= 0.59$$

$$\text{UCL} = D_0 + 3\sigma_{0u} \qquad \text{LCL} = D_0 - 3\sigma_{0u}$$
$$= 5.2 + 3(0.59) \qquad = 5.2 - 3(0.59)$$
$$= 7.0 \qquad = 3.4$$

The central line and control limits are illustrated in Figure 5-13. Calculations for the May 25 subgroup are

$$D_{\text{May 25}} = 9u_c + 3u_{ma} + 1u_{mi}$$
$$= 9\left(\frac{2}{40}\right) + 3\left(\frac{26}{40}\right) + 1\left(\frac{160}{40}\right)$$
$$= 6.4 \quad \text{(in control)}$$

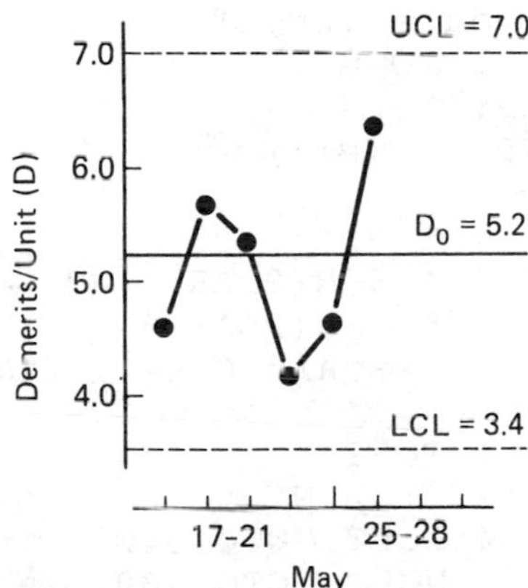

Figure 5-13 Demerit-per-unit chart (D chart).

Quality rating systems based on demerits per unit are useful for performance control and can be an important feature of a total quality control system.

COMPUTER PROGRAM

The computer program given in Figure 5-14 computes the central line and control limits for a fraction defective chart for a fixed subgroup size. If it is desired to print out the incoming data, an LPRINT statement can be added after statement 210. Data used for the program are from Problem 2 at the end of the chapter. The program can be enhanced by graphing the chart and plotting the actual points. This activity is a function of the available graphical output device.

```
1Ø REM                                  p CHART
2Ø REM                            Fixed Subgroup Size
3Ø REM
4Ø REM              N    = Sample Size(n)
5Ø REM              P    = Fraction Defective of Sample(p)
6Ø REM              NP   = Number Defective in Sample(np)
7Ø REM              G    = Number of Subgroups(g)
8Ø REM              PBAR= Average Fraction Defective(p bar)
9Ø REM              UCL  = Upper Control Limit
1ØØ REM             LCL  = Lower Control Limit
11Ø REM             PO   = Standard Value or Central Line
12Ø REM
13Ø DIM NP(3Ø), P(3Ø)
14Ø PRINT " Enter subgroup size." : INPUT N
15Ø LPRINT TAB(5); " n = ";N : LPRINT
16Ø PRINT " Enter number of subgroups." : INPUT G
17Ø REM                 Trial Central Line and Control Limits
18Ø NPS = Ø
19Ø PRINT " Enter data (np)."
2ØØ          FOR I = 1 TO G
21Ø          INPUT NP(I)
22Ø          NPS = NPS + NP(I)
23Ø          NEXT I
24Ø PBAR = NPS / (N * G)
25Ø UCLT = PBAR + 3 * SQR(PBAR * (1 - PBAR) / N)
26Ø LCLT = PBAR - 3 * SQR(PBAR * (1 - PBAR) / N)
27Ø REM                 Discard Out-of-Control Points
28Ø D = G
29Ø          FOR I = 1 TO G
3ØØ          P(I) = NP(I) / N
31Ø          IF P(I) < LCLT GOTO 34Ø
32Ø          IF P(I) > UCLT GOTO 4ØØ
```

Figure 5-14 Computer program in BASIC to calculate the central line and control limits for a *p* chart.

```
330        GOTO 430
340        PRINT " Subgroup number = ";I
350        PRINT " p < LCL ; Enter 0 to discard, else 1."
360        INPUT K
370        IF K = 1 GOTO 430
380        IF K = 0 THEN NPS = NPS - NP(I)
390        D = D - 1 : GOTO 430
400        PRINT " Subgroup number = ";I
410        PRINT " p > UCL ; Enter 0 to discard, else 1."
420        INPUT K : GOTO 370
430        NEXT I
440 REM                Revised Central Line and Control Limits
450 PO = NPS / (N * D)
460 UCL = PO + 3 * SQR(PO * (1 - PO) / N)
470 LCL = PO - 3 * SQR(PO * (1 - PO) / N)
480 LPRINT TAB(5); " Standard Value and Central Line = ";PO
490 LPRINT TAB(5); " Upper Control Limit = ";UCL
500 LPRINT TAB(5); " Lower Control Limit = ";LCL
510 END

n =  1750

Standard Value and Central Line =  .0261863
Upper Control Limit =  .0376382
Lower Control Limit =  .0147344
```

Figure 5-14 Continued.

PROBLEMS

1. Determine the trial central line and control limits for a p chart using the data in the table. If there are any out-of-control points, assume an assignable cause and determine the revised central line and control limits.

Subgroup Number	*Number Inspected*	*Number Defective*	*Subgroup Number*	*Number Inspected*	*Number Defective*
1	300	3	14	300	6
2	300	6	15	300	7
3	300	4	16	300	4
4	300	6	17	300	5
5	300	20	18	300	7
6	300	2	19	300	5
7	300	6	20	300	0
8	300	7	21	300	2
9	300	3	22	300	3
10	300	0	23	300	6
11	300	6	24	300	1
12	300	9	25	300	8
13	300	5			

2. Inspection results of safety hats for 25 consecutive days are given in the table. What central line and control limits should be established and posted if it is assumed that any out-of-control points have assigned causes? The number of inspections each day is constant and equals 1750.

Date	Number Defective	Date	Number Defective
July 6	47	July 23	37
7	42	26	39
8	48	27	51
9	58	28	44
12	32	29	61
13	38	30	48
14	53	Aug. 2	56
15	68	3	48
16	45	4	40
19	37	5	47
20	57	6	25
21	38	9	35
22	53		

3. Fifty motor generators are inspected per day. The best estimate of the population fraction defective is 0.076. Determine the central line and control limits. On a particular day 5 defective generators were discovered. Is this in control or out of control?

4. The performance of the first shift is reflected in the inspection results of electric carving knives. Determine the central line and the trial control limits for each subgroup. Assume that any out-of-control points have assignable causes and determine the standard value for the fraction defective for the next production period.

Date	Number Inspected	Number Defective	Date	Number Inspected	Number Defective
Sept. 6	500	5	Sept. 23	525	10
7	550	6	24	650	3
8	700	8	27	675	8
9	625	9	28	450	23
10	700	7	29	500	2
13	550	8	30	375	3
14	450	16	Oct. 1	550	8
15	600	6	4	600	7
16	475	9	5	700	4
17	650	6	6	600	9
20	650	7	7	450	8
21	550	8	8	500	6
22	525	7	11	525	1

5. Daily inspection results for the model 305 electric range assembly line are given in the table. Determine trial control limits for each subgroup. Assume

that any out-of-control points have assignable causes and determine the standard value for the fraction defective for December.

Date and Shift		Number Inspected	Number Defective	Date and Shift		Number Inspected	Number Defective
Nov. 8	I	171	31	Nov. 17	I	165	16
	II	167	6		II	170	35
9	I	170	8	18	I	175	12
	II	135	13		II	167	6
10	I	137	26	19	I	141	50
	II	170	30		II	159	26
11	I	45	3	22	I	181	16
	II	155	11		II	195	38
12	I	195	30	23	I	165	33
	II	180	36		II	140	21
15	I	181	38	24	I	162	18
	II	115	33		II	191	22
16	I	165	26	25	I	139	16
	II	189	15		II	181	27

6. Control limits are to be established based on the average number inspected from the information of Problem 5. What are these control limits and the central line? Describe the cases where individual control limits will need to be calculated.

7. Control charts are to be established on the manufacture of backpack frames. The population fraction defective is 0.08. Determine control limit lines for inspection rates of 1000 per day, 1500 per day, and 2000 per day. Draw the control chart. Why are the control limits unequally spaced?

8. Determine the revised central line and control limits for a percent defective chart for the information in:
(a) Problem 1
(b) Problem 2

9. For the information of Problem 1, determine the revised central line and control limits for an *np* chart.

10. For the information of Problem 2, determine the revised central line and control limits for an *np* chart. Which chart is more meaningful to operating personnel?

11. An *np* chart is to be established on a painting process that is in statistical control. If 35 pieces are to be inspected every 4 hours and the population fraction defective is 0.06 determine the control limits and central line.

12. Determine the revised central line and control limits for *fraction good, percent good,* and *number good* charts for the information in:
(a) Problem 1
(b) Problem 2

13. Using the data of Figure 5-9, construct a run chart for *percent good.*

14. The count of surface defects in 1000 square meters of 20-kg kraft paper is given in the table. Determine the trial central line and control limits and the revised central line and control limits assuming that out-of-control points have assignable causes.

Lot Number	*Count of Defects*	*Lot Number*	*Count of Defects*
20	10	35	30
21	8	36	2
22	6	37	12
23	6	38	0
24	2	39	6
25	10	40	14
26	8	41	10
27	10	42	8
28	0	43	6
29	2	44	2
30	8	45	14
31	2	46	16
32	20	47	10
33	10	48	2
34	6	49	5
		50	3

15. The data in the table give the count of defects in double-pedestal office desks for the month of January. What control limits and central line are recommended for the control chart for February?

Serial Number	*Count of defects*	*Serial Number*	*Count of Defects*
301	8	314	17
302	19	315	14
303	14	316	9
304	18	317	7
305	11	318	15
306	16	319	22
307	8	320	19
308	15	321	38
309	21	322	12
310	8	323	13
311	23	324	5
312	10	325	2
313	9	326	16

16. An inspector has collected data on the count of rivet defects in 4-m travel trailers. After 30 trailers, the total count of defects is 316. Trial control limits have been determined and a comparison with the data shows no out-of-control points. What is the recommendation for the central line and the revised control limits for a count of defects chart?

17. Determine the trial control limits and revised control limits for a u chart using the data in the table for the surface finish of rolls of white paper.

Lot Number	*Sample Size*	*Total Defects*	*Lot Number*	*Sample Size*	*Total Defects*
1	10	45	15	10	48
2	10	51	16	10	35
3	10	36	17	10	39
4	10	48	18	10	29
5	10	42	19	10	37
6	10	5	20	10	33
7	10	33	21	10	15
8	10	27	22	10	33
9	10	31	23	10	27
10	10	22	24	10	23
11	10	25	25	10	25
12	10	35	26	10	41
13	10	32	27	10	37
14	10	43	28	10	28

18. A process has been in statistical control and control limits are needed for the next period. If the subgroup size is 100, the total count of defects is 835, and the number of subgroups is 22, what are the new control limits and central line?

19. Assuming that a 10:5:1 demerit weighting system is used, determine the central line and control limits when $\mu_c = 0.11$, $\mu_{ma} = 0.70$, $\mu_{mi} = 4.00$, and $n = 50$. If the subgroup inspection results for a particular day are 1 critical, 35 major, and 110 minor defects, determine if the results are in control or out of control.

20. Test, and if necessary rewrite, the computer program for your computer.

21. Modify the computer program to output the central line and control limits for your graphical output device. Also, write the program to plot the subgroup values.

22. Write a computer program for:
(a) c and u charts
(b) D chart
(c) p chart for a variable subgroup size
(c) np chart

6 LOT-BY-LOT ACCEPTANCE SAMPLING BY ATTRIBUTES

FUNDAMENTAL CONCEPTS

Description

Lot-by-lot acceptance sampling by attributes is the most common type of sampling. With this type of sampling, a predetermined number of units (sample) from each lot is inspected by attributes. If the amount defective is less than the prescribed minimum, the lot is accepted; if not, the lot is rejected as being below standard. Each lot in the shipment or order is sampled and either rejected or accepted. Acceptance sampling can be used either for the amount defective or for defects per unit. To simplify the presentation in this chapter, the amount defective is used; however, it is understood that the information is also applicable to defects per unit. Sampling plans are established for each class of defect severity (critical, major, minor) or on a demerit-per-unit basis.

A single sampling plan is defined by the lot size, N, the sample size, n, and the acceptance number, c. Thus, the plan

$$N = 9000$$

$$n = 300$$

$$c = 7$$

means that a lot of 9000 units has 300 units inspected. And if seven or less defectives are found in the 300-unit sample, the lot is accepted. If eight or more defectives are found in the 300-unit sample, the lot is rejected.

Acceptance sampling can be performed in a number of different situations where there is a consumer-producer relationship. The consumer and producer can be from two different companies, two plants within the same company, or two departments within the same plant. In any case, there is always the problem associated with the acceptance of goods.

Acceptance sampling of the product is most likely to be used in one of five situations.

1. When the test is destructive (such as a test on an electrical fuse or a tensile test), sampling is necessary; otherwise, all of the product will be destroyed by testing.
2. When the cost of 100% inspection is high in relation to the cost of passing a defective item.
3. When there are many similar items to be inspected, sampling will produce as good, if not better, results than 100% inspection. This is true because with manual inspection, fatigue and boredom cause a higher percentage of defective material to be passed than would occur on the average using a sampling plan.
4. When information concerning producer's quality, $\overline{X}$ and R or p charts, are not available.
5. When automated inspection is not used.

Advantages and Disadvantages of Sampling

When sampling is compared with 100% inspection, it has the following advantages:

1. More economical, owing to fewer inspections.
2. Less handling damage during inspection.
3. Fewer inspectors, thereby simplifying recruiting, training, and supervising.
4. Upgrading the inspection job from monotonous piece-by-piece decisions to lot-by-lot decisions.
5. Applicable to destructive testing.
6. Rejection of entire lots rather than the return of defectives, thereby providing stronger motivation for improvement.

Inherent disadvantages of acceptance sampling are:

1. There are certain risks of accepting defective lots and rejecting good lots.
2. More time and effort is devoted to planning and documentation.
3. Less information is usually provided about the product.[1]

[1]J. M. Juran, ed., *Quality Control Handbook*, 3rd ed. (New York: McGraw-Hill Book Company, 1974), Sec. 24, p. 2.

Types of Sampling Plans

There are three types of sampling plans: single, double, and multiple. In the single sampling plan, one sample is taken from the lot and a decision to reject or accept the lot is made based on the inspection results of that sample. This type of sampling plan was described earlier in the chapter.

Double sampling plans are somewhat more complicated. On the initial sample a decision, based on the inspection results, is made whether (1) to accept the lot, (2) to reject the lot, or (3) to take another sample. If a second sample is required, the results of that inspection and the first inspection are used to reject or accept the lot. A double sampling plan is defined by

N = lot size
n_1 = sample size on the first sample
c_1 = acceptance number on the first sample (sometimes the symbol Ac is used)
r_1 = rejection number on the first sample (sometimes the symbol Re is used)
n_2 = sample size on the second sample
c_2 = acceptance number for *both* samples
r_2 = rejection number for *both* samples

If values are not given for r_1 and r_2, they are equal to $c_2 + 1$.

An illustrative example will help to clarify the double sampling plan: $N = 9000$, $n_1 = 60$, $c_1 = 1$, $r_1 = 5$, $n_2 = 150$, $c_2 = 6$, and $r_2 = 7$. An initial sample (n_1) of 60 is selected from the lot (N) of 9000 and inspected. One of the following judgments is made:

1. If there are 1 or less defectives (c_1), the lot is accepted.
2. If there are 5 or more defectives (r_1), the lot is rejected.
3. If there are 2, 3, or 4 defectives, no decision is made and a second sample is taken.

A second sample of 150 (n_2) from the lot (N) is inspected, and one of the following judgments is made:

1. If there are 6 or less defectives (c_2) in both samples, the lot is accepted. This number (6 or less) is obtained by 2 in the first sample and 4 or less in the second sample, by 3 in the first sample and 3 or less in the second sample, or by 4 in the first sample and 2 or less in the second sample.

2. If there are 7 or more defectives (r_2) in both samples, the lot is rejected. This number (7 or more) is obtained by 2 in the first sample and 5 or more in the second sample, by 3 in the first sample and 4 or more in the second sample, or by 4 in the first sample and 3 or more in the second sample.

A multiple sampling plan is a continuation of double sampling in that three, four, five, or as many samples as desired can be established. Sample sizes are much smaller. The technique is the same as that described for double sampling; therefore, a detailed description is not given. Multiple sampling plans can be truncated after any specific number of samples or can continue until the lot is exhausted or a decision made. Examples of multiple sampling plans are illustrated later in the chapter.

All three types of sampling plans can give the same results; for example, the chance of a lot being accepted under a single sampling plan is the same under the appropriate double or multiple sampling plan. Therefore, the type of plan for a particular producer or product is based on factors other than effectiveness. These factors are administrative costs, quality information, number of units inspected, and psychological impact.

Administrative costs for training, inspection, record keeping, and so on, are least for single sampling, greater for double sampling, and greatest for multiple sampling.

Single sampling provides more information concerning the quality level in each lot than double sampling and much more than multiple sampling.

In general, the number of pieces inspected is more under single sampling than double sampling provided the lot quality is such that second samples are needed only occasionally. Multiple sampling generally requires fewer pieces inspected than double sampling provided that the decision to accept or reject the lot is made at an early stage in the sampling process.

A fourth factor concerns the psychological impact of the three types of sampling plans. Under single sampling there is no second chance; however, in double sampling, if the first sample is borderline, a second chance is possible by taking another sample. Many producers like the second-chance psychology provided by the double sample. In multiple sampling there is a number of "second chances"; therefore, the psychological impact is less than with double sampling.

Careful consideration of the four factors is necessary to select a type of sampling plan that will be best for the particular situation.

Formation of Lots

Lot formation can influence the effectiveness of the sampling plan. Guidelines for their formation are as follows:

1. Lots should be homogeneous, which means that all product in the lot is produced by the same machine, same operator, same input material, and so on. When product from different sources is mixed, the sampling plan does not function properly. Also, it is difficult to take corrective action to eliminate the source of defective product.

2. Lots should be as large as possible. Since sample sizes do not increase

as rapidly as lot sizes, a lower inspection cost results with larger lot sizes. For example, a lot of 2000 would have a sample size of 125 (6.25%), while an equally effective sampling plan for a lot of 4000 would have a sample size of 200 (5.00%).

The reader is cautioned not to confuse the packaging requirements for shipment and materials handling with the concept of a homogeneous lot. In other words, a lot may consist of a number of packages and may also constitute of a number of shipments. If two different machines and/or two different operators are included in a shipment, they are separate lots and should be so identified.

Sample Selection

The sample pieces selected for inspection should be representative of the entire lot. All sampling plans are based on the premise that each piece in the lot has an equal likelihood of being selected. This is referred to as *random sampling*.

The basic technique of random sampling is to assign a number to each piece in the lot. Then a series of random numbers is generated that tells which of the numbered pieces are to be sampled and inspected. Random numbers can be generated from a computer, electronic hand calculator, 20-sided random-number die, numbered chips in a bowl, and so on. They may be used to select the sample or to develop a table of random numbers.

A random-number table that was generated from an electronic hand calculator is shown in Table D of the Appendix. A portion of Table D is reproduced here as Table 6-1. To use the table it is entered at random and numbers selected sequentially from one direction, such as up, down, left, or right. Any number that is not appropriate is discarded. For locating convenience, the table is established in eight columns. Any number of digits can be used for a random number.

An example will help to illustrate the technique. Assume that a lot of 90 pieces has been assigned numbers from 1 to 90 and it is desired to select a sample of 8. A two-digit number is selected at random, as indicated by the underlined number, 55. Numbers are selected downward and the first three numbers are 55, 90, and 61. Starting at the top of the next column the numbers 37, 12, 76, and 71 are obtained. The next number is 76, and a repeat, so it is discarded. Starting at the top again is the number 92, which is too high and therefore is discarded. The next and eighth number is 62. Pieces with the numbers 55, 90, 61, 37, 12, 76, 71, and 62 comprise the sample.

TABLE 6-1 Random Numbers Generated from an Electronic Hand Calculator

9069	7629	5756	2237	3069	6004	3792	2530
4321	5890	0822	5994	9996	8961	1262	5870
4195	5124	9161	6899	6857	6455	7662	7035
8589	4464	0905	8676	4514	8790	7186	4591
1007	3877	2592	8860	5753	8661	7694	5013

Many products have serial numbers that can be used as the assigned number. This avoids the difficult process of assigning numbers to each piece. In many situations, pieces are systematically packed in a container and the assigned number can be designated by the location. A three-digit number would represent the length, width, and depth in a container. Thus, the random number 328 could specify the piece located at the third level, second row, and eighth column. For fluid or other well-mixed products, the sample can be taken from any location, since the product is homogeneous.

It is not always practical to assign a number to each piece, utilize a serial number, or utilize a locational number. Stratification of the lot or package with samples drawn from each stratum can be an effective substitute for random sampling. The technique is to divide the lot or package into strata or layers as shown in Figure 6-1. Each stratum is further subdivided into cubes, as illustrated by stratum 1. Within each cube, samples are drawn from the entire volume. The dividing of the lot or package into strata and cubes within each stratum is an imaginary process done by the inspector. By this technique pieces are selected from all locations in the lot or package.

Unless an adequate sampling method is used, a variety of biases can occur. An example of a biased sample occurs when the operator makes sure that pieces on the top of a lot are the best quality, and the inspector selects his sample from the same location. Adequate supervision of inspectors is necessary to ensure that no bias occurs.

Rejected Lots

Once a lot has been rejected, there are a number of courses of action that can be taken.

1. The rejected lot can be passed to the production facilities and the defective pieces sorted by production personnel. This is not a satisfactory alter-

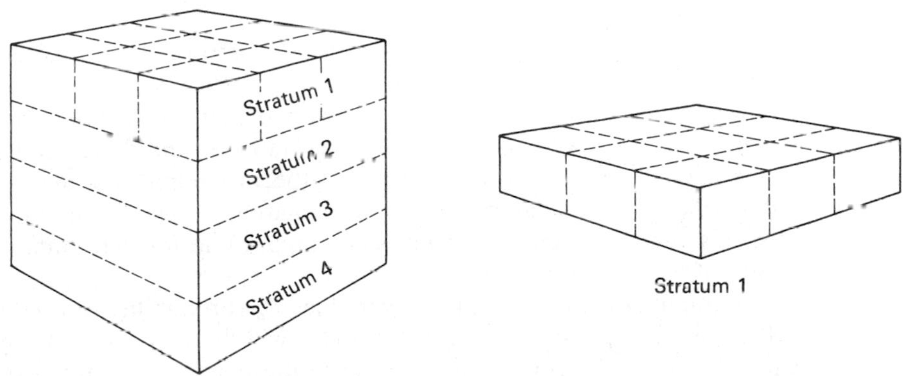

Figure 6-1 Dividing a lot for stratified sampling.

native, since it defeats the purpose of sampling inspection and slows production. However, if the pieces are badly needed, there may be no other choice.

2. The rejected lot can be rectified at the consumer's plant by personnel from either the producer's or the consumer's plant. While shipping costs are saved, there is a psychological disadvantage since all of the consumer's personnel are aware that producer *X* had product rejected. This fact may be used as a crutch to explain poor performance when using producer *X*'s material at a future time. In addition, space at the consumer's plant must be provided for personnel to perform the sorting operation.

3. The rejected lot can be returned to the producer for rectification. This is the only appropriate course of action, since it results in long-run improvement in the quality. Since shipping costs are paid in both directions for a rejected lot, cost becomes a motivating factor to improve the quality. Also, when the lot is sorted in the producer's plant, all the employees are aware that consumer *Y* expects to receive a quality product. This, too, is a motivating factor for quality improvement the next time an order is run for consumer *Y*.

It is assumed that rejected lots will receive 100% inspection and the defective pieces discarded. A resubmitted lot is not normally reinspected, but if it is, the inspection should be confined to the original defect. Since the defective pieces are discarded, a resubmitted lot will have fewer pieces than the original.

STATISTICAL ASPECTS

OC Curve for Single Sampling Plans

An excellent evaluation technique is an *operating characteristic* (OC) *curve*. In judging a particular sampling plan, it is desirable to know the probability that a lot submitted with a certain percent defective, $100p_0$, will be accepted or rejected. The OC curve will provide this information, and a typical OC curve is shown in Figure 6-2.

The construction of an OC curve can be illustrated by a concrete example. A single sampling plan has a lot of size $N = 3000$, a sample size $n = 89$, and an acceptance number $c = 2$. It is assumed that the lots are from a steady stream of product which can be considered infinite, and therefore the binomial probability distribution can be used for the probability calculations. Fortunately, the Poisson is an excellent approximation to the binomial for almost all sampling plans; therefore, the Poisson is applicable for determining the probability of the acceptance of a lot.

In graphing the curve with the variables P_a (probability of acceptance) and $100p_0$ (percent defective), one value $100p_0$ will be assumed and the other calculated. Since the curve is asymptotic to the percent defective axis, it is best to determine the limiting value for $100p_0$, which is obtained by trial and error.

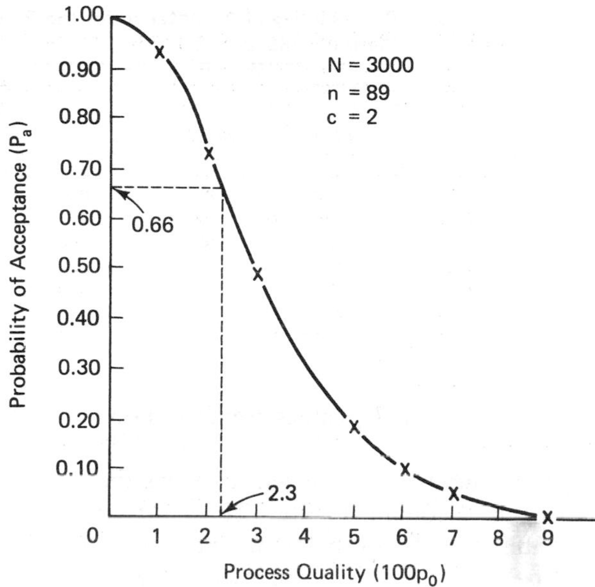

Figure 6-2 OC curve for the single sampling plan $N = 3000$, $n = 89$, and $c = 2$.

Acceptance of the lot is based on the acceptance number $c = 2$ and is possible when there is 0 defective in the sample, 1 defective in the sample, or 2 defectives in the sample. Assuming a trial-and-error value of $100p_0 = 9\%$ and using Table C for the Poisson distribution, the probability of acceptance of a lot with a percent defective of 9% is

$$np_0 = (89)(0.09) = 8.0$$

$$P_a = P(0) + P(1) + P(2) = P(2 \text{ or less})$$

$$= 0.014$$

A p_a value of 0.014 is very close to 0, which indicates that the curve is asymptotic at approximately 9% defective. Therefore, the curve has a range of 0–9% defective.

Approximately seven points are needed to describe the curve with a greater concentration of points occurring where the curve changes direction. A table can be used to assist with the calculations of the seven points, as shown in Table 6-2. The first five assumed values for p_0 are spaced within the range of 0–9% and the last two assumed values of p_0 are located where it is necessary to obtain a smooth curve. Information from the table is plotted to obtain the OC curve shown in Figure 6-2. The steps are: (1) assume p_0 values, (2) calculate np_0

TABLE 6-2 Probabilities of Acceptance for the Single Sampling Plan: $n = 89$, $c = 2$

Assumed Process Quality				
p_0	$100p_0$	*Sample Size, n*	np_0	*Probability of Acceptance,* P_a
0.09	9.0	89	8.0	0.014
0.07	7.0	89	6.2	0.055[a]
0.05	5.0	89	4.5	0.174
0.03	3.0	89	2.7	0.494
0.01	1.0	89	0.9	0.938
0.02	2.0	89	1.8	0.731
0.06	6.0	89	5.3	0.106[a]

[a]By interpolation.

values, and (3) attain P_a values from the Poisson table using the applicable c and np_0 values.

Once the curve is constructed, it shows the chance of a lot being accepted for a particular incoming quality. Thus, if the incoming process quality is 2.3%, the probability of the lot being accepted is 0.66. Similarly, if 55 lots, from a process that is 2.3% defective, are inspected using this sampling plan, 36 [(55)(0.66) = 36.3] will be accepted and 19 (55 − 36 = 19) will be rejected.

OC Curve for Double Sampling Plans

The construction of an OC curve for double sampling plans is somewhat more involved, since two curves must be determined. One curve is for the probability of acceptance on the first sample; the second curve is the probability of acceptance on the combined samples.

A typical OC curve is shown in Figure 6-4 for the double sampling plan $N = 2400$, $n_1 = 150$, $c_1 = 1$, $r_1 = 4$, $n_2 = 200$, $c_2 = 4$, and $r_2 = 5$. The first step in the construction of the OC curve is to determine the equations. If there is one or less defectives on the first sample, the lot is accepted. Symbolically, the equation is

$$(P_a)_{\text{I}} = (P_{1 \text{ or less}})_{\text{I}}$$

To obtain the equation for the second sample, the number of different ways in which the lot can be accepted is determined. A second sample is taken only if there are two or three defectives on the first sample. If there is one or less, the lot is accepted; if there are four or more, the lot is rejected. Therefore, the lot can be accepted by obtaining:

1. Two defectives on the first sample *and* two or less defectives on the second sample
2. *Or* three defectives on the first sample *and* one or less defectives on the second sample

The and's and or's are emphasized above to illustrate the use of the additive and multiplicative theorems, which were discussed in Chapter 4. Where an "and" occurs, multiply, and where an "or" occurs, add and the equation becomes

$$(P_a)_{II} = (P_2)_I(P_{2 \text{ or less}})_{II} + (P_3)_I(P_{1 \text{ or less}})_{II}$$

Roman numerals are used as a subscript for the sample number. The equations derived above are applicable only to this double sampling plan; another plan will require a different set of equations. Figure 6-3 graphically illustrates the technique. Note that the number of defectives in each term in the second equation is equal to or less than the acceptance number, c_2. By combining the equations, the probability of acceptance for the combined samples is obtained:

$$(P_a)_{\text{combined}} = (P_a)_I + (P_a)_{II}$$

Once the equations are obtained, the OC curves are found by assuming various p_0 values and calculating the respective first and second sample P_a values. For

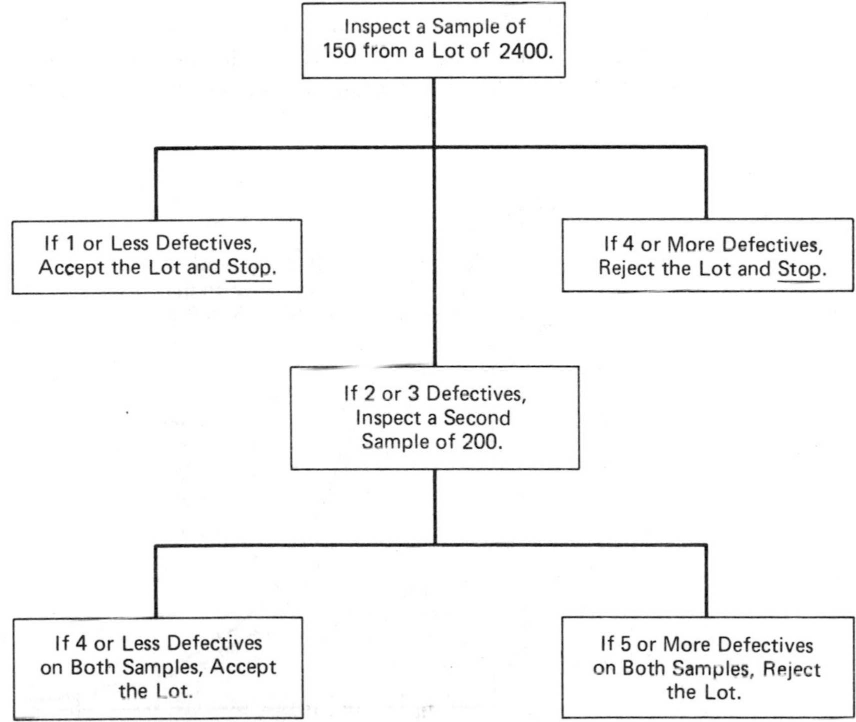

Figure 6-3 Graphical description of the double sampling plan: $N = 2400$, $n_1 = 150$, $c_1 = 1$, $r_1 = 4$, $n_2 = 200$, $c_2 = 4$, and $r_2 = 5$.

example, using Table C of the Appendix and assuming a p_0 value of 0.01 ($100p_0 = 1.0\%$),

$$(np_0)_{\text{I}} = (150)(0.01) = 1.5$$

$$(P_a)_{\text{I}} = (P_{1 \text{ or less}})_{\text{I}} = 0.558$$

$$(np_0)_{\text{II}} = (200)(0.01) = 2.0$$

$$(P_a)_{\text{II}} = (P_2)_{\text{I}}(P_{2 \text{ or less}})_{\text{II}} + (P_3)_{\text{I}}(P_{1 \text{ or less}})_{\text{II}}$$

$$(P_a)_{\text{II}} = (0.251)(0.677) + (0.126)(0.406)$$

$$(P_a)_{\text{II}} = 0.221$$

$$(P_a)_{\text{combined}} = (P_a)_{\text{I}} + (P_a)_{\text{II}}$$

$$(P_a)_{\text{combined}} = 0.558 + 0.221$$

$$(P_a)_{\text{combined}} = 0.779$$

These results are illustrated in Figure 6-4. When the two sample sizes are different, the np_0 values are different, which can cause a calculating error. Another source of error is neglecting to use the "or less" probabilities. Cal-

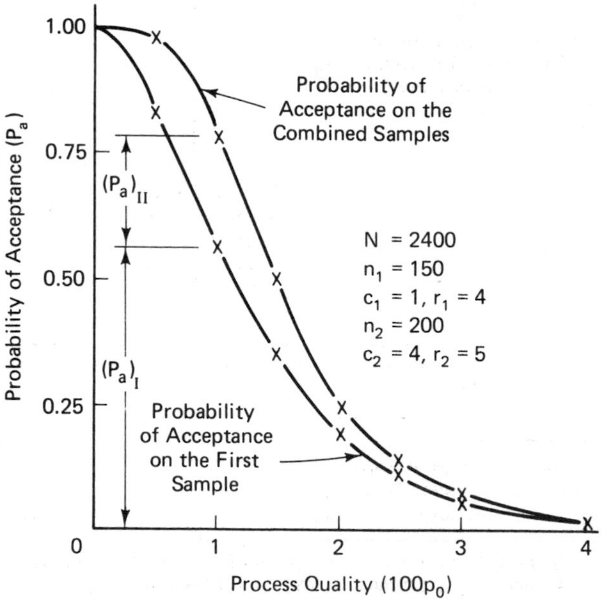

Figure 6-4 OC curve for double sampling plan.

culations are usually to three decimal places. The remaining calculations for other points on the curve are:

For $p_0 = 0.005$ ($100p_0 = 0.5\%$),

$$(np_0)_{\text{I}} = (150)(0.005) = 0.75 \qquad (np_0)_{\text{II}} = (200)(0.005) = 1.00$$

$$(P_a)_{\text{I}} = 0.826$$

$$(P_a)_{\text{II}} = (0.133)(0.920) + (0.034)(0.736) = 0.147$$

For $p_0 = 0.015$ ($100p_0 = 1.5\%$),

$$(np_0)_{\text{I}} = (150)(0.015) = 2.25 \qquad (np_0)_{\text{II}} = (200)(0.015) = 3.00$$

$$(P_a)_{\text{I}} = 0.343$$

$$(P_a)_{\text{II}} = (0.266)(0.423) + (0.200)(0.199) = 0.152$$

For $p_0 = 0.020$ ($100p_0 = 2.0\%$),

$$(np_0)_{\text{I}} = (150)(0.020) = 3.00 \qquad (np_0)_{\text{II}} = (200)(0.020) = 4.00$$

$$(P_a)_{\text{I}} = 0.199$$

$$(P_a)_{\text{II}} = (0.224)(0.238) + (0.224)(0.091) = 0.074$$

For $p_0 = 0.025$ ($100p_0 = 2.5\%$),

$$(np_0)_{\text{I}} = (150)(0.025) = 3.75 \qquad (np_0)_{\text{II}} = (200)(0.025) = 5.00$$

$$(P_a)_{\text{I}} = 0.112$$

$$(P_a)_{\text{II}} = (0.165)(0.125) + (0.207)(0.041) = 0.029$$

For $p_0 = 0.030$ ($100p_0 = 3.0\%$),

$$(np_0)_{\text{I}} = (150)(0.030) = 4.5 \qquad (np_0)_{\text{II}} = (200)(0.030) = 6.0$$

$$(P_a)_{\text{I}} = 0.061$$

$$(P_a)_{\text{II}} = (0.013)(0.062) + (0.169)(0.017) = 0.010$$

For $p_0 = 0.040$ ($100p_0 = 4.0\%$),

$$(np_0)_{\text{I}} = (150)(0.040) = 6.0 \qquad (np_0)_{\text{II}} = (200)(0.040) = 8.0$$

$$(P_a)_{\text{I}} = 0.017$$

$$(P_a)_{\text{II}} = (0.045)(0.014) + (0.089)(0.003) = 0.001$$

Similar to the construction of the OC curve for single sampling, points are plotted as they are calculated, with the last few calculations used for locations where the curve changes direction. Whenever possible, both sample sizes should be the same value to simplify the calculations and the inspector's job. Also, if r_1 and r_2 are not given, they are equal to $c_2 + 1$.

OC Curve for Multiple Sampling Plans

The construction of an operating characteristic (OC) curve for multiple sampling plans is more involved than double or single sampling plans; however, the technique is the same. A multiple sampling plan with four samples is illustrated in Figure 6-5 and is specified as:

$$N = 3000$$

$$n_1 = 30 \quad c_1 = 0 \quad r_1 = 4$$

$$n_2 = 30 \quad c_2 = 2 \quad r_2 = 5$$

$$n_3 = 30 \quad c_3 = 3 \quad r_3 = 5$$

$$n_4 = 30 \quad c_4 = 4 \quad r_4 = 5$$

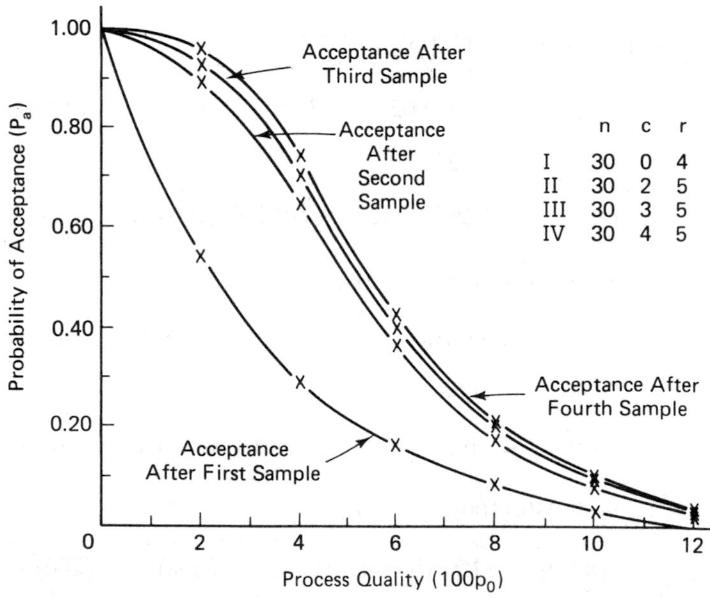

Figure 6-5 OC curve for multiple sampling plan.

Equations for this multiple sampling plan are:

$$(P_a)_{\text{I}} = (P_0)_{\text{I}}$$

$$(P_a)_{\text{II}} = (P_1)_{\text{I}}(P_{1 \text{ or less}})_{\text{II}} + (P_2)_{\text{I}}(P_0)_{\text{II}}$$

$$(P_a)_{\text{III}} = (P_1)_{\text{I}}(P_2)_{\text{II}}(P_0)_{\text{III}} + (P_2)_{\text{I}}(P_1)_{\text{II}}(P_0)_{\text{III}} + (P_3)_{\text{I}}(P_0)_{\text{II}}(P_0)_{\text{III}}$$

$$\begin{aligned}(P_a)_{\text{IV}} = {} & (P_1)_{\text{I}}(P_2)_{\text{II}}(P_1)_{\text{III}}(P_0)_{\text{IV}} + (P_1)_{\text{I}}(P_3)_{\text{II}}(P_0)_{\text{III}}(P_0)_{\text{IV}} \\ & + (P_2)_{\text{I}}(P_1)_{\text{II}}(P_1)_{\text{III}}(P_0)_{\text{IV}} + (P_2)_{\text{I}}(P_2)_{\text{II}}(P_0)_{\text{III}}(P_0)_{\text{IV}} \\ & + (P_3)_{\text{I}}(P_0)_{\text{II}}(P_1)_{\text{III}}(P_0)_{\text{IV}} + (P_3)_{\text{I}}(P_1)_{\text{II}}(P_0)_{\text{III}}(P_0)_{\text{IV}}\end{aligned}$$

Using the equations above and varying the fraction defective p_0, the OC curve of Figure 6-5 is constructed. This is a tedious task and one that is ideally suited for the computer.

Comment

An operating characteristic curve evaluates the effectiveness of a particular sampling plan. If that sampling plan is not satisfactory, as shown by the OC curve, another one should be selected and its OC curve constructed.

Since the process quality or lot quality is usually not known, the OC curve (as well as other curves in this chapter) are "what if" curves. In other words, if the quality is a particular percent defective, its probability of acceptance can be obtained from the curve.

Difference Between Type A and Type B OC Curves

The OC curves that were constructed in the previous sections are type B curves. It was assumed that the lots came from a continuous stream of product, and therefore the calculations are based on an infinite lot size. The binomial is the exact distribution for calculating the acceptance probabilities; however, the Poisson was used, since it is a good approximation. Type B curves are continuous.

Type A OC curves give the probability of accepting an isolated finite lot. With a finite situation the hypergeometric is used to calculate the acceptance probabilities. As the lot size of a type A curve increases, it approaches the type B curve and will become almost identical when the lot size is at least 10 times the sample size ($n/N \leqq 0.10$). A type A curve is shown in Figure 6-6, with the small circles representing the discrete data and a discontinuous curve. The curve is drawn as a continuous one by joining the small circles with lines. Thus, a 4% value is impossible, since it represents 2.6 defective in the lot of 65 [(0.04)(65) = 2.6], but 4.6% defective is possible, as it represents 3 defective in the lot of 65 [(0.046)(65) = 3.0]. Therefore, the "curve" only exists where the small circles are located.

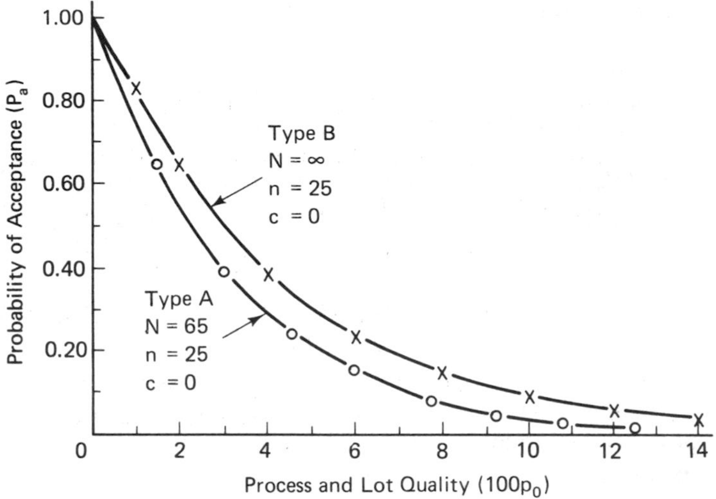

Figure 6-6 Types A and B OC curves.

In comparing the type A and type B curves of Figure 6-6, the type A curve is always lower than the type B curve. When the lot size is small in relation to the sample size, the difference between the curves is significant enough to warrant the extra effort needed to construct the type A curve.

Unless otherwise stated, all discussion of OC curves will be in terms of type B curves.

OC Curve Properties

Acceptance sampling plans with similar properties can give different OC curves. Four of these properties and the OC curve information are given in the information that follows.

1. *Sample size as a fixed percentage of lot size.* Prior to the use of statistical concepts for acceptance sampling, inspectors were usually instructed to sample a fixed percentage of the lot. If this value is, say, 10% of the lot size, plans for lot sizes of 900, 300, and 90 are:

$$N = 900 \qquad n = 90 \qquad c = 0$$

$$N = 300 \qquad n = 30 \qquad c = 0$$

$$N = 90 \qquad n = 9 \qquad c = 0$$

Figure 6-7 shows the OC curves for the three plans, and it is evident that they offer different levels of protection. For example, lots from a process that is 5%

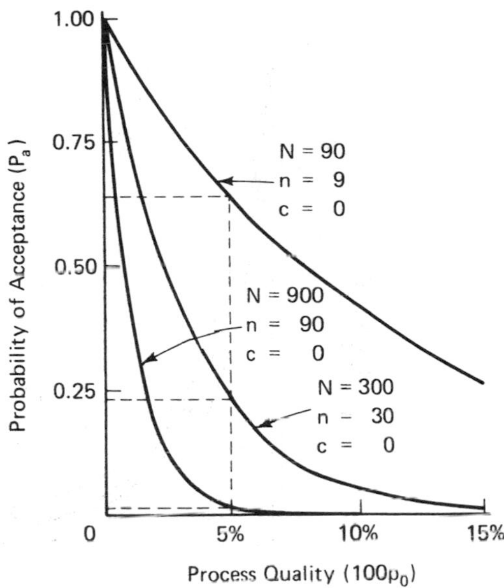

Figure 6-7 OC curves for sample sizes that are 10% of the lot size.

defective will be accepted 2% of the time for lot sizes of 900, 22% of the time for lot sizes of 300, and 63% of the time for lot sizes of 90.

2. *Fixed sample size.* When a fixed or constant sample size is used, the OC curves are very similar. Figure 6-8 illustrates this property for the type A situation were $n \geqq 10\%$ of N. Naturally, for type B curves or when $n < 10\%$ of N, the curves are identical. The sample size has more to do with the shape of the OC curve and the resulting quality protection than does the lot size.

3. *As sample size increases, the curve becomes steeper.* Figure 6-9 illustrates the change in the shape of the OC curve. As the sample size increases, the slope of the curve becomes steeper and approaches a straight vertical line. Sampling plans with large sample sizes are better able to discriminate between acceptable and unacceptable quality. Therefore, the consumer has fewer lots of bad quality accepted and the producer fewer lots of good quality rejected.

4. *As the acceptance number decreases, the curve becomes steeper.* The change in the shape of the OC curve as the acceptance number changes is shown in Figure 6-10. As the acceptance number decreases, the curve becomes steeper. This fact has frequently been used to justify the use of sampling plans with acceptance numbers of zero. However, the OC curve for $N = 2000$, $n = 300$, and $c = 2$, which is shown by the dashed line, is steeper than the plan with $c = 0$. A disadvantage of sampling plans with $c = 0$ is the fact that their curves drop sharply down rather than have a horizontal plateau before descending.

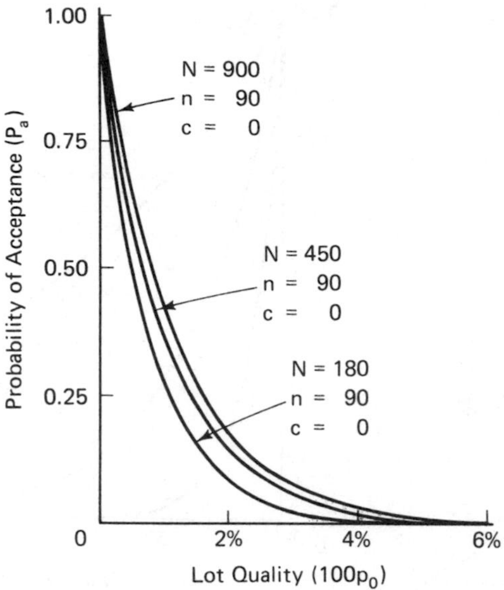

Figure 6-8 OC curves for constant sample size (type A).

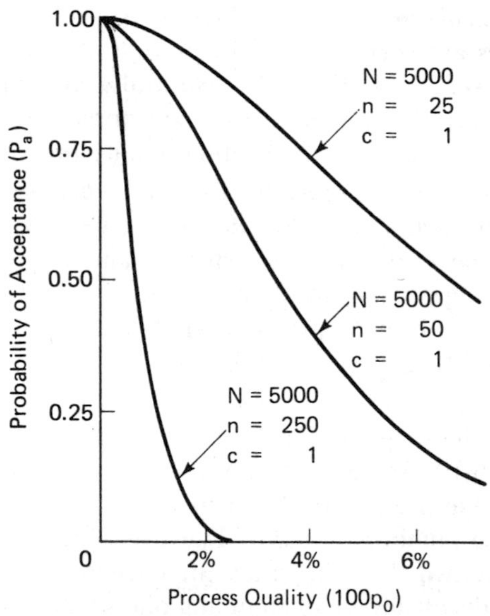

Figure 6-9 OC curves illustrating change in sample size.

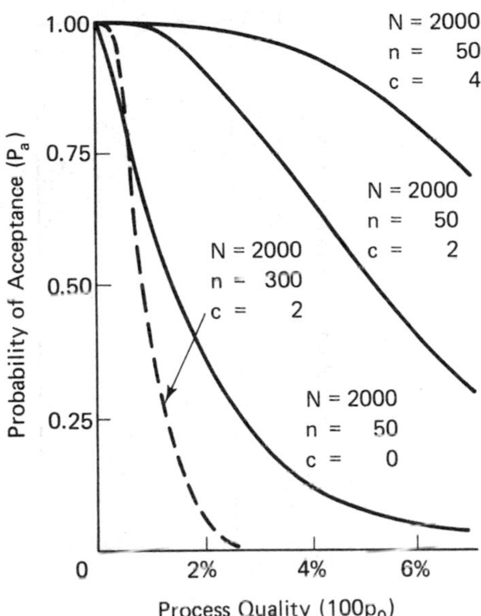

Figure 6-10 OC curves illustrating change in acceptance number.

Since this is the area of the producer's risk (discussed in the next section) sampling plans with $c = 0$ are more demanding of the producer. Sampling plans with acceptance numbers greater than zero can actually be superior to those with zero; however, these require a larger sample size which is more costly. In addition, many producers have a psychological aversion to plans that reject lots when only one defective is found in the sample. The primary advantage of sampling plans with $c = 0$ is the perception that defective product will not be tolerated.

Consumer-Producer Relationship

When acceptance sampling is used, there is a conflicting interest between the consumer and the producer. The producer wants all good lots accepted and the consumer wants all defective lots rejected. Only an ideal sampling plan which has an OC curve that is a vertical line can satisfy both the producer and consumer. An "ideal" OC curve, as shown in Figure 6-11, can only be achieved with 100% inspection, and the pitfalls of this type of inspection were mentioned earlier in the chapter. Therefore, sampling carries risks of rejecting good lots and of accepting defective lots. Because of the seriousness of these risks, various terms and concepts have been standardized.

The *producer's risk*, which is represented by the symbol α, is the probability of rejection of a good or acceptable lot. This risk is frequently given as 0.05, but it can range from 0.01 to 0.10. Since α is expressed in terms of the probability

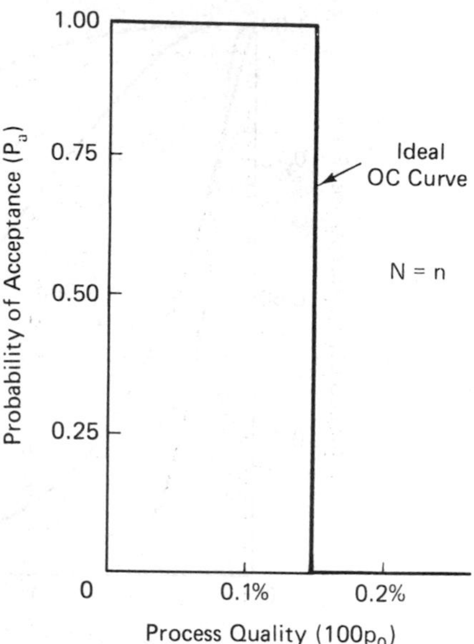

Figure 6-11 Ideal OC curve.

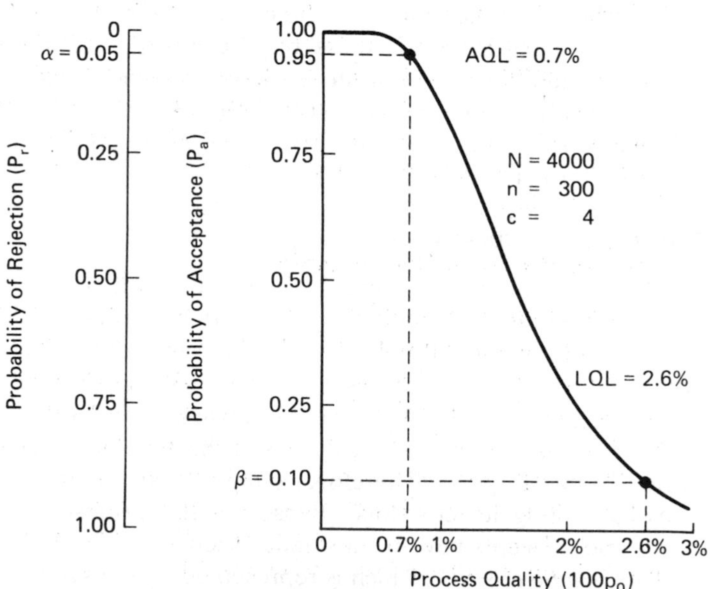

Figure 6-12 Consumer–producer relationship.

of rejection, it cannot be located on an OC curve unless specified in terms of the probability of acceptance. This conversion is accomplished by substracting from 1. Thus, $P_a = 1 - \alpha$, and for $\alpha = 0.05$, $P_a = 1 - 0.05 = 0.95$. Figure 6-12 shows the producer's risk, α, of 0.05 on an imaginary axis labeled probability of rejection.

Associated with the producer's risk is a numerical definition of a good lot which is called *acceptable quality level* (AQL). The AQL is the maximum percent defective that can be considered satisfactory for the purposes of acceptance sampling. It is a reference point on the OC curve and is not meant to convey to the producer that any percent defective is acceptable. The only way the producer can be guaranteed that a lot will be accepted is to have 0% defective or to have the number defective in the lot less than the acceptance number. In other words, the producer's quality goal is to meet or exceed the specifications or requirements so that no defectives are present in the lot.

For the sampling plan $N = 4000$, $n = 300$, and $c = 4$, the AQL = 0.7% for $\alpha = 0.05$, as shown in Figure 6-12. In other words, product that is 0.7% defective will have a rejection probability of 0.05, or 5%. Or, stated another way, 1 out of 20 lots that are 0.7% defective will be rejected by the sampling plan.

The *consumer's risk*, represented by the symbol β, is the probability of acceptance of a defective or unacceptable lot. This risk is frequently given as 0.10. Since β is expressed in terms of probability of acceptance, no conversion is necessary.

Associated with the consumer's risk is a numerical definition of a defective lot, called *limiting quality level* (LQL). The LQL is the percent defective in a lot or batch which, for acceptance sampling purposes, the consumer wishes the probability of acceptance to be low. For the sampling plan in Figure 6-12, the LQL = 2.6% for $\beta = 0.10$. In other words, lots that are 2.6% defective will have an acceptance probability of 0.10, or 10%. Or, stated another way, 1 out of 10 lots that are 2.6% defective will be accepted by the sampling plan.

Average Outgoing Quality

The *average outgoing quality* (AOQ) is another technique for the evaluation of a sampling plan. Figure 6-13 shows an AOQ curve for the sampling plan $N = 3000$, $n = 89$, and $c = 2$. This is the same plan as the one for the OC curve shown in Figure 6-2.

The information for the construction of an average outgoing quality curve is obtained by adding one column (an AOQ column) to the table used to construct an OC curve. Table 6-3 shows the information for the OC curve and the additional column for the AOQ curve. The average outgoing quality in percent defective is determined by the formula $AOQ = 100\, p_0 \cdot P_a$. This formula does not account for the discarded defectives; however, it is close enough for practical purposes and is much simpler to use.

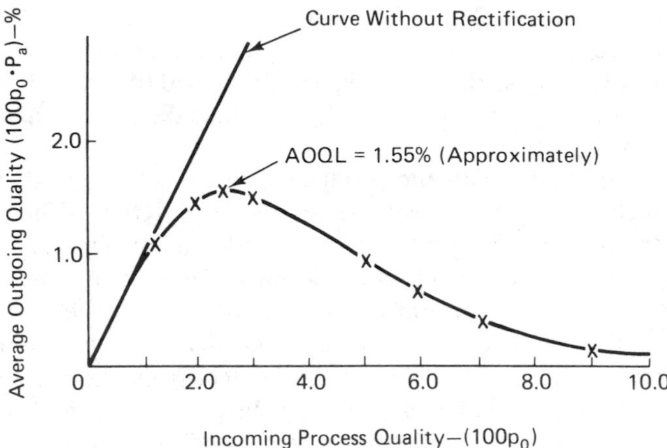

Figure 6-13 Average outgoing quality curve for the sampling plan $N = 3000$, $n = 89$, and $c = 2$.

TABLE 6-3 Average Outgoing Quality (AOQ) for the Sampling Plan $N = 3000$, $n = 89$, and $c = 2$

Process Quality $100\,p_0$	*Sample Size,* n	np_0	*Probability of Acceptance,* P_a	*AOQ,* $100p_0 \cdot P_a$
1.0	89	0.9	0.938	0.938
2.0	89	1.8	0.731	1.462
3.0	89	2.7	0.494	1.482
5.0	89	4.5	0.174	0.870
6.0	89	5.3	0.106	0.636
7.0	89	6.2	0.055	0.385
9.0	89	8.0	0.014	0.126
2.5[a]	89	2.2	0.623	1.558

[a]Additional point where curve changes direction.

Note that to present a more readable graph, the AOQ scale is much larger than the incoming process quality scale. The curve is constructed by plotting the incoming process quality ($100p_0$) with its corresponding AOQ value.

The average outgoing quality is the quality that leaves the inspection operation. It is assumed that any rejected lots have been rectified or sorted and returned with 100% good product. When rectification does not occur, the AOQ is the same as the incoming quality, and this condition is represented by the straight line in Figure 6-13.

Analysis of the curve shows that when the incoming quality is 2.0% defective, the average outgoing quality is 1.46% defective, and when the incoming quality is 6.0% defective, the average outgoing quality is 0.64% defective. Therefore, because rejected lots are rectified, the average outgoing quality is always better than the incoming quality. In fact, there is a limit which is given the name average outgoing quality limit (AOQL). Thus, for this sampling plan, as the percent defective of the incoming quality changes, the average outgoing quality never exceeds the limit of approximately 1.55% defective.

A better understanding of the concept of acceptance sampling can be obtained from an example. Suppose that over a period of time 15 lots of 3000 each are shipped by the producer to the consumer. The lots are 2% defective and a sampling plan of $n = 89$ and $c = 2$ is used to determine acceptance. Figure 6-14 shows this information by a solid line. The OC curve for this sampling plan (Figure 6-2) shows that the probability of acceptance for a 2% defective lot is 0.731. Thus, 11 lots ($15 \times 0.731 = 10.97$) are accepted by the consumer, as indicated by the wavy line. Four lots are rejected by the sampling plan and returned to the producer for rectification, as shown by the dashed line. These four lots receive 100% inspection and are returned to the consumer with 0% defective, as shown by a dashed line.

A summary of what the consumer actually receives is shown at the bottom of the figure. Two percent or 240 of the four rectified lots are discarded by the producer, which gives 11,760 rather than 12,000. The calculations show that the consumer actually receives 1.47% defective, whereas the producer's quality is 2% defective.

It should be emphasized that the acceptance sampling system works only when rejected lots are returned to the producer and rectified. The AQL for this particular sampling plan at $\alpha = 0.05$ is 0.9%; therefore, the producer at 2% defective is not achieving the required quality level.

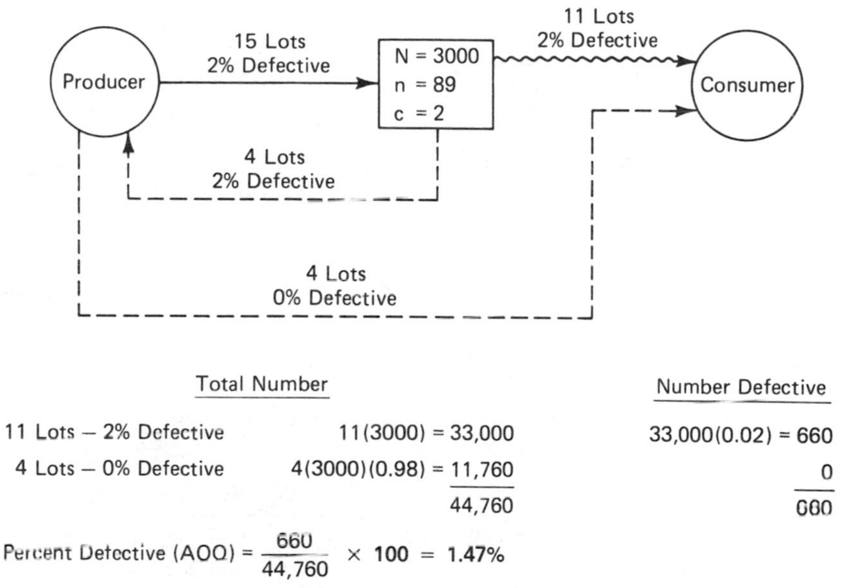

Figure 6-14 How acceptance sampling works.

The AOQ curve, in conjunction with the OC curve, provides two powerful tools for describing and analyzing acceptance sampling plans.

Average Sample Number

The average sample number (ASN) is a comparison of the average amount inspected per lot by the consumer for single, double, and multiple sampling. Figure 6-15 shows the comparison for the three different but equally effective sampling plan types. In single sampling the ASN is constant and equal to the sample size, n. For double sampling the process is somewhat more complicated because a second sample may or may not be taken.

The formula for double sampling is

$$\text{ASN} = n_1 + n_2(1 - P_1)$$

where P_1 is the probability of a decision on the first sample. An example problem will illustrate the concept.

Example Problem

Given the single sampling plan $n = 80$ and $c = 2$ and the equally effective double sampling plan $n_1 = 50$, $c_1 = 0$, $r_1 = 3$, $n_2 = 50$, $c_2 = 3$, and $r_2 = 4$, compare the ASN of the two by constructing their curves.

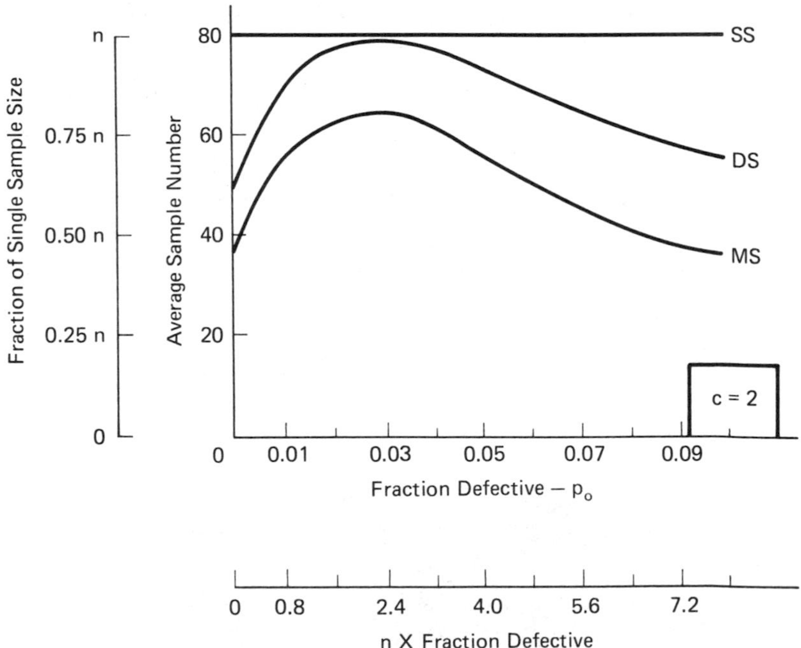

Figure 6-15 ASN curves for single, double, and multiple sampling.

For single sampling the ASN is the straight line at $n = 80$. For double sampling the solution is

$$P_1 = (P_0)_I + (P_3 \text{ or more})_I$$

Assume that $P_0 = 0.01$; then $np_0 = 50(0.01) = 0.5$. From Appendix C:

$$(P_0)_I = 0.607$$

$$(P_3 \text{ or more})_I = 1 - (P_2 \text{ or less})_I = 1 - 0.986 = 0.014$$

$$\begin{aligned} \text{ASN} &= n_1 + n_2[1 - (P_0)_I - (P_3 \text{ or more})_I] \\ &= 50 + 50[1 - (0.607) - (0.014)] \\ &= 69 \end{aligned}$$

Repeating for different values of P_0, the double sampling plan is plotted as shown in Figure 6-15.

The formula assumes that inspection continues even after the rejection number is reached. It is frequently the practice to discontinue inspection after the rejection number is reached on either the first or second sample. This practice is called curtailed inspection and the formula is much more complicated. Thus, the ASN curve for double sampling is somewhat lower than what actually occurs.

An analysis of the ASN curve for double sampling in Figure 6-15 shows that at a fraction defective of 0.03, the single and double sampling plans have about the same amount of inspection. For fraction defectives less than 0.03, double sampling has less inspection because a decision to accept on the first sample is more likely. Similarly, for fraction defectives greater than 0.03, double sampling has less inspection because a decision to reject on the first sample is more likely and a second sample is not required. It should be noted that in most ASN curves the double sample curve does not get close to the single sample one.

Calculation of the ASN curve for multiple sampling is much more involved than double sampling. The formula is

$$\text{ASN} = n_1P_1 + (n_1 + n_2)P_2 + \cdots + (n_1 + n_2 + \cdots + n_k)P_k$$

where n_k is the sample size of the last level and P_k the probability of a decision at the last level.

Determining the probabilities of a decision at each level is quite involved—more so than for the OC curve since the probability of rejection must also be determined.

Figure 6-15 shows the ASN curve for an equivalent multiple sampling plan with seven levels. As expected, the average amount inspected is much less than single or double sampling.

The reader may have been curious concerning the two extra scales in Figure 6-15. Since we are comparing equivalent sampling plans, the double and multiple plans can be related to the single sampling plans where $c = 2$ and n is the equivalent single sample size by the additional scales. To use the horizontal scale, multiply the single sample size n by the fraction defective. The ASN value is found from the vertical scale by multiplying the scale fraction with the single sample size.

Figure 6-16, which is taken from MIL-STD-105D (to be discussed), shows a number of ASN curve comparisons indexed by the acceptance number, c. These curves assume no curtailment of inspection and are approximate to the extent that they are based on the Poisson distribution, and that the sample sizes for double and multiple sampling are assumed to be $0.631n$ and $0.25n$, respectively. Therefore, these curves can be used to find the amount inspected per lot for different process quality levels without having to make the calculations. The arrow indicates the location of the AQL.

When inspection costs are great due to inspection time, equipment costs, or equipment availability, the ASN curves are a valuable tool for justifying double or multiple sampling.

Average Total Inspection

The average total inspection (ATI) is another technique for evaluating a sampling plan. ATI is the amount inspected by both the consumer and the producer. Like the ASN curve, it is a curve that provides information on the amount inspected and not on the effectiveness. For single sampling the formula is

$$\text{ATI} = n + (1 - P_a)(N - n)$$

It assumes that rectified lots will receive 100% inspection. If lots are submitted with 0 defective, the amount inspected is equal to n, and if lots are submitted that are 100% defective, the amount inspected is equal to N. Since neither of these possibilities is likely to occur,then the amount inspected is a function of the probability of rejection $(1 - P_a)$. An example problem will illustrate the calculation.

Example Problem

Determine the ATI curve for the single sampling plan $N = 3000$, $n = 89$, and $c = 2$.

Assume that $p_0 = 0.02$. From the OC curve (Figure 6-2), $P_a = 0.731$.

$$\begin{aligned}\text{ATI} &= n + (1 - P_a)(N - n)\\ &= 89 + (1 - 0.731)(3000 - 89)\\ &= 872\end{aligned}$$

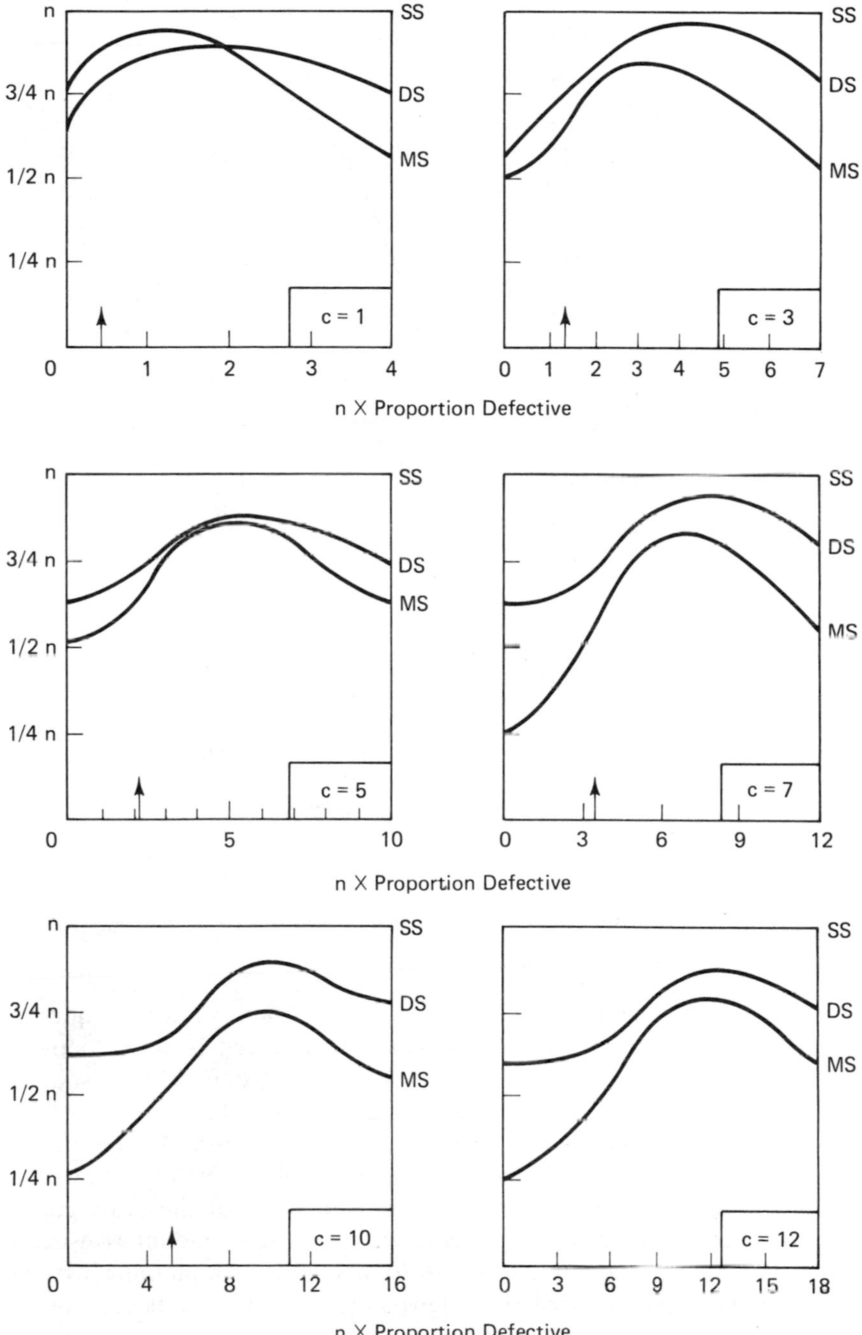

Figure 6-16 Typical ASN curves from MIL-STD-105D.

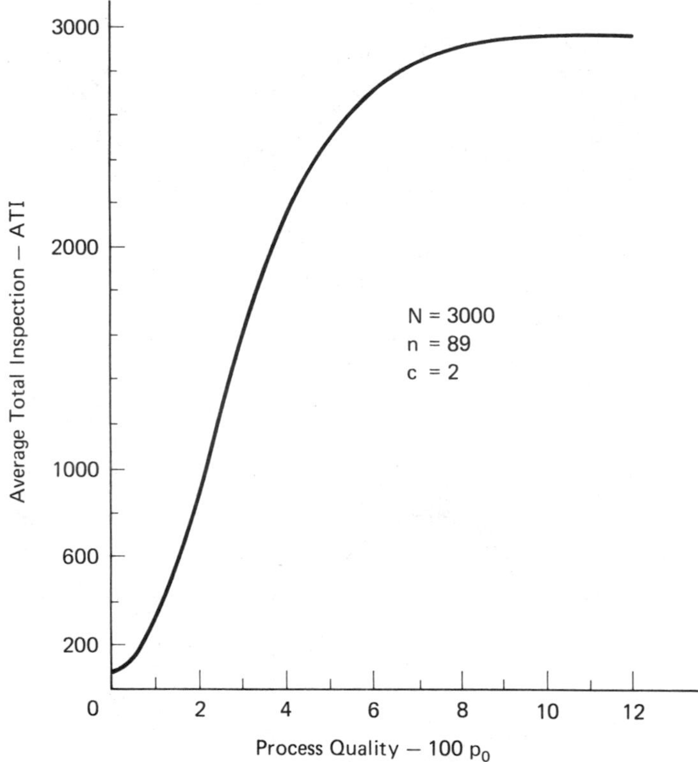

Figure 6-17 ATI curve for $N = 3000$, $n = 89$, $c = 2$.

Repeat for other p_0 values until a smooth curve is obtained, as shown in Figure 6-17.

Examination of the curve shows that when the process quality is close to 0% defective, the average total amount inspected is close to the sample size n. When process quality is very poor, at say 9% defective, most all lots are rejected and the ATI curve becomes asymptotic to 3000.

Double sampling and multiple sampling formulas for the ATI curves are more complicated. These ATI curves will be slightly below the one for single sampling. The amount below is a function of the ASN curve, which is the amount inspected by the consumer, and this amount is usually very small in relation to the ATI, which is dominated by the amount inspected by the producer. From a practical viewpoint, the ATI curves for double and multiple sampling are not necessary.

SAMPLING PLAN DESIGN

Sampling Plans for Stipulated Producer's Risk

When the producer's risk α and its corresponding acceptable quality level (AQL) are specified, a sampling plan or, more precisely, a family of sampling plans, can be determined. For a producer's risk, α, of say 0.05 and an AQL of 1.2%, the OC curves for a family of sampling plans as shown in Figure 6-18 are obtained. Each of the plans passes through the point defined by $P_a = 0.95$ ($\alpha = 0.05$) and $p_{0.95} = 0.012$. Therefore, each of the plans will ensure that product 1.2% defective will be rejected 5% of the time or, conversely, accepted 95% of the time.

The sampling plans are obtained by assuming a value for c and finding its corresponding np_0 value from Table C. Then knowing np_0 and p_0, the sample size n is obtained. In order to find the np_0 values using Table C, interpolation is required. To eliminate the interpolation operation, np_0 values for $\alpha = 0.05$ and $\beta = 0.10$ are reproduced in Table 6-4. In this table, c is cumulative, which means that a c value of 2 represents 2 or less.

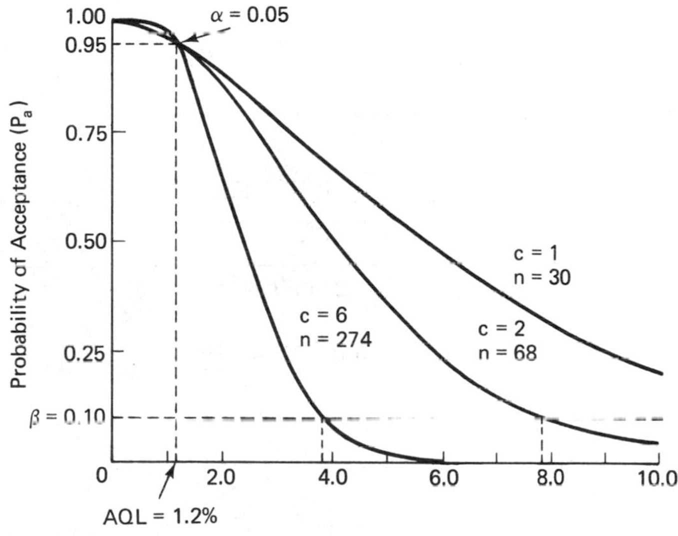

Figure 6-18 Single sampling plans for stipulated producer's risk and AQL.

TABLE 6-4 ***np* Values for Corresponding *c* Values and Typical Producer's and Consumer's Risks**

c	$P_a = 0.95$ ($\alpha = 0.05$)	$P_a = 0.10$ ($\beta = 0.10$)	Ratio of $p_{0.10}/p_{0.95}$
0	0.051	2.303	44.890
1	0.355	3.890	10.946
2	0.818	5.322	6.509
3	1.366	6.681	4.890
4	1.970	7.994	4.057
5	2.613	9.275	3.549
6	3.286	10.532	3.206
7	3.981	11.771	2.957
8	4.695	12.995	2.768
9	5.426	14.206	2.618
10	6.169	15.407	2.497
11	6.924	16.598	2.397
12	7.690	17.782	2.312
13	8.464	18.958	2.240
14	9.246	20.128	2.177
15	10.035	21.292	2.122

Source: Extracted by permission from J. M. Cameron, "Tables for Constructing and for Computing the Operating Characteristics of Single-Sampling Plans," *Industry Quality Control*, 9, No. 1 (July 1952), 39.

Calculations to obtain the three sampling plans of Figure 6-18 are as follows:

$$P_a = 0.95 \qquad p_{0.95} = 0.012$$

For $c = 1$, $np_{0.95} = 0.355$ (from Table 6-4) and

$$n = \frac{np_{0.95}}{p_{0.95}} = \frac{0.355}{0.012} = 29.6 \quad \text{or} \quad 30$$

For $c = 2$, $np_{0.95} = 0.818$ (from Table 6-4) and

$$n = \frac{np_{0.95}}{p_{0.95}} = \frac{0.818}{0.012} = 68.2 \quad \text{or} \quad 68$$

For $c = 6$, $np_{0.95} = 3.286$ (from Table 6-4) and

$$n = \frac{np_{0.95}}{p_{0.95}} = \frac{3.286}{0.012} = 273.9 \quad \text{or} \quad 274$$

The sampling plans for $c = 1$, $c = 2$, and $c = 6$ were arbitrarily selected to illustrate the technique.

While all the plans provide the same protection for the producer, the consumer's risk, at say $\beta = 0.10$, is quite different. From Figure 6-18 for the plan $c = 1$, $n = 30$, product that is 13% defective will be accepted 10% ($\beta = 0.10$) of the time; for the plan $c = 2$, $n = 68$, the product that is 7.8% defective will be accepted 10% ($\beta = 0.10$) of the time; and for the plan $c = 6$, $n = 274$, product that is 3.8% defective will be accepted 10% ($\beta = 0.10$) of the time. From the consumer's viewpoint the latter plan provides better protection; however, the sample size is greater, which increases the inspection cost. The selection of the appropriate plan to use is a matter of judgment which usually involves the lot size.

Sampling Plans for Stipulated Consumer's Risk

When the consumer's risk β and its corresponding limiting quality level (LQL) are specified, a family of sampling plans can be determined. For a consumer's risk, β, of say 0.10 and a LQL of 6.0%, the OC curves for a family of sampling plans as shown in Figure 6-19 are obtained. Each of the plans pass through the point defined by $P_a = 0.10$ ($\beta = 0.10$) and $p_{0.10} = 0.060$. Therefore, each of the plans will ensure that product 6.0% defective (unacceptable product) will be accepted 10% of the time.

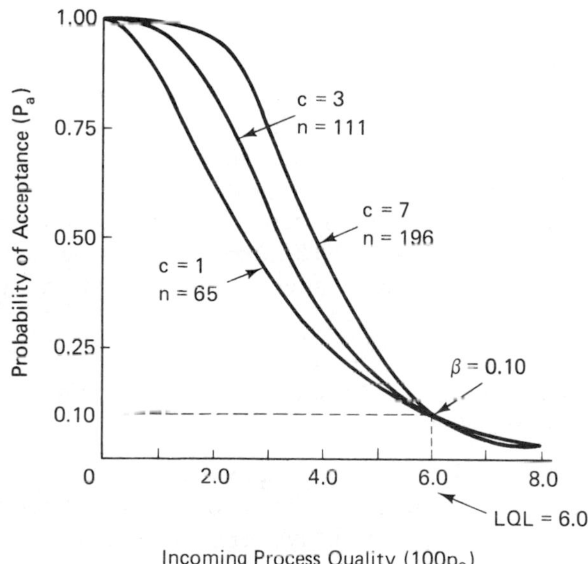

Figure 6-19 Single sampling plans for stipulated consumer's risk and LQL.

The sampling plans are determined in the same manner as used for a stipulated producer's risk. Calculations are as follows:

$$P_a = 0.10 \qquad p_{0.10} = 0.060$$

For $c = 1$, $np_{0.10} = 3.890$ (from Table 6-4) and

$$n = \frac{np_{0.10}}{p_{0.10}} = \frac{3.890}{0.060} = 64.8 \quad \text{or} \quad 65$$

For $c = 3$, $np_{0.10} = 6.681$ (from Table 6-4) and

$$n = \frac{np_{0.10}}{p_{0.10}} = \frac{6.681}{0.060} = 111.4 \quad \text{or} \quad 111$$

For $c = 7$, $np_{0.10} = 11.771$ (from Table 6-4) and

$$n = \frac{np_{0.10}}{p_{0.10}} = \frac{11.771}{0.060} = 196.2 \quad \text{or} \quad 196$$

The sampling plans for $c = 1$, $c = 3$, and $c = 7$ were arbitrarily selected to illustrate the technique.

While all the plans provide the same protection for the consumer, the producer's risk, at say $\alpha = 0.05$, is quite different. From Figure 6-19 for the plan $c = 1$, $n = 65$, product that is 0.5% defective will be rejected 5% ($\alpha = 0.05$) of the time; for the plan $c = 3$, $n = 111$, product that is 1.2% defective will be rejected 5% ($\alpha = 0.05$) of the time; and for the plan $c = 7$, $n = 196$, product that is 2.0% defect will be rejected 5% ($\alpha = 0.05$) of the time. From the producer's viewpoint the latter plan provides better protection; however, the sample size is greater, which increases the inspection costs. The selection of the appropriate plan is a matter of judgment, which usually involves the lot size.

Sampling Plans for Stipulated Producer's and Consumer's Risk

Sampling plans are also stipulated for both the consumer's risk and the producer's risk. It is difficult to obtain an OC curve that will satisfy both conditions. More than likely there will be four sampling plans that are close to meeting the consumer's and producer's stipulations. Figure 6-20 shows four plans that are close to meeting the stipulations of $\alpha = 0.05$, AQL $= 0.9$ and $\beta = 0.10$, LQL $= 7.8$. The OC curves of two plans meet the consumer's stipulation that product which is 7.8% defective (LQL) will be accepted 10% ($\beta =$

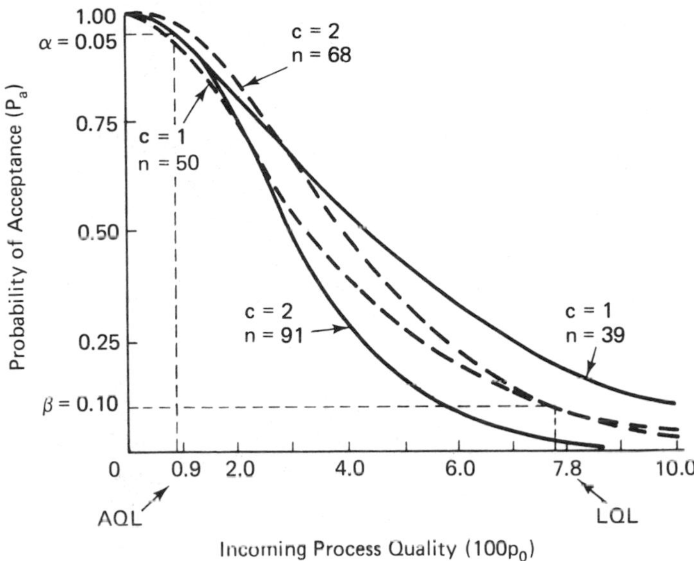

Figure 6-20 Sampling plans for stipulated producer's and consumer's risk.

0.10) of the time and comes close to the producer's stipulation. These two plans are shown by the dashed lines in Figure 6-20 and are $c = 1$, $n = 50$, and $c = 2$, $n = 68$. The two other plans exactly meet the producer's stipulation that product which is 0.9% defective (AQL) will be rejected 5% ($\alpha = 0.05$) of the time. These two plans are shown by the solid lines and are $c = 1$, $n = 39$, and $c = 2$, $n = 91$.

In order to determine the plans, the first step is to find the ratio of $p_{0.10}/p_{0.95}$, which is

$$\frac{p_{0.10}}{p_{0.95}} = \frac{0.078}{0.009} = 8.667$$

From the ratio column of Table 6-4, the ratio of 8.667 falls between the row for $c = 1$ and the row for $c = 2$. Thus, plans that exactly meet the consumer's stipulation of LQL = 7.8% for $\beta = 0.10$ are:

For $c = 1$,

$$p_{0.10} = 0.078$$

$$np_{0.10} = 3.890 \text{ (from Table 6-4)}$$

$$n = \frac{np_{0.10}}{p_{0.10}} = \frac{3.890}{0.078} = 49.9 \quad \text{or} \quad 50$$

For $c = 2$,

$$p_{0.10} = 0.078$$

$$np_{0.10} = 5.322 \text{ (from Table 6-4)}$$

$$n = \frac{np_{0.10}}{p_{0.10}} = \frac{5.322}{0.078} = 68.2 \quad \text{or} \quad 68$$

Plans that exactly meet the producer's stipulation of AQL = 0.9% for $\alpha = 0.05$ are:

For $c = 1$,

$$p_{0.95} = 0.009$$

$$np_{0.95} = 0.355 \text{ (from Table 6-4)}$$

$$n = \frac{np_{0.95}}{p_{0.95}} = \frac{0.355}{0.009} = 39.4 \quad \text{or} \quad 39$$

For $c = 2$,

$$p_{0.95} = 0.009$$

$$np_{0.95} = 0.818 \text{ (from Table 6-4)}$$

$$n = \frac{np_{0.95}}{p_{0.95}} = \frac{0.818}{0.009} = 90.8 \quad \text{or} \quad 91$$

Which of the four plans to select is based on one of four additional criteria. The first additional criterion is the stipulation that the plan with the lowest sample size be selected. The plan with the lowest sample size is one of the two with the lowest acceptance number. Thus, for the example problem, only the two plans for $c = 1$ are calculated, and $c = 1$, $n = 39$ is the sampling plan selected. A second additional criterion is the stipulation that the plan with the greatest sample size be selected. The plan with the greatest sample size is one of two with the largest acceptance number. Thus, for the example problem, only the two plans for $c = 2$ are calculated; and $c = 2$, $n = 91$ is the sampling plan selected.

A third additional criterion is the stipulation that the plan exactly meet the consumer's stipulation and come as close as possible to the producer's stipulation. The two plans that exactly meet the consumer's stipulation are $c = 1$, $n = 50$ and $c = 2$, $n = 68$. Calculations to determine which plan is closest to the producer's stipulation of AQL = 0.9%, $\alpha = 0.05$, are

For $c = 1, n = 50$,

$$p_{0.95} = \frac{np_{0.95}}{n} = \frac{0.355}{50} = 0.007$$

For $c = 2, n = 68$,

$$p_{0.95} = \frac{np_{0.95}}{n} = \frac{0.818}{68} = 0.012$$

Since $p_{0.95} = 0.007$ is closest to the stipulated value of 0.009, the plan of $c = 1, n = 50$ is selected.

The fourth additional criterion for the selection of one of the four sampling plans is the stipulation that the plan exactly meet the producer's stipulation and comes as close as possible to the consumer's stipulation. The two plans that are applicable are $c = 1, n = 39$ and $c = 2, n = 91$. Calculations to determine which is the closest to the consumer's stipulation of LQL = 7.8%, $\beta = 0.10$ are:

For $c = 1, n = 39$,

$$p_{0.10} = \frac{np_{0.10}}{n} = \frac{3.890}{39} = 0.100$$

For $c = 2, n = 91$,

$$p_{0.10} = \frac{np_{0.10}}{n} = \frac{5.322}{91} = 0.058$$

Since $p_{0.10} = 0.058$ is closest to the stipulated value of 0.078, the plan of $c = 2, n = 91$ is selected.

Some Comments

The previous discussions have concerned single sampling plans. Double and multiple sampling plan design, although more difficult, would follow similar techniques.

In the previous discussion a producer's risk of 0.05 and a consumer's risk of 0.10 were used to illustrate the technique. The producer's risk is usually set at 0.05, but can be as small as 0.01 or as high as 0.15. And the consumer's risk is usually set at 0.10, but can be as low as 0.01 or as high as 0.20.

Sampling plans can also be specified by the average outgoing quality limit

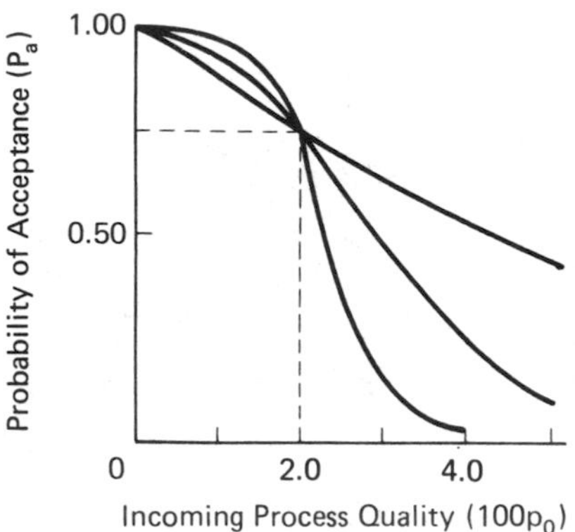

Figure 6-21 AOQL sampling plans.

(AOQL). If an AOQL of 1.5% for an incoming quality of, say, 2.0% is stipulated, the probability of acceptance is

$$\text{AOQL} = 100p_0 \cdot P_a$$

$$1.5 = 2.0P_a$$

$$P_a = 0.75$$

Figure 6-21 shows a family of OC curves for various sampling plans which satisfy the AOQL criteria.

To design a sampling plan, some initial stipulations are necessary by the producer, consumer, or both. These stipulations are decisions based on historical data, experimentation, or engineering judgment. In many cases the stipulations are negotiated as part of the purchasing contract.

The task of designing a sampling plan system is a tedious one. Fortunately, sampling plan systems are available. One such system which is almost universally used for the acceptance of product is MIL-STD-105D. This system is an AQL, or producer's risk system. Another system, Dodge-Romig, uses the LQL or consumer's risk and AOQL methods for determining the sampling plan.

MIL-STD-105D[2]

Introduction

An acceptance sampling plan for lot-by-lot inspection by attributes for use by the government was first devised in 1942 by a group of engineers at Bell Telephone Laboratories. It was designated JAN-STD-105. Since that time,

[2]Copies of MIL-STD-105D may be obtained by directing requests to Commanding Officer, U.S. Naval Supply Depot, Attn. Code DMD, 5801 Tabor Avenue, Philadelphia, PA 19120.

there have been four revisions, the last one occurring in 1963. The last revision was accomplished by a team of American, British, and Canadian personnel and is, therefore, a common standard for the three countries. In 1973, it was adopted by the International Organization for Standardization and designated International Standard ISO/DIS-2859. While MIL-STD-105D was developed for government procurement, it has become the standard for attribute inspection for all industry.

The standard is applicable, but not limited, to attribute inspection of the following: (1) end items, (2) components and raw materials, (3) operations, (4) materials in process, (5) supplies in storage, (6) maintenance operations, (7) data or records, and (8) administrative procedures. Sampling plans of this standard are intended to be used for a continuing series of lots, but plans may be designed for isolated lots by consulting the OC curve to determine the plan with the desired protection.

The standard provides for three types of sampling: single, double, and multiple. For each type of sampling plan, provision is made for normal, tightened, or reduced inspection. Tightened inspection is used when the producer's recent quality history has deteriorated. Acceptance requirements under tightened inspection are more stringent than under normal inspection. Reduced inspection is used when the producer's recent quality history has been exceptionally good. Figure 6-22 illustrates the differences among the OC curves for normal (N), tightened (T), and reduced (R) inspection.

The number inspected under reduced inspection is less than under normal

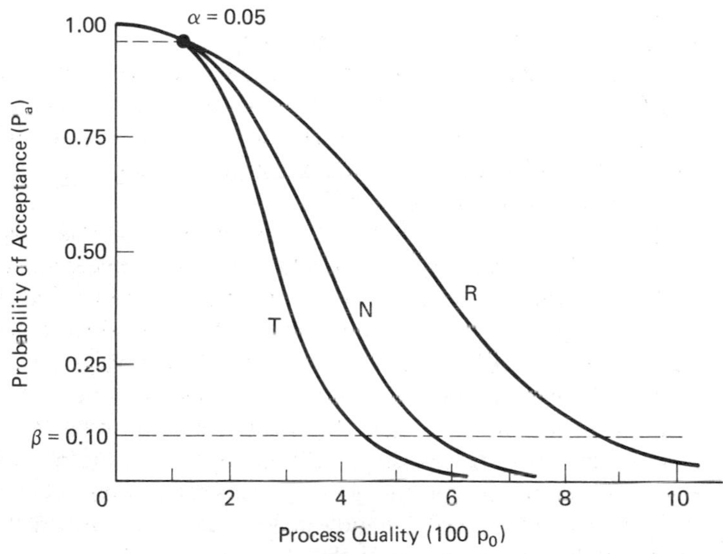

Figure 6-22 Comparison of normal (N), tightened (T), and reduced (R) inspection.

inspection. The decision as to the type of plan to use (single, double, or multiple) is left to the responsible authority (consumer) but should be based on information given earlier in the chapter. Normal inspection is used at the start of inspection with changes to tightened or reduced inspection being a function of the quality.

Defects are classified as critical, major, or minor. These classifications are given in Chapter 5. Defectives are also classified as critical, major, or minor. A critical defective contains one or more critical defects and may contain major or minor defects. A major defective contains one or more major defects and may contain minor defects. A minor defective contains one or more minor defects.

Product is submitted in homogeneous lots with the manner of presentation and identification designated or approved by the responsible authority (consumer). Samples are selected at random without regard to their quality. Rejected lots are resubmitted after all defective units are removed or defects corrected. The responsible authority will determine whether reinspection should include all types or classes of defects or for the particular types or classes of defects that caused initial rejection.

Acceptable Quality Level

The acceptable quality level (AQL) is the most important part of the standard, because the AQL and the sample-size code letter index the sampling plan. AQL is defined as the maximum percent defective (or the maximium number of defects per hundred units) that, for purposes of sampling inspection, can be considered satisfactory as a process average. The phrase "can be considered satisfactory" is interpreted as a producer's risk, α, equal to 0.05; actually, α varies from 0.01 to 0.10 in the standard.

When the standard is used for percent defective plans, the AQLs range from 0.010% to 10.0%. For defect-per-unit plans, there are additional AQLs so AQLs are possible from 0.010 defects per 100 units to 1000 defects per 100 units. The AQLs are in a geometric progression, each being approximately 1.585 times the preceding one.

The AQL is designated in the contract or by the responsible authority. Different AQLs may be designated for groups of defects considered collectively or for individual defects. Critical, major, and minor defects or defectives can have different AQLs, with lower values for critical ones and higher values for minor ones. AQLs are determined from (1) historical data; (2) empirical judgment; (3) engineering information, such as function, safety, interchangeable manufacturing, life testing, etc.; (4) experimentation by testing lots with various percent defective or defects per 100 units, (5) producer's capability, and (6) in some situations the consumer's requirements. AQL determination is a best-judgment decision. The standard helps to determine the AQL since only a finite number are available in the standard.

The AQL is a reference point on the OC curve. It does not imply that any percent defective or defects per 100 units is tolerable.

Sample Size

The sample size is determined by the lot size and the inspection level. The inspection level to be used for a particular requirement will be prescribed by the responsible authority. Three general inspection levels (I, II, and III) are given in Table 6-5. The different levels of inspection provide approximately the same protection to the producer, but different protections to the consumer. Inspection level II is the norm, with level I providing about $\frac{1}{2}$ the amount of inspection and level III providing about twice the amount of inspection. Thus, level III gives a steeper OC curve and consequently more discrimination and increased inspection costs. Figure 6-23 illustrates the differences among the OC curves for inspection levels I, II, and III.

The decision on the inspection level is also a function of the type of product. For inexpensive items, for destructive testing, or for harmful testing, inspection level II should be considered. When subsequent production costs are high or when the items are complex and expensive, inspection level III may be applicable.

Four additional special levels (S-1, S-2, S-3, and S-4) are given in Table 6-5 and may be used where relatively small sample sizes are necessary and large sampling risks can or must be tolerated.

Table 6-5 does not immediately provide the sample size based on the lot size and inspection level, but does give a sample-size code letter. The sample-size code letter and the AQL index the desired sampling plan.

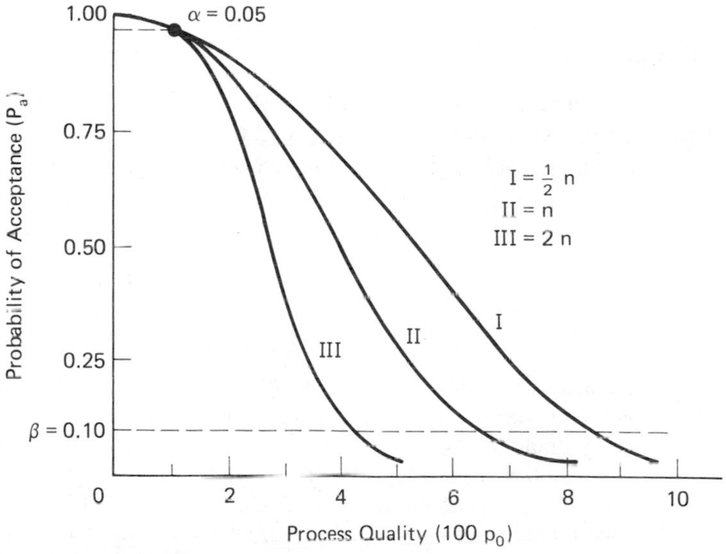

Figure 6-23 Comparison of inspection levels I, II, and III.

TABLE 6-5 Sample-Size code Letters[a] (Table I of MIL-STD-105D)

	Special Inspection Levels				*General Inspection Levels*		
Lot or Batch Size	*S-1*	*S-2*	*S-3*	*S-4*	*I*	*II*	*III*
2–8	A	A	A	A	A	A	B
9–15	A	A	A	A	A	B	C
16–25	A	A	B	B	B	C	D
26–50	A	B	B	C	C	D	E
51–90	B	B	C	C	C	E	F
91–150	B	B	C	D	D	F	G
151–280	B	C	D	E	E	G	H
281–500	B	C	D	E	F	H	J
501–1200	C	C	E	F	G	J	K
1201–3200	C	D	E	G	H	K	L
3201–10,000	C	D	F	G	J	L	M
10,001–35,000	C	D	F	H	K	M	N
35,001–150,000	D	E	G	J	L	N	P
150,001–500,000	D	E	G	J	M	P	Q
500,001 and over	D	E	H	K	N	Q	R

[a]*Note:*

Small sample inspection levels of MIL-STD-105C:	*Convert to these special inspection levels:*
L–1 and L–2	S–1
L–3 and L–6	S–2
L–5 and L–6	S–3
L–7 and L–8	S–4

Single Sampling Plans

The single sampling plans of the standard are given in Tables 6-6, 6-7, and 6-8 for normal, tightened, and reduced inspection, respectively. In order to use the tables, the AQL, lot size, inspection level, and type of sampling plan are needed. An example problem will illustrate the technique.

Example Problem

For a lot size of 2000, an AQL of 0.65%, and an inspection level of III, determine the single sampling plans for normal, tightened, and reduced inspection.

Normal. Using the lot size $N = 2000$ and inspection level III, the sample-size code letter L is obtained from Table 6-5. From Table 6-6 (Single Sampling Plans for Normal Inspection), the desired plan is obtained for code letter L and AQL 0.65%. It is $n = 200$, $Ac = 3$, $Re = 4$. Thus, from a lot of 2000, a random sample of 200 is inspected. If 3 or less defectives are found, the lot is accepted; if 4 or more defectives are found, the lot is rejected.

Tightened. The sample-size code letter, L, is the same as the one for normal

TABLE 6-6 Single Sampling Plans for Normal Inspection (Table II-A of MIL-STD-105D)

Sample size code letter	Sample size	Acceptable Quality Levels (normal inspection)																									
		0.010	0.015	0.025	0.040	0.065	0.10	0.15	0.25	0.40	0.65	1.0	1.5	2.5	4.0	6.5	10	15	25	40	65	100	150	250	400	650	1000
		Ac Re	Ac Re	Ac Re	Ac Re	Ac Re	Ac Re	Ac Re	Ac Re	Ac Re	Ac Re	Ac Re	Ac Re	Ac Re	Ac Re	Ac Re	Ac Re	Ac Re	Ac Re	Ac Re	Ac Re	Ac Re	Ac Re	Ac Re	Ac Re	Ac Re	Ac Re
A	2	↓	↓	↓	↓	↓	↓	↓	↓	↓	↓	↓	↓	↓	↓	0 1	↓	↓	1 2	2 3	3 4	5 6	7 8	10 11	14 15	21 22	30 31
B	3	↓	↓	↓	↓	↓	↓	↓	↓	↓	↓	↓	↓	↓	0 1	↑	↓	1 2	2 3	3 4	5 6	7 8	10 11	14 15	21 22	30 31	44 45
C	5	↓	↓	↓	↓	↓	↓	↓	↓	↓	↓	↓	↓	0 1	↑	↓	1 2	2 3	3 4	5 6	7 8	10 11	14 15	21 22	30 31	44 45	↑
D	8	↓	↓	↓	↓	↓	↓	↓	↓	↓	↓	↓	0 1	↑	↓	1 2	2 3	3 4	5 6	7 8	10 11	14 15	21 22	30 31	44 45	↑	↑
E	13	↓	↓	↓	↓	↓	↓	↓	↓	↓	↓	0 1	↑	↓	1 2	2 3	3 4	5 6	7 8	10 11	14 15	21 22	30 31	44 45	↑	↑	↑
F	20	↓	↓	↓	↓	↓	↓	↓	↓	↓	0 1	↑	↓	1 2	2 3	3 4	5 6	7 8	10 11	14 15	21 22	↑	↑	↑	↑	↑	↑
G	32	↓	↓	↓	↓	↓	↓	↓	↓	0 1	↑	↓	1 2	2 3	3 4	5 6	7 8	10 11	14 15	21 22	↑	↑	↑	↑	↑	↑	↑
H	50	↓	↓	↓	↓	↓	↓	↓	0 1	↑	↓	1 2	2 3	3 4	5 6	7 8	10 11	14 15	21 22	↑	↑	↑	↑	↑	↑	↑	↑
J	80	↓	↓	↓	↓	↓	↓	0 1	↑	↓	1 2	2 3	3 4	5 6	7 8	10 11	14 15	21 22	↑	↑	↑	↑	↑	↑	↑	↑	↑
K	125	↓	↓	↓	↓	↓	0 1	↑	↓	1 2	2 3	3 4	5 6	7 8	10 11	14 15	21 22	↑	↑	↑	↑	↑	↑	↑	↑	↑	↑
L	200	↓	↓	↓	↓	0 1	↑	↓	1 2	2 3	3 4	5 6	7 8	10 11	14 15	21 22	↑	↑	↑	↑	↑	↑	↑	↑	↑	↑	↑
M	315	↓	↓	↓	0 1	↑	↓	1 2	2 3	3 4	5 6	7 8	10 11	14 15	21 22	↑	↑	↑	↑	↑	↑	↑	↑	↑	↑	↑	↑
N	500	↓	↓	0 1	↑	↓	1 2	2 3	3 4	5 6	7 8	10 11	14 15	21 22	↑	↑	↑	↑	↑	↑	↑	↑	↑	↑	↑	↑	↑
P	800	↓	0 1	↑	↓	1 2	2 3	3 4	5 6	7 8	10 11	14 15	21 22	↑	↑	↑	↑	↑	↑	↑	↑	↑	↑	↑	↑	↑	↑
Q	1250	0 1	↑	↓	1 2	2 3	3 4	5 6	7 8	10 11	14 15	21 22	↑	↑	↑	↑	↑	↑	↑	↑	↑	↑	↑	↑	↑	↑	↑
R	2000	↑	↑	1 2	2 3	3 4	5 6	7 8	10 11	14 15	21 22	↑	↑	↑	↑	↑	↑	↑	↑	↑	↑	↑	↑	↑	↑	↑	↑

↓ = Use first sampling plan below arrow. If sample size equals, or exceeds, lot or batch size, do 100 percent inspection.

↑ = Use first sampling plan above arrow.

Ac = Acceptance number.

Re = Rejection number.

TABLE 6-7 Single Sampling Plans for Tightened Inspection (Table II-B of MIL-STD-105D)

Acceptable Quality Levels (tightened inspection)

Sample size code letter	Sample size	0.010 Ac Re	0.015 Ac Re	0.025 Ac Re	0.040 Ac Re	0.065 Ac Re	0.10 Ac Re	0.15 Ac Re	0.25 Ac Re	0.40 Ac Re	0.65 Ac Re
A	2	↓	↓	↓	↓	↓	↓	↓	↓	↓	↓
B	3	↓	↓	↓	↓	↓	↓	↓	↓	↓	↓
C	5	↓	↓	↓	↓	↓	↓	↓	↓	↓	↓
D	8	↓	↓	↓	↓	↓	↓	↓	↓	↓	↓
E	13	↓	↓	↓	↓	↓	↓	↓	↓	↓	↓
F	20	↓	↓	↓	↓	↓	↓	↓	↓	↓	↓
G	32	↓	↓	↓	↓	↓	↓	↓	↓	↓	0 1
H	50	↓	↓	↓	↓	↓	↓	↓	↓	0 1	↓
J	80	↓	↓	↓	↓	↓	↓	↓	0 1	↓	↓
K	125	↓	↓	↓	↓	↓	↓	0 1	↓	↓	1 2
L	200	↓	↓	↓	↓	↓	0 1	↓	↓	1 2	2 3
M	315	↓	↓	↓	↓	0 1	↓	↓	1 2	2 3	3 4
N	500	↓	↓	↓	0 1	↓	↓	1 2	2 3	3 4	5 6
P	800	↓	↓	0 1	↓	↓	1 2	2 3	3 4	5 6	8 9
Q	1250	↓	0 1	↓	↓	1 2	2 3	3 4	5 6	8 9	12 13
R	2000	0 1	↑	↓	1 2	2 3	3 4	5 6	8 9	12 13	18 19
S	3150			1 2							

Sample size code letter	Sample size	1.0 Ac Re	1.5 Ac Re	2.5 Ac Re	4.0 Ac Re	6.5 Ac Re	10 Ac Re	15 Ac Re	25 Ac Re	40 Ac Re	65 Ac Re	100 Ac Re	150 Ac Re	250 Ac Re	400 Ac Re	650 Ac Re	1000 Ac Re
A	2	↓	↓	↓	↓	↓	↓	↓	↓	1 2	2 3	3 4	5 6	8 9	12 13	18 19	27 28
B	3	↓	↓	↓	↓	0 1	↓	↓	1 2	2 3	3 4	5 6	8 9	12 13	18 19	27 28	41 42
C	5	↓	↓	↓	0 1	↓	↓	1 2	2 3	3 4	5 6	8 9	12 13	18 19	27 28	41 42	↑
D	8	↓	↓	0 1	↓	↓	1 2	2 3	3 4	5 6	8 9	12 13	18 19	27 28	41 42	↑	↑
E	13	↓	0 1	↓	↓	1 2	2 3	3 4	5 6	8 9	12 13	18 19	27 28	41 42	↑	↑	↑
F	20	0 1	↓	↓	1 2	2 3	3 4	5 6	8 9	12 13	18 19	↑	↑	↑	↑	↑	↑
G	32	↓	↓	1 2	2 3	3 4	5 6	8 9	12 13	18 19	↑	↑	↑	↑	↑	↑	↑
H	50	↓	1 2	2 3	3 4	5 6	8 9	12 13	18 19	↑	↑	↑	↑	↑	↑	↑	↑
J	80	1 2	2 3	3 4	5 6	8 9	12 13	18 19	↑	↑	↑	↑	↑	↑	↑	↑	↑
K	125	2 3	3 4	5 6	8 9	12 13	18 19	↑	↑	↑	↑	↑	↑	↑	↑	↑	↑
L	200	3 4	5 6	8 9	12 13	18 19	↑	↑	↑	↑	↑	↑	↑	↑	↑	↑	↑
M	315	5 6	8 9	12 13	18 19	↑	↑	↑	↑	↑	↑	↑	↑	↑	↑	↑	↑
N	500	8 9	12 13	18 19	↑	↑	↑	↑	↑	↑	↑	↑	↑	↑	↑	↑	↑
P	800	12 13	18 19	↑	↑	↑	↑	↑	↑	↑	↑	↑	↑	↑	↑	↑	↑
Q	1250	18 19	↑	↑	↑	↑	↑	↑	↑	↑	↑	↑	↑	↑	↑	↑	↑
R	2000	↑	↑	↑	↑	↑	↑	↑	↑	↑	↑	↑	↑	↑	↑	↑	↑
S	3150																

↓ = Use first sampling plan below arrow. If sample size equals or exceeds lot or batch size, do 100 percent inspection.
↑ = Use first sampling plan above arrow.
Ac = Acceptance number.
Re = Rejection number.

TABLE 6-8 Single Sampling Plans for Reduced Inspection (Table II-C of MIL-STD-105D)

Sample size code letter	Sample size	Acceptable Quality Levels (reduced inspection)†																									
		0.010	0.015	0.025	0.040	0.065	0.10	0.15	0.25	0.40	0.65	1.0	1.5	2.5	4.0	6.5	10	15	25	40	65	100	150	250	400	650	1000
		Ac Re	Ac Re	Ac Re	Ac Re	Ac Re	Ac Re	Ac Re	Ac Re	Ac Re	Ac Re	Ac Re	Ac Re	Ac Re	Ac Re	Ac Re	Ac Re	Ac Re	Ac Re	Ac Re	Ac Re	Ac Re	Ac Re	Ac Re	Ac Re	Ac Re	Ac Re
A	2	↓	↓	↓	↓	↓	↓	↓	↓	↓	↓	↓	↓	↓	↓	0 1	↓	↓	1 2	2 3	3 4	5 6	7 8	10 11	14 15	21 22	30 31
B	2	↓	↓	↓	↓	↓	↓	↓	↓	↓	↓	↓	↓	↓	0 1	↑	↓	0 2	1 3	2 4	3 5	5 6	7 8	10 11	14 15	21 22	30 31
C	2	↓	↓	↓	↓	↓	↓	↓	↓	↓	↓	↓	↓	0 1	↑	↓	0 2	1 3	1 4	2 5	3 6	5 8	7 10	10 13	14 17	21 24	↑
D	3	↓	↓	↓	↓	↓	↓	↓	↓	↓	↓	↓	0 1	↑	↓	0 2	1 3	1 4	2 5	3 6	5 8	7 10	10 13	14 17	21 24	↑	↑
E	5	↓	↓	↓	↓	↓	↓	↓	↓	↓	↓	0 1	↑	↓	0 2	1 3	1 4	2 5	3 6	5 8	7 10	10 13	14 17	21 24	↑	↑	↑
F	8	↓	↓	↓	↓	↓	↓	↓	↓	↓	0 1	↑	↓	0 2	1 3	1 4	2 5	3 6	5 8	7 10	10 13	↑	↑	↑	↑	↑	↑
G	13	↓	↓	↓	↓	↓	↓	↓	↓	0 1	↑	↓	0 2	1 3	1 4	2 5	3 6	5 8	7 10	10 13	↑	↑	↑	↑	↑	↑	↑
H	20	↓	↓	↓	↓	↓	↓	↓	0 1	↑	↓	0 2	1 3	1 4	2 5	3 6	5 8	7 10	10 13	↑	↑	↑	↑	↑	↑	↑	↑
J	32	↓	↓	↓	↓	↓	↓	0 1	↑	↓	0 2	1 3	1 4	2 5	3 6	5 8	7 10	10 13	↑	↑	↑	↑	↑	↑	↑	↑	↑
K	50	↓	↓	↓	↓	↓	0 1	↑	↓	0 2	1 3	1 4	2 5	3 6	5 8	7 10	10 13	↑	↑	↑	↑	↑	↑	↑	↑	↑	↑
L	80	↓	↓	↓	↓	0 1	↑	↓	0 2	1 3	1 4	2 5	3 6	5 8	7 10	10 13	↑	↑	↑	↑	↑	↑	↑	↑	↑	↑	↑
M	125	↓	↓	↓	0 1	↑	↓	0 2	1 3	1 4	2 5	3 6	5 8	7 10	10 13	↑	↑	↑	↑	↑	↑	↑	↑	↑	↑	↑	↑
N	200	↓	↓	0 1	↑	↓	0 2	1 3	1 4	2 5	3 6	5 8	7 10	10 13	↑	↑	↑	↑	↑	↑	↑	↑	↑	↑	↑	↑	↑
P	315	↓	0 1	↑	↓	0 2	1 3	1 4	2 5	3 6	5 8	7 10	10 13	↑	↑	↑	↑	↑	↑	↑	↑	↑	↑	↑	↑	↑	↑
Q	500	0 1	↑	↓	0 2	1 3	1 4	2 5	3 6	5 8	7 10	10 13	↑	↑	↑	↑	↑	↑	↑	↑	↑	↑	↑	↑	↑	↑	↑
R	800	↑	↑	0 2	1 3	1 4	2 5	3 6	5 8	7 10	10 13	↑	↑	↑	↑	↑	↑	↑	↑	↑	↑	↑	↑	↑	↑	↑	↑

↓ = Use first sampling plan below arrow. If sample size equals or exceeds lot or batch size, do 100 percent inspection.
↑ = Use first sampling plan above arrow.
Ac = Acceptance number.
Re = Rejection number.
† = If the acceptance number has been exceeded, but the rejection number has not been reached, accept the lot, but reinstate normal inspection (see 10.1.4).

inspection. From Table 6-7 (Single Sampling Plans for Tightened Inspection), the desired plan is obtained for code letter L and AQL 0.65%. It is $n = 200$, $Ac = 2$, $Re = 3$. Thus, from a lot of 2000, a random sample of 200 is inspected. If 2 or less defectives are found, the lot is accepted; if 3 or more defectives are found, the lot is rejected.

Reduced. The sample-size code letter, L, is the same as the one for normal inspection. From Table 6-8 (Single Sampling Plans for Reduced Inspection), the desired plan is obtained for code letter L and AQL 0.65%. It is $n = 80$, $Ac = 1$, $Re = 4$. Thus, from a lot of 2000, a random sample of 80 is inspected. If 1 or fewer defectives are found, the lot is accepted; if 4 or more defectives are found, the lot is rejected. If 2 or 3 defectives are found, the lot is accepted, but the type of inspection changes from reduced to normal. A change to normal inspection is also required when a lot is rejected.

In comparing the three plans, notice that the acceptance requirements are more stringent for tightened than for normal inspection. In fact, a sample with 3 defectives is accepted under normal inspection but rejected under tightened inspection. The sample size for reduced inspection is approximately 40% of the sample size of normal or tightened inspection, which represents a considerable saving in sampling costs.

If a vertical arrow is encountered, the first sampling plan above or below the arrow is used. When this occurs, the sample-size code letter and the sample size change. For example, if a single sample tightened plan (Table 6-7) is indexed by an AQL of 4.0% and a code letter D, the code letter changes to F and the sample size changes from 8 to 20. If the vertical arrow points down, it means that the sample size is too small to make a decision; if the vertical arrow points up, it means that a decision can be made with a smaller sample size. In some cases the sample size will exceed the lot size and in those cases 100% inspection is required.

Double Sampling Plans

The double sampling plans of the standard are given in Tables 6-9, 6-10, and 6-11 for normal, tightened, and reduced inspection, respectively. Use of the tables is similar to the techique described under single sampling plans. An example problem will illustrate the technique.

Example Problem

For a lot size of 20,000, an AQL of 1.5%, and an inspection level of I, determine the double sampling plans for normal, tightened, and reduced inspection.

Normal. Using the lot size $N = 20{,}000$ and inspection level I, the sample-size code letter K is obtained form Table 6-5. From Table 6-9 (Double

TABLE 6-9 Double Sampling Plans for Normal Inspection (Table III-A of MIL-STD-105D)

Acceptable Quality Levels (normal inspection)

Sample size code letter	Sample	Sample size	Cumulative sample size	0.010		0.015		0.025		0.040		0.065		0.10		0.15		0.25		0.40		0.65	
				Ac	Re	Ac	Re	Ac	Re	Ac	Re	Ac	Re	Ac	Re	Ac	Re	Ac	Re	Ac	Re	Ac	Re
A				↓		↓		↓		↓		↓		↓		↓		↓		↓		↓	
B	First	2	2	↓		↓		↓		↓		↓		↓		↓		↓		↓		↓	
	Second	2	4																				
C	First	3	3	↓		↓		↓		↓		↓		↓		↓		↓		↓		↓	
	Second	3	6																				
D	First	5	5	↓		↓		↓		↓		↓		↓		↓		↓		↓		↓	
	Second	5	10																				
E	First	8	8	↓		↓		↓		↓		↓		↓		↓		↓		↓		↓	
	Second	8	16																				
F	First	13	13	↓		↓		↓		↓		↓		↓		↓		↓		↓		*	
	Second	13	26																				
G	First	20	20	↓		↓		↓		↓		↓		↓		↓		↓		*		↑	
	Second	20	40																				
H	First	32	32	↓		↓		↓		↓		↓		↓		↓		*		↑		↓	
	Second	32	64																				
J	First	50	50	↓		↓		↓		↓		↓		↓		*		↑		↓		0	2
	Second	50	100																			1	2
K	First	80	80	↓		↓		↓		↓		↓		*		↑		↓		0	2	0	3
	Second	80	160																	1	2	3	4
L	First	125	125	↓		↓		↓		↓		*		↑		↓		0	2	0	3	1	4
	Second	125	250															1	2	3	4	5	4
M	First	200	200	↓		↓		↓		*		↑		↓		0	2	0	3	1	4	2	5
	Second	200	400													1	2	3	4	4	5	6	7
N	First	315	315	↓		↓		*		↑		↓		0	2	0	3	1	4	2	5	3	7
	Second	315	630											1	2	3	4	4	5	6	7	8	9
P	First	500	500	↓		*		↑		↓		0	2	0	3	1	4	2	5	3	7	5	9
	Second	500	1000									1	2	3	4	4	5	6	7	8	9	12	13
Q	First	800	800	*		↑		↓		0	2	0	3	1	4	2	5	3	7	5	9	7	11
	Second	800	1600							1	2	3	4	4	5	6	7	8	9	12	13	18	19
R	First	1250	1250	↑		↑		0	2	0	3	1	4	2	5	3	7	5	9	7	11	11	16
	Second	1250	2500					1	2	3	4	4	5	6	7	8	9	12	13	18	19	26	27

Sample size code letter	Sample	1.0		1.5		2.5		4.0		6.5		10		15		25		40		65		100		150		250		400		650		1000	
		Ac	Re	Ac	Re	Ac	Re	Ac	Re	Ac	Re	Ac	Re	Ac	Re	Ac	Re	Ac	Re	Ac	Re	Ac	Re	Ac	Re	Ac	Re	Ac	Re	Ac	Re	Ac	Re
A		↓		↓		↓		↓		*		↓		↓		*		*		*		*		*		*		*		*		*	
B	First	↓		↓		↓		*		↑		↓		0	2	0	3	1	4	2	5	3	7	5	9	7	11	11	16	17	22	25	31
	Second													1	2	3	4	4	5	6	7	8	9	12	13	18	19	26	27	37	38	56	57
C	First	↓		↓		*		↑		↓		0	2	0	3	1	4	2	5	3	7	5	9	7	11	11	16	17	22	25	31	↑	
	Second											1	2	3	4	4	5	6	7	8	9	12	13	18	19	26	27	37	38	56	57		
D	First	↓		*		↑		↓		0	2	0	3	1	4	2	5	3	7	5	9	7	11	11	16	17	22	25	31	↑		↑	
	Second									1	2	3	4	4	5	6	7	8	9	12	13	18	19	26	27	37	38	56	57				
E	First	*		↑		↓		0	2	0	3	1	4	2	5	3	7	5	9	7	11	11	16	17	22	25	31	↑		↑		↑	
	Second							1	2	3	4	4	5	6	7	8	9	13	12	18	19	26	27	37	38	56	57						
F	First	↑		↓		0	2	0	3	1	4	2	5	3	7	5	9	7	11	11	16	↑		↑		↑		↑		↑		↑	
	Second					1	2	3	4	4	5	6	7	8	9	12	13	18	19	26	27												
G	First	↓		0	2	0	3	1	4	2	5	3	7	5	9	7	11	11	16	↑		↑		↑		↑		↑		↑		↑	
	Second			1	2	3	4	4	5	6	7	8	9	12	13	18	19	26	27														
H	First	0	2	0	3	1	4	2	5	3	7	5	9	7	11	11	16	↑		↑		↑		↑		↑		↑		↑		↑	
	Second	1	2	3	4	4	5	6	7	8	9	12	13	18	19	26	27																
J	First	0	3	1	4	2	5	3	7	5	9	7	11	11	16	↑		↑		↑		↑		↑		↑		↑		↑		↑	
	Second	3	4	4	5	6	7	8	9	12	13	18	19	26	27																		
K	First	1	4	2	5	3	7	5	9	7	11	11	16	↑		↑		↑		↑		↑		↑		↑		↑		↑		↑	
	Second	4	5	6	7	8	9	12	13	18	19	26	27																				
L	First	2	5	3	7	5	9	7	11	11	16	↑		↑		↑		↑		↑		↑		↑		↑		↑		↑		↑	
	Second	6	7	8	9	12	13	18	19	26	27																						
M	First	3	7	5	9	7	11	11	16	↑		↑		↑		↑		↑		↑		↑		↑		↑		↑		↑		↑	
	Second	8	9	12	13	18	19	26	27																								
N	First	5	9	7	11	11	16	↑		↑		↑		↑		↑		↑		↑		↑		↑		↑		↑		↑		↑	
	Second	12	13	18	19	26	27																										
P	First	7	11	11	16	↑		↑		↑		↑		↑		↑		↑		↑		↑		↑		↑		↑		↑		↑	
	Second	18	19	26	27																												
Q	First	11	16	↑		↑		↑		↑		↑		↑		↑		↑		↑		↑		↑		↑		↑		↑		↑	
	Second	26	27																														
R	First	↑		↑		↑		↑		↑		↑		↑		↑		↑		↑		↑		↑		↑		↑		↑		↑	
	Second																																

↓ = Use first sampling plan below arrow. If sample size equals or exceeds lot or batch size, do 100 percent inspection.

↑ = Use first sampling plan above arrow.

Ac = Acceptance number.

Re = Rejection number.

* = Use corresponding single sample plan (or alternatively, use double sampling plan below, where available).

TABLE 6-10 Double Sampling Plans for Tightened Inspection (Table III-B of MIL-STD-105D)

Sample size code letter	Sample	Sample size	Cumulative sample size	Acceptable Quality Levels (tightened inspection)																									
				0.010	0.015	0.025	0.040	0.065	0.10	0.15	0.25	0.40	0.65	1.0	1.5	2.5	4.0	6.5	10	15	25	40	65	100	150	250	400	650	1000
				Ac Re	Ac Re	Ac Re	Ac Re	Ac Re	Ac Re	Ac Re	Ac Re	Ac Re	Ac Re	Ac Re	Ac Re	Ac Re	Ac Re	Ac Re	Ac Re	Ac Re	Ac Re	Ac Re	Ac Re	Ac Re	Ac Re	Ac Re	Ac Re	Ac Re	Ac Re
A				↓	↓	↓	↓	↓	↓	↓	↓	↓	↓	↓	↓	↓	↓	↓	↓	↓	↓	*	*	*	*	*	*	*	*
B	First	2	2	↓	↓	↓	↓	↓	↓	↓	↓	↓	↓	↓	↓	↓	↓	*	↓	↓	0 2	0 3	1 4	2 5	3 7	6 10	9 14	15 20	23 24
	Second	2	4																		1 2	3 4	4 5	6 7	11 12	15 16	23 24	34 35	52 53
C	First	3	3	↓	↓	↓	↓	↓	↓	↓	↓	↓	↓	↓	↓	↓	*	↓	↓	0 2	0 3	1 4	2 5	3 7	6 10	9 14	15 20	23 24	↑
	Second	3	6																	1 2	3 4	4 5	6 7	11 12	15 16	23 24	34 35	52 53	
D	First	5	5	↓	↓	↓	↓	↓	↓	↓	↓	↓	↓	↓	↓	*	↓	↓	0 2	0 3	1 4	2 5	3 7	6 10	9 14	15 20	23 24	↑	↑
	Second	5	10															1 2	3 4	4 5	6 7	11 12	15 16	23 24	34 35	52 53		
E	First	8	8	↓	↓	↓	↓	↓	↓	↓	↓	↓	↓	↓	*	↓	↓	0 2	0 3	1 4	2 5	3 7	6 10	9 14	15 20	23 24	↑	↑	↑
	Second	8	16														1 2	3 4	4 5	6 7	11 12	15 16	23 24	34 35	52 53			
F	First	13	13	↓	↓	↓	↓	↓	↓	↓	↓	↓	↓	*	↓	↓	0 2	0 3	1 4	2 5	3 7	6 10	9 14	↑	↑	↑	↑	↑	↑
	Second	13	26													1 2	3 4	4 5	6 7	11 12	15 16	23 24						
G	First	20	20	↓	↓	↓	↓	↓	↓	↓	↓	↓	*	↓	↓	0 2	0 3	1 4	2 5	3 7	6 10	9 14	↑	↑	↑	↑	↑	↑	↑
	Second	20	40												1 2	3 4	4 5	6 7	11 12	15 16	23 24							
H	First	32	32	↓	↓	↓	↓	↓	↓	↓	↓	*	↓	↓	0 2	0 3	1 4	2 5	3 7	6 10	9 14	↑	↑	↑	↑	↑	↑	↑	↑
	Second	32	64											1 2	3 4	4 5	6 7	11 12	15 16	23 24								
J	First	50	50	↓	↓	↓	↓	↓	↓	↓	*	↓	↓	0 2	0 3	1 4	2 5	3 7	6 10	9 14	↑	↑	↑	↑	↑	↑	↑	↑	↑
	Second	50	100										1 2	3 4	4 5	6 7	11 12	15 16	23 24									
K	First	80	80	↓	↓	↓	↓	↓	↓	*	↓	↓	0 2	0 3	1 4	2 5	3 7	6 10	9 14	↑	↑	↑	↑	↑	↑	↑	↑	↑	↑
	Second	80	160									1 2	3 4	4 5	6 7	11 12	15 16	23 24										
L	First	125	125	↓	↓	↓	↓	↓	*	↓	↓	0 2	0 3	1 4	2 5	3 7	6 10	9 14	↑	↑	↑	↑	↑	↑	↑	↑	↑	↑	↑
	Second	125	250								1 2	3 4	4 5	6 7	11 12	15 16	23 24											
M	First	200	200	↓	↓	↓	↓	*	↓	↓	0 2	0 3	1 4	2 5	3 7	6 10	9 14	↑	↑	↑	↑	↑	↑	↑	↑	↑	↑	↑	↑
	Second	200	400							1 2	3 4	4 5	6 7	11 12	15 16	23 24												
N	First	315	315	↓	↓	↓	*	↓	↓	0 2	0 3	1 4	2 5	3 7	6 10	9 14	↑	↑	↑	↑	↑	↑	↑	↑	↑	↑	↑	↑	↑
	Second	315	630							1 2	3 4	4 5	6 7	11 12	15 16	23 24													
P	First	500	500	↓	↓	*	↓	↓	0 2	0 3	1 4	2 5	3 7	6 10	9 14	↑	↑	↑	↑	↑	↑	↑	↑	↑	↑	↑	↑	↑	↑
	Second	500	1000						1 2	3 4	4 5	6 7	11 12	15 16	23 24														
Q	First	800	800	↓	*	↓	↓	0 2	0 3	1 4	2 5	3 7	6 10	9 14	↑	↑	↑	↑	↑	↑	↑	↑	↑	↑	↑	↑	↑	↑	↑
	Second	800	1600					1 2	3 4	4 5	6 7	11 12	15 16	23 24															
R	First	1250	1250	*	↑	↓	0 2	0 3	1 4	2 5	3 7	6 10	9 14	↑	↑	↑	↑	↑	↑	↑	↑	↑	↑	↑	↑	↑	↑	↑	↑
	Second	1250	2500				1 2	3 4	4 5	6 7	11 12	15 16	23 24																
S	First	2000	2000			0 2																							
	Second	2000	4000			1 2																							

↓ Use first sampling plan below arrow. If sample size equals or exceeds lot or batch size, do 100 percent inspection.

↑ Use first sampling plan above arrow.

Ac Acceptance number.

Re Rejection number.

* Use corresponding single sampling plan (or alternatively, use double sampling plan below, where available).

TABLE 6-11 Double Sampling Plans for Reduced Inspection (Table III-C of MIL-STD-105D)

Sample size code letter	Sample	Sample size	Cumulative sample size	Acceptable Quality Levies (reduced inspection) †																									
				0.010	0.015	0.025	0.040	0.065	0.10	0.15	0.25	0.40	0.65	1.0	1.5	2.5	4.0	6.5	10	15	25	40	65	100	150	250	400	650	1000
				Ac Re	Ac Re	Ac Re	Ac Re	Ac Re	Ac Re	Ac Re	Ac Re	Ac Re	Ac Re	Ac Re	Ac Re	Ac Re	Ac Re	Ac Re	Ac Re	Ac Re	Ac Re	Ac Re	Ac Re	Ac Re	Ac Re	Ac Re	Ac Re	Ac Re	Ac Re
A				↓	↓	↓	↓	↓	↓	↓	↓	↓	↓	↓	↓	↓	↓	*	↓	↓	*	*	*	*	*	*	*	*	*
B				↓	↓	↓	↓	↓	↓	↓	↓	↓	↓	↓	↓	↓	*	↑	↓	*	*	*	*	*	*	*	*	*	*
C				↓	↓	↓	↓	↓	↓	↓	↓	↓	↓	↓	↓	*	↑	↓	*	*	*	*	*	*	*	*	*	*	↑
D	First	2	2	↓	↓	↓	↓	↓	↓	↓	↓	↓	↓	↓	*	↑	↓	0 2	0 3	0 4	0 4	1 5	2 7	3 8	5 10	7 12	11 17	↑	↑
	Second	2	4															0 2	0 4	1 5	3 6	4 7	6 9	8 12	12 16	18 22	26 30		
E	First	3	3	↓	↓	↓	↓	↓	↓	↓	↓	↓	↓	*	↑	↓	0 2	0 3	0 4	0 4	1 5	2 7	3 8	5 10	7 12	11 17	↑	↑	↑
	Second	3	6														0 2	0 4	1 5	3 6	4 7	6 9	8 12	12 16	18 22	26 30			
F	First	5	5	↓	↓	↓	↓	↓	↓	↓	↓	↓	*	↑	↓	0 2	0 3	0 4	0 4	1 5	2 7	3 8	5 10	↑	↑	↑	↑	↑	↑
	Second	5	10													0 2	0 4	1 5	3 6	4 7	6 9	8 12	12 16						
G	First	8	8	↓	↓	↓	↓	↓	↓	↓	↓	*	↑	↓	0 2	0 3	0 4	0 4	1 5	2 7	3 8	5 10	↑	↑	↑	↑	↑	↑	↑
	Second	8	8												0 2	0 4	1 5	3 6	4 7	6 9	8 12	12 16							
H	First	13	13	↓	↓	↓	↓	↓	↓	↓	*	↑	↓	0 2	0 3	0 4	0 4	1 5	2 7	3 8	5 10	↑	↑	↑	↑	↑	↑	↑	↑
	Second	13	26											0 2	0 4	1 5	3 6	4 7	6 9	8 12	12 16								
J	First	20	20	↓	↓	↓	↓	↓	↓	*	↑	↓	0 2	0 3	0 4	0 4	1 5	2 7	3 8	5 10	↑	↑	↑	↑	↑	↑	↑	↑	↑
	Second	20	40										0 2	0 4	1 5	3 6	4 7	6 9	8 12	12 16									
K	First	32	32	↓	↓	↓	↓	↓	*	↑	↓	0 2	0 3	0 4	0 4	1 5	2 7	3 8	5 10	↑	↑	↑	↑	↑	↑	↑	↑	↑	↑
	Second	32	64									0 2	0 4	1 5	3 6	4 7	6 9	8 12	12 16										
L	First	50	50	↓	↓	↓	↓	*	↑	↓	0 2	0 3	0 4	0 4	1 5	2 7	3 8	5 10	↑	↑	↑	↑	↑	↑	↑	↑	↑	↑	↑
	Second	50	100								0 2	0 4	1 5	3 6	4 7	6 9	8 12	12 16											
M	First	80	80	↓	↓	↓	*	↑	↓	0 2	0 3	0 4	0 4	1 5	2 7	3 8	5 10	↑	↑	↑	↑	↑	↑	↑	↑	↑	↑	↑	↑
	Second	80	160							0 2	0 4	1 5	3 6	4 7	6 9	8 12	12 16												
N	First	125	125	↓	↓	*	↑	↓	0 2	0 3	0 4	0 4	1 5	2 7	3 8	5 10	↑	↑	↑	↑	↑	↑	↑	↑	↑	↑	↑	↑	↑
	Second	125	250						0 2	0 4	1 5	3 6	4 7	6 9	8 12	12 16													
P	First	200	200	↓	*	↑	↓	0 2	0 3	0 4	0 4	1 5	2 7	3 8	5 10	↑	↑	↑	↑	↑	↑	↑	↑	↑	↑	↑	↑	↑	↑
	Second	200	400					0 2	0 4	1 5	3 6	4 7	6 9	8 12	12 16														
Q	First	315	315	*	↑	↓	0 2	0 3	0 4	0 4	1 5	2 7	3 8	5 10	↑	↑	↑	↑	↑	↑	↑	↑	↑	↑	↑	↑	↑	↑	↑
	Second	315	630				0 2	0 4	1 5	3 6	4 7	6 9	8 12	12 16															
R	First	500	500	↑	↑	0 2	0 3	0 4	0 4	1 5	2 7	3 8	5 10	↑	↑	↑	↑	↑	↑	↑	↑	↑	↑	↑	↑	↑	↑	↑	↑
	Second	500	1000			0 2	0 4	1 5	3 6	4 7	6 9	8 12	12 16																

↓ = Use first sampling plan below arrow. If sample size equals or exceeds lot or batch size, do 100 percent inspection.

↑ = Use first sampling plan above arrow.

Ac = Acceptance number.

Re = Rejection number.

* = Use corresponding single sampling plan (or alternatively, use double sampling plan below, when available).

† = If, after the second sample, the acceptance number has been exceeded, but the rejection number has not been reached, accept the lot, but reinstate normal inspection (see 10.14).

Sampling Plans for Normal Inspection), the desired plan is obtained for code letter K and AQL 1.5%. It is:

n	Ac	Re
80	2	5
80	6	7

Thus, from a lot of 20,000, a random sample of 80 is inspected. If 2 or less are defective, the lot is accepted; if 5 or more are defective, the lot is rejected. When 3 or 4 defectives are found in the first sample, a second sample of 80 is inspected. If the total number of defectives is 6 or less on both samples, the lot is accepted; if 7 or more, the lot is rejected.

Tightened. The sample-size code letter, K, is the same as the one for normal inspection. From Table 6-10 (Double Sampling Plans for Tightened Inspection), the desired plan is obtained for code letter K and AQL 1.5%. It is:

n	Ac	Re
80	1	4
80	4	5

Thus, from a lot of 20,000, a random sample of 80 is inspected. If 1 or less is defective, the lot is accepted; if 4 or more are defective, the lot is rejected. When 2 or 3 defectives are found in the first sample, a second sample of 80 is inspected. If the total number of defectives is 4 or less, the lot is accepted; if 5 or more, the lot is rejected.

Reduced. The sample-size code letter, K, is the same as the one for normal inspection. From Table 6-11 (Double Sampling Plans for Reduced Inspection), the desired plan is obtained for code letter K and AQL 1.5%. It is:

n	Ac	Re
32	0	4
32	3	6

Thus, from a lot of 20,000, a random sample of 32 is inspected. If 0 defective is found, the lot is accepted; if 4 or more defectives, the lot is rejected. When 1, 2, or 3 defectives are found in the first sample, a second sample of 32 is inspected. If the total number of defectives is 3 or less, the lot is accepted; if the total number of defectives is 4 or 5, the lot is accepted, but normal inspection is reinstated; and if the total number of defectives is 6 or more, the lot is rejected and normal inspection is reinstated.

The same comparisons among normal, tightened, and reduced inspection that were given for single sampling plans are applicable to double sampling plans. A change in the sample-size code letter and the sample size as a result of a vertical arrow has the same interpretation for double sampling plans as for single sampling plans.

An asterisk, *, is used in the double sampling tables. In most cases where an asterisk is encountered, the corresponding single sampling plan is applicable because the relationship between the acceptance number and the sample size is unrealistic. In other cases the double sampling plan immediately below the asterisk is applicable, as illustrated in Table 6-9 for plans with code letter A and AQLs from 25 to 1000.

Multiple Sampling Plans

The multiple sampling plans of the standard provide for seven samples and are given in Tables 6-12, 6-13, and 6-14 for normal, tightened, and reduced inspection, respectively. Use of the tables is similar to the technique described under single and double sampling plans. Because of the similarity, a detailed explanation is not given.

Example Problem

For a lot size of 430, an AQL of 4.0%, and an inspection level of II, determine the multiple sampling plans for normal, tightened, and reduced inspection.

Sample-size code letter = H (from Table 6-5). Normal inspection (from Table 6-12):

n	Ac	Re
13	#	4
13	1	5
13	2	6
13	3	7
13	5	8
13	7	9
13	9	10

Tightened inspection (from Table 6-13):

n	*Ac*	*Re*
13	#	3
13	0	3
13	1	4
13	2	5
13	3	6
13	4	6
13	6	7

TABLE 6-12 Multiple Sampling Plans for Normal Inspection (Table IV-A of MIL-STD-105D)

Sample size code letter	Sample	Sample size	Cumulative sample size	Acceptable Quality Levels (normal inspection)																									
				0.010	0.015	0.025	0.040	0.065	0.10	0.15	0.25	0.40	0.65	1.0	1.5	2.5	4.0	6.5	10	15	25	40	65	100	150	250	400	650	1000
				Ac Re	Ac Re	Ac Re	Ac Re	Ac Re	Ac Re	Ac Re	Ac Re	Ac Re	Ac Re	Ac Re	Ac Re	Ac Re	Ac Re	Ac Re	Ac Re	Ac Re	Ac Re	Ac Re	Ac Re	Ac Re	Ac Re	Ac Re	Ac Re	Ac Re	Ac Re
A				↓	↓	↓	↓	↓	↓	↓	↓	↓	↓	↓	↓	↓	↓	•	↓	↓	•	•	•	•	•	•	•	•	•
B																	•	↑		++	++	++	++	++	++	++	++	++	++
C																•	↑	↓	++	++	++	++	++	++	++	++	++	++	↑
D	First	2	2	↓	↓	↓	↓	↓	↓	↓	↓	↓	↓	↓	•	↑	↓	# 2	# 2	# 3	# 4	0 4	0 5	1 7	2 9	4 12	6 16	↑	↑
	Second	2	4															# 2	0 3	0 3	1 5	1 6	3 8	4 10	7 14	11 19	17 27		
	Third	2	6															0 2	0 3	1 4	2 6	3 8	6 10	8 13	13 19	19 27	29 39		
	Fourth	2	8															0 3	1 4	2 5	3 7	5 10	8 13	12 17	19 25	27 34	40 49		
	Fifth	2	10															1 3	2 4	3 6	5 8	7 11	11 15	17 20	25 29	36 40	53 58		
	Sixth	2	12															1 3	3 5	4 6	7 9	10 12	14 17	21 23	31 33	45 47	65 68		
	Seventh	2	14															2 3	4 5	6 7	9 10	13 14	18 19	25 26	37 38	53 54	77 78		
E	First	3	3	↓	↓	↓	↓	↓	↓	↓	↓	↓	↓	•	↑	↓	# 2	# 2	# 3	# 4	0 4	0 5	1 7	2 9	4 12	6 16	↑	↑	↑
	Second	3	6														# 2	0 3	0 3	1 5	1 6	3 8	4 10	7 14	11 19	17 27			
	Third	3	9														0 2	0 3	1 4	2 6	3 8	6 10	8 13	13 19	19 27	29 39			
	Fourth	3	12														0 3	1 4	2 5	3 7	5 10	8 13	12 17	19 25	27 34	40 49			
	Fifth	3	15														1 3	2 4	3 6	5 8	7 11	11 15	17 20	25 29	36 40	53 58			
	Sixth	3	18														1 3	3 5	4 6	7 9	10 12	14 17	21 23	31 33	45 47	65 68			
	Seventh	3	21														2 3	4 5	6 7	9 10	13 14	18 19	25 26	37 38	53 54	77 78			
F	First	5	5	↓	↓	↓	↓	↓	↓	↓	↓	↓	•	↑	↓	# 2	# 2	# 3	# 4	0 4	0 5	1 7	2 9	↑	↑	↑	↑	↑	↑
	Second	5	10													# 2	0 3	0 3	1 5	1 6	3 8	4 10	7 14						
	Third	5	15													0 2	0 3	1 4	2 6	3 8	6 10	8 13	13 19						
	Fourth	5	20													0 3	1 4	2 5	3 7	5 10	8 13	12 17	19 25						
	Fifth	5	25													1 3	2 4	3 6	5 8	7 11	11 15	17 20	25 29						
	Sixth	5	30													1 3	3 5	4 6	7 9	10 12	14 17	21 23	31 33						
	Seventh	5	35													2 3	4 5	6 7	9 10	13 14	18 19	25 26	37 38						
G	First	8	8	↓	↓	↓	↓	↓	↓	↓	↓	•	↑	↓	# 2	# 2	# 3	# 4	0 4	0 5	1 7	2 9	↑	↑	↑	↑	↑	↑	↑
	Second	8	16												# 2	0 3	0 3	1 5	1 6	3 8	4 10	7 14							
	Third	8	24												0 2	0 3	1 4	2 6	3 8	6 10	8 13	13 19							
	Fourth	8	32												0 3	1 4	2 5	3 7	5 10	8 13	12 17	19 25							
	Fifth	8	40												1 3	2 4	3 6	5 8	7 11	11 15	17 20	25 29							
	Sixth	8	48												1 3	3 5	4 6	7 9	10 12	14 17	21 23	31 33							
	Seventh	8	56												2 3	4 5	6 7	9 10	13 14	18 19	25 26	37 38							
H	First	13	13	↓	↓	↓	↓	↓	↓	↓	•	↑	↓	# 2	# 2	# 3	# 4	0 4	0 5	1 7	2 9	↑	↑	↑	↑	↑	↑	↑	↑
	Second	13	26											# 2	0 3	0 3	1 5	1 6	3 8	4 10	7 14								
	Third	13	39											0 2	0 3	1 4	2 6	3 8	6 10	8 13	13 19								
	Fourth	13	52											0 3	1 4	2 5	3 7	5 10	8 13	12 17	19 25								
	Fifth	13	65											1 3	2 4	3 6	5 8	7 11	11 15	17 20	25 29								
	Sixth	13	78											1 3	3 5	4 6	7 9	10 12	14 17	21 23	31 33								
	Seventh	13	91											2 3	4 5	6 7	9 10	13 14	18 19	25 26	37 38								
J	First	20	20	↓	↓	↓	↓	↓	↓	•	↑	↓	# 2	# 2	# 3	# 4	0 4	0 5	1 7	2 9	↑	↑	↑	↑	↑	↑	↑	↑	↑
	Second	20	40										# 2	0 3	0 3	1 5	1 6	3 8	4 10	7 14									
	Third	20	60										0 2	0 3	1 4	2 6	3 8	6 10	8 13	13 19									
	Fourth	20	80										0 3	1 4	2 5	3 7	5 10	8 13	12 17	19 25									
	Fifth	20	100										1 3	2 4	3 6	5 8	7 11	11 15	17 20	25 29									
	Sixth	20	120										1 3	3 5	4 6	7 9	10 12	14 17	21 23	31 33									
	Seventh	20	140										2 3	4 5	6 7	9 10	13 14	18 19	25 26	37 38									

↓ = Use first sampling plan below arrow (refer to continuation of table on following page, when necessary). If sample size equals or exceeds lot or batch size, do 100 percent inspection.
↑ = Use first sampling plan above arrow.
Ac = Acceptance number.
Re = Rejection number.
• = Use corresponding single sampling plan (or alternatively, use multiple sampling plan below, where available).
++ = Use corresponding double sampling plan (or alternatively, use multiple sampling plan below, where available).
# = Acceptance not permitted at this sample size.

TABLE 6-12 (continued)

Sample size code letter	Sample	Sample size	Cumulative sample size	Acceptable Quality Levels (normal inspection)																									
				0.010	0.015	0.025	0.040	0.065	0.10	0.15	0.25	0.40	0.65	1.0	1.5	2.5	4.0	6.5	10	15	25	40	65	100	150	250	400	650	1000
				Ac Re	Ac Re	Ac Re	Ac Re	Ac Re	Ac Re	Ac Re	Ac Re	Ac Re	Ac Re	Ac Re	Ac Re	Ac Re	Ac Re	Ac Re	Ac Re	Ac Re	Ac Re	Ac Re	Ac Re	Ac Re	Ac Re	Ac Re	Ac Re	Ac Re	Ac Re
K	First	32	32	↓	↓	↓	↓	↓	•	↑	↓	* 2	* 2	* 3	* 4	0 4	0 5	1 7	2 9	↑	↑	↑	↑	↑	↑	↑	↑	↑	↑
	Second	32	64									* 2	0 3	0 3	1 5	1 6	3 8	4 10	7 14										
	Third	32	96									0 2	0 3	1 4	2 6	3 8	6 10	8 13	13 19										
	Fourth	32	128									0 3	1 4	2 5	3 7	5 10	8 13	12 17	19 25										
	Fifth	32	160									1 3	2 4	3 6	5 8	7 11	11 15	17 20	25 29										
	Sixth	32	192									1 3	3 5	4 6	7 9	10 12	14 17	21 23	31 33										
	Seventh	32	224									2 3	4 5	6 7	9 10	13 14	18 19	25 26	37 38										
L	First	50	50	↓	↓	↓	↓	•	↑	↓	* 2	* 2	* 3	* 4	0 4	0 5	1 7	2 9	↑	↑	↑	↑	↑	↑	↑	↑	↑	↑	↑
	Second	50	100								* 2	0 3	0 3	1 5	1 6	3 8	4 10	7 14											
	Third	50	150								0 2	0 3	1 4	2 6	3 8	6 10	8 13	13 19											
	Fourth	50	200								0 3	1 4	2 5	3 7	5 10	8 13	12 17	19 25											
	Fifth	50	250								1 3	2 4	3 6	5 8	7 11	11 15	17 20	25 29											
	Sixth	50	300								1 3	3 5	4 6	7 9	10 12	14 17	21 23	31 33											
	Seventh	50	350								2 3	4 5	6 7	9 10	13 14	18 19	25 26	37 38											
M	First	80	80	↓	↓	↓	•	↑	↓	* 2	* 2	* 3	* 4	0 4	0 5	1 7	2 9	↑	↑	↑	↑	↑	↑	↑	↑	↑	↑	↑	↑
	Second	80	160							* 2	0 3	0 3	1 5	1 6	3 8	4 10	7 14												
	Third	80	240							0 2	0 3	1 4	2 6	3 8	6 10	8 13	13 19												
	Fourth	80	320							0 3	1 4	2 5	3 7	5 10	8 13	12 17	19 25												
	Fifth	80	400							1 3	2 4	3 6	5 8	7 11	11 15	17 20	25 29												
	Sixth	80	480							1 3	3 5	4 6	7 9	10 12	14 17	21 23	31 33												
	Seventh	80	560							2 3	4 5	6 7	9 10	13 14	18 19	25 26	37 38												
N	First	125	125	↓	↓	•	↑	↓	* 2	* 2	* 3	* 4	0 4	0 5	1 7	2 9	↑	↑	↑	↑	↑	↑	↑	↑	↑	↑	↑	↑	↑
	Second	125	250						* 2	0 3	0 3	1 5	1 6	3 8	4 10	7 14													
	Third	125	375						0 2	0 3	1 4	2 6	3 8	6 10	8 13	13 19													
	Fourth	125	500						0 3	1 4	2 5	3 7	5 10	8 13	12 17	19 25													
	Fifth	125	625						1 3	2 4	3 6	5 8	7 11	11 15	17 20	25 29													
	Sixth	125	750						1 3	3 5	4 6	7 9	10 12	14 17	21 23	31 33													
	Seventh	125	875						2 3	4 5	6 7	9 10	13 14	18 19	25 26	37 38													
P	First	200	200	↓	•	↑	↓	* 2	* 2	* 3	* 4	0 4	0 5	1 7	2 9	↑	↑	↑	↑	↑	↑	↑	↑	↑	↑	↑	↑	↑	↑
	Second	200	400					* 2	0 3	0 3	1 5	1 6	3 8	4 10	7 14														
	Third	200	600					0 2	0 3	1 4	2 6	3 8	6 10	8 13	13 19														
	Fourth	200	800					0 3	1 4	2 5	3 7	5 10	8 13	12 17	19 25														
	Fifth	200	1000					1 3	2 4	3 6	5 8	7 11	11 15	17 20	25 29														
	Sixth	200	1200					1 3	3 5	4 6	7 9	10 12	14 17	21 23	31 33														
	Seventh	200	1400					2 3	4 5	6 7	9 10	13 14	18 19	25 26	37 38														
Q	First	315	315	•	↑	↓	* 2	* 2	* 3	* 4	0 4	0 5	1 7	2 9	↑	↑	↑	↑	↑	↑	↑	↑	↑	↑	↑	↑	↑	↑	↑
	Second	315	630				* 2	0 3	0 3	1 5	1 6	3 8	4 10	7 14															
	Third	315	945				0 2	0 3	1 4	2 6	3 8	6 10	8 13	13 19															
	Fourth	315	1260				0 3	1 4	2 5	3 7	5 10	8 13	12 17	19 25															
	Fifth	315	1575				1 3	2 4	3 6	5 8	7 11	11 15	17 20	25 29															
	Sixth	315	1890				1 3	3 5	4 6	7 9	10 12	14 17	21 23	31 33															
	Seventh	315	2205				2 3	4 5	6 7	9 10	13 14	18 19	25 26	37 38															
R	First	500	500	↑	↑	* 2	* 2	* 3	* 4	0 4	0 5	1 7	2 9	↑	↑	↑	↑	↑	↑	↑	↑	↑	↑	↑	↑	↑	↑	↑	↑
	Second	500	1000			* 2	0 3	0 3	1 5	1 6	3 8	4 10	7 14																
	Third	500	1500			0 2	0 3	1 4	2 6	3 8	6 10	8 13	13 19																
	Fourth	500	2000			0 3	1 4	2 5	3 7	5 10	8 13	12 17	19 25																
	Fifth	500	2500			1 3	2 4	3 6	5 8	7 11	11 15	17 20	25 29																
	Sixth	500	3000			1 3	3 5	4 6	7 9	10 12	14 17	21 23	31 33																
	Seventh	500	3500			2 3	4 5	6 7	9 10	13 14	18 19	25 26	37 38																

↓ = Use first sampling plan below arrow. If sample size equals or exceeds lot or batch size, do 100 percent inspection.
↑ = Use first sampling plan above arrow (refer to preceding page, when necessary).
Ac = Acceptance number.
Re = Rejection number.
• = Use corresponding single sampling plan (or alternatively, use multiple plan below, where available).
* = Acceptance not permitted at this sample size.

TABLE 6-13 Multiple Sampling Plans for Tightened Inspection (Table IV-B of MIL-STD-105D)

Sample size code letter	Sample	Sample size	Cumulative sample size	Acceptable Quality Levels (tightened inspection)																									
				0.010	0.015	0.025	0.040	0.065	0.10	0.15	0.25	0.40	0.65	1.0	1.5	2.5	4.0	6.5	10	15	25	40	65	100	150	250	400	650	1000
				Ac Re	Ac Re	Ac Re	Ac Re	Ac Re	Ac Re	Ac Re	Ac Re	Ac Re	Ac Re	Ac Re	Ac Re	Ac Re	Ac Re	Ac Re	Ac Re	Ac Re	Ac Re	Ac Re	Ac Re	Ac Re	Ac Re	Ac Re	Ac Re	Ac Re	Ac Re
A				↓	↓	↓	↓	↓	↓	↓	↓	↓	↓	↓	↓	↓	↓	↓	↓	↓	↓	*	*	*	*	*	*	*	*
B				↓	↓	↓	↓	↓	↓	↓	↓	↓	↓	↓	↓	↓	↓	*	↓	↓	↔	↔	↔	↔	↔	↔	↔	↔	↔
C				↓	↓	↓	↓	↓	↓	↓	↓	↓	↓	↓	↓	↓	*	↓	↓	↔	↔	↔	↔	↔	↔	↔	↔	↔	↑
D	First	2	2	↓	↓	↓	↓	↓	↓	↓	↓	↓	↓	↓	↓	*	↓	↓	# 2	# 2	# 3	# 4	0 4	0 6	1 8	3 10	6 15	↑	↑
	Second	2	4																# 2	0 3	0 3	1 5	2 7	3 9	6 12	10 17	16 25		
	Third	2	6																0 2	0 3	1 4	2 6	4 9	7 12	11 17	17 24	26 36		
	Fourth	2	8																0 3	1 4	2 5	3 7	6 11	10 15	16 22	24 31	37 46		
	Fifth	2	10																1 3	2 4	3 6	5 8	9 12	14 17	22 25	32 37	49 55		
	Sixth	2	12																1 3	3 5	4 6	7 9	12 14	18 20	27 29	40 43	61 64		
	Seventh	2	14																2 3	4 5	6 7	9 10	14 15	21 22	32 33	48 49	72 73		
E	First	3	3	↓	↓	↓	↓	↓	↓	↓	↓	↓	↓	↓	*	↓	↓	# 2	# 2	# 3	# 4	0 4	0 6	1 8	3 10	6 15	↑	↑	↑
	Second	3	6															# 2	0 3	0 3	1 5	2 7	3 9	6 12	10 17	16 25			
	Third	3	9															0 2	0 3	1 4	2 6	4 9	7 12	11 17	17 24	26 36			
	Fourth	3	12															0 3	1 4	2 5	3 7	6 11	10 15	16 22	24 31	37 46			
	Fifth	3	15															1 3	2 4	3 6	5 8	9 12	14 17	22 25	32 37	49 55			
	Sixth	3	18															1 3	3 5	4 6	7 9	12 14	18 20	27 29	40 43	61 64			
	Seventh	3	21															2 3	4 5	6 7	9 10	14 15	21 22	32 33	48 49	72 73			
F	First	5	5	↓	↓	↓	↓	↓	↓	↓	↓	↓	↓	*	↓	↓	# 2	# 2	# 3	# 4	0 4	0 6	1 8	↑	↑	↑	↑	↑	↑
	Second	5	10														# 2	0 3	0 3	1 5	2 7	3 9	6 12						
	Third	5	15														0 2	0 3	1 4	2 6	4 9	7 12	11 17						
	Fourth	5	20														0 3	1 4	2 5	3 7	6 11	10 15	16 22						
	Fifth	5	25														1 3	2 4	3 6	5 8	9 12	14 17	22 25						
	Sixth	5	30														1 3	3 5	4 6	7 9	12 14	18 20	27 29						
	Seventh	5	35														2 3	4 5	6 7	9 10	14 15	21 22	32 33						
G	First	8	8	↓	↓	↓	↓	↓	↓	↓	↓	↓	*	↓	↓	# 2	# 2	# 3	# 4	0 4	0 6	1 8	↑	↑	↑	↑	↑	↑	↑
	Second	8	16												# 2	0 3	0 3	1 5	2 7	3 9	6 12							
	Third	8	24												0 2	0 3	1 4	2 6	4 9	7 12	11 17							
	Fourth	8	32												0 3	1 4	2 5	3 7	6 11	10 15	16 22							
	Fifth	8	40												1 3	2 4	3 6	5 8	9 12	14 17	22 25							
	Sixth	8	48												1 3	3 5	4 6	7 9	12 14	18 20	27 29							
	Seventh	8	56												2 3	4 5	6 7	9 10	14 15	21 22	32 33							
H	First	13	13	↓	↓	↓	↓	↓	↓	↓	↓	*	↓	↓	# 2	# 2	# 3	# 4	0 4	0 6	1 8	↑	↑	↑	↑	↑	↑	↑	↑
	Second	13	26											# 2	0 3	0 3	1 5	2 7	3 9	6 12								
	Third	13	39											0 2	0 3	1 4	2 6	4 9	7 12	11 17								
	Fourth	13	52											0 3	1 4	2 5	3 7	6 11	10 15	16 22								
	Fifth	13	65											1 3	2 4	3 6	5 8	9 12	14 17	22 25								
	Sixth	13	78											1 3	3 5	4 6	7 9	12 14	18 20	27 29								
	Seventh	13	91											2 3	4 5	6 7	9 10	14 15	21 22	32 33								
J	First	20	20	↓	↓	↓	↓	↓	↓	↓	*	↓	↓	# 2	# 2	# 3	# 4	0 4	0 6	1 8	↑	↑	↑	↑	↑	↑	↑	↑	↑
	Second	20	40										# 2	0 3	0 3	1 5	2 7	3 9	6 12									
	Third	20	60										0 2	0 3	1 4	2 6	4 9	7 12	11 17									
	Fourth	20	80										0 3	1 4	2 5	3 7	6 11	10 15	16 22									
	Fifth	20	100										1 3	2 4	3 6	5 8	9 12	14 17	22 25									
	Sixth	20	120										1 3	3 5	4 6	7 9	12 14	18 20	27 29									
	Seventh	20	140										2 3	4 5	6 7	9 10	14 15	21 22	32 33									

↓ = Use first sampling plan below arrow (refer to continuation of table on following page, when necessary). If sample size equals or exceeds lot or batch size, do 100 percent inspection.
↑ = Use first sampling plan above arrow.
Ac = Acceptance number
Re = Rejection number
* = Use corresponding single sampling plan (or alternatively, use multiple sampling plan below, where available).
↔ = Use corresponding double sampling plan (or alternatively, use multiple sampling plan below, where available).
= Acceptance not permitted at this sample size.

TABLE 6-13 *(continued)*

Sample size code letter	Sample	Sample size	Cumulative sample size	Acceptable Quality Levels (tightened inspection)																									
				0.010	0.015	0.025	0.040	0.065	0.10	0.15	0.25	0.40	0.65	1.0	1.5	2.5	4.0	6.5	10	15	25	40	65	100	150	250	400	650	1000
				Ac Re	Ac Re	Ac Re	Ac Re	Ac Re	Ac Re	Ac Re	Ac Re	Ac Re	Ac Re	Ac Re	Ac Re	Ac Re	Ac Re	Ac Re	Ac Re	Ac Re	Ac Re	Ac Re	Ac Re	Ac Re	Ac Re	Ac Re	Ac Re	Ac Re	Ac Re
K	First	32	32	↓	↓	↓	↓	↓	↓	*	↓	↓	• 2	• 2	• 3	• 4	0 4	0 6	1 8	↑	↑	↑	↑	↑	↑	↑	↑	↑	↑
	Second	32	64										• 2	0 3	0 3	1 5	2 7	3 9	6 12										
	Third	32	96										0 2	0 3	1 4	2 6	4 9	7 12	11 17										
	Fourth	32	128										0 3	1 4	2 5	3 7	6 11	10 15	16 22										
	Fifth	32	160										1 3	2 4	3 6	5 8	9 12	14 17	22 25										
	Sixth	32	192										1 3	3 5	4 6	7 9	12 14	18 20	27 29										
	Seventh	32	224										2 3	4 5	6 7	9 10	14 15	21 22	32 33										
L	First	50	50	↓	↓	↓	↓	↓	*	↓	↓	• 2	• 2	• 3	• 4	0 4	0 6	1 8	↑										
	Second	50	100									• 2	0 3	0 3	1 5	2 7	3 9	6 12											
	Third	50	150									0 2	0 3	1 4	2 6	4 9	7 12	11 17											
	Fourth	50	200									0 3	1 4	2 5	3 7	6 11	10 15	16 22											
	Fifth	50	250									1 3	2 4	3 6	5 8	9 12	14 17	22 25											
	Sixth	50	300									1 3	3 5	4 6	7 9	12 14	18 20	27 29											
	Seventh	50	350									2 3	4 5	6 7	9 10	14 15	21 22	32 33											
M	First	80	80	↓	↓	↓	↓	*	↓	↓	• 2	• 2	• 3	• 4	0 4	0 6	1 8	↑											
	Second	80	160								• 2	0 3	0 3	1 5	2 7	3 9	6 12												
	Third	80	240								0 2	0 3	1 4	2 6	4 9	7 12	11 17												
	Fourth	80	320								0 3	1 4	2 5	3 7	6 11	10 15	16 22												
	Fifth	80	400								1 3	2 4	3 6	5 8	9 12	14 17	22 25												
	Sixth	80	480								1 3	3 5	4 6	7 9	12 14	18 20	27 29												
	Seventh	80	560								2 3	4 5	6 7	9 10	14 15	21 22	32 33												
N	First	125	125	↓	↓	↓	*	↓	↓	• 2	• 2	• 3	• 4	0 4	0 6	1 8	↑												
	Second	125	250							• 2	0 3	0 3	1 5	2 7	3 9	6 12													
	Third	125	375							0 2	0 3	1 4	2 6	4 9	7 12	11 17													
	Fourth	125	500							0 3	1 4	2 5	3 7	6 11	10 15	16 22													
	Fifth	125	625							1 3	2 4	3 6	5 8	9 12	14 17	22 25													
	Sixth	125	750							1 3	3 5	4 6	7 9	12 14	18 20	27 29													
	Seventh	125	875							2 3	4 5	6 7	9 10	14 15	21 22	32 33													
P	First	200	200	↓	↓	*	↓	↓	• 2	• 2	• 3	• 4	0 4	0 6	1 8	↑													
	Second	200	400						• 2	0 3	0 3	1 5	2 7	3 9	6 12														
	Third	200	600						0 2	0 3	1 4	2 6	4 9	7 12	11 17														
	Fourth	200	800						0 3	1 4	2 5	3 7	6 11	10 15	16 22														
	Fifth	200	1000						1 3	2 4	3 6	5 8	9 12	14 17	22 25														
	Sixth	200	1200						1 3	3 5	4 6	7 9	12 14	18 20	27 29														
	Seventh	200	1400						2 3	4 5	6 7	9 10	14 15	21 22	32 33														
Q	First	315	315	↓	*	↓	↓	• 2	• 2	• 3	• 4	0 4	0 6	1 8	↑														
	Second	315	630					• 2	0 3	0 3	1 5	2 7	3 9	6 12															
	Third	315	945					0 2	0 3	1 4	2 6	4 9	7 12	11 17															
	Fourth	315	1260					0 3	1 4	2 5	3 7	6 11	10 15	16 22															
	Fifth	315	1575					1 3	2 4	3 6	5 8	9 12	14 17	22 25															
	Sixth	315	1890					1 3	3 5	4 6	7 9	12 14	18 20	27 29															
	Seventh	315	2205					2 3	4 5	6 7	9 10	14 15	21 22	32 33															
R	First	500	500	*	↑	↓	• 2	• 2	• 3	• 4	0 4	0 6	1 8	↑															
	Second	500	1000				• 2	0 3	0 3	1 5	2 7	3 9	6 12																
	Third	500	1500				0 2	0 3	1 4	2 6	4 9	7 12	11 17																
	Fourth	500	2000				0 3	1 4	2 5	3 7	6 11	10 15	16 22																
	Fifth	500	2500				1 3	2 4	3 6	5 8	9 12	14 17	22 25																
	Sixth	500	3000				1 3	3 5	4 6	7 9	12 14	18 20	27 29																
	Seventh	500	3500				2 3	4 5	6 7	9 10	14 15	21 22	32 33																
S	First	800	800			• 2																							
	Second	800	1600			• 2																							
	Third	800	2400			0 2																							
	Fourth	800	3200			0 3																							
	Fifth	800	4000			1 3																							
	Sixth	800	4800			1 3																							
	Seventh	800	5600			2 3																							

↓ = Use first sampling plan below arrow. If sample size equals or exceeds lot or batch size, do 100 percent inspection.
↑ = Use first sampling plan above arrow (refer to preceding page, when necessary)
Ac = Acceptance number
Re = Rejection number
* = Use corresponding single sampling plan (or alternatively, use multiple sampling plan below, where available)
• = Acceptance not permitted at this sample size.

TABLE 6-14 Multiple Sampling Plans for Reduced Inspection (Table IV-C of MIL-STD-105D)

Sample size code letter	Sample	Sample size	Cumulative sample size	Acceptable Quality Levels (reduced inspection) †																									
				0.010	0.015	0.025	0.040	0.065	0.10	0.15	0.25	0.40	0.65	1.0	1.5	2.5	4.0	6.5	10	15	25	40	65	100	150	250	400	650	1000
				Ac Re	Ac Re	Ac Re	Ac Re	Ac Re	Ac Re	Ac Re	Ac Re	Ac Re	Ac Re	Ac Re	Ac Re	Ac Re	Ac Re	Ac Re	Ac Re	Ac Re	Ac Re	Ac Re	Ac Re	Ac Re	Ac Re	Ac Re	Ac Re	Ac Re	Ac Re
A				↓	↓	↓	↓	↓	↓	↓	↓	↓	↓	↓	↓	↓	↓	*	↓	↓	*	*	*	*	*	*	*	*	*
B				↓	↓	↓	↓	↓	↓	↓	↓	↓	↓	↓	↓	↓	*	↑	↓	*	*	*	*	*	*	*	*	*	*
C				↓	↓	↓	↓	↓	↓	↓	↓	↓	↓	↓	↓	*	↑	↓	*	*	*	*	*	*	*	*	*	*	↑
D				↓	↓	↓	↓	↓	↓	↓	↓	↓	↓	↓	*	↑	↓	↔	↔	↔	↔	↔	↔	↔	↔	↔	↔	↑	↑
E				↓	↓	↓	↓	↓	↓	↓	↓	↓	↓	*	↑	↓	↔	↔	↔	↔	↔	↔	↔	↔	↔	↔	↑	↑	↑
F	First	2	2	↓	↓	↓	↓	↓	↓	↓	↓	↓	*	↑	↓	# 2	# 2	# 3	# 3	# 4	# 4	0 5	0 6	↑	↑	↑	↑	↑	↑
	Second	2	4	↓	↓	↓	↓	↓	↓	↓	↓	↓		↑	↓	# 2	# 3	# 3	0 4	0 5	1 6	1 7	3 9	↑	↑	↑	↑	↑	↑
	Third	2	6	↓	↓	↓	↓	↓	↓	↓	↓	↓		↑	↓	0 2	0 3	0 4	0 5	1 6	2 8	3 9	6 12	↑	↑	↑	↑	↑	↑
	Fourth	2	8	↓	↓	↓	↓	↓	↓	↓	↓	↓		↑	↓	0 3	0 4	0 5	1 6	2 7	3 10	5 12	8 15	↑	↑	↑	↑	↑	↑
	Fifth	2	10	↓	↓	↓	↓	↓	↓	↓	↓	↓		↑	↓	0 3	0 4	1 6	2 7	3 8	5 11	7 13	11 17	↑	↑	↑	↑	↑	↑
	Sixth	2	12	↓	↓	↓	↓	↓	↓	↓	↓	↓		↑	↓	0 3	1 5	1 6	3 7	4 9	7 12	10 15	14 20	↑	↑	↑	↑	↑	↑
	Seventh	2	14	↓	↓	↓	↓	↓	↓	↓	↓	↓		↑	↓	1 3	1 5	2 7	4 8	6 10	9 14	13 17	18 22	↑	↑	↑	↑	↑	↑
G	First	3	3	↓	↓	↓	↓	↓	↓	↓	↓	*	↑	↓	# 2	# 2	# 3	# 3	# 4	# 4	0 5	0 6	↑	↑	↑	↑	↑	↑	↑
	Second	3	6	↓	↓	↓	↓	↓	↓	↓	↓		↑	↓	# 2	# 3	# 3	0 4	0 5	1 6	1 7	3 9	↑	↑	↑	↑	↑	↑	↑
	Third	3	9	↓	↓	↓	↓	↓	↓	↓	↓		↑	↓	0 2	0 3	0 4	0 5	1 6	2 8	3 9	6 12	↑	↑	↑	↑	↑	↑	↑
	Fourth	3	12	↓	↓	↓	↓	↓	↓	↓	↓		↑	↓	0 3	0 4	0 5	1 6	2 7	3 10	5 12	8 15	↑	↑	↑	↑	↑	↑	↑
	Fifth	3	15	↓	↓	↓	↓	↓	↓	↓	↓		↑	↓	0 3	0 4	1 6	2 7	3 8	5 11	7 13	11 17	↑	↑	↑	↑	↑	↑	↑
	Sixth	3	18	↓	↓	↓	↓	↓	↓	↓	↓		↑	↓	0 3	1 5	1 6	3 7	4 9	7 12	10 15	14 20	↑	↑	↑	↑	↑	↑	↑
	Seventh	3	21	↓	↓	↓	↓	↓	↓	↓	↓		↑	↓	1 3	1 5	2 7	4 8	6 10	9 14	13 17	18 22	↑	↑	↑	↑	↑	↑	↑
H	First	5	5	↓	↓	↓	↓	↓	↓	↓	*	↑	↓	# 2	# 2	# 3	# 3	# 4	# 4	0 5	0 6	↑	↑	↑	↑	↑	↑	↑	↑
	Second	5	10	↓	↓	↓	↓	↓	↓	↓		↑	↓	# 2	# 3	# 3	0 4	0 5	1 6	1 7	3 9	↑	↑	↑	↑	↑	↑	↑	↑
	Third	5	15	↓	↓	↓	↓	↓	↓	↓		↑	↓	0 2	0 3	0 4	0 5	1 6	2 8	3 9	6 12	↑	↑	↑	↑	↑	↑	↑	↑
	Fourth	5	20	↓	↓	↓	↓	↓	↓	↓		↑	↓	0 3	0 4	0 5	1 6	2 7	3 10	5 12	8 15	↑	↑	↑	↑	↑	↑	↑	↑
	Fifth	5	25	↓	↓	↓	↓	↓	↓	↓		↑	↓	0 3	0 4	1 6	2 7	3 8	5 11	7 13	11 17	↑	↑	↑	↑	↑	↑	↑	↑
	Sixth	5	30	↓	↓	↓	↓	↓	↓	↓		↑	↓	0 3	1 5	1 6	3 7	4 9	7 12	10 15	14 20	↑	↑	↑	↑	↑	↑	↑	↑
	Seventh	5	35	↓	↓	↓	↓	↓	↓	↓		↑	↓	1 3	1 5	2 7	4 8	6 10	9 14	13 17	18 22	↑	↑	↑	↑	↑	↑	↑	↑
J	First	8	8	↓	↓	↓	↓	↓	↓	*	↑	↓	# 2	# 2	# 3	# 3	# 4	# 4	0 5	0 6	↑	↑	↑	↑	↑	↑	↑	↑	↑
	Second	8	16	↓	↓	↓	↓	↓	↓		↑	↓	# 2	# 3	# 3	0 4	0 5	1 6	1 7	3 9	↑	↑	↑	↑	↑	↑	↑	↑	↑
	Third	8	24	↓	↓	↓	↓	↓	↓		↑	↓	0 2	0 3	0 4	0 5	1 6	2 8	3 9	6 12	↑	↑	↑	↑	↑	↑	↑	↑	↑
	Fourth	8	32	↓	↓	↓	↓	↓	↓		↑	↓	0 3	0 4	0 5	1 6	2 7	3 10	5 12	8 15	↑	↑	↑	↑	↑	↑	↑	↑	↑
	Fifth	8	40	↓	↓	↓	↓	↓	↓		↑	↓	0 3	0 4	1 6	2 7	3 8	5 11	7 13	11 17	↑	↑	↑	↑	↑	↑	↑	↑	↑
	Sixth	8	48	↓	↓	↓	↓	↓	↓		↑	↓	0 3	1 5	1 6	3 7	4 9	7 12	10 15	14 20	↑	↑	↑	↑	↑	↑	↑	↑	↑
	Seventh	8	56	↓	↓	↓	↓	↓	↓		↑	↓	1 3	1 5	2 7	4 8	6 10	9 14	13 17	18 22	↑	↑	↑	↑	↑	↑	↑	↑	↑
K	First	13	13	↓	↓	↓	↓	↓	*	↑	↓	# 2	# 2	# 3	# 3	# 4	# 4	0 5	0 6	↑	↑	↑	↑	↑	↑	↑	↑	↑	↑
	Second	13	26	↓	↓	↓	↓	↓		↑	↓	# 2	# 3	# 3	0 4	0 5	1 6	1 7	3 9	↑	↑	↑	↑	↑	↑	↑	↑	↑	↑
	Third	13	39	↓	↓	↓	↓	↓		↑	↓	0 2	0 3	0 4	0 5	1 6	2 8	3 9	6 12	↑	↑	↑	↑	↑	↑	↑	↑	↑	↑
	Fourth	13	52	↓	↓	↓	↓	↓		↑	↓	0 3	0 4	0 5	1 6	2 7	3 10	5 12	8 15	↑	↑	↑	↑	↑	↑	↑	↑	↑	↑
	Fifth	13	65	↓	↓	↓	↓	↓		↑	↓	0 3	0 4	1 6	2 7	3 8	5 11	7 13	11 17	↑	↑	↑	↑	↑	↑	↑	↑	↑	↑
	Sixth	13	78	↓	↓	↓	↓	↓		↑	↓	0 3	1 5	1 6	3 7	4 9	7 12	10 15	14 20	↑	↑	↑	↑	↑	↑	↑	↑	↑	↑
	Seventh	13	91	↓	↓	↓	↓	↓		↑	↓	1 3	1 5	2 7	4 8	6 10	9 14	13 17	18 22	↑	↑	↑	↑	↑	↑	↑	↑	↑	↑

↓ = Use first sampling plan below arrow (refer to continuation of table on following page, when necessary). If sample size equals, or exceeds lot or batch size, do 100 percent inspection.

↑ = Use first sampling plan above arrow.

Ac = Acceptance number

Re = Rejection number

* = Use corresponding single sampling plan (or alternatively, use multiple sampling plan below, where available).

↔ = Use corresponding double sampling plan (or alternatively, use multiple sampling plan below, where available).

\# = Acceptance not permitted at this sample size.

† = If, after the final sample, the acceptance number has been exceeded, but the rejection number has not been reached, accept the lot but reinstate normal inspection (see 10.1.4).

TABLE 6-14 (continued)

Sample size code letter	Sample	Sample size	Cumulative sample size	Acceptable Quality Levels (reduced inspection)†																									
				0.010	0.015	0.025	0.040	0.065	0.10	0.15	0.25	0.40	0.65	1.0	1.5	2.5	4.0	6.5	10	15	25	40	65	100	150	250	400	650	1000
				Ac Re	Ac Re	Ac Re	Ac Re	Ac Re	Ac Re	Ac Re	Ac Re	Ac Re	Ac Re	Ac Re	Ac Re	Ac Re	Ac Re	Ac Re	Ac Re	Ac Re	Ac Re	Ac Re	Ac Re	Ac Re	Ac Re	Ac Re	Ac Re	Ac Re	Ac Re
L	First	20	20	↓	↓	↓	↓	*	↑	↓	# 2	# 2	# 3	# 3	# 4	# 4	0 5	0 6	↑	↑	↑	↑	↑	↑	↑	↑	↑	↑	↑
	Second	20	40								# 2	# 3	# 3	0 4	0 5	1 6	1 7	3 9											
	Third	20	60								0 2	0 3	0 4	0 5	1 6	2 8	3 9	6 12											
	Fourth	20	80								0 3	0 4	0 5	1 6	2 7	3 10	5 12	8 15											
	Fifth	20	100								0 3	0 4	1 6	2 7	3 8	5 11	7 13	11 17											
	Sixth	20	120								0 3	1 5	1 6	3 7	4 9	7 12	10 15	14 20											
	Seventh	20	140								1 3	1 5	2 7	4 8	6 10	9 14	13 17	18 22											
M	First	32	32				*	↑	↓	# 2	# 2	# 3	# 3	# 4	# 4	0 5	0 6	↑											
	Second	32	64							# 2	# 3	# 3	0 4	0 5	1 6	1 7	3 9												
	Third	32	96							0 2	0 3	0 4	0 5	1 6	2 8	3 9	6 12												
	Fourth	32	128							0 3	0 4	0 5	1 6	2 7	3 10	5 12	8 15												
	Fifth	32	160							0 3	0 4	1 6	2 7	3 8	5 11	7 13	11 17												
	Sixth	32	192							0 3	1 5	1 6	3 7	4 9	7 12	10 15	14 20												
	Seventh	32	224							1 3	1 5	2 7	4 8	6 10	9 14	13 17	18 22												
N	First	50	50			*	↑	↓	# 2	# 2	# 3	# 3	# 4	# 4	0 5	0 6	↑												
	Second	50	100						# 2	# 3	# 3	0 4	0 5	1 6	1 7	3 9													
	Third	50	150						0 2	0 3	0 4	0 5	1 6	2 8	3 9	6 12													
	Fourth	50	200						0 3	0 4	0 5	1 6	2 7	3 10	5 12	8 15													
	Fifth	50	250						0 3	0 4	1 6	2 7	3 8	5 11	7 13	11 17													
	Sixth	50	300						0 3	1 5	1 6	3 7	4 9	7 12	10 15	14 20													
	Seventh	50	350						1 3	1 5	2 7	4 8	6 10	9 14	13 17	18 22													
P	First	80	80		*	↑	↓	# 2	# 2	# 3	# 3	# 4	# 4	0 5	0 6	↑													
	Second	80	160					# 2	# 3	# 3	0 4	0 5	1 6	1 7	3 9														
	Third	80	240					0 2	0 3	0 4	0 5	1 6	2 8	3 9	6 12														
	Fourth	80	320					0 3	0 4	0 5	1 6	2 7	3 10	5 12	8 15														
	Fifth	80	400					0 3	0 4	1 6	2 7	3 8	5 11	7 13	11 17														
	Sixth	80	480					0 3	1 5	1 6	3 7	4 9	7 12	10 15	14 20														
	Seventh	80	560					1 3	1 5	2 7	4 8	6 10	9 14	13 17	18 22														
Q	First	125	125	*	↑	↓	# 2	# 2	# 3	# 3	# 4	# 4	0 5	0 6	↑														
	Second	125	250				# 2	# 3	# 3	0 4	0 5	1 6	1 7	3 9															
	Third	125	375				0 2	0 3	0 4	0 5	1 6	2 8	3 9	6 12															
	Fourth	125	500				0 3	0 4	0 5	1 6	2 7	3 10	5 12	8 15															
	Fifth	125	625				0 3	0 4	1 6	2 7	3 8	5 11	7 13	11 17															
	Sixth	125	750				0 3	1 5	1 6	3 7	4 9	7 12	10 15	14 20															
	Seventh	125	875				1 3	1 5	2 7	4 8	6 10	9 14	13 17	18 22															
R	First	200	200	↑		# 2	# 2	# 3	# 3	# 4	# 4	0 5	0 6	↑															
	Second	200	400			# 2	# 3	# 3	0 4	0 5	1 6	1 7	3 9																
	Third	200	600			0 2	0 3	0 4	0 5	1 6	2 8	3 9	6 12																
	Fourth	200	800			0 3	0 4	0 5	1 6	2 7	3 10	5 12	8 15																
	Fifth	200	1000			0 3	0 4	1 6	2 7	3 8	5 11	7 13	11 17																
	Sixth	200	1200			0 3	1 5	1 6	3 7	4 9	7 12	10 15	14 20																
	Seventh	200	1400			1 3	1 5	2 7	4 8	6 10	9 14	13 17	18 22																

↓ = Use first sampling plan below arrow. If sample size equals, or exceeds, lot or batch size, do 100 percent inspection.
↑ = Use first sampling plan above arrow (refer to preceding page when necessary).
Ac = Acceptance number
Re = Rejection number
# = Acceptance not permitted at this sample size.
† = If, after the final sample, the acceptance number has been exceeded, but the rejection number has not been reached, accept the lot, but reinstate normal inspection (see 10.1.4).

Reduced inspection (from Table 6-14):

n	Ac	Re
5	#	3
5	0	4
5	0	5
5	1	6
5	2	7
5	3	7
5	4	8

Two different symbols are used in the multiple sampling tables. The symbol # is used to indicate that acceptance is not permitted at this time because the sample size is too small. When the symbol †† is encountered in the table, it indicates that the corresponding double sampling plan should be used. Or the multiple sampling plan immediately below can be used, where available.

Normal, Tightened, and Reduced Inspection

Unless otherwise directed by the responsible authority, inspection starts with the normal inspection condition. Normal, tightened, or reduced inspection will continue unchanged for each class of defects or defectives or until the switching procedures given below require a change.

Normal to Tightened. When normal inspection is in effect, tightened inspection shall be instituted when 2 out of 5 consecutive lots or batches have been rejected on original inspection (i.e., ignoring resubmitted lots).

Tightened to Normal. When tightened inspection is in effect, normal inspection shall be instituted when 5 consecutive lots or batches are accepted on original inspection.

Normal to Reduced. When normal inspection is in effect, reduced inspection shall be instituted provided all four of the following conditions are satisfied.

1. The preceding 10 lots or batches have been on normal inspection and none of the lots has been rejected on original inspection. In some cases more than 10 lots are necessary to obtain a sufficient number of sample units for a particular AQL, as indicated by the note of Table 6-15.

2. The total number of defectives (defects) in the samples from the preceding 10 lots or batches is equal to or less than the applicable number given in Table 6-15. For example, if the total number inspected for the past 10 lots or batches is 600 and the AQL is 2.5%, the limit number is 7. Therefore, to qualify for reduced inspection, the number defective in the 600 inspected must be equal to or less than 7. In some cases more than 10 lots or batches are necessary to obtain a sufficient number of sample units for a particular AQL, as indicated by the note of Table 6-15.

TABLE 6-15 Limit Numbers for Reduced Inspection (Table VIII of MIL-STD-105D)

Number of sample units from last 10 lots or batches	Acceptable Quality Level																								
	0.010	0.015	0.025	0.040	0.065	0.10	0.15	0.25	0.40	0.65	1.0	1.5	2.5	4.0	6.5	10	15	25	40	65	100	150	250	400	650	1000
20 - 29	*	*	*	*	*	*	*	*	*	*	*	*	*	*	*	0	0	2	4	8	14	22	40	68	115	181
30 - 49	*	*	*	*	*	*	*	*	*	*	*	*	*	*	0	0	1	3	7	13	22	36	63	105	178	277
50 - 79	*	*	*	*	*	*	*	*	*	*	*	*	*	0	0	2	3	7	14	25	40	63	110	181	301	
80 - 129	*	*	*	*	*	*	*	*	*	*	*	*	0	0	2	4	7	14	24	42	68	105	181	297		
130 - 199	*	*	*	*	*	*	*	*	*	*	*	0	0	2	4	7	13	25	42	72	115	177	301	490		
200 - 319	*	*	*	*	*	*	*	*	*	*	0	0	2	4	8	14	22	40	68	115	181	277	471			
320 - 499	*	*	*	*	*	*	*	*	*	0	0	1	4	8	14	24	39	68	113	189						
500 - 799	*	*	*	*	*	*	*	*	0	0	2	3	7	14	25	40	63	110	181							
800 - 1249	*	*	*	*	*	*	*	0	0	2	4	7	14	24	42	68	105	181								
1250 - 1999	*	*	*	*	*	*	0	0	2	4	7	13	24	40	69	110	169									
2000 - 3149	*	*	*	*	*	0	0	2	4	8	14	22	40	68	115	181										
3150 - 1999	*	*	*	*	0	0	1	4	8	14	24	38	63	111	186											
5000 - 7999	*	*	*	0	0	2	3	7	14	25	40	63	110	181												
8000 - 12499	*	*	0	0	2	4	7	14	24	42	68	105	181													
12500 - 19999	*	0	0	2	4	7	13	24	40	69	110	169														
20000 - 31499	0	0	2	4	8	14	22	40	68	115	181															
31500 - 49999	0	1	4	8	14	24	38	67	111	186																
50000 & Over	2	3	7	14	25	40	63	110	181	301																

*Denotes that the number of sample units from the last ten lots or batches is not sufficient for reduced inspection for this AQL. In this instance more than ten lots or batches may be used for the calculation, provided that the lots or batches used are the most recent ones in sequence, that they have all been on normal inspection, and that none has been rejected while on original inspection.

3. Production is at a steady rate. In other words, no difficulties, such as machine breakdowns, material shortages, or labor problems, have occurred recently.

4. Reduced inspection is considered desirable by the responsible authority (consumer). The consumer must decide if the savings from fewer inspections warrants the additional record-keeping and inspector training expenses.

Reduced to Normal. When reduced inspection is in effect, normal inspection shall be instituted provided any of the four conditions below are satisfied on original inspection.

1. A lot or batch is rejected.
2. When the sampling procedure terminates with neither acceptance nor rejection criteria having been met, the lot or batch is accepted, but normal inspection is reinstated starting with the next lot.
3. Production is irregular or delayed.
4. Other conditions warrant that normal inspection will be instituted.

In the event that 10 consecutive lots or batches remain on tightened inspection (or such other number as may be designated by the responsible authority), inspection under the provisions of this document should be discontinued pending action to improve the quality of submitted material.

Supplementary Information

The standard includes operating characteristic curves for single sampling plans with normal inspection which indicate the percentage of lots or batches that may be expected to be accepted under the various sampling plans for a given process quality. OC curves for double and multiple sampling plans are not given in the standard but are matched as closely as practical.

Table V (not reproduced in this text) of the standard gives the average outgoing quality limit for single sampling plans with normal and tightened inspection.

Average sample-size curves for double and multiple sampling as a function of the equivalent single sample size are shown in Table IX and are reproduced in Figure 6-16. These show the average sample sizes that may be expected to occur under the various sampling plans for a given process quality.

MIL-STD-105D is designed for use where the units of product are produced in a continuing series of lots or batches. However, if a sampling plan is desirable for a lot or batch of an isolated nature, it should be chosen based on the limiting quality level (LQL) and consumer's risk. Tables (not reproduced in this text) for consumer's risks of 0.05 and 0.10 are included in the standard. Therefore, a sampling plan for isolated lots can be obtained which will come close to both the producer's and consumer's criteria.

COMPUTER PROGRAM

The computer program given in Figure 6-24 calculates the probability of acceptance (P_a) for the process quality as given by the fraction defective (p) for an OC curve for single sampling. It is based on the calculated value of the Poisson probability formula rather than the table value. Therefore, it is more accurate because there are no rounding errors as occur with the table values. The reader may wish to check the P_a values with Table 6-2. If more plotted points are desired, the increment in statement 180 can be reduced to, say, 0.005.

```
10Ø REM                                   OC CURVE - SS PLAN
2Ø REM                                     Based on Poisson
3Ø REM
4Ø REM            N  = Sample Size
5Ø REM            P  = Process Quality(Fraction Defective)
6Ø REM            C  = Acceptance Number
7Ø REM            PA = Probability of Acceptance
8Ø REM
9Ø PRINT " Enter the Sample Size." : INPUT N
1ØØ LPRINT TAB(5);" n = ";N
11Ø PRINT "Enter the Acceptance Number." : INPUT K
12Ø LPRINT TAB(5);" c = ";K : LPRINT
13Ø P = Ø
14Ø LPRINT TAB(5);" p "; TAB(15); " Pa"
15Ø P = P + .Ø1
16Ø NP = N * P
17Ø PA = Ø
18Ø       FOR C = K TO Ø STEP -1
19Ø       CF = C
2ØØ       IF C < 1 THEN CF = 1
21Ø       IF C < 3 THEN 26Ø
22Ø       CF = 2
23Ø             FOR J = 3 TO C
24Ø             CF = CF * J
25Ø             NEXT J
26Ø       PA = PA + NP^C / (CF * 2.71828^NP)
27Ø       NEXT C
28Ø LPRINT TAB(4);P;TAB(12);PA
29Ø IF PA < .Ø5 GOTO 31Ø
3ØØ GOTO 15Ø
31Ø END
```

Figure 6-24 Computer program in BASIC for the OC curve for a single sampling plan.

```
n =  89
c =  2

 p          Pa
.01       .93878
.02       .735971
.03       .501003
.04       .309893
.05       .179281
.06       .0987847
.07       .0524594
.08       .0270673
```

Figure 6-24 Continued.

PROBLEMS

1. Construct the OC curve for the single sampling plan $N = 9000$, $n = 110$, and $c = 3$. Use about seven points.

2. Construct the OC curve for the single sampling plan $N = 830$, $n = 62$, and $c = 1$. Use about seven points.

3. Determine the equation for the OC curve for the sampling plan $N = 10{,}000$, $n_1 = 200$, $c_1 = 2$, $r_1 = 6$, $n_2 = 350$, $c_2 = 6$, and $r_2 = 7$. Construct the curve using about five points.

4. Determine the equation for the OC curve for the following sampling plans:
   (a) $N = 500$, $n_1 = 50$, $c_1 = 0$, $r_1 = 3$, $n_2 = 70$, $c_2 = 2$, $r_2 = 3$
   (b) $N = 6000$, $n_1 = 80$, $c_1 = 2$, $r_1 = 4$, $n_2 = 160$, $c_2 = 5$, $r_2 = 6$
   (c) $N = 22{,}000$, $n_1 = 260$, $c_1 = 5$, $r_1 = 9$, $n_2 = 310$, $c_2 = 8$, $r_2 = 9$
   (d) $N = 10{,}000$, $n_1 = 300$, $c_1 = 4$, $n_2 = 300$, $c_2 = 8$
   (e) $N = 800$, $n_1 = 1000$, $c_1 = 0$, $n_2 = 100$, $c_2 = 4$

5. Construct the ASN curves for the single sampling plan $n = 200$, $c = 5$, and the equally effective double sampling plan $n_1 = 125$, $c_1 = 2$, $r_1 = 5$, $n_2 = 125$, $c_2 = 6$, $r_2 = 7$. Compare with Figure 6-16.

6. Construct the ASN curves for the single sampling plan $n = 80$, $c = 3$, and the equally effective double sampling plan $n_1 = 50$, $c_1 = 1$, $r_1 = 4$, $n_2 = 50$, $c_2 = 4$, $r_2 = 5$. Compare with Figure 6-16.

7. Construct the ATI curve for $N = 500$, $n = 80$, $c = 0$.

8. Construct the ATI curve for $N = 10{,}000$, $n = 315$, $c = 5$.

9. For the sampling plan of Problem 1, determine the AOQ curve and the AOQL.

10. Determine the AOQ curve and the AOQL for the single sampling plan $N = 16{,}000$, $n = 280$, $c = 4$.

11. Using $c = 1$, $c = 5$, and $c = 8$, determine three sampling plans which ensure that product 0.8% defective (good product) will be rejected 5.0% of the time.

12. For $c = 3$, $c = 6$, and $c = 12$, determine the sampling plans for AQL = 1.5% and $\alpha = 0.05$.

13. For a consumer's risk of 0.10 and a LQL of 6.5%, determine the sampling plans for $c = 2$, 6, and 14.

14. If product that is 8.3% defective is accepted 10% of the time, determine three sampling plans which meet this criteria. Use $c = 0$, 3, and 7.

15. A single sampling plan is desired with a consumer's risk of 0.10 of accepting 3.0% defective product and a producer's risk of 0.05 of rejecting 0.7% defective product. Select the plan with the lowest sample size.

16. The producer's risk is defined by $\alpha = 0.05$ for 1.5% defective product and the consumer's risk is defined by $\beta = 0.10$ for 4.6% defective product. Select a sampling plan that exactly meets the producer's stipulation and comes as close as possible to the consumer's stipulation.

17. For the information of Problem 15, select the plan that exactly meets the consumer's stipulation and comes as close as possible to the producer's stipulation.

18. For the information of Problem 16, select the plan with the smallest sample size.

19. Give $p_{0.10} = 0.053$ and $p_{0.95} = 0.014$, determine the single sampling plan which exactly meets the consumer's stipulation and comes as close as possible to the producer's stipulation.

20. For the information of Problem 19, select the plan that meets the producer's stipulation and comes as close as possible to the consumer's stipulation.

21. If a single sampling plan is desired with an AOQL of 1.8% at an incoming quality of 2.6%, what is the common point on the OC curves for a family of sampling plans that meet the AOQL and $100p_0$ stipulation?

22. Using MIL-STD-105D, determine the single sampling plans for the following information.

	Inspection Level	*Inspection*	*AQL*	*Lot Size*
(a)	II	Tightened	1.5%	1,400
(b)	I	Normal	65	115
(c)	III	Reduced	0.40%	160,000
(d)	III	Normal	2.5%	27

23. Explain the meaning of the sampling plan determined in Problem 22(c) if (a) 6 defectives are found in the sample, (b) if 8 defectives are found, and (c) if 4 defectives are found.

24. Using MIL-STD-105D, determine the double sampling plans for the information below.

	Inspection Level	*Inspection*	*AQL*	*Lot Size*
(a)	I	Normal	150	145
(b)	II	Reduced	0.15%	1,150
(c)	II	Tightened	2.5%	65
(d)	III	Reduced	15	8,050
(e)	III	Tightened	0.40%	24,000

25. Describe the double sampling plan of Problem 24(d).

26. Write the equations for the OC curves for the double sampling plan of problem 24(e).

27. Using MIL-STD-105D, determine the multiple sampling plans for the following information.

	Inspection Level	*Inspection*	*AQL*	*Lot Size*
(a)	III	Tightened	0.25%	70
(b)	I	Normal	0.25%	12,500
(c)	III	Reduced	1.5%	3,400

28. Inspection results for the last 8 lots using the single sampling plan of $n = 225$, $c = 3$ are

I. 1 defective	V. 3 defectives
II. 4 defectives	VI. 0 defective
III. 5 defectives	VII. 2 defectives
IV. 1 defective	VIII. 2 defectives

If normal inspection was used for lot I, what inspection should be used for lot IX?

29. Using the information from Problem 28, what was the status after lot III? Lot VII?

30. For a double sampling plan, code letter L, normal inspection, and AQL = 2.5%, the number inspected and the number defective for the last 10 lots are

	n	*np*		*n*	*np*
I.	125	0	VI.	125	1
II.	125	2	VII.	125	1
III.	125	0	VIII.	125	2
IV.	250	6	IX.	125	3
V.	125	1	X.	125	1

If production is at a steady rate and reduced inspection is authorized, can a change from normal to reduced inspection be initiated?

31. If lot IX of Problem 30 has 9 defectives rather than 3 defectives, is a change from normal to reduced inspection warranted?

32. For a single sampling plan, code letter C, normal inspection, and AQL = 25 defects/100 units, the number inspected and the count of defects for the last 10 lots are:

	n	*c*		*n*	*c*
I.	5	0	VI.	5	3
II.	5	1	VII.	5	0
III.	5	2	VIII.	5	2
IV.	5	2	IX.	5	0
V.	5	1	X.	5	1

If production is at a steady rate and reduced inspection is authorized, can a change from normal to reduced inspection be initiated?

33. Test, and if necessary rewrite, the computer program for your computer.

34. Modify the computer program to output the answer for your graphical output device.

35. Write a computer program for:
(a) OC curve for multiple sampling
(b) AOQ curve
(c) ASN curve for double sampling
(d) ASN curve for multiple sampling
(e) ATI curve

7 ADDITIONAL ACCEPTANCE SAMPLING PLAN SYSTEMS

Chapter 6 covered the principles of acceptance sampling and provided a detailed description of MIL-STD-105D. MIL-STD-105D is the most common type of lot-by-lot acceptance sampling plan for attributes and is well suited for receiving inspection. There are, however, other types of acceptance sampling plans. It is the purpose of this chapter to discuss these other acceptance sampling plans with sufficient depth to provide the reader with an adequate background.

The chapter covers three different types of acceptance sampling plans: (1) lot-by-lot acceptance sampling for attributes, (2) continuous production acceptance sampling for attributes, and (3) acceptance sampling for variables.

LOT-BY-LOT ACCEPTANCE SAMPLING PLANS FOR ATTRIBUTES

Dodge–Romig Tables

In the 1920s H.F. Dodge and H.G. Romig developed a set of inspection tables for the lot-by-lot acceptance of product by sampling for attributes. These tables are based on two concepts that were discussed in Chapter 6, limiting quality level (LQL)[1] and average outgoing quality limit (AOQL). For each of these concepts there are tables for single and double sampling. No provision is made for multiple sampling.

The principal advantage of the Dodge–Romig tables is a minimum amount of inspection for a given inspection procedure. This advantage makes the tables desirable for within-plant inspection.

[1]Dodge used the term "lot tolerance percent defective" (LTPD). In this text, "limiting quality level" (LQL) has been substituted since it is the appropriate present-day term.

1. *Limiting quality level* (LQL). These tables are based on the probability that a particular lot, which has a percent defective equal to the LQL, will be accepted. This probability is the consumer's risk, β, and is equal to 0.10. LQL plans give assurance that individual lots of poor material will rarely be accepted.

There are two sets of LQL tables, one set for single sampling and one set for double sampling. Each set has tables for LQL values of 0.5, 1.0, 2.0, 3.0, 4.0, 5.0, 7.0, and 10.0%, making a total of 16 tables. For explanatory purposes, Tables 7-1 and 7-2 are shown for single and double sampling, respectively, using a LQL = 1.0%.

To use the tables, an initial decision concerning single sampling or double sampling is required. This decision can be based on the information presented in Chapter 6. In addition, the LQL needs to be determined which can be accomplished in a manner similar to that used for the AQL. The type of sampling (single or double) and the limiting quality level (LQL) indicate the table to use.

Knowing the lot size and the process average, the acceptance sampling plan is easily obtained. For example, if the lot size, N, is 1500 and the process average, $100\bar{p}$, is 0.25, the required single sampling plan for a LQL = 1.0% is found in Table 7-1 and is

$$N = 1500$$

$$n = 490$$

$$c = 2$$

The table also gives the average outgoing quality limit (AOQL) for each plan, which for this example is 0.21%.

In a similar manner, an acceptance sampling plan for double sampling can be obtained. For example, if $N = 4400$ and $100\bar{p} = 0.15\%$, the required double sampling plan for a LQL = 1.0% is found in Table 7-2 and is

$$N = 4400$$

$$n_1 = 275$$

$$c_1 = 0$$

$$n_2 = 565$$

$$c_2 = 4$$

The table also gives the AOQL for each double sampling plan, which for this example is 0.28%.

TABLE 7-1 Dodge–Romig Single Sampling Lot Inspection Table, Based on Limiting Quality Level[a]
LQL = 1.0%

	Process Average (%)																	
	0–0.010			0.011–0.10			0.11–0.20			0.21–0.30			0.31–0.40			0.41–0.50		
Lot Size	*n*	*c*	AOQL (%)	*n*	*c*	AOQL (%)	*n*	*c*	AOQL (%)	*n*	*c*	AOQL (%)	*n*	*c*	AOQL (%)	*n*	*c*	AOQL (%)
1–120	All	0	0	All	0	0	All	0	0	All	0	0	All	0	0	All	0	0
121–150	120	0	0.06	120	0	0.06	120	0	0.06	120	0	0.06	120	0	0.06	120	0	0.06
151–200	140	0	0.08	140	0	0.08	140	0	0.08	140	0	0.08	140	0	0.08	140	0	0.08
201–300	165	0	0.10	165	0	0.10	165	0	0.10	165	0	0.10	165	0	0.10	165	0	0.10
301–400	175	0	0.12	175	0	0.12	175	0	0.12	175	0	0.12	175	0	0.12	175	0	0.12
401–500	180	0	0.13	180	0	0.13	180	0	0.13	180	0	0.13	180	0	0.13	180	0	0.13
501–600	190	0	0.13	190	0	0.13	190	0	0.13	190	0	0.13	190	0	0.13	305	1	0.14
601–800	200	0	0.14	200	0	0.14	200	0	0.14	330	1	0.15	330	1	0.15	330	1	0.15
801–1,000	205	0	0.14	205	0	0.14	205	0	0.14	335	1	0.17	335	1	0.17	335	1	0.17
1,001–2,000	220	0	0.15	220	0	0.15	360	1	0.19	490	2	0.21	490	2	0.21	610	3	0.22
2,001–3,000	220	0	0.15	375	1	0.20	505	2	0.23	630	3	0.24	745	4	0.26	870	5	0.26
3,001–4,000	225	0	0.15	380	1	0.20	510	2	0.24	645	3	0.25	880	5	0.28	1,000	6	0.29
4,001–5,000	225	0	0.16	380	1	0.20	520	2	0.24	770	4	0.28	895	5	0.29	1,120	7	0.31
5,001–7,000	230	0	0.16	385	1	0.21	655	3	0.27	780	4	0.29	1,020	6	0.32	1,260	8	0.34
7,001–10,000	230	0	0.16	520	2	0.25	660	3	0.28	910	5	0.32	1,150	7	0.34	1,500	10	0.37
10,001–20,000	390	1	0.21	525	2	0.26	785	4	0.31	1,040	6	0.35	1,400	9	0.39	1,980	14	0.43
20,001–50,000	390	1	0.21	530	2	0.26	920	5	0.34	1,300	8	0.39	1,890	13	0.44	2,570	19	0.48
50,001–100,000	390	1	0.21	670	3	0.29	1,040	6	0.36	1,420	9	0.41	2,120	15	0.47	3,150	23	0.50

[a]*n*, size of sample; entry of "All" indicates that each piece in lot is to be inspected. *c*, allowable defect number for sample. AOQL, average outgoing quality limit.

Source: Reproduced by permission from H. F. Dodge and H. G. Romig, *Sampling Inspection Tables—Single and Double Sampling*, 2nd ed. (New York: John Wiley & Sons, Inc., 1959).

An analysis of the LQL tables shows the following:

a. As the lot size increases, the relative sample size decreases. Thus, for a process average of 0.25%, a lot size of 1000 has a sample size of 335, while a lot size of 4000 has a sample size of 645. The lot size increased by a factor of 4 while the sample size increased by a factor of about 2. Therefore, inspection costs are more economical with large lot sizes.
b. The tables extend until the process average is one-half of the LQL. Provision for additional process averages is unnecessary since 100% inspection becomes more economical than sampling inspection when the process average exceeds one-half of the LQL.
c. As the process average increases, a corresponding increase occurs in the amount inspected. Therefore, an improvement in the process average results in fewer inspections and a lower sampling inspection cost.

2. *Average outgoing quality limit* (AOQL). Sampling plans for the AOQL concept were developed as a practical need in certain manufacturing situations. When the lot quantity is specified, as is the case with customer lots (homogeneous), the LQL concept is applicable; however, when the inspected lot is a convenient subdivision of a flow of product for materials-handling purposes (nonhomogeneous), the AOQL concept is applicable. AOQL plans limit the amount of poor outgoing quality on an average basis, but give no assurance on individual lots. Tables for the AOQL have one set for single sampling and one set for double sampling. Each set has tables for AOQL values of 0.1, 0.25, 0.5, 0.75, 1.0, 1.5, 2.0, 2.5, 3.0, 4.0, 5.0, 7.0, and 10.0%, making a total of 26 tables. For explanatory purposes, tables of single and double sampling are shown in Tables 7-3 and 7-4, respectively, using an AOQL = 3.0%.

In addition to determining whether single or double sampling is to be used, the AOQL is required. This can be accomplished using the same techniques as those used for finding the AQL, which was described in Chapter 6. The type of sampling (single or double) and the AOQL indicate the table to use.

Knowing the lot size and the process average, the acceptance sampling plan can be obtained. For example, if the lot size, N, is 1500 and the process average, $100\bar{p}$, is 1.60%, then the required single sampling plan for an AOQL = 3.0% is found in Table 7-3 and is

$$N = 1500$$
$$n_1 = 65$$
$$c_1 = 3$$

The corresponding LQL for this plan is 10.2%.

In a similar manner an acceptance sampling plan for double sampling can be obtained. For exmple, if $N = 6000$, and $100\bar{p} = 0.50\%$, then the required

TABLE 7-2 Dodge–Romig Double Sampling Lot Inspection Table, Based on Limiting Quality Level[a]

LQL = 1.0%

	Process Average (%)																				
	0–0.010						0.011–0.10						0.11–0.20								
	Trial 1		Trial 2			AOQL	Trial 1		Trial 2			AOQL	Trial 1		Trial 2			AOQL			
Lot Size	n_1	c_1	n_2	$n_1 + n_2$	c_2	(%)	n_1	c_1	n_2	$n_1 + n_2$	c_2	(%)	n_1	c_1	n_2	$n_1 + n_2$	c_2	(%)			
1–120	All	0	—	—	—	0	All	0	—	—	—	0	All	0	—	—	—	0			
121–150	120	0	—	—	—	0.06	120	0	—	—	—	0.06	120	0	—	—	—	0.06			
151–200	140	0	—	—	—	0.08	140	0	—	—	—	0.08	140	0	—	—	—	0.08			
201–260	165	0	—	—	—	0.10	165	0	—	—	—	0.10	165	0	—	—	—	0.10			
261–300	180	0	75	255	1	0.10	180	0	75	255	1	0.10	180	0	75	255	1	0.10			
301–400	200	0	90	290	1	0.12	200	0	90	290	1	0.12	200	0	90	290	1	0.12			
401–500	215	0	100	315	1	0.14	215	0	100	315	1	0.14	215	0	100	315	1	0.14			
501–600	225	0	115	340	1	0.15	225	0	115	340	1	0.15	225	0	115	340	1	0.15			
601–800	235	0	125	360	1	0.16	235	0	125	360	1	0.16	235	0	125	360	1	0.16			
801–1,000	245	0	135	380	1	0.17	245	0	135	380	1	0.17	245	0	250	495	2	0.19			
1,001–2,000	265	0	155	420	1	0.18	265	0	155	420	1	0.18	265	0	285	550	2	0.21			
2,001–3,000	270	0	160	430	1	0.19	270	0	300	570	2	0.22	270	0	420	690	3	0.25			
3,001–4,000	275	0	160	435	1	0.19	275	0	305	580	2	0.22	275	0	435	710	3	0.25			
4,001–5,000	275	0	165	440	1	0.19	275	0	310	585	2	0.23	275	0	565	840	4	0.28			
5,001–7,000	275	0	170	445	1	0.20	275	0	315	590	2	0.23	275	0	580	855	4	0.29			
7,001–10,000	280	0	320	600	1	0.24	280	0	460	740	3	0.26	280	0	590	870	4	0.30			
10,001–20,000	280	0	325	605	1	0.24	280	0	465	745	3	0.27	450	1	700	1,150	6	0.33			
20,001–50,000	280	0	325	605	1	0.25	280	0	605	885	4	0.30	450	1	830	1,280	7	0.36			
50,001–100,000	280	0	325	605	1	0.25	280	0	605	885	4	0.30	450	1	960	1,410	8	0.38			

TABLE 7-2 *(Continued)*

Lot Size	Process Average (%) 0.21–0.30						0.31–0.40						0.41–0.50					
	Trial 1		Trial 2			AOQL	Trial 1		Trial 2			AOQL	Trial 1		Trial 2			AOQL
	n_1	c_1	n_2	$n_1 + n_2$	c_2	(%)	n_1	c_1	n_2	$n_1 + n_2$	c_2	(%)	n_1	c_1	n_2	$n_1 + n_2$	c_2	(%)
1–120	All	0	—	—	—	0	All	0	—	—	—	0	All	0	—	—	—	0
121–150	120	0	—	—	—	0.06	120	0	—	—	—	0.06	120	0	—	—	—	0.06
151–200	140	0	—	—	—	0.08	140	0	—	—	—	0.08	140	0	—	—	—	0.08
201–260	165	0	—	—	—	0.10	165	0	—	—	—	0.10	165	0	—	—	—	0.10
261–300	180	0	75	255	1	0.10	180	0	75	255	1	0.10	180	0	75	255	1	0.10
301–400	200	0	90	290	1	0.12	200	0	90	290	1	0.12	200	0	90	290	1	0.12
401–500	215	0	100	315	1	0.14	215	0	100	315	1	0.14	215	0	100	315	1	0.14
501–600	225	0	115	340	1	0.15	225	0	115	340	1	0.15	225	0	205	430	2	0.16
601–800	235	0	230	465	2	0.18	235	0	230	465	2	0.18	235	0	230	465	2	0.18
801–1,000	245	0	250	495	2	0.19	245	0	250	495	2	0.19	245	0	250	495	2	0.19
1,001–2,000	265	0	405	670	3	0.23	265	0	515	780	4	0.24	265	0	515	780	4	0.24
2,001–3,000	270	0	545	815	4	0.26	430	1	620	1,050	6	0.28	430	1	830	1,260	8	0.30
3,001–4,000	435	1	645	1,080	6	0.29	435	1	865	1,300	8	0.30	580	2	940	1,520	10	0.33
4,001–5,000	440	1	660	1,100	6	0.30	440	1	1,000	1,440	9	0.33	585	2	1,075	1,660	11	0.35
5,001–7,000	445	1	785	1,230	7	0.33	590	2	990	1,580	10	0.36	730	3	1,190	1,920	13	0.38
7,001–10,000	450	1	920	1,370	8	0.35	600	2	1,240	1,840	12	0.39	870	4	1,540	2,410	17	0.41
10,001–20,000	605	2	1,035	1,640	10	0.39	745	3	1,485	2,230	15	0.43	1,150	6	1,990	3,140	23	0.44
20,001–50,000	605	2	1,295	1,900	12	0.42	885	4	1,845	2,730	19	0.47	1,280	7	2,600	3,880	29	0.52
50,001–100,000	605	2	1,545	2,150	14	0.44	885	4	2,085	2,970	21	0.49	1,410	8	3,280	4,690	36	0.55

[a] n_1, size of first sample; n_2 = size of second sample; entry of "All" indicates that each piece in lot is to be inspected. c_1, allowable defect number for first sample; c_2 = allowable defect number for first and second samples combined. AOQL, average outgoing quality limit.

Source: Reproduced by permission from H. F. Dodge and H. G. Romig, *Sampling Inspection Tables—Single and Double Sampling*, 2nd ed. (New York: John Wiley & Sons, Inc., 1959).

TABLE 7-3 Dodge–Romig Single Sampling Lot Inspection Table, Based on Average Outgoing Quality Limit[a]
AOQL = 3.0%

	Process Average (%)																	
	0–0.06			*0.07–0.60*			*0.61–1.20*			*1.21–1.80*			*1.81–2.40*			*2.41–3.00*		
Lot Size	*n*	*c*	*LQL (%)*	*n*	*c*	*LQL (%)*	*n*	*c*	*LQL (%)*	*n*	*c*	*LQL (%)*	*n*	*c*	*LQL (%)*	*n*	*c*	*LQL (%)*
1–10	All	0	—	All	0	—	All	0	—	All	0	—	All	0	—	All	0	—
11–50	10	0	19.0	10	0	19.0	10	0	19.0	10	0	19.0	10	0	19.0	10	0	19.0
51–100	11	0	18.0	11	0	18.0	11	0	18.0	11	0	18.0	11	0	18.0	22	1	16.4
101–200	12	0	17.0	12	0	17.0	12	0	17.0	25	1	15.1	25	1	15.1	25	1	15.1
201–300	12	0	17.0	12	0	17.0	26	1	14.6	26	1	14.6	26	1	14.6	40	2	12.8
301–400	12	0	17.1	12	0	17.1	26	1	14.7	26	1	14.7	41	2	12.7	41	2	12.7
401–500	12	0	17.2	27	1	14.1	27	1	14.1	42	2	12.4	42	2	12.4	42	2	12.4
501–600	12	0	17.3	27	1	14.2	27	1	14.2	42	2	12.4	42	2	12.4	60	3	10.8
601–800	12	0	17.3	27	1	14.2	27	1	14.2	43	2	12.1	60	3	10.9	60	3	10.9
801–1,000	12	0	17.4	27	1	14.2	44	2	11.8	44	2	11.8	60	3	11.0	80	4	9.8
1,001–2,000	12	0	17.5	28	1	13.8	45	2	11.7	65	3	10.2	80	4	9.8	100	5	9.1
2,001–3,000	12	0	17.5	28	1	13.8	45	2	11.7	65	3	10.2	100	5	9.1	140	7	8.2
3,001–4,000	12	0	17.5	28	1	13.8	65	3	10.3	85	4	9.5	125	6	8.4	165	8	7.8
4,001–5,000	28	1	13.8	28	1	13.8	65	3	10.3	85	4	9.5	125	6	8.4	210	10	7.4
5,001–7,000	28	1	13.8	45	2	11.8	65	3	10.3	105	5	8.8	145	7	8.1	235	11	7.1
7,001–10,000	28	1	13.9	46	2	11.6	65	3	10.3	105	5	8.8	170	8	7.6	280	13	6.8
10,001–20,000	28	1	13.9	46	2	11.7	85	4	9.5	125	6	8.4	215	10	7.2	380	17	6.2
20,001–50,000	28	1	13.9	65	3	10.3	105	5	8.8	170	8	7.6	310	14	6.5	560	24	5.7
50,001–100,000	28	1	13.9	65	3	10.3	125	6	8.4	215	10	7.2	385	17	6.2	690	29	5.4

[a]*n*, size of sample; entry of "All" indicates that each piece in lot is to be inspected. *c*, allowable defect number for sample. LQL, limiting quality level corresponding to a consumer's risk (β) = 0.10.

Source: Reproduced by permission from H. F. Dodge and H. G. Romig, *Sampling Inspection Tables—Single and Double Sampling*, 2nd ed. (New York: John Wiley & Sons, Inc., 1959).

double sampling plan for an AOQL = 3.0% is found in Table 7-4 and is

$$N = 6000$$
$$n_1 = 26$$
$$c_1 = 0$$
$$n_2 = 44$$
$$c_2 = 3$$

The table also gives the LQL for each double sampling plan which, in this case, is 11.0%.

An analysis of the AOQL tables shows the following:

a. As the lot size increases, the relative sample size decreases.

b. Plans are not given for process averages which exceed the AOQL, since sampling is uneconomical when the average incoming quality is poorer than the specified AOQL.

c. The lower the process average, the smaller the sample size, resulting in lower sampling inspection cost.

3. *Additional comments on the Dodge–Romig tables.* The process average $100\bar{p}$ is obtained by the same techniques used for the p chart. Using the first 25 lots, the average percent defective is obtained. For double sampling only the first sample is included in the computation. Any lot percent defective ($100p$) which exceeds the limit of $100\bar{p} + 3\sqrt{100\bar{p}(1 - 100\bar{p})/n}$ is discarded (if it has an assignable cause) and a new process average calculated. However, until it is possible to obtain a process average by the technique above, the largest possible process average should be used. Thus, the last column in the tables is used until $100\bar{p}$ can be determined from the first 25 lots.

The Dodge–Romig tables do not make a provision for the type of defect, although different LQL or AOQL values can be used—lower ones for critical defects and higher ones for minor defects. No provision is made for tightened or reduced inspection, although different LQL or AOQL values can also be used. Defects/100 units rather than percent defective can be used for the process average; however, this is limited to values of 10 or less.

Philips Standard Sampling System

The Philips Standard Sampling System was developed by H. C. Hamaker for the Philips Company in Holland. It is a split-risk system, wherein the operating characteristic (OC) curves pass through a particular point. This point of control is defined by the product quality, $p_{0.50}$, at a probability of acceptance

TABLE 7-4 Dodge–Romig double Sampling Lot Inspection Table, Based on Average Outgoing Quality Limit[a]
AOQL = 3.0%

	Process Average (%)																	
	0–0.06						0.07–0.60						0.61–1.20					
	Trial 1		Trial 2			LQL	Trial 1		Trial 2			LQL	Trial 1		Trial 2			LQL
Lot Size	n_1	c_1	n_2	n_1+n_2	c_2	(%)	n_1	c_1	n_2	n_1+n_2	c_2	(%)	n_1	c_1	n_2	n_1+n_2	c_2	(%)
1–10	All	0	—	—	—	—	All	0	—	—	—	—	All	0	—	—	—	—
11–50	10	0	—	—	—	19.0	10	0	—	—	—	19.0	10	0	—	—	—	19.0
51–100	16	0	9	25	1	16.4	16	0	9	25	1	16.4	16	0	9	25	1	16.4
101–200	17	0	9	26	1	16.0	17	0	9	26	1	16.0	17	0	9	26	1	16.0
201–300	18	0	10	28	1	15.5	18	0	10	28	1	15.5	21	0	23	44	2	13.3
301–400	18	0	11	29	1	15.2	21	0	24	45	2	13.2	23	0	37	60	3	12.0
401–500	18	0	11	29	1	15.2	21	0	25	46	2	13.0	24	0	36	60	3	11.7
501–600	18	0	12	30	1	15.0	21	0	25	46	2	13.0	24	0	41	65	3	11.5
601–800	21	0	25	46	2	13.0	21	0	25	46	2	13.0	24	0	41	65	3	11.5
801–1,000	21	0	26	47	2	12.8	21	0	26	47	2	12.8	25	0	40	65	3	11.4
1,001–2,000	22	0	26	48	2	12.6	22	0	26	48	2	12.6	27	0	58	85	4	10.3
2,001–3,000	22	0	26	48	2	12.6	25	0	40	65	3	11.4	28	0	62	90	4	10.0
3,001–4,000	23	0	26	49	2	12.4	25	0	45	70	3	11.0	29	0	76	105	5	9.6
4,001–5,000	23	0	26	49	2	12.4	26	0	44	70	3	11.0	30	0	75	105	5	9.5
5,001–7,000	23	0	27	50	2	12.2	26	0	44	70	3	11.0	30	0	80	110	5	9.4
7,001–10,000	23	0	27	50	2	12.2	27	0	43	70	3	11.0	30	0	80	110	5	9.4
10,001–20,000	23	0	27	50	2	12.2	27	0	43	70	3	11.0	31	0	94	125	6	9.2
20,001–50,000	23	0	27	50	2	12.2	28	0	67	95	4	9.7	55	1	120	175	8	8.0
50,001–100,000	23	0	27	50	2	12.2	31	0	84	115	5	9.0	60	1	140	200	9	7.6

[a] n_1, size of sample; n_2, size of second sample; entry of "All" indicates that each piece in lot is to be inspected. c_1, allowable defect number for sample; c_2, allowable defect number for first and second samples combined. LQL, limiting quality level corresponding to a consumer's risk (β) = 0.10.

Source: Reproduced by permission from H. F. Dodge and H. G. Romig, *Sampling Inspection Tables—Single and Double Sampling*, 2nd ed. (New York: John Wiley & Sons, Inc., 1959).

TABLE 7-4 *(continued)*

	Process Average (%)																	
	1.21–1.80						1.81–2.40						2.41–3.00					
	Trial 1		Trial 2			LQL	Trial 1		Trial 2			LQL	Trial 1		Trial 2			LQL
Lot Size	n_1	c_1	n_2	$n_1 + n_2$	c_2	(%)	n_1	c_1	n_2	$n_1 + n_2$	c_2	(%)	n_1	c_1	n_2	$n_1 + n_2$	c_2	(%)
1–10	All	0	—	—	—	—	All	0	—	—	—	—	All	0	—	—	—	—
11–50	10	0	—	—	—	19.0	10	0	—	—	—	19.0	10	0	—	—	—	19.0
51–100	17	0	17	34	2	15.8	17	0	17	34	2	15.8	17	0	17	34	2	15.8
101–200	20	0	21	41	2	13.7	22	0	33	55	3	12.4	22	0	33	55	3	12.4
201–300	23	0	37	60	3	12.0	23	0	37	60	3	12.0	24	0	51	75	4	11.1
301–400	23	0	37	60	3	12.0	25	0	55	80	4	10.8	42	1	63	105	6	10.4
401–500	24	0	36	60	3	11.7	25	0	55	80	4	10.8	46	1	79	125	7	9.7
501–600	26	0	54	80	4	10.7	46	1	69	115	6	9.7	48	1	97	145	8	9.2
601–800	26	0	54	80	4	10.7	49	1	81	130	7	9.4	50	1	115	165	9	8.9
801–1,000	27	0	58	85	4	10.3	49	1	86	135	7	9.2	70	2	120	190	10	8.4
1,001–2,000	49	1	76	125	6	9.1	50	1	150	200	10	8.0	100	3	180	280	14	7.5
2,001–3,000	50	1	95	145	7	8.7	80	2	165	245	12	7.6	130	4	260	390	19	6.9
3,001–4,000	55	1	110	165	8	8.5	105	3	200	305	14	7.0	155	5	330	485	23	6.5
4,001–5,000	60	1	135	195	9	7.8	110	3	225	335	15	6.7	215	7	390	605	27	6.0
5,001–7,000	60	1	165	225	10	7.3	110	3	250	360	16	6.6	270	9	505	775	34	5.7
7,001–10,000	85	2	160	245	11	7.2	115	3	290	405	18	6.5	285	9	680	965	41	5.4
10,001–20,000	85	2	180	265	12	7.2	140	4	315	455	20	6.3	315	10	805	1,120	47	5.3
20,001–50,000	85	2	205	290	13	7.0	170	5	420	590	26	6.0	390	13	940	1,330	56	5.2
50,001–100,000	90	2	245	335	15	6.8	200	6	505	705	30	5.7	445	15	1,105	1,550	65	5.1

of 0.50. While the system is popular in Europe, it has had limited acceptance in North America.

The system is comprised of one table, which is shown by Table 7-5. This table is indexed by the lot size and the specified product quality or point of control. There are eleven lot-size groupings with single sampling being required for lots which are 1000 or less. Double sampling is required whenever the lot is greater than 1000. The table provides plans for eight different quality levels: 0.25, 0.5, 1.0, 2.0, 3.0, 5.0, 7.0, and 10.0%.

An example problem will illustrate the simplicity of the system. For a lot size of 3500 and a desired split-risk product quality, $100p_{0.50} = 3.0\%$, the sampling plan is

$$n_1 = 70$$

$$c_1 = 1$$

$$n_2 = 140$$

$$c_2 = 5$$

Note, the second sample is not specified in the table since it is always twice as large as the first sample.

In addition to the simplicity of the Philips system, another important feature is the relationship between sample size and the specified quality (point of control). As the specified quality increases, there is a decrease in the sample size. Thus, for a lot size of 750, the sample size is 225 for a specified quality of 0.5% and is 55 for a specified quality of 5%. The poorer the quality that can be tolerated, the smaller the sample size that is needed.

Chain Sampling Inspection Plan[2]

A special type of lot-by-lot acceptance sampling plan for attributes was developed by H. F. Dodge. The plan was designated "Chain Sampling Plan ChSP-1." It is applicable to quality characteristics which involve destructive or costly tests.

When tests are destructive or very costly, sampling plans with a small sample size are used as a matter of practical necessity. Plans with sample sizes of 5, 10, 15, etc., usually have acceptance numbers of zero ($c = 0$).

Single sampling plans for $c = 0$ have an undesirable feature. It is the poor shape of the OC curve, which gives poor discrimination between good and defective lots. Figure 7-1 shows the general shape of single sampling plans for $c = 0$ and $c = 1$ or more. The comparison shows the desirability (from a producer's viewpoint) of plans with acceptance numbers equal to 1 or more.

[2]For more information, see H. F. Dodge, "Chain Sampling Inspection Plan," *Industrial Quality Control,* 11, No. 4 (January 1955), 10–13.

TABLE 7-5 Philips Standard Sampling System[a]

Lot Size	0.25%			0.5%			1%			2%			3%			5%			7%			10%		
Single sampling	n		c	n		c	n		c	n		c	n		c	n		c	n		c	n		c
20–50	A			A			A			30		0	20		0	13		0	10		0	7		0
51–100	A			A			60		0	30		0	20		0	13		0	10		0	7		0
101–200	A			100		0	60		0	35		0	55		1	35		1	25		1	17		1
201–500	175		0	100		0	135		1	75		1	55		1	35		1	40		2	25		2
501–1,000	225		0	225		1	150		1	85		1	85		2	55		2	55		3	35		3
Double sampling	n_1	c_1	c_2	n_1	c_1	c_2	n_1	c_1	c_2	n_1	c_1	c_2	n_1	c_1	c_2	n_1	c_1	c_2	n_1	c_1	c_2	n_1	c_1	c_2
1,001–2,000	330	0	1	150	0	1	110	0	2	55	0	2	45	0	3	25	0	3	30	1	5	22	1	5
2,001–5,000	425	0	2	200	0	2	135	0	3	70	0	3	70	1	5	45	1	5	55	2	10	40	2	10
5,001–10,000	525	0	3	260	0	3	220	1	5	110	1	5	125	2	10	75	2	10	75	3	15	55	3	15
10,001–20,000	875	1	5	440	1	5	380	2	10	190	2	10	180	3	15	110	3	15	100	4	20	70	4	20
20,001–50,000	1,500	2	10	750	2	10	540	3	15	270	3	15	240	4	20	140	4	20	120	5	25	85	5	25
50,001–100,000	2,200	3	15	1,100	3	15	700	4	20	390	4	20	290	5	25	175	5	25	145	6	30	105	6	30

Point of Control: 0.25% through 10%.

[a]Second sample $n_2 = 2n_1$ "A" means inspect entire lot.

Source: Reproduced by permission from H. C. Hamaker, J. J. M. Taudin Chabot, and F. G. Willemze, "The Practical Application of Sampling Inspection Plans and Tables," *Philips Technical Review*, 11 (June 1950), 362-370.

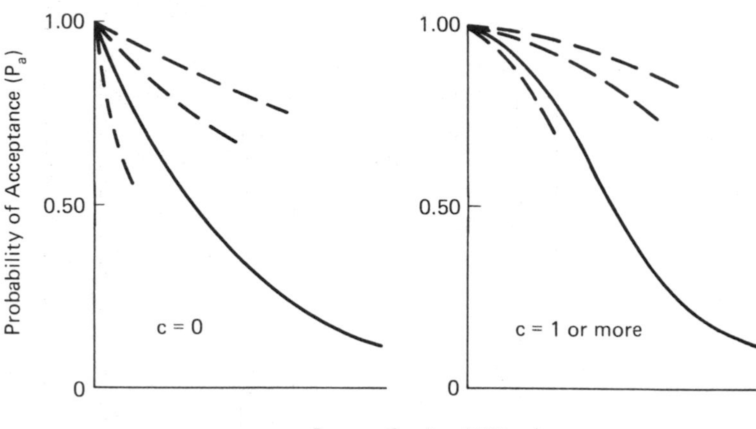

Figure 7-1 General shape of OC curves for single sampling plans. [Reproduced by permission from H. F. Dodge, "Chain Sampling Inspection Plan," *Industrial Quality Control*, 11, No. 4 (January 1955), 10–13.]

Chain sampling plans make use of the cumulative results of several preceding samples. The procedure is as follows:

1. For each lot, select a sample of size n and test each for conformance to specifications.
2. If the sample has 0 defectives, accept the lot; if the sample has 2 or more defectives, reject the lot; and if the sample has 1 defective, it may be accepted provided that there is no defective in the previous i samples of size n.

Thus, for a chain sampling plan given by $n = 8, i = 3$, the lot would be accepted (1) by no defectives in the sample of 8, or (2) by 1 defective in the sample of 8 and no defectives in the previous 3 samples of 8.

The value of i, the number of previous samples, is determined by analysis of the operating characteristic (OC) curves for a given sample size. Figure 7-2 shows the OC curve for the single sample plan $n = 5, c = 0$, and the OC curves for ChSP-1 plans for $i = 1, 2, 3$, and 5. The OC curves for the ChSP-1 plans are obtained from the general formula

$$P_a = P_0 + P_1[P_0]^i$$

An example will illustrate the technique. For the ChSP-1 plan $n = 5, c = 0, i = 2$, the calculations for $p_0 = 0.15$ are

$$P_0 = \frac{n!}{d!(n-d)!} p_0^d q_0^{n-d} = q_0^n = (0.85)^5 = 0.444$$

$$P_1 = \frac{n!}{d!(n-d)!} p_0^d q_0^{n-d} = np_0 q_0^{n-d} = 5(0.15)(0.85)^{5-1} = 0.392$$

$$P_a = P_0 + P_1[P_0]^i = 0.444 + (0392)(0.444)^2 = 0.521$$

The point $P_a = 0.521$ is shown in Figure 7-2.

The curve for $i = 1$ is shown dashed, since it is not a preferred choice. In practice i values of from 3 to 5 will be the most used, since their OC curves approximate the single sampling plan OC curve. Where the percent defective is small, the ChSP-1 plans increase the probability that a sample with one defective will be accepted. This provides for the occasional defective that is expected every now and then.

For appropriate use of the chain sampling technique, the following conditions should be met:

1. The lot should be one of a continuing series of product which is sampled in substantially the order of its production.
2. The consumer can normally expect the lots to be essentially the same quality.
3. The consumer has confidence in the producer, that he would not occasionally send an unacceptable lot which would have the optimum chance of acceptance.

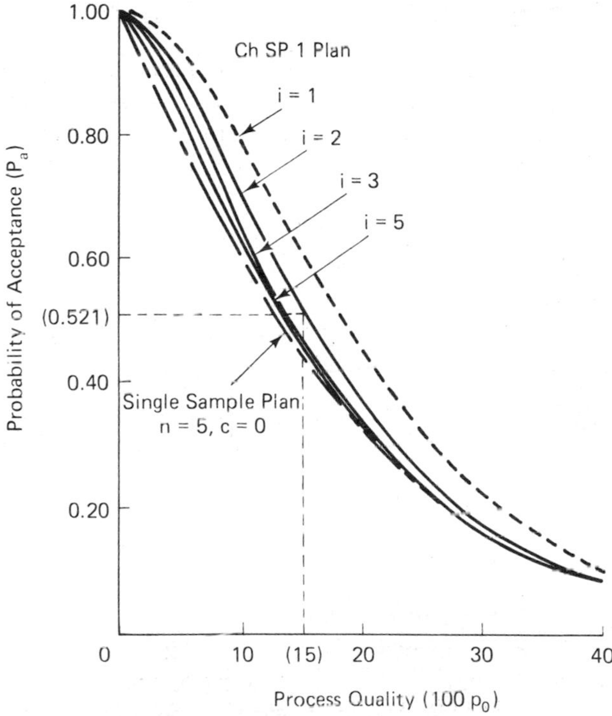

Figure 7-2 OC curves for ChSP-1 plans with values 1, 2, 3, 5, and for single sampling plan $n = 5$, $c = 0$. [Reproduced by permission from H. F. Dodge, "Chain Sampling Inspection Plan," *Industrial Quality Control*, 11, No. 4 (January 1955), 10–13.]

4. The quality characteristic is one that involves destructive or costly tests, thereby dictating a small sample size.

Sequential Sampling

Sequential sampling is similar to multiple sampling except that the sequential sampling can theoretically continue indefinitely. In practice the plan is truncated after the number inspected is equal to three times the number inspected by a corresponding single sampling plan. Sequential sampling, which is used for costly or destructive tests, usually has a subgroup size of 1, thereby making it an item-by-item plan.

Item-by-item sequential sampling is based on the concept of the sequential probability ratio test (SPRT), which was developed by Wald.[3] Figure 7-3 illustrates the sampling plan technique. The "stepped" line shows the number defective for the total number inspected and is updated with the inspection results of each item. If the cumulative results equal or are greater than the upper line, the lot is rejected. If the cumulative results equal or are less than the lower line, the lot is accepted. If neither decision is possible, another item is inspected. Thus, if the 20th sample is found to be defective, the cumulative number of defectives will be five. Since five defectives exceeds the rejection line for 20 inspections, the lot is rejected, as shown by the dashed line in Figure 7.3.

The sequential sampling plan is defined by the producer's risk, α, and its process quality, p_α, and by the consumer's risk, β, and its process quality, p_β. Using these requirements, the equations (slope intercept form) can be determined for the acceptance line and rejection line using the following formulas:

$$h_a = \log\left(\frac{1-\alpha}{\beta}\right) \Big/ \left[\log\left(\frac{p_\beta}{p_\alpha}\right) + \log\left(\frac{1-p_\alpha}{1-p_\beta}\right)\right]$$

$$h_r = \log\left(\frac{1-\beta}{\alpha}\right) \Big/ \left[\log\left(\frac{p_\beta}{p_\alpha}\right) + \log\left(\frac{1-p_\alpha}{1-p_\beta}\right)\right]$$

$$s = \log\left(\frac{1-p_\alpha}{1-p_\beta}\right) \Big/ \left[\log\left(\frac{p_\beta}{p_\alpha}\right) + \log\left(\frac{1-p_\alpha}{1-p_\beta}\right)\right]$$

$$d_a = -h_a + sn$$

$$d_r = h_r + sn$$

where s = slope of the lines
h_r = intercept for the rejection line
h_a = intercept for the acceptance line
p_β = fraction defective for the consumer's risk
p_α = fraction defective for the producer's risk
β = consumer's risk

[3]For more information, see Abraham Wald, *Sequential Analysis* (New York: John Wiley & Sons, Inc., 1947).

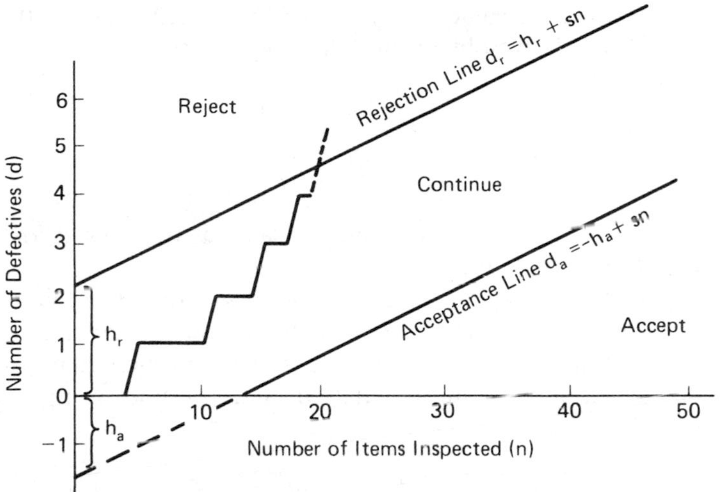

Figure 7-3 Graphical presentation of an item-by-item sequential plan.

α = producer's risk
d_a = number of defectives for acceptance
d_r = number of defectives for rejection
n = number of units inspected

Thus, the equations for the sequential plan, which is defined by $\alpha = 0.05$, $p_\alpha = 0.06$, $\beta = 0.10$, and $p_\beta = 0.20$, is obtained by the following calculations:

$$h_a = \log\left(\frac{1-\alpha}{\beta}\right) \Big/ \left[\log\left(\frac{p_\beta}{p_\alpha}\right) + \log\left(\frac{1-p_\alpha}{1-p_\beta}\right)\right]$$

$$= \log\left(\frac{1-0.05}{0.10}\right) \Big/ \left[\log\left(\frac{0.20}{0.06}\right) + \log\left(\frac{0.94}{0.80}\right)\right]$$

$$= 1.65$$

$$h_r = \log\left(\frac{1-\beta}{\alpha}\right) \Big/ \left[\log\left(\frac{p_\beta}{p_\alpha}\right) + \log\left(\frac{1-p_\alpha}{1-p_\beta}\right)\right]$$

$$= \log\left(\frac{1-0.10}{0.05}\right) \Big/ \left[\log\left(\frac{0.20}{0.06}\right) + \log\left(\frac{0.94}{0.80}\right)\right]$$

$$= 2.12$$

$$s = \log\left(\frac{1-p_\alpha}{1-p_\beta}\right) \Big/ \left[\log\left(\frac{p_\beta}{p_\alpha}\right) + \log\left(\frac{1-p_\alpha}{1-p_\beta}\right)\right]$$

$$= \log\left(\frac{1-0.06}{1-0.20}\right) \Big/ \left[\log\left(\frac{0.20}{0.06}\right) + \log\left[\frac{0.94}{0.80}\right)\right]$$

$$= 0.12$$

Substituting the values of $h_a = 1.65$, $h_r = 2.12$, and $s = 0.12$ into the formulas for d_a and d_r, we obtain the following equations:

$$d_a = -1.65 + 0.12n$$

$$d_r = 2.12 + 0.12n$$

The previous equations are the same as those used for the acceptance and rejection lines of Figure 7-3.

While the graphical presentation of Figure 7-3 can be used as the sampling plan, it is usually more convenient to use the tabular form. This is easily accomplished by substituting values of n into the equations for the acceptance and rejection lines and calculate d_a and d_r. For example, the calculations for $n = 17$ are:

$$\begin{aligned} d_a &= -1.65 + 0.12n & d_r &= 2.12 + 0.12n \\ &= -1.65 + (0.12)(17) & &= 2.12 + (0.12)(17) \\ &= 0.39 & &= 4.16 \end{aligned}$$

Since number of defectives (d_a and d_r) are whole numbers, the rejection number is the next whole number above d_r and the acceptance number is the next whole number below d_a. Thus, for $n = 17$, $d_a = 0$, and $d_r = 5$. Table 7-6 illustrates the sampling plan for the first 30 samples. The plan would normally be truncated at $n = 150$, since this value is 3 times the value of n for an equivalent single sampling plan.

It is sometimes preferable to take the sample in groups rather than singly. This is accomplished by using multiples of the desired sample size. Therefore, if the sample size is 5, the acceptance and rejection numbers are determined for n values of 5, 10, 15, ...

Sequential sampling is used to reduce the number inspected for items that require costly or destructive testing. It is also applicable for any situation since the average amount inspected will be less than for multiple sampling.

Skip-Lot Sampling

Skip-lot sampling was devised by H. F. Dodge in 1955.[4] It is a single sampling plan for minimizing inspection costs when there is a continuing supply of lots of raw material, component parts, subassemblies, and finished parts from the same source. It is particularly applicable to chemical and physical characteristics that requrie laboratory analyses.

The skip-lot sampling plan designated SkSP-1 is based on the AOQL. However, the AOQL refers to units rather than lots, as discussed in Chapter

[4] H. F. Dodge, "Skip-Lot Sampling Plans," *Industriual Quality Control*, 11, No. 5 (February 1955), 3–5.

TABLE 7-6 Unit by Unit Sequential Sampling Plan (First 30 Samples) $\alpha = 0.05$, $p_{1-\alpha} = 0.06$, $\beta = 0.10$, and $p_\beta = 0.20$

Number of Units Inspected, n	Acceptance Number, d_a	Rejection Number, d_r	Number of Units Inspected, n	Acceptance Number, d_a	Rejection Number, d_r
1	[a]	[b]	18	0	5
2	[a]	[b]	19	0	5
3	[a]	3	20	0	5
4	[a]	3	21	0	5
5	[a]	3	22	0	5
6	[a]	3	23	1	5
7	[a]	3	24	1	5
8	[a]	4	25	1	6
9	[a]	4	26	1	6
10	[a]	4	27	1	6
11	[a]	4	28	1	6
12	[a]	4	29	1	6
13	[a]	4	30	1	6
14	0	4	·	·	·
15	0	4	·	·	·
16	0	5	·	·	·
17	0	5			

[a]Acceptance not possible.
[b]Rejection not possible.

6. Thus, an AOQL of 1% means that on the average the plan will accept no more than 1% of the lots that are nonconforming (defective) for the characteristic under consideration.

The SkSP-1 plan begins with the inspection of every lot. When a prescribed number of lots have been accepted, a sampling of lots occurs. Figure 7-4 describes the SkSP-1 in a flow-chart format. When a lot is rejected while in the sampling mode, the plan reverts to inspecting every lot.

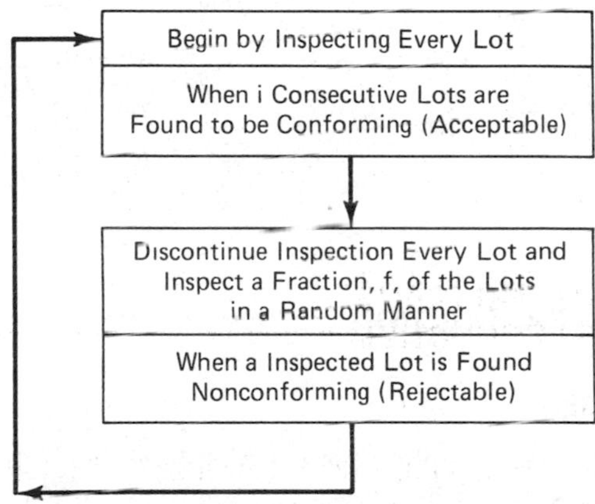

Figure 7-4 Procedure for SkSP-1 plans.

The plan is a modification of a continuous sampling plan, CSP-1, the primary difference being that SkSP-1 refers to lots and CSP-1 refers to units. Table 7-7 is used for both plans to provide a family of i and f values for each AOQL value. Thus, for an AOQL of 1.22% any of the following i and f values could be used.

f	i
$\frac{1}{2}$	23
$\frac{1}{3}$	38
$\frac{1}{4}$	49
.	.
.	.
.	.
$\frac{1}{200}$	255

In general, f values will be those at the top of the table.

The best way to select lots to be inspected, while in the sampling mode, is to use a known probability sampling method. Thus, if $f = \frac{1}{2}$, then a head on the flip of a coin would decide if the lot is inspected; if $f = \frac{1}{3}$, a 1 or 2 on the roll of a six-sided die would determine if the lot is inspected; or if $f = \frac{1}{4}$, a spade on a draw from a deck of cards would determine if the lot is inspected.

The plans assume that nonconforming (rejected) lots will be rectified. If this does not occur, then the i value has to be increased by 1.

TABLE 7-7 Values of *i* for CSP-1 plans

	AOQL (%)															
f	0.018	0.033	0.046	0.074	0.113	0.143	0.198	0.33	0.53	0.79	1.22	1.90	2.90	4.94	7.12	11.46
$\frac{1}{2}$	1,540	840	600	375	245	194	140	84	53	36	23	15	10	6	5	3
$\frac{1}{3}$	2,550	1,390	1,000	620	405	321	232	140	87	59	38	25	16	10	7	5
$\frac{1}{4}$	3,340	1,820	1,310	810	530	420	303	182	113	76	49	32	21	13	9	6
$\frac{1}{5}$	3,960	2,160	1,550	965	630	498	360	217	135	91	58	38	25	15	11	7
$\frac{1}{7}$	4,950	2,700	1,940	1,205	790	623	450	270	168	113	73	47	31	18	13	8
$\frac{1}{10}$	6,050	3,300	2,370	1,470	965	762	550	335	207	138	89	57	38	22	16	10
$\frac{1}{15}$	7,390	4,030	2,890	1,800	1,180	930	672	410	255	170	108	70	46	27	19	12
$\frac{1}{25}$	9,110	4,970	3,570	2,215	1,450	1,147	828	500	315	210	134	86	57	33	23	14
$\frac{1}{50}$	11,730	6,400	4,590	2,855	1,870	1,477	1,067	640	400	270	175	110	72	42	29	18
$\frac{1}{100}$	14,320	7,810	5,600	3,485	2,305	1,820	1,302	790	500	330	215	135	89	52	36	22
$\frac{1}{200}$	17,420	9,500	6,810	4,235	2,760	2,178	1,583	950	590	400	255	165	106	62	43	26

ACCEPTANCE SAMPLING PLANS FOR CONTINUOUS PRODUCTION

Introduction

Acceptance sampling plans which have been discussed in this chapter and in Chapter 6 were lot-by-lot plans. Many manufacturing operations do not create lots as a normal part of the production process, since they are produced by a continuous process on a conveyor or other straight-line system. In such cases acceptance sampling plans for continuous production are required.

Plans for continuous production consist of alternating sequences of sampling inspection and screening (100%) inspection. These plans usually begin with 100% inspection, and if a stated number of units (clearance number, i) are free of defects, sampling inspection is instituted. Sampling continues until a specific number of defective units are found, at which time 100% inspection is reinstated.

Sampling plans for continuous production are applicable to attribute, nondestructive inspection of moving product. The inspection must be of such a nature that it is relatively easy and rapid so that no "bottlenecks" occur because of the inspection activity. In addition, the process must be capable of manufacturing homogeneous product.

The concept of sampling for continuous production was first devised by H. F. Dodge in 1943, with a sampling plan that has been commonly referred to as CSP-1. This plan and two additional plans, CSP-2 and CSP-3, are categorized as single-level plans. In 1955 the theory of multilevel continuous plans was presented by G. Licherman and H. Soloman. Multilevel plans provide for reduced levels of sampling inspection when the quality continues to be superior.[5] Much of this early work was incorporated into MIL-STD-1235 (ORD), which was superseded by MIL-STD-1235A (MU) on June 28, 1974.

CSP-1[6] Plans

This plan begins by 100% inspection (screening) of the product in the order of production until a certain number of successive units are free of defects. When that number is obtained, 100% inspection is discontinued and sampling inspection begun. The sample is a fraction of the flow of the product and is selected in such a manner as to minimize any bias. If a defect occurs, sampling inspection is discontinued and 100% inspection begins. Figure 7-5 shows the procedure for CSP-1 plans. The clearance number i is the number of defect-free units in 100% inspection, and the sampling frequency f is the ratio of units inspected to the total units passing an inspection station during periods of sampling inspection. Thus, an f value of $\frac{1}{20}$ means that 1 sampling inspection is made for every 20 units of product.

CSP-1 plans are indexed by an average outgoing quality limit (AOQL). For a particular AOQL, there are different combinations of i and f which are given in Table 7-7. Thus, one plan for an AOQL of 0.79 is $i = 59$ and $f = \frac{1}{3}$. This plan specifies that sampling inspection of 1 out of every 3 products is instigated after 59 defect-free products. Sampling continues until a defect is found, at which time screening inspection is reinstated. Some other plans for an AOQL

[5]G. Licherman and H. Soloman, "Multi-level Continuous Sampling Plans, *Annals of Mathematical Statistics*, 26 (December 1955), 686–704.

[6]H. F. Dodge, "A Sampling Inspection Plan for Continuous Production," *Annals of Mathematical Statistics*, 14 (September 1943), 264–279.

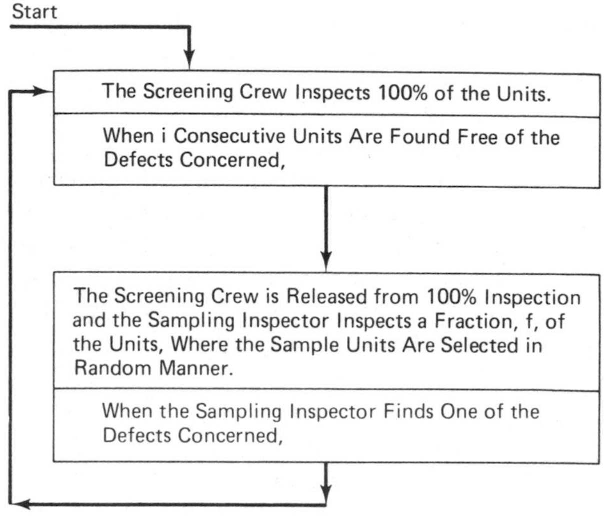

Figure 7-5 Procedure for CSP-1 plans.

of 0.79 are:

$$i = 113 \qquad f = \tfrac{1}{7}$$
$$= 270 \qquad = \tfrac{1}{50}$$

Analysis of the table shows that as the sampling frequency, f, decreases, the number of defect-free inspections, i, increases.

Values of f and i for an AOQL are based on practical considerations. As f gets smaller, the protection from spotty quality decreases, especially for values less than $\frac{1}{50}$. Another practical consideration is the amount of production per shift; as the amount increases, the value of f decreases. Also, the value of f can be influenced by the sampling inspector's work load.

CSP-2 Plans

Continuous sampling inspection plan designated CSP-2 is a modification of CSP-1. Plan CSP-1 requires a return to 100% inspection wherever a defect is found during the sampling inspection. CSP-2, however, does not require a return to 100% inspection unless a second defect is found in the next i or fewer sample units.[7] Figure 7-6 gives the procedure for CSP-2 plans.

The purpose of CSP-2 plans is to provide protection against the occurrence of an isolated defect that would initiate a return to 100% inspection.

[7]H. F. Dodge and M. N. Torrey, "Additional Continuous Sampling Inspection Plans, *Industrial Quality Control*, 7, No. 5 (March 1951), 7–12.

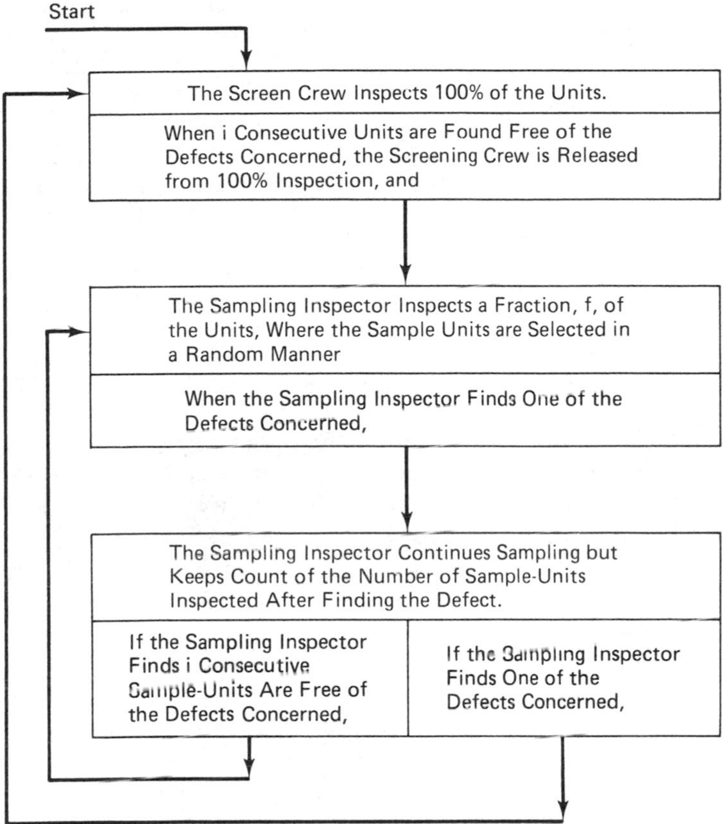

Figure 7-6 Procedure for CSP-2 plans.

Plans are indexed by a specific AOQL which provides for different combinations of i and f, as shown in Table 7-8. Thus, $i = 35, f = \frac{1}{5}$ and $i = 59, f = \frac{1}{15}$ are two of many plans for an AOQL of 2.90.

For the latter plan, $i = 59$ and $f = \frac{1}{15}$, sampling inspection of 1 out of every 15 continues after one defect is found. If a second defect is found in the next 59 sample units, 100% inspection is invoked. If a second defect does not occur, sampling continues without the conditional stipulation.

MIL-STD-1235A (MU)[8]

As previously stated, this standard supersedes MIL-STD-1235 (ORD). The standard is composed of five different continuous sampling plans. Inspection is by attributes for defects or defectives using the three classes of severity: critical, major, and minor.

[8]Copies of MIL-STD-1235A (MU) may be obtained by directing requests to Commanding Officer, U.S. Naval Supply Depot, Attn. Code DMD, 5801 Tabor Avenue, Philadelphia, PA 19120.

TABLE 7-8 Values of *i* for CSP-2 Plans

	AOQL (%)							
f	*0.53*	*0.79*	*1.22*	*1.90*	*2.90*	*4.94*	*7.12*	*11.46*
$\frac{1}{2}$	80	54	35	23	15	9	7	4
$\frac{1}{3}$	128	86	55	36	24	14	10	7
$\frac{1}{4}$	162	109	70	45	30	18	12	8
$\frac{1}{5}$	190	127	81	52	35	20	14	9
$\frac{1}{7}$	230	155	99	64	42	25	17	11
$\frac{1}{10}$	275	185	118	76	50	29	20	13
$\frac{1}{15}$	330	220	140	90	59	35	24	15
$\frac{1}{25}$	395	265	170	109	71	42	29	18
$\frac{1}{50}$	490	330	210	134	88	52	36	22

Continuous sampling plans are designed based on the average outgoing quality limit (AOQL). In order to be comparable with MIL-STD-105D, the plans are also indexed by the acceptable quality level (AQL). The AQL is merely an index to the plans and has no other meaning.

The standard has a special provision for critical defects. Only two plans, CSP-1 and CSP-F, can be used for critical defects. Even in these cases the responsible authority (consumer) can require 100% inspection at all times.

In each of the five sampling plans, provision is made for the discontinuation of inspection. The consumer can suspend product acceptance when the product quality is such that 100% inspection continues beyond a prescribed number of units, s. In other words, if sampling inspection does not occur within s units, the product quality is below standard and product acceptance can be suspended. The table for s values is not reproduced in the text.

Sampling plans are designated by code letters. Table 7-9 provides a range of permissible code letters based on the number of units in the production interval (usually an 8-hour shift). Factors that influence the selection of the code letter are inspection time per unit of product, production rate, and proximity to other inspection stations. When idle inspection time is a significant consideration, a plan with a higher sampling frequency and lower clearance number is usually preferred.

TABLE 7-9 Sampling-Frequency Code Letters

Number of Units in Production Interval	*Permissible Code Letters*
2–8	A, B
9–25	A–C
26–90	A–D
91–500	A–E
501–1,200	A–F
1,201–3,200	A–G
3,201–10,000	A–H
10,001–35,000	A–I
35,001–150,000	A–J
150,001–up	A–K

CSP-1 and CSP-2 Plans. Both of Dodge's plans, CSP-1 and CSP-2, are incorporated into the standard; therefore, additional discussion is not necessary.

CSP-F Plans. CSP-F is a single-level continuous sampling procedure which provides for alternating sequences of 100% inspection and sampling inspection. The procedure is the same as the CSP-1 plan, which is shown in Figure 7-5. CSP-F plans are indexed by the AOQL and also by the amount of product manufactured in a production interval. This allows smaller clearance numbers to be used, which permits CSP-F plans to be applied for short-production-run situations or to be applied where the inspection operation is time consuming.

There are 12 tables for the CSP-F plans; each table represents a different AOQL value. Table 7-10 is an example of the table for AOQL = 0.33%. The *i* values in the last row of the table are the same as those given for CSP-1 plans.

The difference between the two plans is illustrated by an example problem. For a production run of 500 with an AOQL of 0.33% and an *f* value of $\frac{1}{4}$, the *i* values are:

CSP-1 $i = 182$

CSP-F $i = 114$

Therefore, when there is a short production run, a CSP-F plan will allow sampling

TABLE 7-10 Values of *i* for CSP-F Plans (AQL,[a] 0.25%; AOQL, 0.33%) [Table 3-A-8 of MIL STD-1235A (MU)]

Sample-Frequency Code Letter	*A*	*B*	*C*	*D*	*E*	*F*	*G*
f	$\frac{1}{2}$	$\frac{1}{3}$	$\frac{1}{4}$	$\frac{1}{5}$	$\frac{1}{7}$	$\frac{1}{10}$	$\frac{1}{15}$
N							
1–500	70	99	114	123	133	140	146
501–1,000	77	116	140	155	174	188	200
1,001–2,000	81	127	158	181	211	236	258
2,001–3,000	82	132	166	192	228	261	291
3,001–4,000	83	134	170	198	237	276	312
4,001–5,000	83	135	173	201	244	286	327
5,001–6,000	84	136	174	204	248	293	338
6,001–7,000	84	137	176	206	251	298	346
7,001–8,000	84	137	177	207	254	302	353
8,001–9,000	84	138	177	209	256	305	358
9,001–10,000	84	138	178	209	257	308	362
10,001–11,000	84	138	178	210	259	310	366
11,001–12,000	84	139	179	211	260	312	369
12,001–15,000	84	139	180	212	262	316	376
15,001–20,000	84	140	181	214	265	320	384
20,001 and over	84	140	182	217	270	335	410

[a]AQLs are provided as indices to simplify use of this table but have no other meaning relative to the plans.

inspection to commence much sooner than a CSP-1 plan. When production runs are long, there is no difference between the two continuous plans.

CSP-T Plans. CSP-T is a multilevel continuous sampling procedure which provides for alternate sequences of 100% inspection and sampling inspection. It differs from the previous inspection plans in that it provides for a reduced sampling frequency upon demonstration of superior product quality. Figure

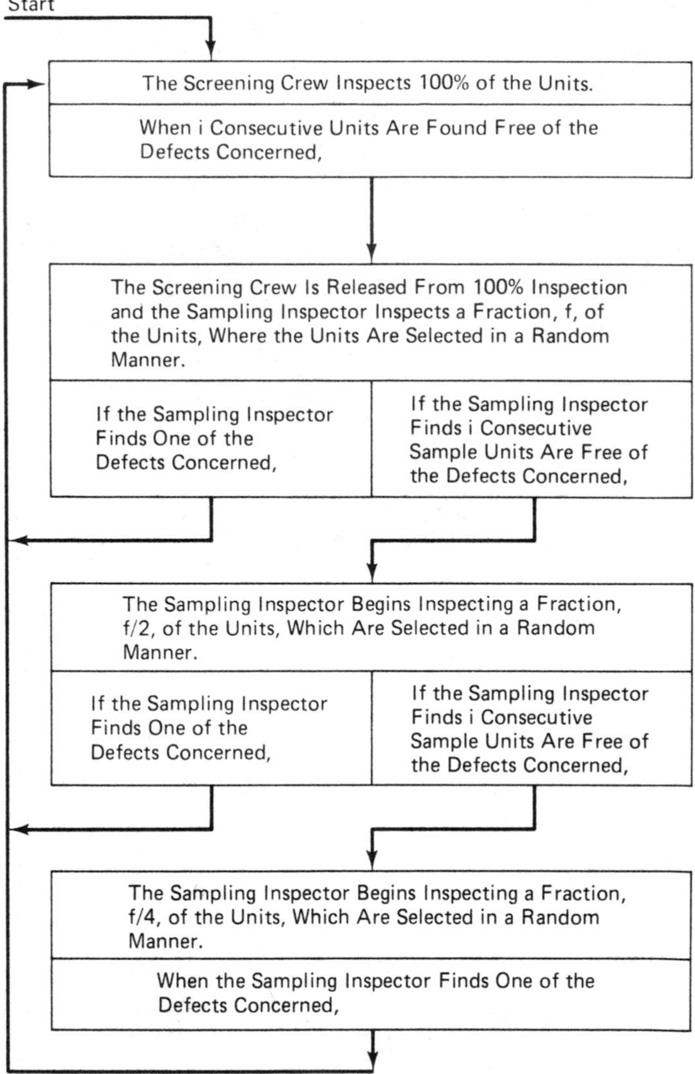

Figure 7-7 Procedure for CSP-T plans.

7-7 shows the CSP-T procedure. Table 7-11 gives the values of i and f for a specified AOQL.

An example problem will illustrate the use of the procedure. For an AOQL value of 2.90% and an f value of $\frac{1}{7}$, the corresponding i value from Table 7-11 is 35. Screening inspection (100%) continues until 35 units are found free of defects, and then sampling inspection with a frequency of $\frac{1}{7}$ commences. If no defects are found in the next 35 sample units, the sample frequency is changed to $f/2$ or $\frac{1}{14}$. Sampling continues with this new frequency of $\frac{1}{14}$ until 35 sample units are found free of defects, at which point the sampling frequency is further reduced. This last reduction is changed to $f/4$ or $\frac{1}{28}$, and sampling continues at this rate until production of the item is completed. Of course, any time a defect is found, 100% inspection is reinstated and the procedure starts over again.

TABLE 7-11 Values of *i* for CSP-T plans [Table 5-A of MIL-STD-1235A (MU)]

Sampling-Frequency Code Letter	*f*	AQL[a] (%) 0.40	0.65	1.0	1.5	2.5	4.0	6.5	10.0
A	$\frac{1}{2}$	87	58	38	25	16	10	7	5
B	$\frac{1}{3}$	116	78	51	33	22	13	9	6
C	$\frac{1}{4}$	139	93	61	39	26	15	11	7
D	$\frac{1}{5}$	158	106	69	44	29	17	12	8
E	$\frac{1}{7}$	189	127	82	53	35	21	14	9
F	$\frac{1}{10}$	224	150	97	63	41	24	17	11
G	$\frac{1}{15}$	226	179	116	74	40	29	20	13
H	$\frac{1}{25}$	324	217	141	90	59	35	24	15
I	$\frac{1}{50}$	409	274	177	114	75	44	30	19
J, K	$\frac{1}{100}$	499	335	217	139	91	53	37	23
AOQL (%)		0.53	0.79	1.22	1.90	2.90	4.94	7.12	11.46

[a]AQLs are provided as indices to simplify use of this table, but have no other meaning relative to the plans.

CSP-V Plans. The fifth plan in MIL-STD-1235A is a single-level continuous sampling procedure. A return to 100% inspection is required whenever a defect is discovered during the inspection of the first i sample units. Once the initial i sample units have passed and a defect occurs, a return to 100% inspection is required; however, the clearance number, i, is reduced by $\frac{2}{3}$. Thus, if the original i value is 39 the clearance number, i, is reduced to 13. This type of plan can be beneficially applied in those situations where there is no advantage to reducing the sampling frequency, f. This situation occurs when the inspector cannot be assigned to other duties.

Additonal details of this type of plan are found in the standard.

ACCEPTANCE SAMPLING PLANS FOR VARIABLES

Introduction

While attribute sampling plans are the most common type of acceptance sampling, there are situations where variable sampling is required. Variable sampling plans are based on the sample statistics of average and/or standard deviation and the type of frequency distribution.

Advantages and Disadvantages. Variable sampling has the principal advantage that the sample size is considerably less than with attribute sampling. In addition, variable sampling provides a better basis for improving quality and gives more information for decision making.

One of the disadvantages of variable sampling is that only one characteristic can be evaluated; a separate plan is required for each quality characteristic. Variable sampling usually involves greater administrative, clerical, and equipment costs. Furthermore, the distribution of the population has to be known or estimated.

Types of Sampling Plans. There are two types of variable plans—percent defective and process parameter. Variable plans for percent defective are designed to determine the proportion of product that is outside specifications. Of the variable plans for percent defective, two will be discussed in this section. These are the Shainin lot plot and MIL-STD-414.

Variable plans for process parameter are designed to control the average and standard deviation of the distribution of the product to specified levels. Plans of this type are acceptance control chart, sequential sampling for variables, and hypothesis testing. Because of the limited application of these plans, they are briefly discussed at the end of this chapter.

Shainin Lot Plot Plan

The Shainin lot plot plan is a variable sampling plan used in many industries. It was developed by Dorian Shainin while he was Chief Inspector at Hamilton Standard Division of United Aircraft Corporation.[9] The plan uses a plotted frequency distribution to evaluate a sample for decisions concerning acceptance or rejection of a lot. The most significant feature of the plan is the fact that it is applicable to both normal and nonnormal frequency distributions. It is a practical plan for in-house inspection as well as receiving inspection.

Lot Plot Method. The method for obtaining the lot plots is as follows:

1. A random sample of 50 items is obtained from the lot. Table 7-12 shows the inspection results.

[9]Dorian Shainin, "The Hamilton Standard Lot Plot Method of Acceptance Sampling by Variables," *Industrial Quality Control*, 7, No. 1 (July 1950), 15–34.

TABLE 7-12 Random Sample of 50 in 10 Subgroups of 5 (Data for the width of a brass plate, in millimeters)

1	2	3	4	5	6	7	8	9	10
96.75	97.04	98.03	97.80	97.54	98.55	98.30	98.28	97.95	97.48
97.78	98.34	99.09	97.24	96.70	97.11	97.70	97.95	97.79	96.55
98.42	97.28	98.32	97.68	98.12	96.81	97.62	97.85	97.80	96.98
97.41	96.52	97.59	98.01	96.69	97.60	98.86	98.10	97.17	97.35
97.08	97.86	97.79	97.48	96.98	98.24	98.04	98.80	98.35	98.48

2. Five pieces are selected from the original 50 and inspected. The average, $\overline{X}$, and range, R, are obtained from the values of the 5 pieces, which are shown in column 1 of Table 7-12. Calculations are as follows:

$$\overline{X} = \frac{\sum X}{n} = \frac{96.75 + 97.78 + 98.42 + 97.41 + 97.08}{5} = 97.49$$

$$R = X_H - X_L = 98.42 - 96.75 = 1.67$$

3. The average of the subgroup of 5 is established as the assumed average, $\overline{X}_a$, for construction of the frequency distribution and is taken as 97.50. A simple procedure is used to determine the cell interval and number of cells using the first subgroup of 5. The range of the lot is assumed to be twice the first subgroup range and is $2R = (2)(1.67) = 3.34$. Knowing the lot range, the cell interval and the number of cells are obtained as discussed in Chapter 2. The plan states that the number of cells should be between 7 and 16. Calculations are

Assume that $i = 0.25$; then

$$\begin{aligned} h &= \frac{R}{i} \\ &= \frac{3.34}{0.25} \\ &= 13 \end{aligned}$$

Therefore, since the number of cells is between 7 and 16, the cell interval of 0.25 is satisfactory.

4. The cell midpoint values[10] of the frequency distribution in Figure 7-8 are established using the assumed average, $\overline{X}_a = 97.50$, and the cell interval, $i = 0.25$. These figures are shown in the first column. Column 2 of Figure 7-8 gives the deviation in cell units of the cell midpoint from the assumed average. If the cell midpoint is greater than $\overline{X}_a$, the deviation in cell units is positive; if less than $\overline{X}_a$ the deviation in cell units is negative.

[10]In the published lot plot method, the upper cell boundary is used rather than the midpoint.

Mid-point	Cell Deviation	Distribution
	+10	
	+9	.... ULL
	+8	
	+7	
99.00	+6	3
98.75	+5	2 7 8
98.50	+4	1 6 10
98.25	+3	2 3 6 7 8 9
98.00	+2	3 4 5 7 8 8 9
97.75	+1	1 3 4 4 5 7 8 9 9 ... $\overline{\overline{X}}$
97.50	0	1 3 4 5 6 7 10
97.25	−1	2 4 9 10
97.00	−2	1 2 5 6 10
96.75	−3	1 5 6
96.50	−4	2 10
	−5	
	−6	
	−7	 LLL
	−8	

	Values in Cell Units		
No	Sum	$\overline{X}$	R
1	0	0	7
2	1	0.2	9
3	12	2.4	6
4	3	0.6	3
5	−2	−0.4	5
6	2	0.4	7
7	11	2.2	5
8	13	2.6	4
9	6	1.2	4
10	−3	−0.6	8
Total		8.6	58
Average		0.86	5.8

Figure 7-8 Example of lot plot for width of brass plate (in millimeters).

5. The first subgroup of 5 is recorded on the frequency distribution with the number 1. Additional subgroups of 5 each are inspected and recorded with the appropriate number.

6. For each subgroup of 5, the sum, average, and range in cell units are recorded in the columns to the right of the frequency distribution. The totals of the subgroup averages and ranges are divided by 10, the number of subgroups, to obtain $\overline{X} = 0.86$ in cell units from $\overline{X}_a$ and $\overline{R} = 5.8$ in cell units. The lot average is shown in Figure 7-8.

7. Using these values, the upper lot limit and lower lot limit in cell units are calculated as follows:

$$\text{ULL} = \overline{\overline{X}} + \frac{3\overline{R}}{d_2} = 0.86 + \frac{(3)(5.8)}{2.326} = 8.3 \text{ cell units}$$

$$\text{LLL} = \overline{\overline{X}} - \frac{3\overline{R}}{d_2} = 0.86 - \frac{(3)(5.8)}{2.326} = -6.6 \text{ cell units}$$

The lot limit values are shown in Figure 7-8.

With electronic calculators and microcomputers the entire method can be simplified. Once the data are collected, the steps are to construct a histogram, calculate $\overline{\overline{X}}$ and $\overline{R}$, and calculate ULL and LLL.

Lot Plan Evaluation. Once the lot plot and the lot limits are obtained, the decision concerning acceptance or rejection is made. This decision is based on a comparison of the lot plot with 11 different types of lot plots which are shown in Figure 7-9.

The first four types are applicable to lot plots which are approximately normally distributed. In the type 1 situation, the lot plot is well within specification

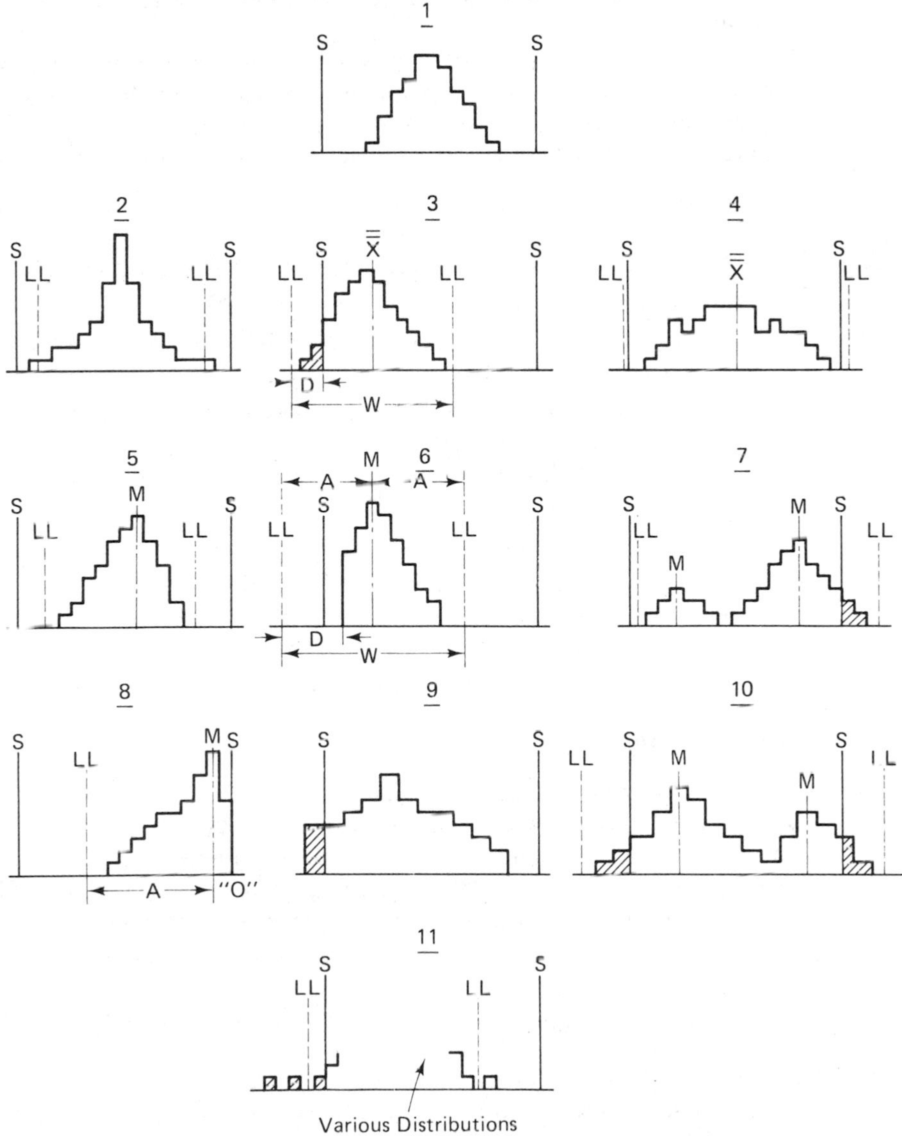

Figure 7-9 Eleven typical types of lot plots. [Reproduced by permission from Dorian Shainin, "The Hamilton Standard Lot Plot Method," *Industrial Quality Control*, 7, No. 1 (July 1950), 17.]

limits, and the lot is accepted without the need to calculate the lot limits. If the lot limits are within the specifications, as illustrated by type 2, the lot is accepted. When the lot limits are outside the specifications as shown by types 3 and 4, the percentage of product beyond specifications is obtained and a review board determines the final disposition of the stock. In some cases an attribute plan is employed to determine the lot acceptability when one or two values are beyond the lot limits.

The other types of lot plots are used for nonnormal distributions. For example, type 5 is skewed; types 6 and 9 indicate that the lot was screened or sorted; types 7 and 10 illustrate the bimodal condition; and type 11 is for stray values. Special techniques are specified for analyzing the nonnormal lot plots.

Comments

1. Once learned, the lot plot procedure is relatively simple and has resulted in improved quality and lower inspection costs.
2. Lot plots are returned to the producer, and this action will cause a subsequent improvement in quality.
3. Inspectors can accept lots; however, disposition of unsatisfactory lots is left to a material-review board.
4. Many users of the lot plot method have modified the Shainin method for their own situation.
5. The major criticism of the plan is that the shape of the lot plot does not always give an accurate indication of the true distribution. Shainin states that the lot plot is close enough to have no practical effect on the final decision or if there are any errors, they are in a safe direction.
6. For additional information, the reader is referred to the published articles.[11]

MIL-STD-414[12]

MIL-STD-414 is a lot-by-lot acceptance sampling plan by variables. The standard is indexed by numerical values of the AQL which range from 0.04 to 15.00%. Provision is made for normal, tightened, and reduced inspection. Sample sizes are a function of the lot size and the inspection level. The standard assumes a normally distributed random variable. Since MIL-STD-414 has limited application and it is 110 pages long, only a portion of the tables and the procedures will be given.

The standard makes provision for nine different procedures which can be

[11]Dorian Shainin, "Recent Lot Plot Experiences Around the Country," *Industrial Quality Control,* 8, No. 5 (March 1952), 22.

[12]Copies of MIL-STD-414 may be obtained by directing requests to Commanding Officer, U.S. Naval Supply Depot, Attn. Code DMD, 5801 Tabor Avenue, Philadelphia, PA 19120.

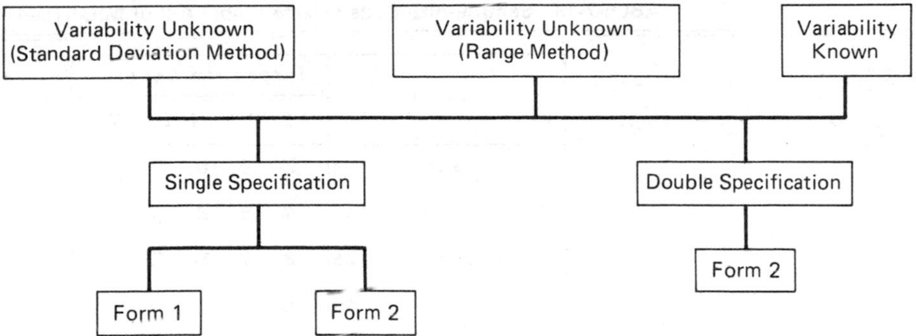

Figure 7-10 Composition of MIL-STD-414.

used to evaluate a lot for acceptance or rejection. Figure 7-10 shows the composition of the standard. If the variability (σ) of the process is known and stable, the variability known plan is the most economical. When the variability is unknown, the standard deviation method or the range method is used. The range method requires a larger sample size; however, the calculations are easier. There are two types of specifications—single and double. Two alternative procedures, Forms 1 and 2, are available and will lead to the same acceptance–rejection decision. While Form 1 is somewhat easier, it is only applicable to single specification situations; in addition, it does not give sufficient information for the normal, tightened, and reduced switching rules. Therefore, Form 2 is the preferred procedure.

MIL-STD-414 is divided into four sections. Section A contains a general description, sample-size code letters, and OC curves for the sampling plans. Procedure and examples for the unknown variability—standard deviation method is given in Section B; procedures and examples for unknown variability—range method is given in Section C; and procedures and examples for known variability are given in Section D.

The sample size for all the methods is designated by code letters. These code letters are based on the lot size and the inspection level as shown in Table 7-13. There are five inspection levels: I, II, III, IV, and V. Unless otherwise specified, inspection level IV will be used. Inspection level V gives a steeper OC curve and therefore reduced consumer's risk. When greater consumer's risks can be tolerated, lower inspection levels can be used.

An example problem for unknown variability—standard deviation method, single specification, and Form 2 is used to demonstrate the procedure.

Example Problem

The minimum temperature of operation for a certain device is specified as 180°C. A lot of 40 items is submitted for inspection where inspection level IV, normal inspection, and AQL = 1.0% are the criteria. From Table

TABLE 7-13 Sample-Size Code Letters (Table A-2 of MIL-STD-414)

Lot Size	Inspection Levels				
	I	II	III	IV	V
3 to 8	B	B	B	B	C
9 to 15	B	B	B	B	D
16 to 25	B	B	B	C	E
26 to 40	B	B	B	D	F
41 to 65	B	B	C	E	G
66 to 110	B	B	D	F	H
111 to 180	B	C	E	G	I
181 to 300	B	D	F	H	J
301 to 500	C	E	G	I	K
501 to 800	D	F	H	J	L
801 to 1,300	E	G	I	K	L
1,301 to 3,200	F	H	J	L	M
3,201 to 8,000	G	I	L	M	N
8,001 to 22,000	H	J	M	N	O
22,001 to 110,000	I	K	N	O	P
110,001 to 550,000	I	K	O	P	Q
550,001 and over	I	K	P	Q	Q

7-13 the code letter is D, which gives a sample size $n = 5$ (from Table 7-14). The temperatures for the five samples are 197°, 188°, 184°, 205°, and 201°C.

$$\overline{X} = \frac{\sum X}{n} = \frac{197 + 188 + 184 + 205 + 201}{5} = 195°\text{C}$$

$$s = \sqrt{\frac{\sum X^2 - \frac{(\sum X)^2}{n}}{n - 1}} = \sqrt{\frac{190{,}435 - 190{,}125}{5 - 1}} = 8.80$$

Lower-quality index:

$$Q_L = \frac{\overline{X} - L}{s} = \frac{195 - 180}{8.80} = 1.70$$

Estimate of lot percent defective below L: p_L

From Table 7-15, $p_L = 0.66\%$

Maximum allowable percent defective: M

From Table 7-14, $M = 3.32\%$

The lot meets acceptance criterion if $p_L \leqq M$:

Since $0.66\% < 3.32\%$, accept lot

Note: If the upper specification is required, use the formula $Q_U = (U - \overline{X})/s$.

The formula for the quantity index, Q, is very similar to the formula for the Z value which is given in Chapter 2. Table 7-15 is based on Q and the sample size, whereas Table A in the Appendix is based on the Z value and the infinite situation. The value of p_L is the estimate of the percent defective which is below the lower specification limit L. As long as this value, p_L, is less than the maximum allowable percent defective, M (for a particular AQL and n), the lot is accepted.

Normal and tightened inspection use the same table. The AQL values for normal inspection are indexed from the top of the table, and for tightened inspection they are indexed from the bottom of the table.

MIL-STD-414 contains a special procedure for application of mixed variable—attribute sampling plans. If the lot does not meet the acceptability criterion of the variable plan, an attribute single sampling plan, with tightened inspection and the same AQL, is obtained from MIL-STD-105D. A lot can be accepted by either of the plans in sequence but must be rejected by both the variable and the attribute plans.

Other Acceptance Sampling Plans for Variables

There are three other types of acceptance sampling plans by variables which are occasionally used. These types of variable plans are concerned with the average quality or the variability in the quality of the product and not with the percent defective. They may be used for sampling bulk material that is shipped in bags, drums, tank cars, and so on. A brief discussion of each is given in this section.

Acceptance control charts provide a technique for rejecting or accepting a lot using the sample average. Acceptance control limits and the sample size are established from the known standard deviation, specification limits, AQL, and values of the consumer and producer risks. The use of a control chart allows personnel to observe quality trends.[13]

[13]For more information, see R. A. Freund, "Acceptance Control Charts," *Industrial Quality Control,* October 1957, 13-23.

TABLE 7-14 Master Table for Normal and Tightened Inspection for Plans Based on Variability Unknown, Standard Deviation Method, Form 2

Sample size code letter	Sample size	Acceptable Quality Levels (normal inspection)													
		.04	.065	.10	.15	.25	.40	.65	1.00	1.50	2.50	4.00	6.50	10.00	15.00
		M	M	M	M	M	M	M	M	M	M	M	M	M	M
B	3	↓	↓	↓	↓	↓	↓	↓	▼	▼	7.59	18.86	26.94	33.69	40.47
C	4	↓	↓	↓	↓	↓	↓	↓	1.53	5.50	10.92	16.45	22.86	29.45	36.90
D	5	↓	↓	↓	↓	↓	↓	1.33	3.32	5.83	9.80	14.39	20.19	26.56	33.99
E	7	↓	↓	↓	↓	0.422	1.06	2.14	3.55	5.35	8.40	12.20	17.35	23.29	30.50
F	10	↓	↓	↓	0.349	0.716	1.30	2.17	3.26	4.77	7.29	10.54	15.17	20.74	27.57
G	15	0.099	0.186	0.312	0.503	0.818	1.31	2.11	3.05	4.31	6.56	9.46	13.71	18.94	25.61
H	20	0.135	0.228	0.365	0.544	0.846	1.29	2.05	2.95	4.09	6.17	8.92	12.99	18.03	24.53
I	25	0.155	0.250	0.380	0.551	0.877	1.29	2.00	2.86	3.97	5.97	8.63	12.57	17.51	23.97
J	30	0.179	0.280	0.413	0.581	0.879	1.29	1.98	2.83	3.91	5.86	8.47	12.36	17.24	23.58
K	35	0.170	0.264	0.388	0.535	0.847	1.23	1.87	2.68	3.70	5.57	8.10	11.87	16.65	22.91
L	40	0.179	0.275	0.401	0.566	0.873	1.26	1.88	2.71	3.72	5.58	8.09	11.85	16.61	22.86
M	50	0.163	0.250	0.363	0.503	0.789	1.17	1.71	2.49	3.45	5.20	7.61	11.23	15.87	22.00
N	75	0.147	0.228	0.330	0.467	0.720	1.07	1.60	2.29	3.20	4.87	7.15	10.63	15.13	21.11
O	100	0.145	0.220	0.317	0.447	0.689	1.02	1.53	2.20	3.07	4.69	6.91	10.32	14.75	20.66
P	150	0.134	0.203	0.293	0.413	0.638	0.949	1.43	2.05	2.89	4.43	6.57	9.88	14.20	20.02
Q	200	0.135	0.204	0.294	0.414	0.637	0.945	1.42	2.04	2.87	4.40	6.53	9.81	14.12	19.92
		.065	.10	.15	.25	.40	.65	1.00	1.50	2.50	4.00	6.50	10.00	15.00	
		Acceptability Quality Levels (tightened inspection)													

All AQL and table values are in percent defective.

↓ Use first sampling plan below arrow, that is, both sample size as well as M value. When sample size equals or exceeds lot size, every item in the lot must be inspected.

TABLE 7-15 Table for Estimating the Lot Percent Defective (p_L or p_U) Using Standard Deviation Method (Values in percent) (Table B-5 of MIL-STD-414[a])

Q_U or Q_L	Sample Size							
	5	10	20	30	40	50	100	200
0	50.00	50.00	50.00	50.00	50.00	50.00	50.00	50.00
0.10	46.44	46.16	46.08	46.05	46.04	46.04	46.03	46.02
0.20	42.90	42.35	42.19	42.15	42.13	42.11	42.09	42.08
0.30	39.37	38.60	38.37	38.31	38.28	38.27	38.24	38.22
0.40	35.88	34.93	34.65	34.58	34.54	34.53	34.49	34.47
0.50	32.44	31.37	31.06	30.98	30.95	30.93	30.89	30.87
0.60	29.05	27.94	27.63	27.55	27.52	27.50	27.46	27.44
0.70	25.74	24.67	24.38	24.31	24.28	24.26	24.23	24.21
0.80	22.51	21.57	21.33	21.27	21.25	21.23	21.21	21.20
0.90	19.38	18.67	18.50	18.46	18.44	18.43	18.42	18.41
1.00	16.36	15.97	15.89	15.88	15.87	15.87	15.87	15.87
1.10	13.48	13.50	13.52	13.53	13.54	13.54	13.55	13.56
1.20	10.76	11.24	11.38	11.42	11.44	11.46	11.48	11.49
1.30	8.21	9.22	9.48	9.55	9.58	9.60	9.64	9.66
1.40	5.88	7.44	7.80	7.90	7.94	7.97	8.02	8.05
1.50	3.80	5.87	6.34	6.46	6.52	6.55	6.62	6.65
1.60	2.03	4.54	5.09	5.23	5.30	5.33	5.41	5.44
1.70	0.66	3.41	4.02	4.18	4.25	4.30	4.38	4.42
1.80	0.00	2.49	3.13	3.30	3.38	3.43	3.51	3.55
1.90	0.00	1.75	2.40	2.57	2.65	2.70	2.79	2.83
2.00	0.00	1.17	1.81	1.98	2.06	2.10	2.19	2.23
2.10	0.00	0.74	1.34	1.50	1.58	1.62	1.71	1.75
2.20	0.00	0.437	0.968	1.120	1.192	1.233	1.314	1.352
2.30	0.00	0.233	0.685	0.823	0.888	0.927	1.001	1.037
2.40	0.00	0.109	0.473	0.594	0.653	0.687	0.755	0.787
2.50	0.00	0.041	0.317	0.421	0.473	0.503	0.563	0.592
2.60	0.00	0.011	0.207	0.293	0.337	0.363	0.415	0.441
2.70	0.00	0.001	0.130	0.200	0.236	0.258	0.302	0.325
2.80	0.00	0.000	0.079	0.133	0.162	0.181	0.218	0.237
2.90	0.00	0.000	0.046	0.087	0.110	0.125	0.155	0.171
3.00	0.00	0.000	0.025	0.055	0.073	0.084	0.109	0.122

[a]The actual Table B-5 of MIL-STD-414 contains more sample sizes and about 10 times as many values for Q_U or Q_L.

Sequential sampling by variables can be used when the quality characteristic is normally distributed and when the standard deviation is known. The technique for this sampling plan is similar to the sequential plan by attributes that was discussed previously. However, the variable plan plots the cumulative sum, $\sum X$, while the attribute plan plots the number of defectives, d. Sequential sampling can result in reduced sampling inspection.[14]

A third type of sampling by variables is referred to as *hypothesis testing*. There are a number of different tests to evaluate the sample average or sample deviation for acceptance or rejection decisions.[15]

[14]For more information, see A. J. Duncan, *Quality Control and Industrial Statistics* (Homewood, Ill.: Richard D. Irwin, Inc., 1974), pp. 309-316.

[15]For more information, see J. M. Juran, ed., *Quality Control Handbook*, 3rd ed. (New York: McGraw-Hill Book Company, 1974), Sec. 22, pp. 33–48.

```
10 REM                    OC CURVE-CHAIN SAMPLING
20 REM                       Based on Binomial
30 REM
40 REM                    N = Sample Size(n)
50 REM                    P = Fraction Defective(p)
60 REM                    I = Number of Previous Lots(i)
70 REM                    PA= Probability of Acceptance(Pa)
80 REM
90 PRINT " Enter the Sample Size or Enter 0 to stop program."
100 INPUT N
110 IF N = 0 GOTO 250
120 LPRINT TAB(5);" n = ";N
130 PRINT " Enter Number of Previous Lots." : INPUT I
140 LPRINT TAB(5);" i = ";I : LPRINT
150 P = .01
160 LPRINT TAB(5);" p";TAB(15);"Pa" : GOTO 180
170 P = P + .04
180 Q = 1 - P
190 P0 = Q^N
200 P1 = N * P * Q^(N-1)
210 PA = P0 + P1 * P0^I
220 LPRINT TAB(4);P;TAB(12);PA
230 IF PA < .1 GOTO 90
240 GOTO 170
250 END
```

```
     n =  8
     i =  5

     p         Pa
    .01       .972627
    .05       .699318
    .09       .478809
    .13       .329706
    .17       .225443
    .21       .151737
    .25       .100116
    .29       .0645756
```

Figure 7-11 Computer program in BASIC for the OC curves for chain sampling.

COMPUTER PROGRAM

The computer program given in Figure 7-11 computes the OC curve for Dodge's chain sampling plan. It is structured so that values of the sample size, n, and the number of previous lots, i, can be changed to achieve the optimum sampling plan without leaving the program. If more plotted points are desired, the increment in statement 220 can be reduced to, say, 0.01.

PROBLEMS

1. Using the Dodge–Romig tables, determine the double sampling plan for AOQL = 3.0% when the process average is 0.80% and the lot size is 2500. What is the LQL?
2. Using the Dodge–Romig tables for LQL, determine the single sampling plan for a LQL = 1.0% when the process average is 0.35% and $N = 502$. What is the AOQL?
3. What would be the sampling plan of Problem 1 if the lot contains a new product and the process average is unknown?
4. If the process average is 0.19% defective, what double sampling plan is recommended using the Dodge–Romig LQL tables? LQL is 1.0% and the lot size is 8000. What is the AOQL?
5. For the information in Problem 4, give the equations for the OC curve.
6. Using the Philips split-risk system, determine the sampling plan for a lot size of 30,000 and a desired split-risk product quality, $100p = 5.0\%$.
7. Determine the sampling plan using the Philips system for a lot size of 800 and a desired split-risk product quality of 2%.
8. Determine the probability of acceptance of product that is 3% defective using the sampling plan for Problem 7.
9. Determine the OC curve for a ChSP-1 where $n = 4$, $c = 0$, and $i = 3$. Use five points to determine the curve.
10. A chain sampling plan ChSP-1 is being used for the inspection of lots of 250 pieces. Six samples are inspected. If none are defective, the lot is accepted; if one defective is found, the lot is accepted if the three previous lot samples were free of defectives. Determine the probability of acceptance of a lot that is 3% defective.
11. A unit sequential sampling plan is defined by $p_\alpha = 0.08$, $\alpha = 0.05$, $p_\beta = 0.18$, and $\beta = 0.10$. Determine the equations for the acceptance and rejection line and draw the graphical plan.

12. For a unit sequential sampling plan that is defined by $\alpha = 0.08$, $p_\alpha = 0.05$, $\beta = 0.15$, and $p_\beta = 0.12$, determine the equations for the acceptance and rejection line. Using these equations establish a table of the rejection number, acceptance number, and number of units inspected. The table can be stopped when the rejection number equals 6.

13. For SkSP-1 determine the i values for $f = \frac{1}{2}$, $\frac{1}{3}$, and $\frac{1}{4}$ using an AOQL of 1.90%.

14. For SkSP-1 determine the i values for $f = \frac{1}{2}$, $\frac{1}{3}$, and $\frac{1}{4}$ using an AOQL of 0.79%.

15. Assuming a continuous process, determine three sampling plans for an AOQL = 0.143% using CSP-1.

16. For Dodge's CSP-2 plan, determine the value of i for an AOQL value of 4.94% and a frequency of 20%.

17. Describe the CSP-2 continuous sampling plan of Problem 16.

18. Using MIL-STD-1235A(MU) and an AOQL of 1.22%, determine the value of i for CSP-T with a sampling frequency of $\frac{1}{15}$.

19. For CSP-1, determine the value of i for an AOQL = 0.198% and a frequency of $\frac{1}{4}$.

20. Using the Shainin lot plot, compute the lot limits and draw the lot plot. The hardness inspection results of 50 sample units using Rockwell-C are as follows:

Subgroup	*Data*	*Average*
1	50, 49, 53, 49, 56	51.4
2	52, 50, 47, 50, 51	50.0
3	49, 49, 53, 51, 48	50.0
4	49, 52, 50, 52, 51	50.8
5	51, 53, 51, 52, 53	52.6
6	54, 50, 54, 53, 52	52.2
7	53, 51, 52, 47, 50	50.6
8	46, 55, 54, 52, 52	51.8
9	49, 53, 51, 51, 50	50.8
10	51, 48, 55, 51, 52	51.4

What type of lot plot does the distribution above represent? Specifications are from 41 to 60. Is the lot accepted or rejected?

21. The diameter of a $\frac{3}{8}$-in. thread has specifications of 9.78 mm and 9.65 mm. Sample results from 50 random inspections are given below. Determine the lot limits and draw the lot plot. What type of lot plot does the distribution below represent?

Subgroup	Data	Average
1	9.77, 9.76, 9.75, 9.76, 9.76	9.760
2	9.73, 9.74, 9.77, 9.74, 9.77	9.750
3	9.73, 9.77, 9.76, 9.77, 9.75	9.756
4	9.78, 9.77, 9.77, 9.76, 9.78	9.772
5	9.72, 9.78, 9.77, 9.78, 9.74	9.758
6	9.75, 9.77, 9.76, 9.77, 9.77	9.764
7	9.78, 9.76, 9.77, 9.76, 9.78	9.770
8	9.77, 9.77, 9.77, 9.78, 9.78	9.774
9	9.78, 9.77, 9.76, 9.76, 9.77	9.768
10	9.76, 9.78, 9.77, 9.78, 9.76	9.768

22. A lot of 480 items is submitted for inspection with an inspection level of II. Determine the sample-size code letter and the sample size for inspection by variables using MIL-STD-414.

23. Assuming normal inspection, MIL-STD-414, variability unknown, standard deviation method, code letter D, AQL = 2.50%, and a single lower specification of 200 g, determine whether the lot is accepted or rejected using Form 2. The inspection results of the 5 samples are: 204, 211, 199, 209, and 208 g.

24. If the lower specification of Problem 23 is 200.5 g, what is the acceptance–rejection decision?

25. For tightened inspection, MIL-STD-414, variability unknown, standard deviation method, code letter F, AQL = 0.65%, and an upper single specification of 4.15 mm, determine whether the lot is accepted or rejected. Use Form 2. The results of the 10 sample inspections are 3.90, 3.70, 3.40, 4.20, 3.60, 3.50, 3.70, 3.60, 3.80, and 3.80 mm.

26. If Problem 25 has normal inspection rather than tightened, what is the decision?

27. Test, and if necessary rewrite, the computer program for your computer.

28. Modify the computer program to output the OC curve for your graphical output device.

29. Write a computer program for:
(a) Sequential sampling by attributes
(b) MIL-STD-414

8 RELIABILITY

FUNDAMENTAL ASPECTS

Definition

Simply stated, *reliability* is quality over the long run. Quality is the condition of the product during manufacturing or immediately afterward, whereas reliability is the ability of the product to perform its intended function over a period of time. A product that "works" for a long period of time is a reliable one. Since all units of a product will fail at different times, reliability is a probability.

A more precise definition is: *Reliability is the probability that a product will perform its intended function satisfactorily for a prescribed life under certain stated environmental conditions*. From the definition, there are four factors associated with reliability: (1) numerical value, (2) intended function, (3) life, and (4) environmental conditions.

The numerical value is the probability that failure of the product will not occur during a particular time. Thus, a value of 0.93 would represent the probability that 93 of 100 products would function after a prescribed period of time and 7 products would fail before the prescribed period of time. Particular probability distributions can be used to describe the failure rate of units of product.

The second factor concerns the intended function of the product. Products are designed for particular applications and are expected to be able to perform those applications. For example, an electric hoist is expected to lift a certain design load; it is not expected to lift a load that exceeds the design specification.

The third factor in the definition of reliability is the intended life of the product; in other words, how long the product is expected to last. Thus, the life of automobile tires is specified by different values, such as 36 months or 48,000 km, depending on the construction of the tire. Product life is specified as a function of usage, time, or both.

The last factor in the definition involves the environmental conditions. A product that is designed to function indoors, such as an upholstered chair, cannot be expected to function reliably outdoors in the sun, wind, and precipitation. Environmental conditions also include the storage and transportation aspects of the product. These aspects may be more severe than the actual use.

Achieving Reliability

Emphasis. Increased emphasis is being given to product reliability. One of the reasons for this emphasis is due to the Consumer Protection Act of 1972, which is discussed in Chapter 10. Another reason is the fact that products are more complicated. At one time the washing machine was a simple device that agitated the clothes in a hot, soapy solution. Today, a washing machine has different agitating speeds, different rinse speeds, different cycle times, different water temperatures, different water levels, and provisions to dispense a number of washing ingredients at precise times in the cycle. An additional reason for the increased emphasis on reliability is due to automation; people are, in many cases, not able to manually operate the product if an automated component fails.

System Reliability. As products become more complex (have more components), the chance of failure increases. The method of arranging the components affects the reliability of the entire system. Components can be arranged in series, parallel, or a combination. Figure 8-1 illustrates the various arrangements.

When components are arranged in series, the reliability of the system is the product of the individual components. Thus, for the series arrangement of Figure 8-1a, the series reliability, R_s, is calculated as follows:

$$\begin{aligned} R_s &= (R_A)(R_B)(R_C) \\ &= (0.95)(0.75)(0.99) \\ &= 0.71 \end{aligned}$$

As components are added to the series, the system reliability decreases.

When components are arranged in series, the failure of any component causes failure of the system. This is not the case when the components are arranged in parallel. When a component fails, the product continues to function using another component until all parallel components have failed. Thus, for the parallel arrangement in Figure 8-1b, the parallel reliability, R_p, is calculated as follows:

$$\begin{aligned} R_p &= 1 - (1 - R_I)(1 - R_J) \\ &= 1 - (1 - 0.75)(1 - 0.84) \\ &= 0.96 \end{aligned}$$

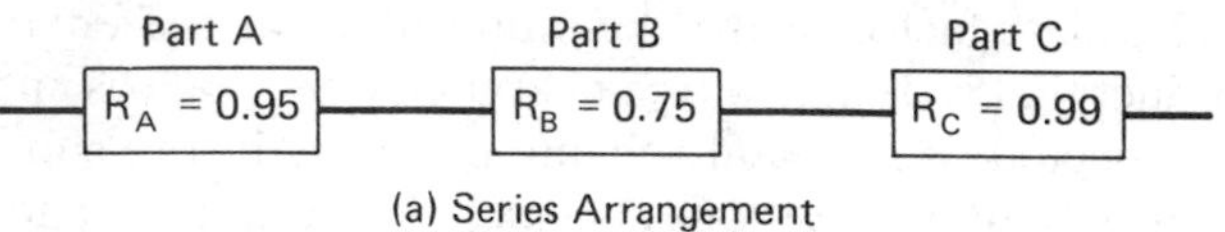

(a) Series Arrangement

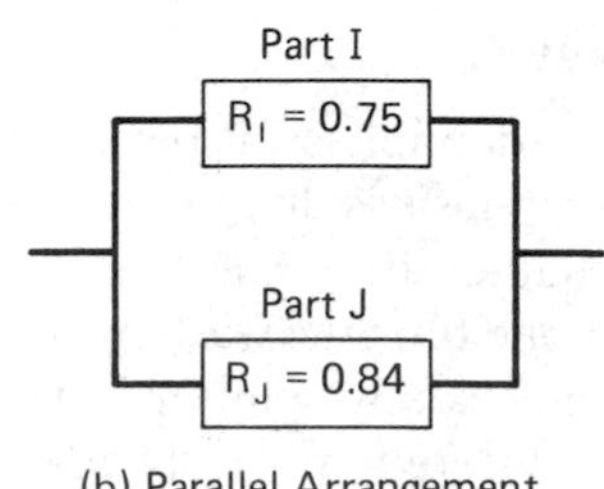

(b) Parallel Arrangement

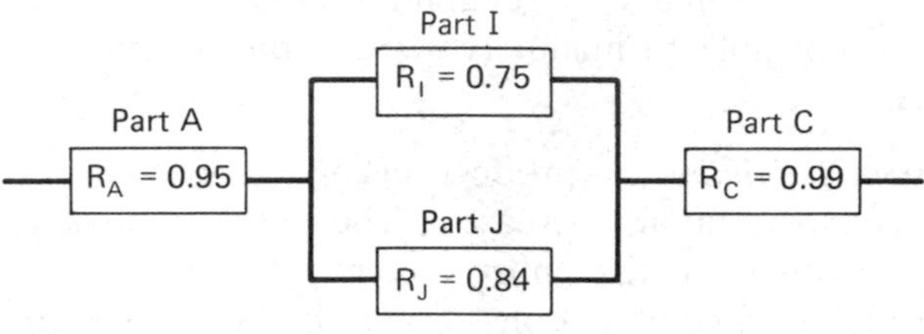

(c) Combination Arrangement

Figure 8-1 Methods of arranging components.

As the number of components in parallel increases, the reliability increases. The reliability for a parellel arrangement of components is greater than the reliability of the individual components.

Most complexed products are a combination of series and parallel arrangements of components. This is illustrated in Figure 8-1c, wherein part B is replaced by the parallel components, part I and part J. The reliability of the combination, R_c, is calculated as follows:

$$\begin{aligned} R_c &= (R_a)(R_{I,J})(R_C) \\ &= (0.95)(0.96)(0.99) \\ &= 0.90 \end{aligned}$$

Product reliability depends on its design, manufacture, transportation, and maintenance.

Design. The most important aspect of reliability is the design. It should be as simple as possible. As previously pointed out, the greater the number of components, the greater the chance of product failure. If a system has 50 components in series, and each component has a reliability of 0.95, the system reliability is

$$R_s = R^n = 0.95^{50} = 0.08$$

The fewer the components, the better the reliability.

Another way of achieving reliability is to have a backup or redundant component. When the primary component fails, another component is activated. This concept was illustrated by the parallel arrangement of components. It is frequently cheaper to have inexpensive redundant components to achieve a particular reliability than to have a single expensive component.

Reliability can also be achieved by overdesign. The use of large factors of safety can increase the reliability of a product. For example, a 1-in. rope may be substituted for a $\frac{1}{2}$-in. rope even though the $\frac{1}{2}$-in. rope would have been sufficient.

When the failure of a product can lead to a fatality or substantial financial loss, a fail-safe type of device should be used. Thus, disabling extremity injuries from power-press operations are minimized by the use of a clutch. The clutch must be engaged for the ram and die to descend. If there is a malfunction of the clutch-activation system, the press will fail to operate.

The maintenance of the system is an important factor in reliability. Products that are easy to maintain will likely receive better maintenance. In some situations it may be more practical to eliminate the need for maintenance. For example, oil-impregnated bearings do not need lubrication for the life of the product.

Environmental conditions such as dust, temperature, moisture, and vibration can be the cause of failure. The designer must protect the product from these conditions. Heat shields, rubber vibration mounts, and filters are used to increase the reliability under adverse environmental conditions.

There is a definite relationship between investment in reliability (cost) and reliability. After a certain point, there is only a slight improvement in reliability for a large increase in product cost. For example, assume that a $50 component has a reliability of 0.75. If the cost is increased to $100, the reliability becomes 0.90; if the cost is increased to $150, the reliability becomes 0.94; and if the cost is increased to $200, the reliability becomes 0.96. As can be seen by this hypothetical example, there is a diminishing reliability return for the investment dollar.

Manufacturing. The manufacturing process is the second most important aspect of reliability. Basic quality control techniques that have been described in earlier chapters will minimize the risk of product failure. Emphasis should be placed on those components which are least reliable.

Manufacturing personnel can take action to ensure that the equipment used is right for the job and investigate new equipment as it becomes available. In addition, they can experiment with process conditions to determine which conditions produce the most reliable product.

Transportation. The third aspects of reliability is the transportation of the product to the customer. No matter how well conceived the design or how carefully manufactured, the actual performance of the product by the customer is the final evaluation. The reliability of the product at the point of use can be greatly affected by the type of handling the product receives in transit. Good packaging techniques and shipment evaluation are essential.

Maintenance. While designers try to eliminate the need for customer maintenance, there are many situations where it is not practical or possible. In such cases, the customer should be given ample warning. For example, a warning light or buzzer when a component needs a lubricant. Maintenance should be simple and easy to perform.

STATISTICAL ASPECTS

Distributions Applicable to Reliability

Types of continuous probability distributions used in reliability studies are exponential, normal, and Weilbull.[1] Their frequency distributions as a function of time are given in Figure 8-2a.

Reliability Curves

Reliability curves for the exponential, normal, and Weilbull distributions as a function of time are given in Figure 8-2b. The formulas for these distributions are also given in the figure. For the exponential and Weilbull curves the formulas are $R_t = e^{-t/\theta}$ and $R_t = e^{\alpha t}$, respectively. The formula for the normal distribution is

$$R_t = 1.0 - \int_0^t f(t)\,dt$$

which requires integration. However, Table A in the Appendix can be used to find the area under the curve, which is the $\int_0^t f(t)\,dt$.

Failure-Rate Curve

Failure-rate is important in describing the life-history curve of a product. The failure-rate curves and formulas for the exponential, normal, and Weibull as a function of time are shown in Figure 8-2c.

[1]A fourth type, the gamma distribution, is not given because of its limited application. Also, the discrete probability distributions, geometric and negative binomial, are not given for the same reason.

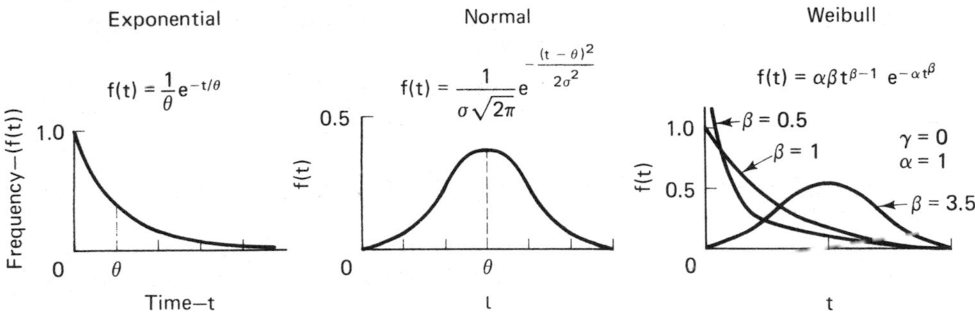

a) Frequency Distribution as a Function of Time

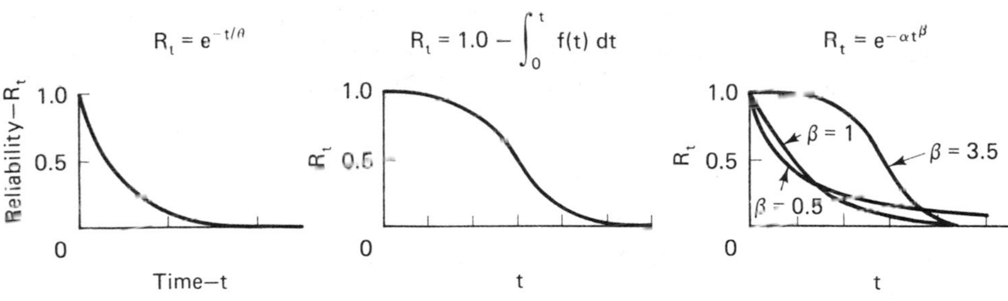

b) Reliability as a Function of Time

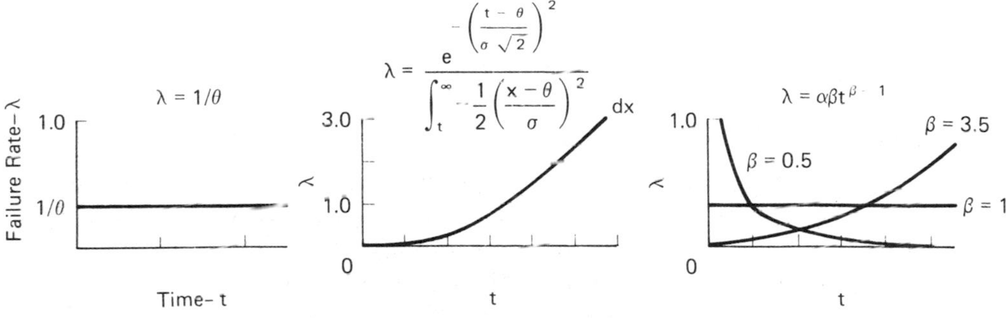

c) Failure Rate as a Function of Time

Figure 8-2 Probability distributions, failure-rate curves, and reliability curves as a function of time.

Failure rate can be estimated from test data by use of the formula

$$\lambda_{\text{estimated}} = \frac{\text{number of item failures}}{\text{sum of test times or cycles}}$$

For example, nine items are tested, with the following results at the end of 22 test hours:

Four items failed after 4, 12, 15, and 21, respectively. Five items were still operating at the end of 22 h.

$$\lambda = \frac{4}{4 + 12 + 15 + 21 + 5(22)} = 0.025$$

For the exponential distribution and for the Weibull distribution when β, the shape parameter, equals 1, there is a constant failure rate. When the failure rate is constant, the relationship between mean life and failure rate is as follows:[2]

$$\lambda = \frac{1}{\theta} \qquad \text{(for constant failure rate)}$$

where λ = failure rate, which is the probability that a unit will fail in a stated unit of time or cycles
θ = mean life or mean time to failure (MTTF)

For the example problem, the mean life θ would be determined by

$$\theta = \frac{1}{\lambda} = \frac{1}{0.025} = 40 \text{ h}$$

Life-History Curve

Figure 8-3 shows a typical life-history curve of a complexed product for an infinite number of items. The curve, sometimes referred to as the "bathtub" curve, is a comparison of failure rate with time. It has three distinct phases: debugging phase, chance failure phase, and the wear-out phase.

The *debugging phase*, which is also called the burn-in or infant-mortality phase, is characterized by marginal and short-life parts that cause a rapid decrease in the failure rate. This phase is depicted by many visits to the repair shop. While the shape of the curve varies somewhat due to the type of product, the Weibull distribution with shaping parameters less than 1, $\beta < 1$, is used to

[2]Failure rate is also equal to $f(t)/R_t$.

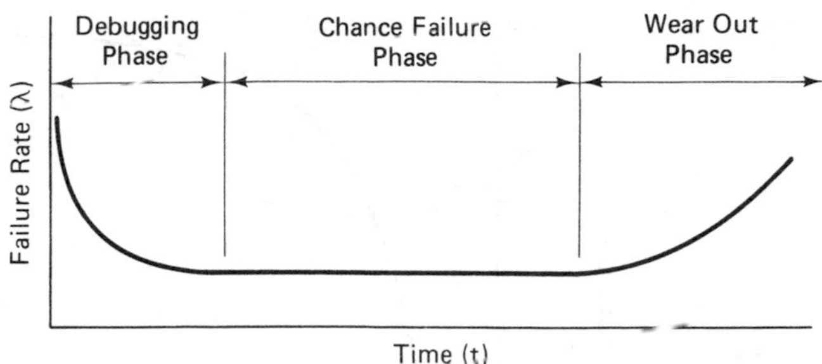

Figure 8-3 Typical life history of a complexed product for an infinite number of items.

describe the occurrence of failures. Since the debugging phase is not necessarily an operational phase, it is rarely studied.

The *chance failure phase* is shown in the figure as a horizontal straight line, thereby making the failure rate constant. Failures occur in a random manner due to the constant failure rate. The assumption of a constant failure rate is valid for most products; however, some products may have a failure rate that decreases or increases with time.

The exponential distribution and the Weibull distribution with shape parameter equal to 1 are used to describe this phase of the life history. When the curve increases or decreases, a Weibull shape parameter greater or less than 1 can be used. Reliability studies and sampling plans are, for the most part, concerned with the chance failure phase.

The third phase is the *wear-out phase*, which is depicted by a sharp rise in the failure rate. Usually the normal distribution is the one that best describes the wear-out phase. However, the Weibull distribution with shape parameters greater or less than 3.5 can be used depending on the type of wear-out distribution.

The curve shown in Figure 8-3 is the type of failure pattern exhibited by most products; however, there will be some products that deviate from this curve. It is important to know the type of failure pattern so that known probability distributions can be used for analysis and prediction of product reliability.

OC Curve Construction

The operating characteristic (OC) curve is constructed in a manner similar to that given in Chapter 6. However, the fraction defective p_0 is replaced by the mean life θ. The shape of the OC curve as shown in Figure 8-4 is different than those of Chapter 6. If lots are submitted with a mean life of 5000 h, the probability of acceptance is 0.697 using the sampling plan described by the OC curve of Figure 8-4.

An example problem for a constant failure rate will be used to illustrate the construction. A lot-by-lot acceptance sampling plan with replacement is as

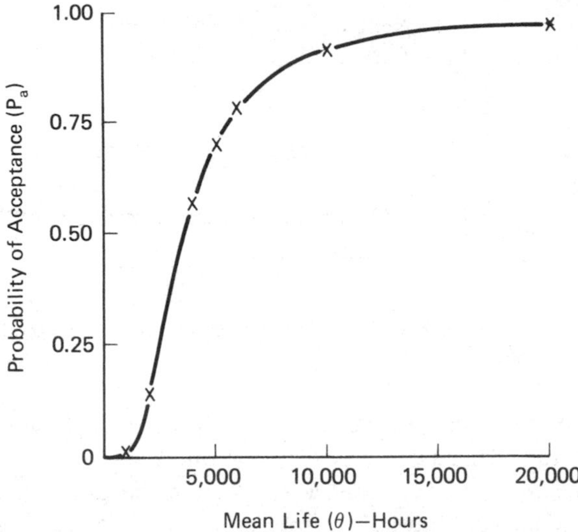

Figure 8-4 OC curve for the sampling plan $n = 16$, $T = 600$ h, $c = 2$, $r = 3$.

follows. Select a sample of 16 units from a lot and test each item for 600 h. If 2 or less items fail, accept the lot; if 3 or more items fail, reject the lot. In symbols, the plan is $n = 16$, $T = 600$ h, $c = 2$, and $r = 3$. When an item fails, it is replaced by another one from the lot. The first step in the construction of the curve is to assume values for the mean life θ. These values are converted to the failure rate, λ, as shown in the second column of Table 8-1. The expected average number of failures is obtained by multiplying a constant [$nT = (16)(600) = 9600$ h] with the failure rate as shown in the third column of the table. This value $nT\lambda$ performs the same function as the value of np_0 which was previously used for the construction of an OC curve. Values for the probability of ac-

TABLE 8-1 Calculations for the OC Curve for the Sampling Plan $n = 16$, $T = 600$ h, $c = 2$, and $r = 3$

Mean Life, θ	*Failure Rate,* $\lambda = 1/\theta$	*Expected Average Number of Failures,* $nT\lambda$	P_a, $c = 2$
20,000	0.00005	0.48	0.983[a]
10,000	0.0001	0.96	0.927[a]
5,000	0.0002	1.92	0.698[a]
2,000	0.0005	4.80	0.142
1,000	0.0010	9.60	0.004
4,000	0.00025	2.40	0.570
6,000	0.00017	1.60	0.783

[a]By interpolation.

ceptance of the lot are found in Table C of the Appendix for $c = 2$. Typical calculations are as follows. Assume that $\theta = 2000$:

$$\lambda = \frac{1}{\theta} = \frac{1}{2000} = 0.0005$$

$$nT\lambda = (16)(600)(0.0005) = 4.80$$

From Table C of the Appendix for $nT\lambda = 4.80$ and $c = 2$,

$$P_a = 0.142$$

Additional calculations for other assumed values of θ are shown in Table 8-1.

Since this OC curve assumes a constant failure rate, the exponential distribution is applicable. The Poisson distribution is used to construct the OC curve since it approximates the exponential.

Because of the constant failure rate, there are other sampling plans that will have the same OC curve. Some of these are:

$$n = 4, \quad T = 2400\text{ h}, \quad c = 2$$
$$n = 8, \quad T = 1200\text{ h}, \quad c = 2$$
$$n = 16, \quad T = 600\text{ h}, \quad c = 2$$
$$n = 24, \quad T = 450\text{ h}, \quad c = 2$$
$$n = 32, \quad T = 300\text{ h}, \quad c = 2$$

OC curves for reliability sampling plans are also plotted as a function of θ/θ_0, which is the actual mean life/acceptable mean life. When the OC curve is constructed in this manner, all OC curves for life tests with or without replacement have one point in common. This point is the producer's risk α and $\theta/\theta_0 = 1.0$.

LIFE AND RELIABILITY TESTING PLANS

Types of Tests

Since reliability testing requires the use of the product and sometimes its destruction, the type of test and the amount of testing is usually an economic decision. Testing is normally done on the end product; however, components and parts can be tested if they are presenting problems. Since testing is usually done in the laboratory, every effort should be made to simulate the real environment under controlled conditions.

Life tests are of three types, as described next.

Failure-Terminated. These life-test sample plans are terminated when a preassigned number of failures occur to the sample. Acceptance criteria for the lot are based on the accumulated item test times when the test is terminated.

Time-Terminated. This type of life-test sampling plan is terminated when the sample obtains a predetermined test time. Acceptance criteria for the lot are based on the number of failures in the sample during the test time.

Sequential. A third type of life-testing plan is a sequential life-test sampling plan whereby neither the number of failures nor the time required to reach a decision are fixed in advance. Instead, decisions depend on the accumulated results of the life test. The sequential life-test plans have the advantage that the expected test time and the expected number of failures required to reach a decision as to lot acceptability are less than the failure-terminated or the time-terminated type.

Testing may be conducted with replacement of a failed unit or without replacement. *With replacement* occurs when a failure is replaced with another unit. Test time continues to be accumulated with the new sample unit. This situation is possible when there is a constant failure rate and the replaced unit has an equal chance of failure. The *without-replacement* situation occurs when the failure is not replaced.

Tests are based on one or more of the following characteristics:

1. *Mean life*—the average life of the product.
2. *Failure rate*—the percentage of failures per unit time or number of cycles.
3. *Hazard rate*—the instantaneous failure rate at a specified time. This varies with age except in the special case of a constant failure rate wherein the failure rate and hazard rate are the same. The Weibull distribution is applicable and the hazard rate increases with age if the shape parameter β is greater than 1 and decreases with age if the shape parameter is less than 1.
4. *Reliable life*—the life beyond which some specified portion of the items in the lot will survive. The Weibull distribution and the normal distribution as they pertain to the wear-out phase are applicable.

Table 8-2 gives a summary of some of the life-testing and reliability plans. The time-terminated tests in terms of mean-life criteria are the most common plans.

Handbook H108[3]

Quality Control and Reliability Handbook H108 gives sampling procedures and tables for life and reliability testing. Sampling plans in the handbook are based on the exponential distribution. The handbook provides for the three

[3]Copies of *Handbook H108* may be obtained by directing requests to Commanding Officer, U.S. Naval Supply Depot, Attn. Code DMD, 5801 Tabor Avenue, Philadelphia, PA 19120.

TABLE 8-2 Summary of Some Life-Testing and Reliability Plans

	Plans in Terms of:					Type of Test		
Document	*Basic Distribution and Type of Plan*	*Mean Life*	*Hazard Rate*	*Reliable Life*	*Failure Rate (FR)*	*Failure-Terminated*	*Time-Terminated*	*Sequential*
H 108[a]	Exponential, lot by lot	X			X	X	X	X
MIL-STD-690B[b]	Exponential, lot by lot				X		X	
MIL-STD-781B[c]	Exponential, sampling scheme	X					X	X
TR-3[d]	Weibull, lot by lot	X					X	
TR-4[e]	Weibull, lot by lot		X				X	
TR-6[f]	Weibull, lot by lot			X			X	
TR-7[g]	Weibull, lot by lot, converts MIL-STD-105D	X	X	X			X	

[a]"H108, Sampling Procedures and Tables for Life and Reliability Testing (Based on Exponential Distribution)," U.S. Department of Defense, Quality Control and Reliability Handbook, Government Printing Office, Washington, D.C., 1960.

[b]"MIL-STD-690B, Failure Rate Sampling Plans and Procedures," U.S. Department of Defense, Military Standard, Government Printing Office, Washington, D.C. 1968.

[c]"MIL-STD-781B, Reliability Tests: Exponential Distribution," U.S. Department of Defense, Military Standard, Government Printing Office, Washington, D.C., 1967.

[d]"TR-3, Sampling Procedures and Tables for Life and Reliability Testing Based on the Weibull Distribution (Mean Life Criterion)," U.S. Department of Defense, Quality Control and Reliability Technical Report, Government Printing Office, Washington, D.C., 1961.

[e]"TR-4, Sampling Procedures and Tables for Life and Reliability Testing Based on the Weibull Distribution (Hazard Rate Criterion)," U.S. Department of Defense, Quality Control and Reliability Technical Report, Government Printing Office, Washington, D.C., 1962.

[f]"TR-6, Sampling Procedures and Tables for Life and Reliability Testing Based on the Weibull Distribution (Reliable Life Criterion)," U.S. Department of Defense, Quality Control and Reliability Technical Report, Government Printing Office, Washington, D.C., 1963.

[g]"TR-7, Factors and Procedures for Applying MIL-STD-105D Sampling Plans to Life and Reliability Testing," U.S. Department of Defense, Quality Control and Reliability Technical Report, Government Printing Office, Washington, D.C., 1965.

Source: Reproduced by permission from J. M. Juran, ed., *Quality Control Handbook* (New York: McGraw-Hill Book Company, 1974), Sec. 25, p. 30.

different types of tests: failure-terminated, time-terminated, and sequential. For each of these types of tests, provision is made for the two situations: with replacement of failed units during the test, or without replacement. Essentially, the plans are based on the mean-life criterion, although failure rate is used in one part of the handbook.

Since the handbook is over 70 pages long, only one of the plans will be illustrated. This plan is a time-terminated, with-replacement, mean-life plan, which is the most common plan. There are three methods of obtaining this plan. Example problems will be used to illustrate the methods.

1. *Stipulated producer's risk, consumer's risk, and sample size.* Determining the time-

terminated, with-replacement, mean-life sampling plan, where the producer's risk, α, of rejecting lots with mean life $\theta_0 = 900$ h is 0.05 and the consumer's risk, β, of accepting lots with mean life $\theta_1 = 300$ h is 0.10. The ratio θ_1/θ_0 is

$$\frac{\theta_1}{\theta_0} = \frac{300}{900} = 0.333$$

From Table 8-3 for $\alpha = 0.05$, $\beta = 0.10$, and $\theta_1/\theta_0 = 0.333$, the code letter B-8 is obtained. Since the calculated ratio will rarely equal the one in the table, the next large one is used.

For each code letter, A, B, C, D, and E there is a table to determine the rejection number and the value of the ratio T/θ_0, where T is the test time. Table 8-4 gives the value for code letter B. Thus, for code B-8, the rejection number r is 8. The value of T/θ_0 is a function of the sample size.

The sample size is selected from one of the multiples of the rejection number: $2r$, $3r$, $4r$, $5r$, $6r$, $7r$, $8r$, $9r$, $10r$, and $20r$. For the life-test plans, the sample size depends on the relative cost of placing large numbers of units of product on test and on the expected length of time the life tests must continue in order to determine acceptability of the lots. Increasing the sample size will, on one hand, cut the average time required to determine acceptability but on the other hand will increase the cost due to placing more units of product on test. For this example problem, the multiple $3r$ is selected which gives a sample size $n = 3(8) = 24$.

TABLE 8-3 Life-Test Sampling Plan code Designation[a] (Table 2A-1 of H108)

$\alpha = 0.01$, $\beta = 0.01$		$\alpha = 0.05$, $\beta = 0.10$		$\alpha = 0.10$, $\beta = 0.10$		$\alpha = 0.25$, $\beta = 0.10$		$\alpha = 0.50$, $\beta = 0.10$	
Code	θ_1/θ_0	*Code*	θ_1/θ_0	*Code*	θ_1/θ_0	*Code*	θ_1/θ_0	*Code*	θ_1/θ_0
A-1	0.004	B-1	0.022	C-1	0.046	D-1	0.125	E-1	0.301
A-2	0.038	B-2	0.091	C-2	0.137	D-2	0.247	E-2	0.432
A-3	0.082	B-3	0.154	C-3	0.207	D-3	0.325	E-3	0.502
A-4	0.123	B-4	0.205	C-4	0.261	D-4	0.379	E-4	0.550
A-5	0.160	B-5	0.246	C-5	0.304	D-5	0.421	E-5	0.584
A-6	0.193	B-6	0.282	C-6	0.340	D-6	0.455	E-6	0.611
A-7	0.221	B-7	0.312	C-7	0.370	D-7	0.483	E-7	0.633
A-8	0.247	B-8	0.338	C-8	0.396	D-8	0.506	E-8	0.652
A-9	0.270	B-9	0.361	C-9	0.418	D-9	0.526	E-9	0.667
A-10	0.291	B-10	0.382	C-10	0.438	D-10	0.544	E-10	0.681
A-11	0.371	B-11	0.459	C-11	0.512	D-11	0.608	E-11	0.729
A-12	0.428	B-12	0.512	C-12	0.561	D-12	0.650	E-12	0.759
A-13	0.470	B-13	0.550	C-13	0.597	D-13	0.680	E-13	0.781
A-14	0.504	B-14	0.581	C-14	0.624	D-14	0.703	E-14	0.798
A-15	0.554	B-15	0.625	C-15	0.666	D-15	0.737	E-15	0.821
A-16	0.591	B-16	0.658	C-16	0.695	D-16	0.761	E-16	0.838
A-17	0.653	B-17	0.711	C-17	0.743	D-17	0.800	E-17	0.865
A-18	0.692	B-18	0.745	C-18	0.774	D-18	0.824	E-18	0.882

[a]Producer's risk α, is the probability of rejecting lots with mean life θ_0; consumer's risk, β, is the probability of accepting lots with mean life θ_1.

TABLE 8-4 Values of T/θ_0 for $\alpha = 0.05$—Time-Terminated, with Replacement Code Letter B [Table 2C-2(b) of H108]

		Sample Size									
Code	*r*	*2r*	*3r*	*4r*	*5r*	*6r*	*7r*	*8r*	*9r*	*10r*	*20r*
B-1	1	0.026	0.017	0.013	0.010	0.009	0.007	0.006	0.006	0.005	0.003
B-2	2	0.089	0.059	0.044	0.036	0.030	0.025	0.022	0.020	0.018	0.009
B-3	3	0.136	0.091	0.068	0.055	0.045	0.039	0.034	0.030	0.027	0.014
B-4	4	0.171	0.114	0.085	0.068	0.057	0.049	0.043	0.038	0.034	0.017
B-5	5	0.197	0.131	0.099	0.079	0.066	0.056	0.049	0.044	0.039	0.020
B-6	6	0.218	0.145	0.109	0.087	0.073	0.062	0.054	0.048	0.044	0.022
B-7	7	0.235	0.156	0.117	0.094	0.078	0.067	0.059	0.052	0.047	0.023
B-8	8	0.249	0.166	0.124	0.100	0.083	0.071	0.062	0.055	0.050	0.025
B-9	9	0.261	0.174	0.130	0.104	0.087	0.075	0.065	0.058	0.052	0.026
B-10	10	0.271	0.181	0.136	0.109	0.090	0.078	0.068	0.060	0.054	0.027
B-11	15	0.308	0.205	0.154	0.123	0.103	0.088	0.077	0.068	0.062	0.031
B-12	20	0.331	0.221	0.166	0.133	0.110	0.095	0.083	0.074	0.066	0.033
B-13	25	0.348	0.232	0.174	0.139	0.116	0.099	0.087	0.077	0.070	0.035
B-14	30	0.360	0.240	0.180	0.144	0.120	0.103	0.090	0.080	0.072	0.036
B-15	40	0.377	0.252	0.189	0.151	0.126	0.108	0.094	0.084	0.075	0.038
B-16	50	0.390	0.260	0.195	0.156	0.130	0.111	0.097	0.087	0.078	0.039
B-17	75	0.409	0.273	0.204	0.164	0.136	0.117	0.102	0.091	0.082	0.041
B-18	100	0.421	0.280	0.210	0.168	0.140	0.120	0.105	0.093	0.084	0.042

The corresponding value of $T/\theta_0 = 0.166$, which gives a test time T of

$$\begin{aligned} T &= 0.166(\theta_0) \\ &= 0.166(900) \\ &= 149.4 \quad \text{say} \quad 149 \text{ h} \end{aligned}$$

A sample of 24 items is selected from a lot and all are tested simultaneously. If the eighth failure occurs before the termination time of 149 h, the lot is rejected; if the eighth failure still has not occurred after 149 test hours, the lot is accepted.

2. *Stipulated producer's risk, rejection number, and sample size.* Determine the time-terminated, with-replacement, mean-life sampling plan where the producer's risk of rejecting lots with mean life $\theta_0 = 1200$ h is 0.05, the rejection number is 5, and the sample size is 10, or $2r$. The same set of tables is used for this method as for the previous one. Table 8-4 is the table for the code letter B designation as well as for $\alpha = 0.05$. Thus, using Table 8-4, the value for $T/\theta_0 = 0.197$ and the value for T is

$$\begin{aligned} T &= 0.197(\theta_0) \\ &= 0.197(1200) \\ &= 236.4 \quad \text{say} \quad 236 \text{ h} \end{aligned}$$

A sample of 10 items is selected from a lot and all are tested simultaneously. If the fifth failure occurs before the termination time of 236 hours, the lot is rejected; if the fifth failure still has not occurred after 236 hours, the lot is accepted.

3. *Stipulated producer's risk, consumer's risk, and test time.* Determine the time-terminated, with-replacment, mean-life sampling plan which is not to exceed 500 h and which will accept a lot with mean life of 10,000 h (θ_0) at least 90% of the time ($\alpha = 0.10$) but will reject a lot with mean life of 2000 h (θ_1) about 95% of the time ($\beta = 0.05$). The first step is to calculate the two ratios, θ_1/θ_1 and T/θ_0.

$$\frac{\theta_1}{\theta_0} = \frac{2000}{10{,}000} = \frac{1}{5}$$

$$\frac{T}{\theta_0} = \frac{500}{10{,}000} = \frac{1}{20}$$

Using the value of θ_1/θ_0, T/θ_0, α, and β, the values of r and n are obtained from Table 8-5 and are $n = 34$ and $r = 4$.

The sampling plan is to select a sample of 34 items from a lot. If the fourth failure occurs before the termination time of 500 h, the lot is rejected; if the fourth failure still has not occurred after 500 h, the lot is accepted.

When using this technique the tables provided for values of $\alpha = 0.01, 0.05, 0.10$, and 0.25; $\beta = 0.01, 0.05, 0.10$, and 0.25; $\theta_1/\theta_0 = \frac{2}{3}, \frac{1}{2}, \frac{1}{3}, \frac{1}{5}, \frac{1}{10}$; and $T\theta_0 = \frac{1}{3}, \frac{1}{5}, \frac{1}{10}$, and $\frac{1}{20}$.

The method to use for obtaining the desired life-test sampling plan is determined by the available information.

PROBLEMS

1. A system has four components, A, B, C, and D, with reliability values of 0.98, 0.89, 0.94, and 0.95, respectively. If the components are in series, what is the system reliability?

2. If component B of Problem 1 is changed to three parallel components and each has the same reliability, what is the system reliability now?

3. A system is composed of five components in series and each has a reliability of 0.96. If the system can be changed to three components in series, what is the change in the reliability?

4. Determine the failure rate for a 150-h test of 9 items where 3 items failed at 5, 76, and 135 hours. What is the mean life?

5. If the mean life is 52 h, what is the failure rate?

6. Construct the OC curve for a sampling plan specified as $n = 24$, $T = 149$, and $r = 8$.

7. Construct the OC curve for a sampling plan specified as $n = 10$, $T = 236$, and $r = 5$.

TABLE 8-5 Sampling Plans for Specified α, β, θ_1/θ_0, and T/θ_0 (Table 2C-4 of H108)

		T/θ_0					T/θ_0			
		1/3	*1/5*	*1/10*	*1/20*		*1/3*	*1/5*	*1/10*	*1/20*
θ_1/θ_0	*r*	*n*	*n*	*n*	*n*	*r*	*n*	*n*	*n*	*n*
		$\alpha = 0.01$		$\beta = 0.01$			$\alpha = 0.05$		$\beta = 0.01$	
2/3	136	331	551	1103	2207	95	238	397	795	1591
1/2	46	95	158	317	634	33	72	120	241	483
1/3	19	31	51	103	206	13	25	38	76	153
1/5	9	10	17	35	70	7	9	16	32	65
1/10	5	4	6	12	25	4	4	6	13	27
		$\alpha = 0.01$		$\beta = 0.05$			$\alpha = 0.05$		$\beta = 0.05$	
2/3	101	237	395	790	1581	67	162	270	541	1082
1/2	35	68	113	227	454	23	47	78	157	314
1/3	15	22	37	74	149	10	16	27	54	108
1/5	8	8	14	29	58	5	6	10	19	39
1/10	4	3	4	8	16	3	3	4	8	16
		$\alpha = 0.01$		$\beta = 0.10$			$\alpha = 0.05$		$\beta = 0.10$	
2/3	83	189	316	632	1265	55	130	216	433	867
1/2	30	56	93	187	374	19	37	62	124	248
1/3	13	18	30	60	121	8	11	19	39	79
1/5	7	7	11	23	46	4	4	7	13	27
1/10	4	2	4	8	16	3	3	4	8	16
		$\alpha = 0.01$		$\beta = 0.25$			$\alpha = 0.05$		$\beta = 0.25$	
2/3	60	130	217	434	869	35	77	129	258	517
1/2	22	37	62	125	251	13	23	38	76	153
1/3	10	12	20	41	82	6	7	13	26	52
1/5	5	4	7	13	25	3	3	4	8	16
1/10	3	2	2	4	8	2	1	2	3	7
		$\alpha = 0.10$		$\beta = 0.01$			$\alpha = 0.25$		$\beta = 0.01$	
2/3	77	197	329	659	1319	52	140	234	469	939
1/2	26	59	98	197	394	17	42	70	140	281
1/3	11	21	35	70	140	7	15	25	50	101
1/5	5	7	12	24	48	3	5	8	17	34
1/10	3	3	5	11	22	2	2	4	9	19
		$\alpha = 0.10$		$\beta = 0.05$			$\alpha = 0.25$		$\beta = 0.05$	
2/3	52	128	214	429	859	32	84	140	280	560
1/2	18	38	64	128	256	11	25	43	86	172
1/3	8	13	23	46	93	5	10	16	33	67
1/5	4	5	8	17	34	2	3	5	10	19
1/10	2	2	3	5	10	2	2	4	9	19
		$\alpha = 0.10$		$\beta = 0.10$			$\alpha = 0.25$		$\beta = 0.10$	
2/3	41	99	165	330	660	23	58	98	196	392
1/2	15	30	51	102	205	8	17	29	59	119
1/3	6	9	15	31	63	4	7	12	25	50
1/5	3	4	6	11	22	2	3	4	9	19
1/10	2	2	2	5	10	1	1	2	3	5
		$\alpha = 0.10$		$\beta = 0.25$			$\alpha = 0.25$		$\beta = 0.25$	
2/3	25	56	94	188	376	12	28	47	95	190
1/2	9	16	27	54	108	5	10	16	33	67
1/3	4	5	8	17	34	2	2	4	9	19
1/5	3	3	5	11	22	1	1	2	3	6
1/10	2	1	2	5	10	1	1	1	2	5

8. Determine the time-terminated, with-replacement, mean-life sampling plan where the producer's risk of rejecting lots with mean life of 800 h is 0.05 and the consumer's risk of accepting lots with mean life $\theta_1 = 220$ is 0.10. The sample size is 30.

9. Determine the time-terminated, with-replacement sampling plan which has the following specifications: $T = 160$, $\theta_1 = 400$, $\beta = 0.10$, $\theta_0 = 800$, $\alpha = 0.05$.

10. Determine the time-terminated, with-replacement sampling plan where the producer's risk of rejecting lots with mean life $\theta_0 = 900$ h is 0.05, the rejection number is 3, and the sample size is 9.

11. Find a replacement life-test sampling plan of 300 h which will accept a lot with mean life of 3,000 h at least 95% of the time but will reject a lot with mean life of 1000 h about 90% of the time.

12. If the probability of accepting a lot with a mean life of 1100 cycles is 0.95 and the probability of rejecting a lot with mean life of 625 cycles is 0.90, what is the sampling plan for a sample size of 60?

13. Find a life-test, time-terminated sampling plan with replacement that will accept a lot with a mean life of 900 h with probability of 0.95 ($\alpha = 0.05$). The test is to be stopped after the occurrence of the second failure and 12 units of product are to be placed on test.

9 QUALITY COSTS

INTRODUCTION

In the preceding chapters, various quality control techniques were emphasized. However, in the final analysis the value of quality control must be based on its ability to contribute to company profits. In our profit oriented society, decisions are between alternatives and the effect each alternative will have on the expense and income of the business entity.

The efficiency of any business is measured in terms of dollars. Therefore, like maintenance, production, design, sales, and other activities, the costs of quality must be known. This cost is no different than other costs. It can be programmed, budgeted, measured, and analyzed to attain the objective of better quality at lower costs.

Quality costs cross department lines by involving all activities of the company—purchasing, manufacturing, design, and service to name a few. Some costs, such as inspection, instrumentation, and quality personnel salaries, are readily identifiable; other costs, such as those associated with scrap and rework, are more difficult to identify and allocate. There are customer-dissatisfaction costs and loss-of-reputation costs which are difficult, if not impossible, to measure.

Quality costs are a significant management tool. They provide:

1. A method of assessing the overall effectiveness of the quality program
2. A means of establishing programs to meet overall needs
3. A method of determining problem areas and action priorities
4. A technique to determine the optimum amount of effort between the various quality activities
5. Information for pricing products or bidding on jobs

The cost of quality (or more appropriately the cost of nonquality) may be as high as 25% of the sales dollar for a manufactured product and as high as 40% for a service. Quality costs are an excellent area for cost reduction, which will lead to increased productivity. Generally speaking, as quality improves, overall cost is reduced. Only in very rare situations would quality improvement result in increased overall cost.

DIRECT QUALITY COSTS

Direct quality costs are separated into the categories of prevention, appraisal, internal failure, and external failure. Each of these four categories are made up of a number of subcategories. The subcategories simplify the collection, reporting, and analysis of the information.

Prevention

These costs are associated with personnel engaged in designing, implementing, and maintaining the quality system. Prevention costs are a measure of the investment made prior to producing a product. These planned costs assure the conformance to quality requirements at economic levels. Subcategories are as follows:

Quality Engineering. This cost includes the activities associated with the creation of the overall quality plan, the inspection plan, the realiability plan, the data system, and miscellaneous special plans. It also includes the implementation and maintenance of the plans and includes the audit of the system.

Design and Development of Equipment. The cost of personnel engaged in the planning of measurement and quality control equipment.

Quality Planning by Others. Represents costs associated with the amount of time spent in quality planning by personnel who are not normally part of the quality control function.

Quality Training. The cost of developing, implementing, operating, and maintaining formal training programs.

Other Prevention Expenses. This subcategory includes the clerical, telecommunications, travel, and supply costs. It is a general office management category.

Prevention activities and their associated costs involve design reviews, vendor qualifications, process-capability studies, process-control planning, and any other activity utilized for the prevention of defects and defectives.

Appraisal

Appraisal costs are associated with measuring, evaluating, or auditing products, components, and purchased materials to assure conformance with quality standards and performance requirements. These costs are incurred to determine the condition of the product and assure that it meets specifications. Subcategories are as follows:

Inspection and Test of Incoming Material. The costs associated with the inspection and test of supplier-made material. This subcategory includes receiving inspection and test, inspection and test at the supplier's plant, and periodic audit of the supplier's quality system.

Inspection and Test. The costs of checking the conformance of the product such as setup, first piece, in-process, final, and shipping. Includes reliability testing and testing done at customer's plant prior to product release.

Product-Quality Audits. This cost includes the expenses involved in performing quality audits on in-process or finished products.

Materials and Services Consumed. This subcategory includes the cost of material and products consumed in destructive tests or devalued by reliability tests.

Equipment Calibration and Maintenance. These costs are associated with the maintenance and calibration of the equipment used in the control of quality.

Essentially the appraisal activities are associated with the assessment and analysis of the product quality.

Internal Failure

Internal failure costs occur when products, components, and materials fail to meet quality requirements prior to transfer of ownership to the customer. These are costs that would disappear if there were no defects in the product. Subcategories are as follows:

Scrap. The net loss in labor, material, and overhead resulting from defective product that cannot economically be repaired or used.

Rework. This is the cost of correcting defective units so that they meet specifications.

Failure Analysis. The costs incurred to determine the cause of product failure.

Reinspection. The costs of reinspection or retest of products that have been reworked.

Fault of Supplier. Unrecovered losses incurred due to failure of supplier's material.

Downgrading. This cost is the price differential between the normal selling price and the reduced price because the product is usable but does not meet specifications.

The internal failure activities are associated with the correction or disposition of defective product which is detected prior to its acceptance by the customer.

External Failure

External failure costs occur when the product does not perform satisfactorily after transfer of ownership to the customer. These costs would also disappear if there were no defects in the product. Subcategories are as follows:

Complaints. This subcategory includes all costs for the adjustment of complaints.

Rejected and Returned. Costs associated with the handling and replacement of returned product.

Repair. The costs resulting from the repair of returned product.

Warranty Charges. This subcategory is for the costs to replace failures within the warranty period.

Errors. The costs associated with product replacement that is caused by an error.

Liability. This cost is incurred as a result of product liability litigation.

The external failure activities are associated with the correction or disposition of defective product after it has been in use by the customer.[1]

The categories and subcategories are representative of those used in all industries. These subcategories can be modified to meet the needs of the individual plant, corporation, or industry. In order to use the cost categories, a procedure manual is required which gives detailed specifications of the cost items to include in each category. It is important that cost items be consistently classified into categories to that comparisons from period to period can be made.

Direct Cost Curves

The operating quality costs of prevention and appraisal are considered to be controllable quality costs, while the internal and external failure costs are uncontrollable. Figure 9-1 illustrates the relationship between the controllable and uncontrollable quality cost curves and the combined direct quality cost curve. As the controllable costs of prevention and appraisal increases, the uncontrollable costs of internal and external failure decrease. At some point the cost of preventing and appraising defective product exceeds the cost of correcting for the product failure. This point is the optimum operating quality cost and will be discussed in greater detail later in the chapter.

[1]For more information about quality cost categories, see Quality Cost–Cost Effectiveness Committee, ASQC, *Quality Costs—What and How*, 2nd ed. (Milwaukee, Wis.: American Society for Quality Control, Inc., 1971).

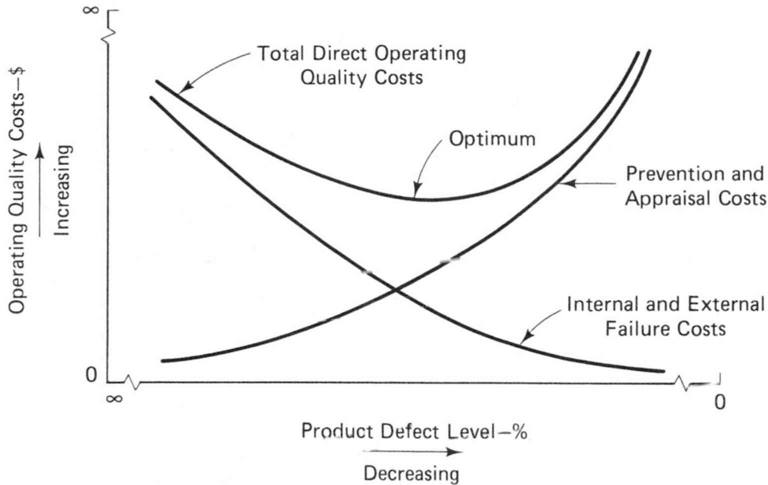

Figure 9-1 Direct operating quality costs.

INDIRECT QUALITY COSTS

In addition to the direct operating quality costs, the indirect quality costs and their effect on the total cost curve must be considered. Indirect quality costs can be divided into three categories: customer-incurred quality costs, customer-dissatisfaction costs, and loss-of-reputation costs.

Customer-Incurred Quality Costs. This category includes costs to the customer due to equipment downtime, repair costs after the warranty period, and transportation costs.

Customer-Dissatisfaction Costs. Customer dissatisfaction is an attribute type of cost; the customer is satisfied or dissatisfied. This cost is high when the defect level is high and low when the defect level is low.

Loss-of-Reputation Costs. These costs reflect the customer's attitude toward a company rather than an individual product line.

These intangible, indirect quality costs are difficult to measure; however, they do affect the total quality cost curve. This influence is apparent when the indirect quality costs are added to the direct cost curve, as shown by Figure 9-2. Note that the optimum point has moved to the right, which indicates the need for a lower product defect level. A lower product defect level can be obtained by increasing the prevention and appraisal costs, which subsequently lowers the external failure cost. A lower external failure cost has a desirable influence on the indirect costs.[2]

[2]H. J. Harrington, "Quality Costs—the Whole and Its Parts, Part II," *Quality*, 15, No. 6 (June 1976).

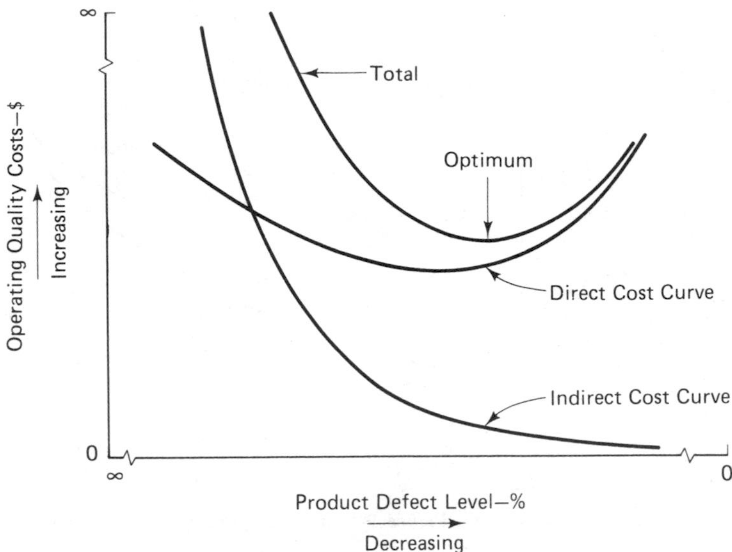

Figure 9-2 Direct and indrect quality costs.

The measurement of the actual indirect costs may be impossible. However, a knowledge that these costs exist and their relationship to the direct costs can aid in their control.

COLLECTION AND EVALUATION

Collecting the Quality Cost Data

The measurement of actual quality costs is essentially an accounting function. However, the development of the quality cost system requires the close interaction of quality control and accounting. Since accounting cost data are established by departmental cost codes, a significant amount of quality cost can be obtained from this source. However, some quality cost data crosses department lines, and it is this type of quality cost that is the most difficult to collect. Thus, special forms may be required to report some quality costs. For example, scrap or rework costs may require analysis by quality control personnel to determine the cause and the department responsible.

In some cases, estimates may be used to allocate costs to the proper account. For example, when the product design department engages in quality activities, it is necessary for the departmental supervisor to estimate the costs relative to that quality activity. Work-sampling techniques can be a valuable tool to assist the departmental supervisor in making the estimate.

Quality costs should be collected by product line, projects, department, operator, defect classification, and work center. This manner of collection provides sufficient information for subsequent quality cost analysis.

Measurement Base

Quality costs by themselves present insufficient information for analysis. A measurement base is required that will relate quality costs to some aspect of the business that is sensitive to change. Typical measurement bases are labor, cost, sales, and unit. When these measurement bases are compared with quality costs, a valuable index is obtained.

Labor. Quality costs per hour of direct labor is a common index. Direct labor information is readily available since it is used for other indexes. Automation affects the base over an extended period of time; therefore, the value of a labor base is limited to comparisons within a short period of time.

Sometimes direct labor dollars are used rather than direct labor hours. This technique eliminates the inflation factor since dollars are divided by dollars.

Costs. Quality costs per dollar of manufacturing cost is another common index. Manufacturing cost is composed of direct labor, direct material, and overhead. Manufacturing cost information is readily available since it is used for other indexes. Since there are three costs involved, this index is not significantly affected by material price fluctuations or by automation.

Sales. Quality costs per dollar of sales income is the most common type of index. It is a valuable tool for higher management decision making. Since sales lag behind production and are frequently subject to seasonal variations, it is sometimes a poor index for short-term analysis. It is also affected by changes in selling price and shifts in available markets.

Unit. Quality cost per unit such as number of boxes, kilograms of aluminum, or meters of cloth is an excellent index where product lines are similar. However, where product lines are dissimilar, comparisons are difficult to make and interpret.

Since each of the various indexes has disadvantages, it is the normal practice to use three indexes. From experience, the most useful indexes are selected and used to compare trends in quality costs. Table 9-1 reports the bases of labor, cost, and sales at the bottom of the table. Figure 9-3b shows a graph of some trends.

The Optimum

In analyzing quality costs management wants to know the optimum cost. This optimum was shown on the quality cost curves of Figures 9-1 and 9-2. Since these cost curves are theoretical, they cannot be related to an individual plant or corporation.

One technique to determine the optimum quality costs is to compare with other companies. Fortunately, more and more companies use sales as the measurement base, which makes comparison somewhat easier. There are, however,

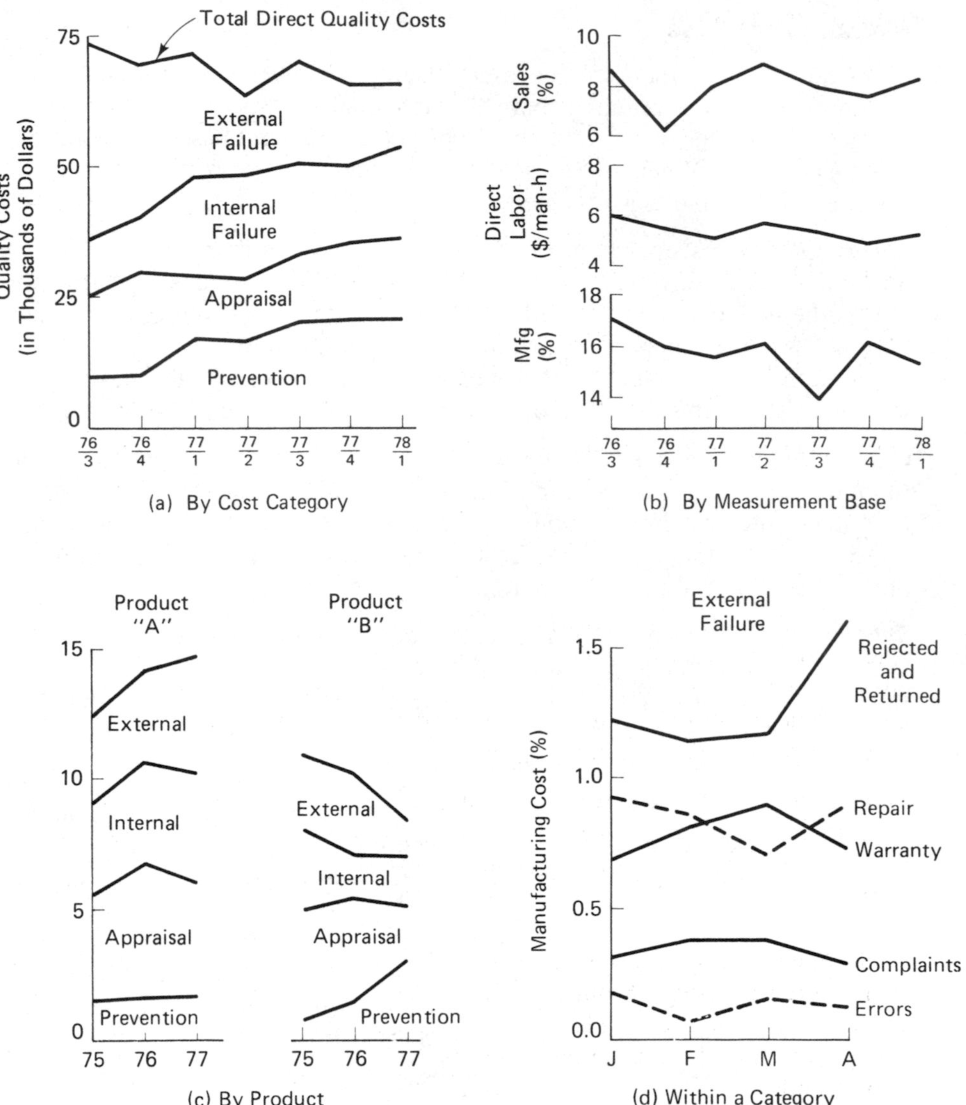

Figure 9-3 Typical trend analysis graphs.

many variations in types of manufacturing and service organizations which cause quality costs to vary appreciably. Where complex, highly reliable products are involved, quality costs may be as high as 20% of sales; whereas in industries that produce simple products with low tolerance requirements, quality costs of less than 2% of sales may be a realistic level.

In 1967 the average cost of quality per company in the ITT Corporation was 10% of sales, and by 1973 it was 5.3% of sales. This improvement was made

TABLE 9-1 Typical Monthly Quality Cost Report (Values in thousands of dollars)

October			Year-to-date	
Actual	*Variance*	*Category*	*Actual*	*Variance*
		A. Prevention cost		
18.3	3.2	1. Quality engineeering	190.1	10.1
4.6	0.6	2. Design and development	61.8	7.5[a]
2.6	0.9	3. Quality planning by others	20.7	7.3
7.3	2.1	4. Quality training	40.8	20.3
2.4	3.4	5. Other	31.2	25.0
35.2	10.2	Total prevention cost	350.6	55.2
7.7%		% of total quality cost	9.4%	
		B. Appraisal cost		
9.6	1.8[a]	1. Inspect and test incoming materials	87.3	7.1[a]
32.5	15.4[a]	2. Inspection and test	323.0	105.0[a]
14.1	27.4	3. Product quality audits	140.9	269.7
1.4	1.1	4. Materials and services consumed	16.5	8.8
4.1	1.6[a]	5. Equipment calibration and maintenance	23.4	0.0
61.7	9.7	Total appraisal cost	591.1	166.4
13.5%		% of total quality cost	15.9%	
		C. Internal failure cost		
14.6	9.6[a]	1. Scrap	50.0	8.0
197.2	124.3[a]	2. Rework	1305.6	557.6[a]
25.2	8.1	3. Failure analysis	185.1	0.4
6.8	2.3	4. Reinspection	88.0	3.0
14.1	6.6[a]	5. Fault of supplier	152.1	77.2[a]
0.8	0.2	6. Downgrading	8.1	1.9
258.7	129.9[a]	Total internal cost	1788.9	621.5[a]
56.4%		% of total quality cost	48.1%	
		D. External failure cost		
8.6	1.6[a]	1. Complaints	75.3	5.3[a]
41.8	1.2	2. Rejected and returned	403.6	26.4
25.6	0.3[a]	3. Repair	256.5	3.5[a]
21.9	27.0	4. Warranty charges	226.6	263.4
4.9	4.0	5. Errors	28.5	10.2
0.0	0.0	6. Liability	0.0	0.0
102.8	30.3	Total external cost	990.5	291.2
22.4%		% of total quality cost	26.6%	
458.4	79.7[a]	Total operating cost	3721.1	108.7[a]
		Measurement bases		
6.5		1. Direct labor ($/man-hour)	5.3	
8.8		2. Sales (%)	9.0	
16.7		3. Manufacturing cost (%)	16.3	

[a]Unfavorable variance.

after the ITT Corporation implemented a quality cost program throughout the worldwide corporation. Interestingly, the product or service of the individual company made little or no difference in the cost improvement.[3]

[3]Quality Costs: The Real Measurement of Performance," *Quality Management and Engineeirng,* January 1975, pp. 26–30.

When comparing quality costs with other companies, it is important to compare the quality cost subcategories. Only when subcategories are being utilized equally will comparisons be valid.

Another technique to determine the optimum is by analysis of the interrelationships among the cost categories. A study of 21 companies showed that on the average 53% of the total quality cost is due to the failure category and 47% of the total quality cost is due to the prevention and appraisal categories. There was wide variation in the individual company data that produced these overall averages. Theoretically, the prevention and appraisal costs should be at least equal to, and possibly greater than, failure costs.[4] While this information gives some idea of the relative percentages for the cost categories, it does not give information concerning the magnitude of the quality costs.

A third technique is to optimize the individual categories. Failure costs are optimized when there are no identifiable and profitable projects for reducing them. Appraisal costs are also optimized when there are no identifiable and profitable projects for reducing them. Prevention costs are optimized when most of the dollar cost is used for improvement projects, when the prevention work itself has been analyzed for improvement, and when nonproject prevention work is controlled by sound budgeting.[5]

There appears to be no single value which a company can point to as the optimum quality cost point; however, continued application of the three techniques will maintain the quality cost at the lowest level.

ANALYSIS

The primary purpose of a quality cost program is to identify areas of opportunity for profit improvement by means of quality improvement. An effective quality cost system will provide a way to determine where and when to take corrective action.

Operating Quality Cost Report

The basic quality cost control instrument is the operating quality cost report, which is usually issued by the accounting department. An example of this type of report is shown in Table 9-1. Provision is made in the report for the monthly cost information and the year-to-date cost information by cost category. A column is included for reporting the variance from the budgeted or planned quality cost. In addition, the percentage of total operating quality costs for each category is reported. Indexes of quality costs per various measurement bases are shown at the bottom of the report.

[4]H. L. Gilmore, "Product Conformance Cost," *Quality Progress,* 7, No. 6 (June 1974), 16–19.

[5]J. M. Juran, ed., *Quality Control Handbook,* 2nd ed. (New York: McGraw-Hill Book Company, 1974), Sec. 5, p. 14.

The monthly operating quality cost report allows actual quality costs to be compared with budgeted quality costs. By comparing actual to budget, a certain amount of control is exercised over the quality costs.

Analysis of the report will indicate the categories where excessive costs have occurred. For example, scrap cost for the month has an unfavorable variance of $9600; however, the year-to-date value has a favorable variance of $8000. While the monthly unfavorable variance needs to be explained, no corrective action would be indicated, at this time, because the year to-date variance is favorable. Similarly, the inspection and test subcategory shows an unfavorable variance for both the month and year-to-date. This set of circumstances would indicate that corrective action is necessary.

There is a tendency to analyze only the unfavorable variances. This practice can be a mistake since the analysis of substantial favorable variances can provide information that might lead to programs that would continue this happy state of affairs.

Accounting maintains the records of the transactions that comprise the total dollar value of any subcategory. Records of these detailed transactions can be invaluable for the investigation of unfavorable and favorable variances.

Trend Analysis

Essentially, the monthly quality cost report is a short-range report. Trend analysis provides information for long-range planning. It also provides information for the instigation and assessment of quality improvement programs. Data for trend analysis comes from the monthly quality cost report and the detailed transactions which make up the subcategory costs.

Trend analysis can be accomplished by cost category, by subcategory, by product, by measurement base, by plant within a corporation, by department, by work center, and by combinations thereof. The graphs of some of these are shown in Figure 9-3. Time scales for the graphs may be by month, quarter, or year depending on the purpose of the analysis.

Figure 9-3a shows a graph of the four cost categories by quarters. This graph is the cumulative type wherein the second line from the bottom includes the prevention and the appraisal costs; the third line includes the internal failure, appraisal, and prevention costs; and the top line includes all of the four cost categories. Figure 9-3a shows that prevention and internal failure costs are increasing, appraisal costs remain unchanged, and external failure and total failure costs are decreasing.

Figure 9-3b shows the trend analysis for three different measurement bases. The differences in the trends of the three bases point up the need for more than one base. A decrease in the percent of sales curve during the fourth quarter of the initial year is due to a seasonal variation, while the variation in manufacturing costs for the third quarter of the following year is due to excessive overtime costs.

Figure 9-3c shows the trend analysis for two different products. The figure shows that the quality costs for product B are better than those for product A. In fact, product B is under control and showing a nice improvement while product A's costs are increasing. An increase in the prevention and appraisal costs will, hopefully, improve the external and internal failure costs of product A. Comparisons between products and plants should be made with extreme caution.

A trend graph for the external failure category is shown in Figure 9-3d. Rejected and internal costs and warranty costs have increased, while costs for the other subcategories have remained unchanged. In this figure the measurement base is by manufacturing costs, and the time period is by months.

Trend analysis is an effective tool provided it is recognized that some period-to-period fluctuations are merely normal variations. These variations are similar to those which occur on an $\overline{X}$ or R chart. The important factor to observe is the quality costs trend.

Pareto Analysis

One of the most effective cost analysis tools is the *Pareto distribution.* A typical Pareto distribution is shown in Figure 9-4 for manufacturing defects as a percent of direct labor. A Pareto distribution has a few items that represent a substantial amount of the total. These items (or departments in this case) are located on the left in Figure 9-4 and are referred to as the "vital few." And a Pareto distribution has many items that represent a small amount of the total. These items are located on the right in Figure 9-4 and are referred to as the "trivial many." Pareto distributions can be established for quality costs by operator, by machine, by department, by type of defect, or by product line.

Once the "vital few" are known, projects can be developed to reduce their costs. In other words, money is spent to control the "vital few"; little or no money is spent to control the "trivial many." In Figure 9-4 the "vital few" would be departments 17, 13, 14, 37, and 33 and the "trivial many" would be those departments to the right of number 23. Departments 26, 15, 22, and 23 would be in a third group, which is between the other two groups. This group would be investigated after efforts to improve the vital few were completed.

In summary, the analysis of quality costs by these three techniques is an effective decision-making tool. Once the causes of excessive quality costs are known, programs for their improvement can be developed.

ADDITIONAL ASPECTS

Program Phases

In a quality cost system, three phases are encountered: the implementation, project, and control phases. These three phases naturally merge into each other.

Implementation Phase. The implementation phase of a quality cost system usually begins by convincing upper management of the need for the program. Once this is accomplished, the extent of the initial effort is determined. The initial

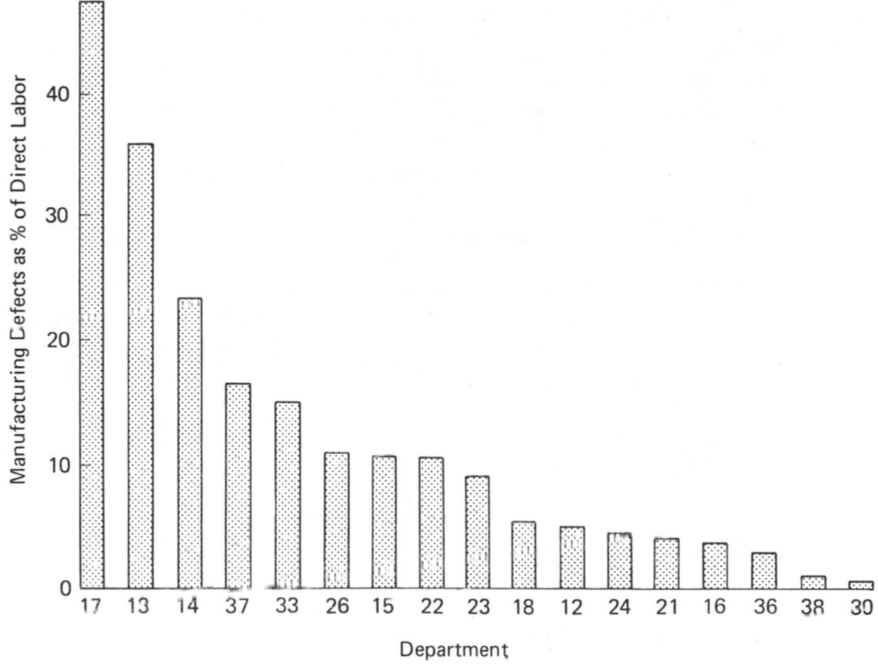

Figure 9-4 Pareto distribution by department.

effort will be a pilot study of a product line or a plant within a corporation. The unit selected should be representative of the company's operation.

Initially, cost subcategories are selected and defined. Collection methods are established using sound accounting techniques; however, some estimates may be necessary at the beginning. All personnel who will be involved with the system are educated and trained.

As soon as possible, reports are issued so that cost analysis techniques can be utilized. Based on these initial experiences, the system is reviewed and, if necessary, revised. Finally, the system is extended to other product lines or plants.

Project Phase. The second phase is the project phase. Based on analysis of the quality costs, improvement projects are begun. Since the analysis and implementation of projects requires additional manpower, prevention costs will increase during this phase. If the business is inspection and test oriented, prevention quality planners might rearrange the appraisal activity with a subsequent reduction in the appraisal cost.

Most of the improvement projects will be directed toward reducing the failure costs. Therefore, external failure costs will be expected to decline. However, this decline will follow other changes depending on the time required for the improved product to reach the customer. Internal failure costs are also expected to decrease.

Control Phase. As the quality costs are brought to a point approaching the optimum, the control phase begins. This phase is essentially a maintenance one wherein standards and budgets are established.

During this phase, inspection and test methods are reviewed to determine if they can be improved. Other appraisal costs and prevention costs are also scrutinized for possible improvement.

Quality Cost Improvement Projects

Most of the cost improvement projects will be based on cost analysis and the creativity of the quality prevention planners. They will be unique to a particular operation, machine, type of defect, product, and so on.

Improvement projects that have general application are:

1. Product design review
2. Process design review
3. Supervisor quality training
4. Zero-defect program
5. Supplier defective material recovery
6. Supplier rating system
7. Sampling plan analysis (double, sequential, chain, etc.)
8. Inspection system analysis (first-piece, in-process, final, route, station)
9. Automatic inspection
10. Operator inspection (before and after processing)

This list represents just a few of the general projects that can reduce quality costs.

Capital Quality Costs

This chapter has been concerned with operating quality costs. There are also capital outlays of money for quality. Most of these capital costs are for inspection equipment, data-processing equipment, or for automatic process control. In some cases production equipment is partially justified on the basis of improved quality and a subsequent reduction in operating quality costs.

Capital quality costs are reported separately from operating quality costs.

10 PRODUCT LIABILITY

INTRODUCTION

Consumers are initiating lawsuits in record numbers as a result of injury, death, and property damage from alleged faulty design or product workmanship. The number of lawsuits in this area has skyrocketed since the mid-1960s. Jury verdicts in favor of the injured party (plaintiff) have risen in recent years. The size of the judgment or settlement has also increased significantly, which has caused an increase in product liability insurance. While the larger manufacturers have been able to absorb the judgment or settlement cost and pass it on to the consumer, smaller manufacturers have occasionally been forced into bankruptcy.

The development of strict liability in product liability law has made it easier for the plaintiff to obtain a favorable judgment. This implies that a manufacturer, retailer, or other member of the distributive chain is legally responsible to any customer who suffers an injury due to a defective product.

History of Product Liability

Historical records indicate that in ancient times, the producers of grain were liable for the quality of their product. This liability was based on a sample, since it was physically impossible to inspect each and every grain. If the sample was of good quality, the entire shipment was considered to be good; if the sample was defective, the entire shipment was defective.

By the fourteenth century, sampling inspection of textiles was commonplace. Seals and official stamps were used by producers, wholesalers, and government inspectors to attest to the quality of the goods. Sampling was used rather than 100% inspection because it was not economically feasible to inspect every yard of cloth. Economic damages were awarded to plaintiffs for defective products, and, in some cases, damages were awarded for injuries sustained as a result of defective products. Since manufactured products were of simple design, handcrafted, and relatively safe to use, lawsuits based on strict liability for injuries were infrequent.

By the middle of the eighteenth century, two concepts had developed which affected product liability litigation for about two centuries. *Caveat emptor* (let the buyer beware) is one of those concepts which resulted from Adam Smith's "invisible hand" theory of commercial regulation. This concept was part of the common law of England.

The other concept resulted from the case of *Winterbottom* v. *Wright.* In this case a defective wheel caused a coach to overturn, and the injured passenger sued the coach owner and the coach manufacturer. The court ruled that the coach owner was not liable because he was not aware that the wheel was defective. And the coach manufacturer was not liable because there was no contractual relationship between the injured party and the manufacturer. This decision brought about the legal concept of *privity of contract,* which required that the manufacturer and the injured party have a contractual relationship. Therefore, the manufacturer was liable to the wholesaler, the wholesaler to the retailer, and the retailer to the customer.

In cases involving food, drugs, firearms, explosives, and other ultrahazardous products, the privity of contract concept was turned aside because the harm done could be substantial. The *MacPherson* v. *Buick Motor Company* case of 1916 marked the beginning of the end of the privity of contract concept. In this case a defective wheel caused an injury and the court ruled that the manufacturer was liable, even in the absence of privity, since there was evidence of negligence in the assembly of the product.

Manufacturers' liability increased with the adoption of the warranty principle. There are two kinds of warranty—expressed and implied. An expressed warranty is part of the conditions of sale; the buyer purchases the product on the reasonable assumption that it is as stated by the seller. An implied warranty is implied by the law rather than the seller; the buyer purchases the product on the reasonable assumption that the product will be reliable and like the sample. Present law is such that an implied warranty is assumed for every sale by a merchant.

During the first half of the twentieth century the emphasis in product liability litigation changed from privity of contract to breach of warranty or to negligence. Negligence in the design or manufacture of the product was an effective argument for the plaintiff. However, since few manufacturers were knowingly derelict, proving negligence was difficult.

In 1965, the American Law Institute issued its Restatement of the Law of Torts Second, which is based on common law (legal decisions of cases called case law). The Restatement declared that:

> If a product because of a defect becomes unreasonably dangerous and causes an injury, it is defectively made. A manufacturer, who makes and sells that defective product, has committed a fault. It is implied that he was negligent and, therefore, strictly liable to the injured party.

This is the definition of strict liability.

On October 27, 1972, the Consumer Product Safety Act was passed. The purpose of this act is to prevent or minimize product-caused injury, illness, or death and to provide substantial civil or criminal penalties for safety violations. Details are given in the next section.

Consumer Product Safety Act

The Consumer Product Safety Act (CPSA) is a significant consumer safety law. It is a part of legislative law and augments the common law and case law of product liability.

The purposes of this act are:

1. To protect the public against unreasonable risks of injury associated with consumer products
2. To assist consumers in evaluating the comparative safety of consumer products
3. To develop uniform safety standards for consumer products and to minimize conflicting state and local regulations
4. To promote research and investigation into the causes and prevention of product-related deaths, illnesses, and injuries

Based on these purposes, it is evident that the intent of the CPSA is to prevent hazardous or defective products from reaching the customer.

A five-member commission appointed by the President with the advice and consent of the Senate, administers this act as well as similar acts, such as the Refrigerator Safety Act and Flammable Fabrics Act. The commission is authorized to establish product safety standards relating to performance, composition, design, construction, finishing, labeling, or packaging of products. All consumer products used in and around a household, school, or for recreation are covered by the CPSA except for products administered by other agencies. Exempted products, which are covered by other agencies, include cars, boats, airplanes, food, drugs, cosmetics, tobacco, and poisons.

The commission is relying principally on the development of voluntary safety standards; however, conditions may warrant a mandatory standard. In extreme cases when a product presents an unreasonable risk of harm and when no feasible standard would adequately protect the public, the commission can declare the product a *banned hazardous product*.

The commission may file in a United States district court an action against an *imminently hazardous product* for condemnation and seizure. An imminently hazardous product is one that presents an imminent and unreasonable risk of death, serious illness, or severe personal injury. If the court declares that the product is imminently hazardous, public notice, recall, repair, replacement, or refund may be required.

A third category of hazard is a *substantial product hazard.* This category includes products that fail to comply with an applicable consumer product safety rule or contain a defect that could create a substantial risk of injury to the public. After notice and a hearing, the commission may determine that a substantial product hazard exists and order one or more of the following actions: (1) public notice of the defect, (2) mail notice to known purchasers, (3) repair of the product, (4) replacement of the product, and/or (5) refund of the purchase price.

Failure to comply with the act can invoke civil or criminal penalties. Any person who knowingly violates the rules is subject to a civil penalty not to exceed $2000 per violation. Any person who knowingly and willfully violates the rules after receiving notice of noncompliance can be fined not more than $50,000 or be imprisoned not more than one year, or both. Such criminal penalties can be imposed on officers of the corporation who knowingly violate the rules in addition to any penalties imposed on the corporation.[1]

The commission is required to maintain an injury information clearinghouse to collect, investigate, analyze, and disseminate injury data. It may conduct reseach and investigations on the safety of consumer products.

For purposes of implementing the act or rules, the commission can inspect manufacturing operations and appropriate records to ensure compliance.

Compliance with a consumer product safety rule does not relieve any person from liability under common law or state legislative law. However, compliance with an applicable federal standard can be an effective defense in a product liability lawsuit.

LEGAL ASPECTS

Product Liability Law

Two types of law are involved in product liability lawsuits: contracts and torts. A *contract* is an agreement between two or more parties which is enforceable in a court of law. Warranties, either expressed or implied, are a part of the contract of sale of property at the time of sale. Lawsuits for a breach of warranty are based on contract law, since there is a contractual relationship between the parties.

A *tort* is a civil wrong committed by the invasion of any personal or private right which each person enjoys by virtue of federal and state laws. The personal or private right affected must be one that is determined by law rather than by contract. In addition to the tortious act, there must also be personal injury or property damage.

The majority of states have adopted the doctrine of strict liability in tort as set forth in the Restatement of the Law of Torts Second. This mean that the injured person need only prove that a product was unreasonably dangerous to

[1]L. J. Lamatina, "The Consumer Product Safety Act," *Journal of Products Liability,* 4 (1981), 275–325.

win his case. Proof that the manufacturer is negligent is not required. Under the doctrine of strict liability, contributory negligence means that the injured party acted in a careless and unreasonable manner while using the product.

While contributory negligence is no longer applicable, some jurisdictions that have not adopted comparative negligence use two very narrow defenses. These occur: (1) when the user of a product knew of a defect and was aware of the danger, but nonetheless proceeded to use it and suffered injury, and (2) when the product was misused in a manner that was not reasonably foreseeable.

Comparative negligence is becoming the most widely accepted defense to a products liability claim where the injured party was negligent in the use of the product. This concept apportions the award on the basis of the degree of negligence or fault of the parties. The adoption of this defense abolishes that of assumption of the risk and diminishes, or completely bars, the recovery of the injured party.[2]

Recent statutory enactments by some state legislatures declare that if a product does not injure a person within a period of 5, 10, 12 years, or within the useful life of the product from the date of manufacture, it is presumed to be free from defect unless the injured party can prove otherwise. The burden of proof that the product was defective lies with the injured party.[3]

It is apparent that product liability law, as with all laws, will vary somewhat from state to state. In all probability the lawsuit will be tried in the state where the injury occurred, which gives the plaintiff's attorney a decided advantage. The Consumer Product Safety Act is a federal law and therefore does not present the same problems of variance from state to state.

The Plaintiff

A lawsuit is a civil suit seeking money damages for injuries to either a person or his/her property or both. It is instigated by the injured party, called the plaintiff, and filed in a court of law as a claim against the responsible parties. The liability may arise as a result of a defect in design or manufacturing, improper service, breach of warranty, or negligence in marketing due to improper directions, warnings, or advertising.

Under the doctrine of strict liability the plantiff must prove that (1) the product was defective and unreasonably dangerous, (2) the defect was present when the product changed ownership, and (3) the defect caused the injury. Some of the facets of the case which are explored to prove that the product was defective and unreasonably dangerous are:

1. The defective aspect of the product
2. The design of similar and safer products, and the elimination of the danger

[2]W. P. Keeton, et al., *Prosser and Keeton on the Law of Torts,* 5th ed (St. Paul, Minn.: West Publishing Co. (1984).

[3]R. K. Herrman, "An Overview of State Statutory Product Liability Law," *Trial Lawyer's Guide,* 7, No. 1 (1983).

3. The public's common knowledge of the product's danger
4. The probability that an injury of this nature could occur assuming that reasonable care is exercised
5. The adequacy of instructions and warnings
6. The environment in which the product was used

Investigation of these facets will usually provide some favorable or unfavorable arguments.

Proof that the product was defective at the time it changed ownership from the producer to the consumer is frequently difficult because the product may be entirely or partly destroyed by the accident. Expert testimony may be needed to ascertain when the defect occurred. This testimony will usually follow the line of reasoning that a microscopic flaw, which was present during the manufacturing operation, caused the product to fail at a future date.

Proof that the product caused the injury can also be difficult to determine if the product has been involved in an accident. One of the trends in product liability litigation is the requirement that the injured party need only show that the defect was the *proximate cause* of the injury. Proximate cause is a legal term which means that the defect need not be the sole cause of the injury but could be a contributing cause.

Before the lawsuit is brought to trial, the plaintiff is entitled to certain information by right of *discovery*. This information includes all records that pertain to the alleged defective product, such as product design, test and inspection results, customer complaints, and sales literature. The plaintiff is also entitled to take depositions of individuals involved with the case. A *deposition* is an oral questioning before a court reporter which permits both sides of the litigation to discover the important facts of the case.

The Defendant

While anyone along the trail of commerce (manufacturer, wholesaler, or retailer) can become a defendant in a lawsuit, it is usually the manufacturer who is held liable to the injured party. The manufacturer is the one with the "deepest pocket" or the one from which the largest award can be obtained.

In general, the defendant tries to prove that the product was not defective and not unreasonably dangerous. The same facets of the case, as those stated for the plaintiff, will be explored by the defendant to find favorable or unfavorable arguments.

The defendant tries to prove that there was no defect in the product at the time of manufacture which could have caused the accident. Test and inspection results and other records that can attest to the integrity, performance, and sales history of a particular product are valid arguments. The use of acceptance sampling plans based on government and industry standards help to build an effective defense.

A substantial portion of the trial is spent determining the cause of the accident. The defendant makes every effort to prove that the defect was not responsible for the injury. Proving that the plaintiff's bad judgment, his failure to properly maintain the product, or his improper use of the product caused the injury are also persuasive arguments that a jury can readily understand. In this regard it may be possible to prove that the plaintiff used the product knowing it was defective. It is also possible that the accident was caused by a change or alteration of the product after it left the hands of the manufacturer.

As the Consumer Product Safety Commission develops product safety standards, it will be an effective defense to prove that the product complies with a federal product design standard.

Expert Witness

Expert witnesses are engaged by both sides of the litigation to prove their arguments. The defendant uses the services of expert technical witnesses within the manufacturing organization as well as outside or independent technical experts. While company experts are usually more knowledgeable about the product, the independent expert is considered to have less bias to his/her opinions.

The first requirement of an expert technical witness is his/her technical competency relative to the area of testimony. Technical competency can be substantiated by impressive credentials such as education, registration, and technical publications. In addition, the technical witness's personal character must be above reproach. Perhaps the most important requirement of an acceptable technical witness is the ability to communicate with the judge and jury. The technical expert must be able to explain and teach nontechnical people the technical aspects of the case. Testimony concerning science, product design, and quality control is given in a simple, truthful, and convincing manner. The objective is to convince the jury that the statements are true.

The technical expert and the lawyer will work together to develop an effective case. It is the duty of the expert to appraise the lawyer of the favorable and unfavorable technical aspects, and it is the duty of the lawyer to appraise the technical expert of the favorable and unfavorable legal aspects. While the lawyer has the primary responsibility for litigation strategy, it should be developed in cooperation with the technical expert.

The Outcome

After all the arguments are presented by the plaintiff and the defendant, the jury or judge returns a verdict. The verdict either absolves the defendant of any fault or requires that the defendant pay the plaintiff a stipulated amount of money.

If an unfavorable verdict is returned, the party can appeal to a higher court. The higher court, which is an odd number of judges, will review the earlier trial. Written and oral arguments are presented by both sides and the court will uphold the decision, overturn the decision, or order a new trial of the entire lawsuit.

Before or during the trial a settlement may be negotiated between the parties. A settlement is a compromise between both sides to reach a middle ground. Since it is never possible to absolutely predict the outcome of a trial, the possibility of a settlement should be continually assessed.

If the defendant loses the case, the effect can be much greater than the loss of one lawsuit. The loss of a lawsuit increases the probability of future successful lawsuits against the same product.

Financial Loss

As a result of a lawsuit or to prevent future ones, there are a number of possible areas of financial loss. These areas include trial expenses, court judgments, bankruptcy, insurance premiums, and recalls.

Regardless of who wins the lawsuit, the defendant has certain legal expenses. These expenses include the attorney's fee, technical expert fees, investigation fees, and court costs if the verdict is unfavorable. In addition, at least one company representative will be present at all times during the trial, which indirectly adds to the expense.

The largest financial loss is the court judgement. When a judge or jury reaches a verdict for the plaintiff, the amount of the monetary award is also specified. Because the public believes that corporate enterprises have an almost unlimited amount of money, the awards have, in recent years, been particularly generous. Awards exceeding $1.5 million are not unusual. While monetary settlements have not been as large as the awards from a completed trial, they have been substantial. In the case of the larger enterprises, the financial loss imposed on the manufacturers is eventually passed on to the customer. However, smaller enterprises may have insufficient assets and/or liability insurance to cover the award and be forced into bankruptcy. This result is unfortunate, since it may affect adversely the competitive nature of a particular product or industry.

Another financial loss is due to the increase in insurance premiums which manufacturers pay for product liability. Product liability insurance has been difficult or impossible to obtain by many small businesses in high-risk areas such as machine tools.

Other financial considerations that may result directly or indirectly from a product liability lawsuit are:

1. Cost of recall, replacement, or repair of a product
2. Cost of damage to a company's reputation and customer dissatisfaction
3. Cost of a hold or delay in production due to a potential defect
4. Cost of increased quality costs for prevention or appraisal

In the long run, these financial losses may be more substantial than a $1.5 million judgment.

Outlook for the Future

Product liability is continually changing. Many states have instituted remedies that prevent manufacturers from going out of business because of (1) excessive court judgments, (2) exhorbitant insurance premiums, or (3) insurance cancellation. These remedies reduce the costs of product liability, which are passed on to the customer by both small and large manufacturers.

A bill, the Federal Product Liability Act, that has been proposed in the U.S. Congress would, if passed into law, supplant all existing state laws in the area of product liability. This law would virtually do away with strict liability claims. Instead, to recover on a claim under this act the plaintiff would have to prove that the product was unreasonably dangerous, that the product was the proximate cause of the injury, and that the product which caused the harm was manufactured by the defendant. Under this act, an unreasonably dangerous product is defined as having one or more of the following attributes: (1) a deficiency in construction, (2) a deficiency in design, (3) a failure to warn of potential danger, and (4) the product failed to conform to an express warranty. The law would have a two-year statute of limitations in which a plaintiff could bring an action against a defendant. The time period for this statute of limitations begins from the point at which the plaintiff discovered or should have discovered the harm. The Act, proposed in 1975, has yet to be passed, though the bill is still pending in Congress.[4]

PREVENTION[5]

The manufacturer of a consumer product must protect himself against the risk of product liability litigation or at least reduce the risk to a level that will allow a reasonable profit and continued growth. To accomplish this protection, a product liability prevention program is required. While these programs will vary from corporation to corporation, certain common elements are essential for an effective program.

Organization

To have an effective product liability prevention program, an organizational structure must be established. This structure will be a function of the size of the company and the talents of available employees. The organizational struc-

[4]G. C. Robb, "The Effect of the Proposed Product Liability Act on Current Law Regarding Liability for Defectively Designed Products," *Journal of Products Liability,* 6 (1983) 147–170.

[5]This section is extracted by permission from W. H. Koch, *Products Liability Risk Control,* Technical Paper IQ75-538 (Dearborn, Mich.: Society of Manufacturing Engineers), pp. 5–12.

ture must specify responsibilities and the necessary authority to achieve those responsibilities.

Education

Education is the cornerstone of an effective program. All employees are made aware of the importance of product safety. An initial effort using available purchased materials, training sessions, and printed materials will educate personnel to the product liability prevention program. As new or transferred employees become part of the organization, they are exposed to the same educational effort.

Some form of continuing education is part of the plan of action. Information such as changes to state and national law, results of relevant lawsuits, and feedback on product audits is especially important to disseminate to employees.

New Product Review

New products are more likely to be involved in product liability litigation than well-established products; therefore, a special review is required before the product can be released to manufacturing. The safety of the consumer is the paramount consideration in the review process, with function, cost, and sales appeal being of secondary importance.

A written description of the product by the designer is the starting point for the review process. This description includes the intended use of the product, expected life, probable failure, limiting design parameters, service environment, development tests, and final acceptance criteria. The design and development of the product are thoroughly documented.

A product review team is established which has no preconceived notions about the product. The review team evaluates the product's compliance with present and foreseeable industry and government standards as well as applicable codes, laws, and regulations. Customer requirements and customers' known or anticipated end use of the item will also be reviewed.

It is frequently impossible to economically design a product with zero safety incident. In these situations the unsafe area is guarded or protected from injury exposure. Product defects can, in some situations, be designed to occur in such a manner that a disabling injury does not occur. If it is not possible or practical to design and/or guard against an injury exposure, then adequate warnings by word, color, or illustration should be permanently attached to the product.

Customer-oriented tests are performed to predict the misuse of the product. Designers test a product to determine if it performs as intended when correctly used. A customer-oriented test tries to determine what happens when the product is misued. Consideration is given to the wide variance in the physical and mental ability of *all* potential customers.

Since minor design and material changes to an existing product can cause disabling injury, the same type of review is necessary for any and all changes.

Initial Production Review

The new product review is usually based on hand-built prototypes. Therefore, a subsequent review is necessary on the first production items to determine if any defects are encountered that did not materialize in the prototypes. For an inherently hazardous product, a limited production run and controlled distribution is recommended. From this limited sample, meaningful information can be obtained from customers while the liability risk exposure is minimized.

The production review will evaluate the manufacturing plan to determine the adequacy of:

1. Tooling and work-holding devices
2. Production machinery
3. Materials handling
4. Test equipment
5. Inspection system
6. Sampling plan
7. Packaging and shipping
8. Operating instructions
9. Safety warnings
10. Advanced service information for distributors and dealers

All personnel who are active in the initial production review process can informally evaluate the product design for safety. The more people evaluating a product for safety, the greater the likelihood that a potential liability exposure will be detected before the product is sold in the marketplace.

Periodic Production Audits

Most manufacturing organizations periodically perform production audits to verify or validate the effectiveness of the quality control system. These audits can be extended to evaluate the safety parameters. The audit should be performed on recently manfactured products, or products that have been through the distribution system, and on products that have been in customer use a substantial period of time. Inspection and testing of the product is based on a simulation of the customer's activities. Feedback of the results of the audit is sent to both manufacturing and product design.

Control of Warranties, Advertisements, Agreements, and the Like

The product liability loss-prevention program must provide for a continual review of warranty, advertising literature, dealer agreements, catalogs, and technical publications. The review should include:

1. A check to determine that the terms and conditions of sale are limited to a statement of *merchantability,* which means that the product is of good material and workmanship. The use of such phrases as "safe" and "ensures the safety of the operator" are to be avoided. If the product is referred to as "safe" and a person is injured, he/she has established that the product was defective.

2. An analysis by legal counsel of all advertising copy, sales brochures, other promotional literature, and technical reports and presentations.

3. An examination of purchase orders to determine the acceptability of any special warranty provisions.

4. An analysis of dealer distributorships and franchise agreements to determine the handling of "defective" items. These agreements are allowed in court and can constitute an admission that the company manufactures "defective" products.

Complaints and Claims

A complaint or a claim is a communication between the marketplace and the manufacturing operations concerning the performance of the product. This information serves to alert the manufacturer to the need for corrective action. Analysis of complaints can lead to a change in product design or manufacturing that will reduce the exposure to disabling injuries.

The investigation of bodily injury or property damage claims or product safety complaints should be acted upon quickly. Usually, the notice of a claim or complaint is given to a dealer, distributor, or employee. This initial notice is sent to the proper department for action. An investigator reviews the situation and determines:

1. The cause of the claim or complaint
2. The nature and seriousness of the injury, if one has occurred
3. The defect that caused the situation, if there was a defect
4. The age of the defect and if it was present when the product was sold
5. The negligence of the parties

An early investigation can lead to quick settlement of reasonable claims or the preparation of defenses for those claims which may require litigation.

The complaint and claim procedure should make provision for notifying the appropriate departments, depending on the seriousness of the claim. It may even be necessary to implement the product-recall plan.

Records Retention

The defense of a product liability lawsuit necessitates the availability of design, production, and sales records. Particular types of records that should be retained are:

1. Product development and test records
2. Results of process, product, and system inspections and audits
3. Records of verbal and written communications with customers relative to requirements, product application, nonstandard materials, and claims
4. Original design data
5. Service-life data
6. Acceptance and approvals by government agencies, customers, or independent testing companies
7. Critical raw material acceptance records

Records are maintained in such a manner that the material or product can be traced to a given shipment, operator, machine, time, and so on.

Records must be protected from loss by storage in fireproof cabinets and by having duplicate sets. The question of how long records should be retained is based on a number of considerations. Usually, records are maintained for the expected useful life of the product plus 18 years, in order to cover the time when an injured minor could bring a lawsuit upon reaching the legal age of 18. Other retention considerations are the inherent risk of the product, the need for records critical to the defense, and the method of storage.

Product-Recall Plan

While the cost of recalling a product varies significantly with the type of product and the quantities involved, the costs are substantial and have forced at least one company into bankruptcy. An effective recall contingency plan helps to minimize the recall costs and the product liability risk.

Once notification of a defective product is received, the company must decide whether or not to recall all product suspected of having the defective condition. Consideration for this decision will be given to:

1. Determination of the maximum exposure to personal injury or property damage if the product is not recalled. This determination will be based on the pattern of defect, the quantity involved, the severity of the risk, and the cost of the recall.
2. The form of communication (radio, TV, newspaper, telephone, and registered letter) to use in contacting the users of the product.
3. Determining if the product will be repaired, or replaced, or if the customer will be reimbursed.

If the defective condition is classified as a substantial product hazard, the Consumer Product Safety Commission may order the manufacturer to take specific action. In such a case the decision is made for the manufacturer.

When a recall is required, it is extremely important to identify those units with the defective condition and correlate this identification with the applicable manufacturing records. This type of identification is referred to as *traceability*. The traceability of a product can have a decided influence on whether 100 or 10,000 units are recalled.

Subrogation

Part of a product liability prevention program involves the raw material, component parts, and subassembly suppliers. The same elements of evaluation and safety criteria that are applicable to the manufacturer are applicable to the supplier. A visit to the supplier's plant and an audit of his prevention program is a necessity. The supplier should also visit the manufacturer's plant to evaluate product safety exposure of the raw material, component part, or subassembly.

All communication between supplier and manufacturer concerning defective raw materials, component parts, and subassembly are made in writing. The manufacturer advises the supplier of all relevant product safety information, such as complaints, audits, warranties, and product reviews.

Risk Criteria

If a company manufactures a broad range of products, it usually has a range of potential product liability loss. Some products, for inherent reasons, pose a much greater risk than others; therefore, products are evaluated based on certain risk criteria. The degree of prevention control is then based on the degree of potential liability loss. This technique enables a company to exert its maximum preventive effort on those products where it is most needed.

Standards

All prevention programs, especially those of large corporations, should make provision for employees to be involved in the development of design and manufacturing standards. Since manufacturers have the most to lose from stringent, unrealistic standards, they should actively be engaged in their evolution and maintenance.

In this connection the legal staff should be actively involved in the evolution of product liability law.

Audit

Periodic audits of the prevention programs are absolutely essential to determine whether or not the program is operating satisfactorily. These audits are for the most part system audits which operate in much the same manner as audits of the total quality control system. Periodic audits are useful tools for measuring progress and for providing feedback to improve the prevention program. The audits are scheduled and performed by internal company personnel or knowledgeable external people. Results of the audit are written and circulated within the company.

In conclusion, it is appropriate to mention the old cliché, "An ounce of prevention is worth a pound of cure." An adequate prevention program can substantially reduce the risk of damaging litigation.

11 COMPUTERS AND QUALITY CONTROL

INTRODUCTION

Computers play an essential role in the quality control function. They perform very simple operations at fast speeds (thousands of operations per second) with an exceptionally high degree of accuracy. The computer must be programmed (told what to do) to execute these simple operations in the correct sequence in order to accomplish a given task. Computers can be programmed to perform complex calculations, to control a process or test, to analyze data, to write reports, and to recall information on command.

There are two classes of computers, digital and analog. Digital computers operate on numbers represented by sequences of digits. The analog computers operate on a continuous input of data such as voltage or angular displacement of a wheel, which represents the variations in the actual data.

Computers range from pocket size to desk size to huge multiprocessing computing centers. The large computers are capable of handling many jobs at the same time and of storing vast amounts of information. As the size of the computer increases, its cost and versatility increase.

Since the use of a computer is a costly proposition, it must be justified. The cost of preparing a program, using the computer, and implementing the results is substantial. This cost has to be less than the potential benefits, which include money or time saved, data created, improved accuracy, and greater control.

Quality control needs served by the computer are (1) data collection, (2) data analysis and reporting, (3) statistical analysis, (4) process control, and (5) test and inspection. The purpose of this chapter is to illustrate the use of the computer as a tool to aid the quality control function.

DATA COLLECTION

Computers are well suited for the collection of data. Principal benefits are faster data transmission, fewer errors, and lower collection costs. Data are transmitted to the computer by punched cards, paper or magnetic tape, optical scanning, typewriter terminals, touch telephone, and voice.

The type and amount of data are the principal problems of data collection. Sources of data are process inspection stations, scrap and waste reports, product audits, testing laboratories, customer complaints, service information, and incoming material inspection. From these sources a vast amount of data can be collected. The decision as to how much data to collect and analyze is based on the reports to be issued, the processes to be controlled, the records to be retained, and the nature of the quality improvement program.

A typical form for collecting data for an internal failure or deficiency is shown in Figure 11-1. In addition to the basic information concerning the internal failure or deficiency, a number of identifiers are used. Typical identifiers are part number, operator, foreman, data, vendor, product line, work center, and department. Identifiers are necessary for data analysis, report preparation, and record traceability. Once the disposition of the defective material is determined, this particular report is routed to accounting, where the failure costs are assigned and the information is transmitted to the computer.

Data can also be transmitted directly to the computer by means of typewriter terminals (with or without visual display), microcomputers, touch telephones, or voice. The touch telephone system is a simple system whereby the inspection results for a particular work center are transmitted to the computer using the touch tone signals to represent the 10 numbers.

The collection, utilization, and dissemination of quality control information is best accomplished when the information is incorporated into a data-base management system. A data-base management system maintains relationships with other activities, such as inventory control, purchasing, accounting, and production control. Linkages are developed between the stored data records of the various activities in order to obtain additional information with a minimum of programming and to improve the storage utilization.

Sometimes information is stored in the computer in order for it to be transmitted efficiently to remote terminals. For example, the operating instructions, specifications, tools, inspection gages, and inspection requirements for a particular job are stored in the computer. This information is then provided to the employee at the same time the work assignment is given. One of the principal advantages of this type of system is the ability to quickly update or change the information. Another advantage is the likelihood of fewer errors, since the operator is using current information rather than obsolete or hard-to-read instructions.

DEFICIENCY REPORT

1. PART NUMBER | 2. ISSUE | SUF.

IDENTIFICATION

3. TELL | HUNT | 4. TELL OPER.# | 4A. RESP. OPER.# | 5. FOREMAN# | 6. DATE WRITTEN (MONTH | DAY | YEAR)

7. PART NAME | 8. MATERIAL LOCATION | 9. DEF. OPN. | SUF. | 10. QTY. REJECTED

11. DEFICIENCY DESCRIPTION
USE STANDARD ABBREVIATIONS

12. SHOP ORDER NUMBER | 13. CLERK# | 14. DATE

15. DEPT.# | 16. SEC.-SH. | 17. DEFECT CODE | 18. LAST OPN. | SUF. | 19. COMPONENT S/N | 20. MODEL/S | 21. SERIAL NUMBER

22. VENDOR NAME | 23. VENDOR CODE | 24. WRITER # | REJECTED BY SIGNATURE

RESPONSIBILITY | 27. **DISPOSITION**

25. DEPT. | 26. ACCOUNT | USE AS IS ☐ | RTV ☐

REWORK ☐ | SCRAP ☐

REPAIR ☐ | HOLD FOR—SORT ☐ | DISP. ☐

28. **ROUTING** | TO 1ST | TO 2ND | TO 3RD | TO 4TH | TO LAST

29. DETAILED DEFICIENCY DESCRIPTION

30. COMMENTS

OPERATOR'S SIGNATURE | FOREMAN'S SIGNATURE

31. DISPOSITION INSTRUCTIONS

32. MFG. SIGNATURE | 33. MFG. ENGR. SIGNATURE | 34. QA SIGNATURE

35. PROD. ENGR. SIGNATURE | 36. APPROVED | 37. APPROVED

38. CANCEL | REPLACE | 39. PREVIOUS DR | 40. PREVIOUS DISP. | 41. PREVIOUS QTY. | 42. UPDATE AUTHORITY—QA

43. REASON FOR UPDATE

Figure 11-1 Deficiency report. (Courtesy of Fiat-Allis Construction Machinery, Inc.)

A computer has a limited amount of storage capacity; therefore, quality control data are periodically analyzed to determine what data to retain in the computer, what data to store by another method, and what data to destroy. Data can be stored on magnetic tape or a disk and reentered into the computer if needed. Product liability requirements determine the amount and type of data to be destroyed.

DATA ANALYSIS, REDUCTION, AND REPORTING

While some of the quality control information is merely stored in the computer for retrieval at a future time, most of the information is analyzed, reduced to a meaningful amount, and disseminated in the form of a report. These activities of analysis, reduction, and reporting are programmed to occur automatically as the data are collected or to occur on command by the computer operator.

Typical reports for scrap and rework as produced by a computer are shown in Figure 11-2. The weekly scrap and rework cost report of Figure 11-2a is a listing by part number of the information transmitted to the computer from the internal failure deficiency report. Identifiers reported for each transaction are a function of the report and the space available. For this report the identifiers are part number, operation code, and deficiency ticket number.

The basic data can be summarized in a number of different ways. Figure 11-2b shows a summary by failure code. Summaries are also compiled by operator, department, work center, defect, product line, part number, subassembly, vendor, and material.

A monthly Pareto analysis of the data by defect for Department 4 is shown in Figure 11-2c. This Pareto analysis is in tabular form; however, the computer could have been programmed to present the information in graphical form, as illustrated by the Pareto analysis in Chapter 10. Pareto analyses could also have been computed for operators, work centers, departments, part numbers, and so on.

The previous paragraphs have described the reports associated with scrap and rework. Reports for inspection results, product audits, service information, customer complaints, vendor evaluation, and laboratory testing are all similar. Information of a graphical nature, such as for a *p* chart can be programmed, displayed at a terminal, and reproduced as shown by Figure 11-3. This particular *p*-chart program uses control limits based on an average subgroup size and then computes individual control limits based on the performance for that day.

Data can be analyzed as they are being accumulated rather than on a weekly or monthly basis. When this technique is practiced, decision rules can be employed in the program which will automatically signal the likelihood of a quality problem. In this manner, information concerning a potential problem is provided and corrective action taken prior to the issuance of the formal report.

SCRAP AND REWORK COST REPORT FOR THE WEEK ENDING 11/26

PART#	CODE	TICKET	QTY	MATERIAL	LABOR	OVERHEAD	TOTAL
1194	E	2387	40000	800.00	.00	24.80	824.80
1275	E	1980	15	31.50	2.28	5.59	39.37
1276	D	2021	7	11.76	.94	2.30	15.00
1276	E	2442	10	16.80	1.34	3.28	21.42
9020	D	608	1	30.79	6.01	14.72	51.52
9600	D	2411	3	48.03	19.00	46.55	113.38
9862	D	2424	1	23.73	4.92	12.05	40.70
TOTAL				$13,627.35	2,103.65	5,153.98	21,307.41

RECAP OF FAILURE CODES SHOWING AMOUNT AND PERCENT OF TOTAL

CODE EXPLANATION	AMOUNT	%
A #OPERATION MISSED	5.36	
B #BROKEN PARTS	.00	
C #MISSING PARTS	.00	
D #IMPROPER MACHINING	11,882.72	56
E #FOUNDRY OR PURCHASING	8,841.79	41
F #MECHANICAL FAILURE	.00	
G #IMPROPER HANDLING	533.10	3
H #OTHER	44.44	
	$21,307.41	100

HIGH DOLLAR DEFECTS DEPARTMENT 4 MONTH OF OCTOBER

RANK	DEF CODE	DEFECT CODE DESCR.	$ SCRAP	$ RWK	TOTAL	%
01	D-T2	TURN	7,500	4,105	11,605	28.5
02	D-H1	HOB	5,810	681	6,491	16.0
03	D-G6	GRIND	4,152	1,363	5,515	13.8
04	D-D4	DRILL	793	3,178	3,971	9.8
05	D-L1	LAP	314	2,831	3,145	7.8

Figure 11-2 Typical scrap and rework reports: weekly cost report, weekly summary by failure code, Pareto analysis by defect code and department.

STATISTICAL ANALYSIS

The first use of the computer in quality control was for statistical analysis. Most of the statistical techniques discussed in this book can be easily programmed. Once programmed, considerable calculation time is saved, and the calculations are error-free. A number of computer programs written in BASIC were given earlier in the book.

Many statistical computer programs have been published in the *Journal of Quality Technology* and can easily be adapted to any computer or programming language. A selected list of these programs is given in Table 11-1. Information on additional statistical analysis techniques has been published in *Applied Statistics* since 1969.

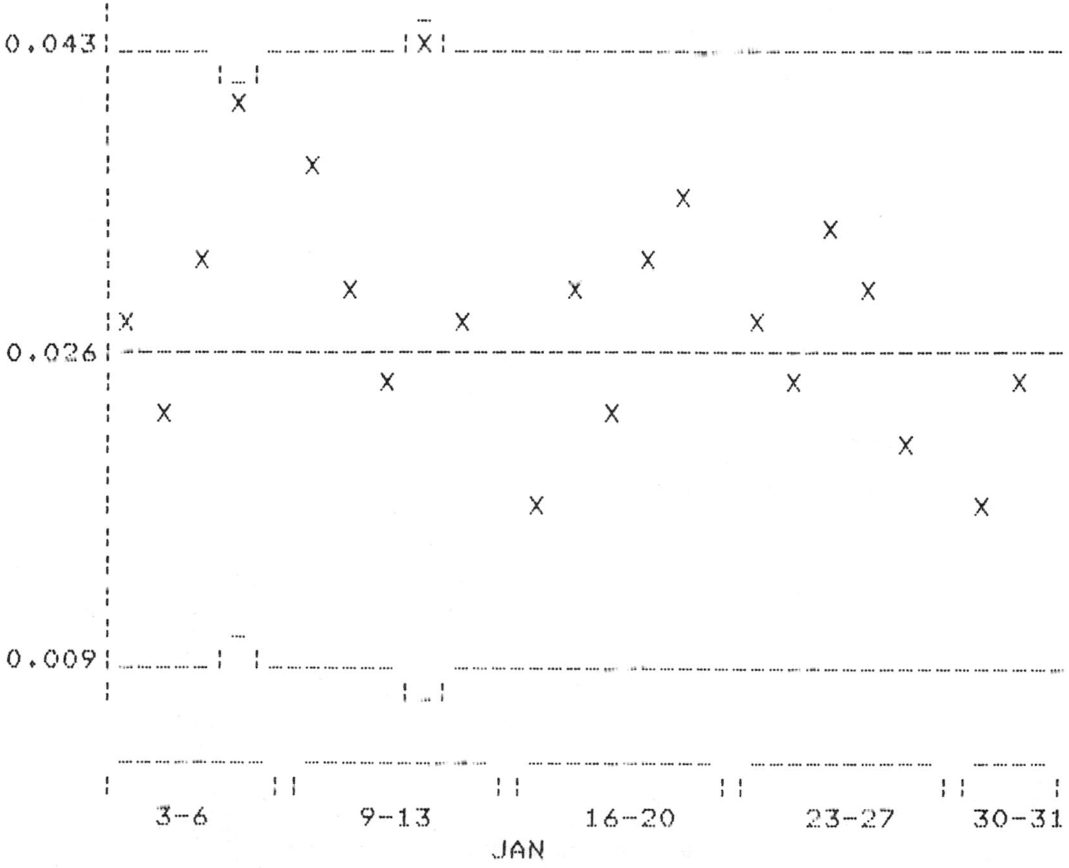

Figure 11-3 Computer-generated *p* chart.

TABLE 11-1 Computer Programs Given in the *Journal of Quality Technology* (Programs in FORTRAN IV)

Contents	*Issue*
Seven statistics (median, mean, etc.) and frequency histogram plots	Jan. 1969
Plots $\overline{X}$ and R charts	Apr. 1969
Plotting p and np charts	July 1969
Plotting c and u charts	Oct. 1969
Plotting cusum charts	Jan. 1970
Algorithm for scale selection in computer plots	Apr. 1970
Two- to five-point Lagrangian interpolation	July 1970
Student's t test	Oct. 1970
Scatter plots (up to 500 pairs)	Jan. 1971
Coefficient of correlation	Apr. 1971
Simple linear regression	July 1971
Multiple linear regression	Oct. 1971
Fitting two widely useful nonlinear models	Apr. 1972
Scaled midpoints for a histogram	Apr. 1972
Single sampling plans given an AQL, LTPD, producer, and consumer risks	July 1972
Double sampling plans	Oct. 1972
Multiple sampling plans	Jan. 1973
Plotting exponentially smoothed average control charts	Apr. 1973
Machine-plotted probability charts	July 1973
One-way analysis of variance	Oct. 1973
Sequential simplex program for solving minimization problems	Jan. 1974
Constructing orthogonal polynomials when the independent variable is unequally spaced	Apr. 1974
The Doolittle technique	July 1974
Single-pass computer algorithms for solution of the shortest-route problem	Oct. 1974
Dodge's continuous sampling plans	Jan. 1975
Analysis of variance of an $n \times n$ Latin square	Apr. 1975
Variance components for unbalanced n-level hierarchic designs	July 1975
A runs test for sample nonrandomness	Oct. 1975
Quadiature approximation for statistical tolerancing	Apr. 1976
Speed and quality of random number for simulation	July 1976
A time-sharing computer laboratory in quality control	Oct. 1976
Tests for outlying observations	Jan. 1977
A computer program for MIL-STD-414: sampling procedures and inspection by variables for percent defective	Apr. 1977
Plotting response surface contours for three-component mixtures	Oct. 1977
Randomized complete block design	Jan. 1978
Replicated randomized complete block design	Apr. 1978
GRASP: a general routine for attribute sampling plan evaluation	July 1978
Orthogonal polynomial regression for unequal spacing and frequencies	Oct. 1978
Computations of a two-tailed Fisher's test	Jan. 1979
A small-sample test for nonnormality	Apr. 1979
Estimation for mixtures of distributions by direct maximization of likelihood function	July 1979
Fitting Johnson's S_B and S_U systems of curves using the method of maximum likelihood	Oct. 1979
Comparison of K samples involving variables or attribute data using the analysis of means	Jan. 1980
A FORTRAN computer program for analysis of variance and analysis of means	Apr. 1980
Interior analysis of the observations in multiple linear regression	July 1980

TABLE 11-1 (Continued)

Contents	*Issue*
Minimum sample-size single sampling plans: a computerized approach	Oct. 1980
Simultaneous pairwise comparison tests among treatment means	Jan. 1981
Computer program for the two-sample Kolmogorov–Smirnov test	Apr. 1981
Response surface contour plots for mixture problems	July 1981
A computer program for simple linear regression with censored data	Oct. 1981
Economic design of an *X* control chart	Jan 1982
Analysis of two-level factorial experiments	Apr. 1982
An algorithm for determining double attribute sampling plans	July 1982
Randomization tests for *K* sample binomial data	Oct. 1982
The analysis of means for balanced experimental designs	Jan. 1983
Computation of the component randomization test for paired comparisons	Apr. 1983
Testing for normality	July 1983
Variance estimation using staggered, nested design	Oct. 1983
Determination of rectifying inspection plans for single sampling by attributes	Jan. 1984
Machine setting to minimize scrap and rework costs	Apr. 1984
Wald sequential sampling for attribute inspection	July 1984
Normal family distribution functions: FORTRAN and BASIC programs	Oct. 1984

Once a statistical package of computer programs is developed, the quality engineer can specify a particular sequence of statistical calculations to use for a given set of conditions. The results of these calculations can provide conclusive evidence or suggest additional statistical calculations for the computer to perform. Many of these tests are too tedious to perform without the use of a computer.

PROCESS CONTROL

The first application of computers in process control was with numerically controlled (N/C) machines. Numerically controlled machines use punched paper or magnetic tape to transmit instructions to the computer, which then controls the sequence of operations. A more sophisticated type of process control measures and controls the process variables to maintain their values within acceptable control limits.

An automatic process control system is illustrated by the flow diagram of Figure 11-4. While the computer is a key part of automatic process control, it is not the only part. There are two major interfacing subsystems between the computer and the process.

One subsystem has a sensor that measures a process variable such as temperature, pressure, voltage, length, weight, moisture content, and so on, and sends an analog signal to the digital computer. However, the digital computer can only receive information in digital form, so the signal is converted by an analog-to-digital interface. The variable value in digit form is evaluated by the computer to determine if the value is within the prescribed limits. If such is

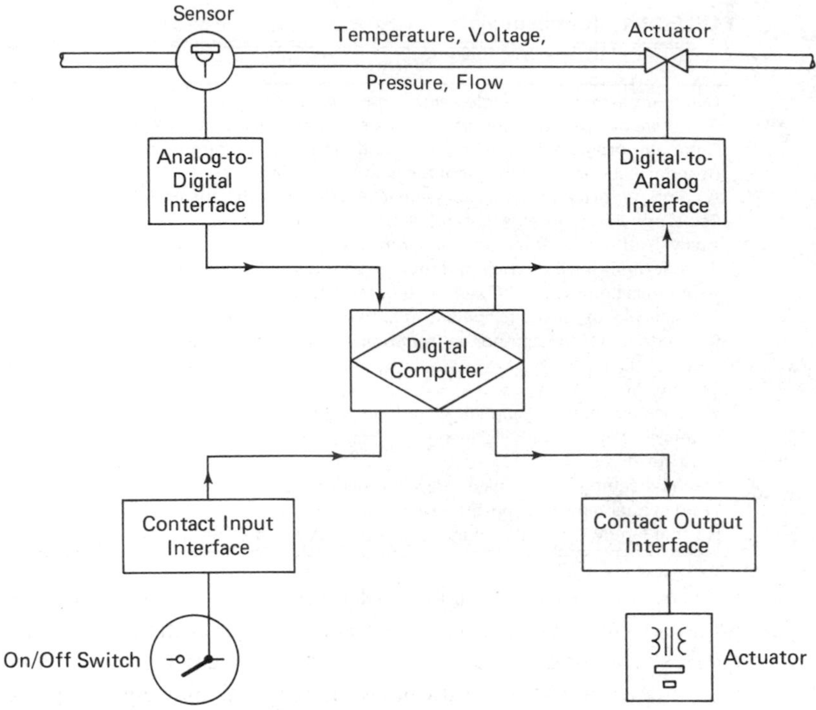

Figure 11-4 Automatic process control system.

the case, no further action is necessary; however, if the digital value is outside the limits, corrective action is required. A corrected digital value is sent to the digital-to-analog interface, which converts to an analog signal that is acceptable to an actuator mechanism, such as a valve. Then the actuator mechanism increases or decreases the variable.

The other subsystem is essentially an attribute type which either determines if a contact is on/off or controls an on/off function. Through the contact input interface, the computer continuously scans the actual on/off status of switches, motors, pumps, and so on, and compares these to the desired contact status. The computer program controls the sequence of events performed during the process cycle. Operating instructions are initiated by specific process conditions or as a function of time and are sent to the contact output interface. This interface activates a solenoid, sounds an alarm, starts a pump, stops a conveyor, and so on.

The four interfaces in Figure 11-4 are capable of handling a number of signals at the same time. Also, the two subsystems can operate independently or in conjunction with each other. Since the computer operates in microseconds and the subsystems operate in milliseconds, a timing problem can occur unless the feedback loops are as tight as possible so that corrective action is immediate.[1] The benefits that are obtained from automatic process control are:

1. Constant product quality, owing to a reduction in process variation
2. More uniform startup and shutdown, since the process can be monitored and controlled during these critical periods
3. Increased productivity, because fewer people are needed to monitor the controls
4. Safer operation for personnel and equipment, by either stopping the process or failing to start the process when an unsafe condition occurs

One of the first automatic process-controlled installations occurred at Western Electric's North Carolina plant in 1960. The product variables were controlled by the computer using $\bar{X}$ and R control chart techniques. For example, the resistance value of deposited carbon resistors coming out of the furnace was controlled by the amount of methane in the furnace and by the speed through the furnace. Since the inspection and packaging operations were also under computer control, the entire production facility was completely automatic.[2]

AUTOMATIC TEST AND INSPECTION

If we consider test and inspection as a process in itself or a part of a manufacturing process, then automatic test and inspection is similar to the previous section on automatic process control. Computer-controlled test and inspection systems offer the following advantages: improved test quality, lower operating cost, better report preparation, improved accuracy, automatic calibration, and malfunction diagnostics. Their primary disadvantage is the high cost of the equipment.

Computer-controlled automatic inspection can be used for go/no-go inspection decisions or for sorting and classifying parts in selective assembly. Automatic inspection systems have the capacity and speed to be used on high-volume production lines.

Automatic test systems can be programmed to perform a complete quality audit of the product. Testing can be sequenced through the various product components and subassemblies. Parameters such as temperature, voltage, and

[1]N. A. Poisson, "Interfaces for Process Control," *Textile Industries,* 134, No. 3 (March 1970), 61–65.

[2]J. H. Boatwright, "Using a Computer for Quality Control of Automated Production," *Computers and Automation,* 13, No. 2 (February 1964), 10–17.

force can be varied to simulate environmental and wear-out conditions. Reports are automatically prepared to reflect the performance of the product.

When automatic test and inspection is applied to automatic or semiautomatic produced product, the computer can generate the inspection instructions at the same time the product is manufactured.

When the computer is used effectively, it becomes a powerful tool to aid in the improvement of the product quality. However, the computer is not a device that can correct a poorly designed manual system. In other words, the use of a computer in quality control is as effective as the people who create the total quality control system.

SELECTED BIBLIOGRAPHY

ASQC Statistics Division, *Glossary and Tables for Statistical Quality Control.* Milwaukee, Wis.: American Society for Quality Control, Inc., 1983.

Crosby, Phillip B., *Quality Is Free.* New York: McGraw-Hill Book Company, 1979.

Crosby, Phillip B., *Quality Without Tears.* New York: McGraw-Hill Book Company, 1984.

Deming, W. Edwards, *Quality, Productivity, and Competitive Position.* Cambridge, Mass.: Massachusetts Institute of Technology, 1982.

Henley, Ernest J., and Hiromitsu Kumamoto, *Reliability Engineering and Risk Assessment.* Englewood Cliffs, N.J.: Prentice-Hall, Inc., 1981.

Juran, Joseph M. (ed.), *Quality Control Handbook*, 3rd ed. New York: McGraw-Hill Book Company, 1974.

Juran, Joseph M., and Frank M. Gryna, Jr., *Quality Planning and Analysis,* 2nd ed. New York: McGraw-Hill Book Company, 1980.

Shapiro, Samuel S., The ASQC Basic References in Quality Control: Statistical Techniques, Edward J. Dudewicz, PhD., Editor, *Volume 3: How to Test Normality and Other Distributional Assumptions.* Milwaukee, Wis.: American Society for Quality Control, Inc., 1980.

Quality Cost Effectiveness Technical Committee, *Quality Costs—What and How,* 2nd ed. Milwaukee, Wis.: American Society for Quality Control, Inc., 1971.

APPENDIX

TABLE A Areas Under the Normal Curve[a]

$\frac{X_i-\mu}{\sigma}$	0.09	0.08	0.07	0.06	0.05	0.04	0.03	0.02	0.01	0.00
−3.5	0.00017	0.00017	0.00018	0.00019	0.00019	0.00020	0.00021	0.00022	0.00022	0.00023
−3.4	0.00024	0.00025	0.00026	0.00027	0.00028	0.00029	0.00030	0.00031	0.00033	0.00034
−3.3	0.00035	0.00036	0.00038	0.00039	0.00040	0.00042	0.00043	0.00045	0.00047	0.00048
−3.2	0.00050	0.00052	0.00054	0.00056	0.00058	0.00060	0.00062	0.00064	0.00066	0.00069
−3.1	0.00071	0.00074	0.00076	0.00079	0.00082	0.00085	0.00087	0.00090	0.00094	0.00097
−3.0	0.00100	0.00104	0.00107	0.00111	0.00114	0.00118	0.00122	0.00126	0.00131	0.00135
−2.9	0.0014	0.0014	0.0015	0.0015	0.0016	0.0016	0.0017	0.0017	0.0018	0.0019
−2.8	0.0019	0.0020	0.0021	0.0021	0.0022	0.0023	0.0023	0.0024	0.0025	0.0026
−2.7	0.0026	0.0027	0.0028	0.0029	0.0030	0.0031	0.0032	0.0033	0.0034	0.0035
−2.6	0.0036	0.0037	0.0038	0.0039	0.0040	0.0041	0.0043	0.0044	0.0045	0.0047
−2.5	0.0048	0.0049	0.0051	0.0052	0.0054	0.0055	0.0057	0.0059	0.0060	0.0062
−2.4	0.0064	0.0066	0.0068	0.0069	0.0071	0.0073	0.0075	0.0078	0.0080	0.0082
−2.3	0.0084	0.0087	0.0089	0.0091	0.0094	0.0096	0.0099	0.0102	0.0104	0.0107
−2.2	0.0110	0.0113	0.0116	0.0119	0.0122	0.0125	0.0129	0.0132	0.0136	0.0139
−2.1	0.0143	0.0146	0.0150	0.0154	0.0158	0.0162	0.0166	0.0170	0.0174	0.0179
−2.0	0.0183	0.0188	0.0192	0.0197	0.0202	0.0207	0.0212	0.0217	0.0222	0.0228
−1.9	0.0233	0.0239	0.0244	0.0250	0.0256	0.0262	0.0268	0.0274	0.0281	0.0287
−1.8	0.0294	0.0301	0.0307	0.0314	0.0322	0.0329	0.0336	0.0344	0.0351	0.0359
−1.7	0.0367	0.0375	0.0384	0.0392	0.0401	0.0409	0.0418	0.0427	0.0436	0.0446
−1.6	0.0455	0.0465	0.0475	0.0485	0.0495	0.0505	0.0516	0.0526	0.0537	0.0548
−1.5	0.0559	0.0571	0.0582	0.0594	0.0606	0.0618	0.0630	0.0643	0.0655	0.0668
−1.4	0.0681	0.0694	0.0708	0.0721	0.0735	0.0749	0.0764	0.0778	0.0793	0.0808
−1.3	0.0823	0.0838	0.0853	0.0869	0.0885	0.0901	0.0918	0.0934	0.0951	0.0968
−1.2	0.0895	0.1003	0.1020	0.1038	0.1057	0.1075	0.1093	0.1112	0.1131	0.1151
−1.1	0.1170	0.1190	0.1210	0.1230	0.1251	0.1271	0.1292	0.1314	0.1335	0.1357
−1.0	0.1379	0.1401	0.1423	0.1446	0.1469	0.1492	0.1515	0.1539	0.1562	0.1587
−0.9	0.1611	0.1635	0.1660	0.1685	0.1711	0.1736	0.1762	0.1788	0.1814	0.1841
−0.8	0.1867	0.1894	0.1922	0.1949	0.1977	0.2005	0.2033	0.2061	0.2090	0.2119
−0.7	0.2148	0.2177	0.2207	0.2236	0.2266	0.2297	0.2327	0.2358	0.2389	0.2420
−0.6	0.2451	0.2483	0.2514	0.2546	0.2578	0.2611	0.2643	0.2676	0.2709	0.2743
−0.5	0.2776	0.2810	0.2843	0.2877	0.2912	0.2946	0.2981	0.3015	0.3050	0.3085
−0.4	0.3121	0.3156	0.3192	0.3228	0.3264	0.3300	0.3336	0.3372	0.3409	0.3446
−0.3	0.3483	0.3520	0.3557	0.3594	0.3632	0.3669	0.3707	0.3745	0.3783	0.3821
−0.2	0.3859	0.3897	0.3936	0.3974	0.4013	0.4052	0.4090	0.4129	0.4168	0.4207
−0.1	0.4247	0.4286	0.4325	0.4364	0.4404	0.4443	0.4483	0.4522	0.4562	0.4602
−0.0	0.4641	0.4681	0.4721	0.4761	0.4801	0.4840	0.4880	0.4920	0.4960	0.5000

[a]Proportion of total area under the curve that is under the portion of the curve from $-\infty$ to $(X_i - \mu)/\sigma$ (X_i represents any desired value of the variable X).

TABLE A *(continued)*

$\frac{X_i - \mu}{\sigma}$	0.00	0.01	0.02	0.03	0.04	0.05	0.06	0.07	0.08	0.09
+0.0	0.5000	0.5040	0.5080	0.5120	0.5160	0.5199	0.5239	0.5279	0.5319	0.5359
+0.1	0.5398	0.5438	0.5478	0.5517	0.5557	0.5596	0.5636	0.5675	0.5714	0.5753
+0.2	0.5793	0.5832	0.5871	0.5910	0.5948	0.5987	0.6026	0.6064	0.6103	0.6141
+0.3	0.6179	0.6217	0.6255	0.6293	0.6331	0.6368	0.6406	0.6443	0.6480	0.6517
+0.4	0.6554	0.6591	0.6628	0.6664	0.6700	0.6736	0.6772	0.6808	0.6844	0.6879
+0.5	0.6915	0.6950	0.6985	0.7019	0.7054	0.7088	0.7123	0.7157	0.7190	0.7224
+0.6	0.7257	0.7291	0.7324	0.7357	0.7389	0.7422	0.7454	0.7486	0.7517	0.7549
+0.7	0.7580	0.7611	0.7642	0.7673	0.7704	0.7734	0.7764	0.7794	0.7823	0.7852
+0.8	0.7881	0.7910	0.7939	0.7967	0.7995	0.8023	0.8051	0.8079	0.8106	0.8133
+0.9	0.8159	0.8186	0.8212	0.8238	0.8264	0.8289	0.8315	0.8340	0.8365	0.8389
+1.0	0.8413	0.8438	0.8461	0.8485	0.8508	0.8531	0.8554	0.8577	0.8599	0.8621
+1.1	0.8643	0.8665	0.8686	0.8708	0.8729	0.8749	0.8770	0.8790	0.8810	0.8830
+1.2	0.8849	0.8869	0.8888	0.8907	0.8925	0.8944	0.8962	0.8980	0.8997	0.9015
+1.3	0.9032	0.9049	0.9066	0.9082	0.9099	0.9115	0.9131	0.9147	0.9162	0.9177
+1.4	0.9192	0.9207	0.9222	0.9236	0.9251	0.9265	0.9279	0.9292	0.9306	0.9319
+1.5	0.9332	0.9345	0.9357	0.9370	0.9382	0.9394	0.9406	0.9418	0.9429	0.9441
+1.6	0.9452	0.9463	0.9474	0.9484	0.9495	0.9505	0.9515	0.9525	0.9535	0.9545
+1.7	0.9554	0.9564	0.9573	0.9582	0.9591	0.9599	0.9608	0.9616	0.9625	0.9633
+1.8	0.9641	0.9649	0.9656	0.9664	0.9671	0.9678	0.9686	0.9693	0.9699	0.9706
+1.9	0.9713	0.9719	0.9726	0.9732	0.9738	0.9744	0.9750	0.9756	0.9761	0.9767
+2.0	0.9773	0.9778	0.9783	0.9788	0.9793	0.9798	0.9803	0.9808	0.9812	0.9817
+2.1	0.9821	0.9826	0.9830	0.9834	0.9838	0.9842	0.9846	0.9850	0.9854	0.9857
+2.2	0.9861	0.9864	0.9868	0.9871	0.9875	0.9878	0.9881	0.9884	0.9887	0.9890
+2.3	0.9893	0.9896	0.9898	0.9901	0.9904	0.9906	0.9909	0.9911	0.9913	0.9916
+2.4	0.9918	0.9920	0.9922	0.9925	0.9927	0.9929	0.9931	0.9932	0.9934	0.9936
+2.5	0.9938	0.9940	0.9941	0.9943	0.9945	0.9946	0.9948	0.9949	0.9951	0.9952
+2.6	0.9953	0.9955	0.9956	0.9957	0.9959	0.9960	0.9961	0.9962	0.9963	0.9964
+2.7	0.9965	0.9966	0.9967	0.9968	0.9969	0.9970	0.9971	0.9972	0.9973	0.9974
+2.8	0.9974	0.9975	0.9976	0.9977	0.9977	0.9978	0.9979	0.9979	0.9980	0.9981
+2.9	0.9981	0.9982	0.9983	0.9983	0.9984	0.9984	0.9985	0.9985	0.9986	0.9986
+3.0	0.99865	0.99869	0.99874	0.99878	0.99882	0.99886	0.99889	0.99893	0.99896	0.99900
+3.1	0.99903	0.99906	0.99910	0.99913	0.99915	0.99918	0.99921	0.99924	0.99926	0.99929
+3.2	0.99931	0.99934	0.99936	0.99938	0.99940	0.99942	0.99944	0.99946	0.99948	0.99950
+3.3	0.99952	0.99953	0.99955	0.99957	0.99958	0.99960	0.99961	0.99962	0.99964	0.99965
+3.4	0.99966	0.99967	0.99969	0.99970	0.99971	0.99972	0.99973	0.99974	0.99975	0.99976
+3.5	0.99977	0.99978	0.99978	0.99979	0.99980	0.99981	0.99981	0.99982	0.99983	0.99983

TABLE B Factors for Computing Central Lines and 3σ Control Limits for $\overline{X}$, s, and R, Charts

Observations in Sample, n	*Chart for Averages*			Chart for Standard Deviations						Chart for Ranges						
	Factors for Control Limits			Factors for Central Line		Factors for Control Limits				Factors for Central Line		Factors for Control Limits				
	A	A_2	A_3	c_4	$1/c_4$	B_3	B_4	B_5	B_6	d_2	$1/d_2$	d_1	D_1	D_2	D_3	D_4
2	2.121	1.880	2.659	0.7979	1.2533	0	3.267	0	2.606	1.128	0.8865	0.853	0	3.686	0	3.267
3	1.732	1.023	1.954	0.8862	1.1284	0	2.568	0	2.276	1.693	0.5907	0.888	0	4.358	0	2.574
4	1.500	0.729	1.628	0.9213	1.0854	0	2.266	0	2.088	2.059	0.4857	0.880	0	4.698	0	2.282
5	1.342	0.577	1.427	0.9400	1.0638	0	2.089	0	1.964	2.326	0.4299	0.864	0	4.918	0	2.114
6	1.225	0.483	1.287	0.9515	1.0510	0.030	1.970	0.029	1.874	2.534	0.3946	0.848	0	5.078	0	2.004
7	1.134	0.419	1.182	0.9594	1.0423	0.118	1.882	0.113	1.806	2.704	0.3698	0.833	0.204	5.204	0.076	1.924
8	1.061	0.373	1.099	0.9650	1.0363	0.185	1.815	0.179	1.751	2.847	0.3512	0.820	0.388	5.306	0.136	1.864
9	1.000	0.337	1.032	0.9693	1.0317	0.239	1.761	0.232	1.707	2.970	0.3367	0.808	0.547	5.393	0.184	1.816
10	0.949	0.308	0.975	0.9727	1.0281	0.284	1.716	0.276	1.669	3.078	0.3249	0.797	0.687	5.469	0.223	1.777
11	0.905	0.285	0.927	0.9754	1.0252	0.321	1.679	0.313	1.637	3.173	0.3152	0.787	0.811	5.535	0.256	1.744
12	0.866	0.266	0.886	0.9776	1.0229	0.354	1.646	0.346	1.610	3.258	0.3069	0.778	0.922	5.594	0.283	1.717
13	0.832	0.249	0.850	0.9794	1.0210	0.382	1.618	0.374	1.585	3.336	0.2998	0.770	1.025	5.647	0.307	1.693
14	0.802	0.235	0.817	0.9810	1.0194	0.406	1.594	0.399	1.563	3.407	0.2935	0.763	1.118	5.696	0.328	1.672
15	0.775	0.223	0.789	0.9823	1.0180	0.428	1.572	0.421	1.544	3.472	0.2880	0.756	1.203	5.741	0.347	1.653
16	0.750	0.212	0.763	0.9835	1.0168	0.448	1.552	0.440	1.526	3.532	0.2831	0.750	1.282	5.782	0.363	1.637
17	0.728	0.203	0.739	0.9845	1.0157	0.466	1.534	0.458	1.511	3.588	0.2787	0.744	1.356	5.820	0.378	1.622
18	0.707	0.194	0.718	0.9854	1.0148	0.482	1.518	0.475	1.496	3.640	0.2747	0.739	1.424	5.856	0.391	1.608
19	0.688	0.187	0.698	0.9862	1.0140	0.497	1.503	0.490	1.483	3.689	0.2711	0.734	1.487	5.891	0.403	1.597
20	0.671	0.180	0.680	0.9869	1.0133	0.510	1.490	0.504	1.470	3.735	0.2677	0.729	1.549	5.921	0.415	1.585
21	0.655	0.173	0.663	0.9876	1.0126	0.523	1.477	0.516	1.459	3.778	0.2647	0.724	1.605	5.951	0.425	1.575
22	0.640	0.167	0.647	0.9882	1.0119	0.534	1.466	0.528	1.448	3.819	0.2618	0.720	1.659	5.979	0.434	1.566
23	0.626	0.162	0.633	0.9887	1.0114	0.545	1.455	0.539	1.438	3.858	0.2592	0.716	1.710	6.006	0.443	1.557
24	0.612	0.157	0.619	0.9892	1.0109	0.555	1.445	0.549	1.429	3.895	0.2567	0.712	1.759	6.031	0.451	1.548
25	0.600	0.135	0.606	0.9896	1.0105	0.565	1.435	0.559	1.420	3.931	0.2544	0.708	1.806	6.056	0.459	1.541

TABLE C The Poisson Distribution $P(c) = (np_0/c!)e^{-np_0}$ (Cumulative Values Are in Parentheses)

c \ np_0	0.1	0.2	0.3	0.4	0.5
0	0.905 (0.905)	0.819 (0.819)	0.741 (0.741)	0.670 (0.670)	0.607 (0.607)
1	0.091 (0.996)	0.164 (0.983)	0.222 (0.963)	0.268 (0.938)	0.303 (0.910)
2	0.004 (1.000)	0.016 (0.999)	0.033 (0.996)	0.054 (0.992)	0.076 (0.986)
3		0.010 (1.000)	0.004 (1.000)	0.007 (0.999)	0.013 (0.999)
4				0.001 (1.000)	0.001 (1.000)

c \ np_0	0.6	0.7	0.8	0.9	1.0
0	0.549 (0.549)	0.497 (0.497)	0.449 (0.449)	0.406 (0.406)	0.368 (0.368)
1	0.329 (0.878)	0.349 (0.845)	0.359 (0.808)	0.366 (0.772)	0.368 (0.736)
2	0.099 (0.977)	0.122 (0.967)	0.144 (0.952)	0.166 (0.938)	0.184 (0.920)
3	0.020 (0.997)	0.028 (0.995)	0.039 (0.991)	0.049 (0.987)	0.061 (0.981)
4	0.003 (1.000)	0.005 (1.000)	0.008 (0.999)	0.011 (0.998)	0.016 (0.997)
5			0.001 (1.000)	0.002 (1.000)	0.003 (1.000)

c \ np_0	1.1	1.2	1.3	1.4	1.5
0	0.333 (0.333)	0.301 (0.301)	0.273 (0.273)	0.247 (0.247)	0.223 (0.223)
1	0.366 (0.699)	0.361 (0.662)	0.354 (0.627)	0.345 (0.592)	0.335 (0.558)
2	0.201 (0.900)	0.217 (0.879)	0.230 (0.857)	0.242 (0.834)	0.251 (0.809)
3	0.074 (0.974)	0.087 (0.966)	0.100 (0.957)	0.113 (0.947)	0.126 (0.935)
4	0.021 (0.995)	0.026 (0.992)	0.032 (0.989)	0.039 (0.986)	0.047 (0.982)
5	0.004 (0.999)	0.007 (0.999)	0.009 (0.998)	0.011 (0.997)	0.014 (0.996)
6	0.001 (1.000)	0.001 (1.000)	0.002 (1.000)	0.003 (1.000)	0.004 (1.000)

c \ np_0	1.6	1.7	1.8	1.9	2.0
0	0.202 (0.202)	0.183 (0.183)	0.165 (0.165)	0.150 (0.150)	0.135 (0.135)
1	0.323 (0.525)	0.311 (0.494)	0.298 (0.463)	0.284 (0.434)	0.271 (0.406)
2	0.258 (0.783)	0.264 (0.758)	0.268 (0.731)	0.270 (0.704)	0.271 (0.677)
3	0.138 (0.921)	0.149 (0.907)	0.161 (0.892)	0.171 (0.875)	0.180 (0.857)
4	0.055 (0.976)	0.064 (0.971)	0.072 (0.964)	0.081 (0.956)	0.090 (0.947)
5	0.018 (0.994)	0.022 (0.993)	0.026 (0.990)	0.031 (0.987)	0.036 (0.983)
6	0.005 (0.999)	0.006 (0.999)	0.008 (0.998)	0.010 (0.997)	0.012 (0.995)
7	0.001 (1.000)	0.001 (1.000)	0.002 (1.000)	0.003 (1.000)	0.004 (0.999)
8					0.001 (1.000)

TABLE C *(continued)*

c \ np_0	2.1		2.2		2.3		2.4		2.5	
0	0.123	(0.123)	0.111	(0.111)	0.100	(0.100)	0.091	(0.091)	0.082	(0.082)
1	0.257	(0.380)	0.244	(0.355)	0.231	(0.331)	0.218	(0.309)	0.205	(0.287)
2	0.270	(0.650)	0.268	(0.623)	0.265	(0.596)	0.261	(0.570)	0.256	(0.543)
3	0.189	(0.839)	0.197	(0.820)	0.203	(0.799)	0.209	(0.779)	0.214	(0.757)
4	0.099	(0.938)	0.108	(0.928)	0.117	(0.916)	0.125	(0.904)	0.134	(0.891)
5	0.042	(0.980)	0.048	(0.976)	0.054	(0.970)	0.060	(0.964)	0.067	(0.958)
6	0.015	(0.995)	0.017	(0.993)	0.021	(0.991)	0.024	(0.988)	0.028	(0.986)
7	0.004	(0.999)	0.005	(0.998)	0.007	(0.998)	0.008	(0.996)	0.010	(0.996)
8	0.001	(1.000)	0.002	(1.000)	0.002	(1.000)	0.003	(0.999)	0.003	(0.999)
9							0.001	(1.000)	0.001	(1.000)

c \ np_0	2.6		2.7		2.8		2.9		3.0	
0	0.074	(0.074)	0.067	(0.067)	0.061	(0.061)	0.055	(0.055)	0.050	(0.050)
1	0.193	(0.267)	0.182	(0.249)	0.170	(0.231)	0.160	(0.215)	0.149	(0.199)
2	0.251	(0.518)	0.245	(0.494)	0.238	(0.469)	0.231	(0.446)	0.224	(0.423)
3	0.218	(0.736)	0.221	(0.715)	0.223	(0.692)	0.224	(0.670)	0.224	(0.647)
4	0.141	(0.877)	0.149	(0.864)	0.156	(0.848)	0.162	(0.832)	0.168	(0.815)
5	0.074	(0.951)	0.080	(0.944)	0.087	(0.935)	0.094	(0.926)	0.101	(0.916)
6	0.032	(0.983)	0.036	(0.980)	0.041	(0.976)	0.045	(0.971)	0.050	(0.966)
7	0.012	(0.995)	0.014	(0.994)	0.016	(0.992)	0.019	(0.990)	0.022	(0.988)
8	0.004	(0.999)	0.005	(0.999)	0.006	(0.998)	0.007	(0.997)	0.008	(0.996)
9	0.001	(1.000)	0.001	(1.000)	0.002	(1.000)	0.002	(0.999)	0.003	(0.999)
10							0.001	(1.000)	0.001	(1.000)

c \ np_0	3.1		3.2		3.3		3.4		3.5	
0	0.045	(0.045)	0.041	(0.041)	0.037	(0.037)	0.033	(0.033)	0.030	(0.030)
1	0.140	(0.185)	0.130	(0.171)	0.122	(0.159)	0.113	(0.146)	0.106	(0.136)
2	0.216	(0.401)	0.209	(0.380)	0.201	(0.360)	0.193	(0.339)	0.185	(0.321)
3	0.224	(0.625)	0.223	(0.603)	0.222	(0.582)	0.219	(0.558)	0.216	(0.537)
4	0.173	(0.798)	0.178	(0.781)	0.182	(0.764)	0.186	(0.744)	0.189	(0.726)
5	0.107	(0.905)	0.114	(0.895)	0.120	(0.884)	0.126	(0.870)	0.132	(0.858)
6	0.056	(0.961)	0.061	(0.956)	0.066	(0.950)	0.071	(0.941)	0.077	(0.935)
7	0.025	(0.986)	0.028	(0.984)	0.031	(0.981)	0.035	(0.976)	0.038	(0.973)
8	0.010	(0.996)	0.011	(0.995)	0.012	(0.993)	0.015	(0.991)	0.017	(0.990)
9	0.003	(0.999)	0.004	(0.999)	0.005	(0.998)	0.006	(0.997)	0.007	(0.997)
10	0.001	(1.000)	0.001	(1.000)	0.002	(1.000)	0.002	(0.999)	0.002	(0.999)
11							0.001	(1.000)	0.001	(1.000)

TABLE C (*continued*)

c \ np_0	3.6		3.7		3.8		3.9		4.0	
0	0.027	(0.027)	0.025	(0.025)	0.022	(0.022)	0.020	(0.020)	0.018	(0.018)
1	0.098	(0.125)	0.091	(0.116)	0.085	(0.107)	0.079	(0.099)	0.073	(0.091)
2	0.177	(0.302)	0.169	(0.285)	0.161	(0.268)	0.154	(0.253)	0.147	(0.238)
3	0.213	(0.515)	0.209	(0.494)	0.205	(0.473)	0.200	(0.453)	0.195	(0.433)
4	0.191	(0.706)	0.193	(0.687)	0.194	(0.667)	0.195	(0.648)	0.195	(0.628)
5	0.138	(0.844)	0 143	(0.830)	0.148	(0.815)	0.152	(0.800)	0.157	(0.785)
6	0.083	(0.927)	0.088	(0.918)	0.094	(0.909)	0.099	(0.899)	0.104	(0.889)
7	0.042	(0.969)	0.047	(0.965)	0.051	(0.960)	0.055	(0.954)	0.060	(0.949)
8	0.019	(0.988)	0.022	(0.987)	0.024	(0.984)	0.027	(0.981)	0.030	(0.979)
9	0.008	(0.996)	0.009	(0.996)	0.010	(0.994)	0.012	(0.993)	0.013	(0.992)
10	0.003	(0.999)	0.003	(0.999)	0.004	(0.998)	0.004	(0.997)	0.005	(0.997)
11	0.001	(1.000)	0.001	(1.000)	0.001	(0.999)	0.002	(0.999)	0.002	(0.999)
12					0.001	(1.000)	0.001	(1.000)	0.001	(1.000)

c \ np_0	4.1		4.2		4.3		4.4		4.5	
0	0.017	(0.017)	0.015	(0.015)	0.014	(0.014)	0.012	(0.012)	0.011	(0.011)
1	0.068	(0.085)	0.063	(0.078)	0.058	(0.072)	0.054	(0.066)	0.050	(0.061)
2	0.139	(0.224)	0.132	(0.210)	0.126	(0.198)	0.119	(0.185)	0.113	(0.174)
3	0.190	(0.414)	0.185	(0.395)	0.180	(0.378)	0.174	(0.359)	0.169	(0.343)
4	0.195	(0.609)	0.195	(0.590)	0.193	(0.571)	0.192	(0.551)	0.190	(0.533)
5	0.160	(0.769)	0.163	(0.753)	0.166	(0.737)	0.169	(0.720)	0.171	(0.704)
6	0.110	(0.879)	0.114	(0.867)	0.119	(0.856)	0.124	(0.844)	0.128	(0.832)
7	0.064	(0.943)	0.069	(0.936)	0.073	(0.929)	0.078	(0.922)	0.082	(0.914)
8	0.033	(0.976)	0.036	(0.972)	0.040	(0.969)	0.043	(0.965)	0.046	(0.960)
9	0.015	(0.991)	0.017	(0.989)	0.019	(0.988)	0.021	(0.986)	0.023	(0.983)
10	0.006	(0.997)	0.007	(0.996)	0.008	(0.996)	0.009	(0.995)	0.011	(0.994)
11	0.002	(0.999)	0.003	(0.999)	0.003	(0.999)	0.004	(0.999)	0.004	(0.998)
12	0.001	(1.000)	0.001	(1.000)	0.001	(1.000)	0.001	(1.000)	0.001	(0.999)
13									0.001	(1.000)

TABLE C *(continued)*

c \ np_0	4.6		4.7		4.8		4.9		5.0	
0	0.010	(0.010)	0.009	(0.009)	0.008	(0.008)	0.008	(0.008)	0.007	(0.007)
1	0.046	(0.056)	0.043	(0.052)	0.039	(0.047)	0.037	(0.045)	0.034	(0.041)
2	0.106	(0.162)	0.101	(0.153)	0.095	(0.142)	0.090	(0.135)	0.084	(0.125)
3	0.163	(0.325)	0.157	(0.310)	0.152	(0.294)	0.146	(0.281)	0.140	(0.265)
4	0.188	(0.513)	0.185	(0.495)	0.182	(0.476)	0.179	(0.460)	0.175	(0.441)
5	0.172	(0.685)	0.174	(0.669)	0.175	(0.651)	0.175	(0.635)	0.176	(0.617)
6	0.132	(0.817)	0.136	(0.805)	0.140	(0.791)	0.143	(0.778)	0.146	(0.763)
7	0.087	(0.904)	0.091	(0.896)	0.096	(0.887)	0.100	(0.878)	0.105	(0.868)
8	0.050	(0.954)	0.054	(0.950)	0.058	(0.945)	0.061	(0.939)	0.065	(0.933)
9	0.026	(0.980)	0.028	(0.978)	0.031	(0.976)	0.034	(0.973)	0.036	(0.969)
10	0.012	(0.992)	0.013	(0.991)	0.015	(0.991)	0.016	(0.989)	0.018	(0.987)
11	0.005	(0.997)	0.006	(0.997)	0.006	(0.997)	0.007	(0.996)	0.008	(0.995)
12	0.002	(0.999)	0.002	(0.999)	0.002	(0.999)	0.003	(0.999)	0.003	(0.998)
13	0.001	(1.000)	0.001	(1.000)	0.001	(1.000)	0.001	(1.000)	0.001	(0.999)
14									0.001	(1.000)

c \ np_0	6.0		7.0		8.0		9.0		10.0	
0	0.002	(0.002)	0.001	(0.001)	0.000	(0.000)	0.000	(0.000)	0.000	(0.000)
1	0.015	(0.017)	0.006	(0.007)	0.003	(0.003)	0.001	(0.001)	0.000	(0.000)
2	0.045	(0.062)	0.022	(0.029)	0.011	(0.014)	0.005	(0.006)	0.002	(0.002)
3	0.089	(0.151)	0.052	(0.081)	0.029	(0.043)	0.015	(0.021)	0.007	(0.009)
4	0.134	(0.285)	0.091	(0.172)	0.057	(0.100)	0.034	(0.055)	0.019	(0.028)
5	0.161	(0.446)	0.128	(0.300)	0.092	(0.192)	0.061	(0.116)	0.038	(0.066)
6	0.161	(0.607)	0.149	(0.449)	0.122	(0.314)	0.091	(0.207)	0.063	(0.129)
7	0.138	(0.745)	0.149	(0.598)	0.140	(0.454)	0.117	(0.324)	0.090	(0.219)
8	0.103	(0.848)	0.131	(0.729)	0.140	(0.594)	0.132	(0.456)	0.113	(0.332)
9	0.069	(0.917)	0.102	(0.831)	0.124	(0.718)	0.132	(0.588)	0.125	(0.457)
10	0.041	(0.958)	0.071	(0.902)	0.099	(0.817)	0.119	(0.707)	0.125	(0.582)
11	0.023	(0.981)	0.045	(0.947)	0.072	(0.889)	0.097	(0.804)	0.114	(0.696)
12	0.011	(0.992)	0.026	(0.973)	0.048	(0.937)	0.073	(0.877)	0.095	(0.791)
13	0.005	(0.997)	0.014	(0.987)	0.030	(0.967)	0.050	(0.927)	0.073	(0.864)
14	0.002	(0.999)	0.007	(0.994)	0.017	(0.984)	0.032	(0.959)	0.052	(0.916)
15	0.001	(1.000)	0.003	(0.997)	0.009	(0.993)	0.019	(0.978)	0.035	(0.951)
16			0.002	(0.999)	0.004	(0.997)	0.011	(0.989)	0.022	(0.973)
17			0.001	(1.000)	0.002	(0.999)	0.006	(0.995)	0.013	(0.986)
18					0.001	(1.000)	0.003	(0.998)	0.007	(0.993)
19							0.001	(0.999)	0.004	(0.997)
20							0.001	(1.000)	0.002	(0.999)
21									0.001	(1.000)

TABLE C *(continued)*

c \ np_0	11.0		12.0		13.0		14.0		15.0	
0	0.000	(0.000)	0.000	(0.000)	0.000	(0.000)	0.000	(0.000)	0.000	(0.000)
1	0.000	(0.000)	0.000	(0.000)	0.000	(0.000)	0.000	(0.000)	0.000	(0.000)
2	0.001	(0.001)	0.000	(0.000)	0.000	(0.000)	0.000	(0.000)	0.000	(0.000)
3	0.004	(0.005)	0.002	(0.002)	0.001	(0.001)	0.000	(0.000)	0.000	(0.000)
4	0.010	(0.015)	0.005	(0.007)	0.003	(0.004)	0.001	(0.001)	0.001	(0.001)
5	0.022	(0.037)	0.013	(0.020)	0.007	(0.011)	0.004	(0.005)	0.002	(0.003)
6	0.041	(0.078)	0.025	(0.045)	0.015	(0.026)	0.009	(0.014)	0.005	(0.008)
7	0.065	(0.143)	0.044	(0.089)	0.028	(0.054)	0.017	(0.031)	0.010	(0.018)
8	0.089	(0.232)	0.066	(0.155)	0.046	(0.100)	0.031	(0.062)	0.019	(0.037)
9	0.109	(0.341)	0.087	(0.242)	0.066	(0.166)	0.047	(0.109)	0.032	(0.069)
10	0.119	(0.460)	0.105	(0.347)	0.086	(0.252)	0.066	(0.175)	0.049	(0.118)
11	0.119	(0.579)	0.114	(0.461)	0.101	(0.353)	0.084	(0.259)	0.066	(0.184)
12	0.109	(0.688)	0.114	(0.575)	0.110	(0.463)	0.099	(0.358)	0.083	(0.267)
13	0.093	(0.781)	0.106	(0.681)	0.110	(0.573)	0.106	(0.464)	0.096	(0.363)
14	0.073	(0.854)	0.091	(0.772)	0.102	(0.675)	0.106	(0.570)	0.102	(0.465)
15	0.053	(0.907)	0.072	(0.844)	0.088	(0.763)	0.099	(0.669)	0.102	(0.567)
16	0.037	(0.944)	0.054	(0.898)	0.072	(0.835)	0.087	(0.756)	0.096	(0.663)
17	0.024	(0.968)	0.038	(0.936)	0.055	(0.890)	0.071	(0.827)	0.085	(0.748)
18	0.015	(0.983)	0.026	(0.962)	0.040	(0.930)	0.056	(0.883)	0.071	(0.819)
19	0.008	(0.991)	0.016	(0.978)	0.027	(0.957)	0.041	(0.924)	0.056	(0.875)
20	0.005	(0.996)	0.010	(0.988)	0.018	(0.975)	0.029	(0.953)	0.042	(0.917)
21	0.002	(0.998)	0.006	(0.994)	0.011	(0.986)	0.019	(0.972)	0.030	(0.947)
22	0.001	(0.999)	0.003	(0.997)	0.006	(0.992)	0.012	(0.984)	0.020	(0.967)
23	0.001	(1.000)	0.002	(0.999)	0.004	(0.996)	0.007	(0.991)	0.013	(0.980)
24			0.001	(1.000)	0.002	(0.998)	0.004	(0.995)	0.008	(0.988)
25					0.001	(0.999)	0.003	(0.998)	0.005	(0.993)
26					0.001	(1.000)	0.001	(0.999)	0.003	(0.996)
27							0.001	(1.000)	0.002	(0.998)
28									0.001	(0.999)
29									0.001	(1.000)

TABLE D Random Numbers (Generated by an Electronic Hand Calculator)

9069	7629	5756	2237	3069	6004	3792	2530
4321	5890	0822	5994	9996	8961	1262	5870
4195	5124	9161	6899	6857	6455	7662	7035
8589	4464	0905	8676	4514	8790	7186	4591
1007	3877	2592	8860	5753	8661	7694	5013
7047	2263	8242	9363	0458	5459	2369	3815
6974	5289	7527	6283	3635	1209	3791	1709
6203	5675	0586	8541	7337	3896	3060	1726
3888	0533	6091	6066	2169	4146	1047	3999
9860	9589	0814	1976	8775	8710	0231	8630
3845	7559	3167	1845	5491	4805	7966	9334
5732	0238	6134	5642	7306	2351	3150	2848
9534	6145	1823	0269	6577	4545	2181	9347
3574	9563	8359	4776	0111	9110	6160	8471
6574	1550	9890	5275	3005	3922	7048	1569
3756	6594	6634	9824	1318	6586	4075	5091
5569	2958	8823	3073	2471	1512	1015	9361
9109	2166	2146	9374	9483	2111	7095	8421
1165	2712	2021	6154	5522	9017	0354	0754
8078	2347	6410	2480	7247	1283	1307	6651
0179	4334	7117	2530	2504	4703	1756	0688
1125	2677	9553	7598	1407	3062	4701	9624
9936	2780	0687	7901	4265	5741	3310	2535
2827	1781	7272	4947	8892	7557	3134	8504
5389	9850	5081	5267	5164	1340	0605	5451
2166	6647	7554	4773	9682	3348	8503	8358
3760	1243	7458	6177	8038	2223	2679	4284
7522	6494	8298	7868	0822	8806	9255	3581
3111	6280	3705	0257	0298	6587	8677	8291
6589	0555	8479	4523	0150	4309	2756	9037
3879	9015	1218	3420	1552	8760	2758	3897
4607	5549	8957	1643	7731	6421	4639	0839
6202	0118	0479	4969	5067	3423	2718	1440
6226	1693	7411	0887	8890	0987	6252	8683
8490	3667	9016	6370	3826	4061	4548	6521
0267	5886	8597	3128	1833	7218	2997	4017
4977	9118	3327	7049	0913	0947	9262	8071
3846	7549	8036	7688	4659	9984	4752	7859
4786	4360	7316	7631	4046	0174	8035	4080
1680	4395	6313	9927	0274	1499	7072	4169

TABLE E Commonly Used Conversion Factors

Quantity	*Conversion*	*Multiply by*
Length	in. to m	2.54[a] E−02
Area	in.^{2} to m^2	6.451 600 E−04
Volume	in.^{3} to m^3	1.638 706 E−05
	U.S. gallon to m^3	3.785 412 E−03
Mass	oz (avoir) to kg	2.834 952 E−02
Acceleration	ft/s^2 to m/s^2	3.048[a] E−01
Force	poundal to N	1.382 550 E−01
Pressure, stress	poundal/ft^2 to Pa	1.488 164 E+00
	lb_f/in^2 to Pa	6.894 757 E+03
Energy, work	ft·lb_f to J	1.355 818 E+00
Power	hp (550 ft·lb_f/s) to W	7.456 999 E+02

[a]Relationship is exact and needs no additional decimal points.

ANSWERS TO SELECTED PROBLEMS

Chapter 2

1. 0.86, 0.63, 0.15, 0.48

3. 66.4, 379.1, 5, 4.652, 6.2×10^2

5. Frequencies starting at 5.94 are 1, 2, 4, 8, 16, 24, 20, 17, 13, 3, 1, 1

9. (a) Relative frequencies starting at 5.94 (in %) are 0.9, 1.8, 3.6, 7.3, 14.5, 21.8, 18.2, 15.4, 11.8, 2.7, 0.9, 0.9
(b) Cumulative frequencies starting at 5.945 are 1, 3, 7, 15, 31, 55, 75, 92, 105, 108, 109, 110
(c) Relative cumulative frequencies starting at 5.945 (in %) are 0.9, 2.7, 6.4, 13.6, 28.2, 50.0, 68.2, 83.6, 95.4, 98.2, 99.1, 100.0

15. 116

17. 95

19. 3264

21. (a) 15; (b) 35.5

23. (a) 55, (b) none, (c) 14, 17

25. (a) 11; (b) 6; (c) 14; (d) 0.11

27. 0.004

29. 19.9

33. (b) Frequencies beginning at 0.55 are 1, 17, 29, 39, 42, 54, 74, 86, 100, 106, 110

37. (b) Relative frequencies beginning at 0.5 (in %) are 0.9, 14.5, 10.9, 9.1, 2.7, 10.9, 18.2, 10.9, 12.7, 5.4, 3.6
(d) Cumulative relative frequencies beginning at 0.55 (in %) are 0.9, 15.4, 26.4, 35.4, 38.2, 49.1, 67.3, 78.2, 90.9, 96.4, 100.0

39. (b) -0.14, 3.11

41. 0.0228, 0.0475, 0.9545

43. 25.37

Chapter 3

1. $\overline{X}_0 = 20.40$; CLs = 20.56, 20.24; $R_0 = 0.34$; CLs = 0.68, 0

3. $\overline{X}_0 = 20.40$; CLs = 20.76, 20.04; $R_0 = 0.36$; CLs = 0.92, 0

5. $\overline{X}_0 = 2.08$; CLs = 2.42, 1.74; $R_0 = 0.47$; CLs = 1.08, 0

7. $\overline{X}_0 = 81.9$; CLs = 82.8, 81.0; $s_0 = 0.7$; CLs = 1.4, 0.0

11. 0.47% scrap, 2.27% rework, $\overline{X}_0 = 305.32$ mm, 6.43% rework

13. 0.27

15. 1.32, 1.67

17. (a) $\sum \overline{X}_0 = 122.40$; CLs = 123.36, 121.44

19. $\overline{\overline{X}} = 4.56$; CLs = 4.74, 4.38; $\overline{R} = 0.25$; CLs = 0.57, 0

21. $\text{Md}_{\text{Md}} = 6.39$; CLs = 6.46, 6.32; $R_{\text{Md}} = 0.08$; CLs = 0.19, 0; pattern is similar

23. $\overline{X}_0 = 25.0$; assume that $n = 4$, CLs = 25.15, 24.85

25. Histogram is symmetrical, while run chart slopes downward.

Chapter 4

1. 1.000, 0

3. 0.50, 0.81

5. 0.57

7. 0.018

9. 720

11. 4845

13. 190

15. If $r = 0$, then $C_0^n = 1$

17. If $r = 1$, then $C_1^n = n$

19. 0.084

21. 0.099

23. 0.859

25. 0.045

27. 0.783

29. 0.359

31. 0.222

Chapter 5

1. p_0 = 0.0154; CLs = 0.0367, 0

3. p_0 = 0.076; CLs = 0.188, 0

5. p_0 = 0.132

7. p_0 = 0.080; CLs (1000) = 0.106, 0.054; CLs (1500) = 0.101, 0.059; CLs (2000) = 0.098, 0.062

9. np_0 = 4.6; CLs = 11, 0

11. np_0 = 2.1; CLs = 6, 0

15. c_0 = 13.24; CLs = 24, 2

17. u_0 = 3.24; CLs = 4.94, 1.53

19. D_0 = 8.6; CLs = 11.02, 6.18; D = 5.9, out of control, exceptional good quality

Chapter 6

1. (p, P_a) pairs are (0.01, 0.972), (0.02, 0.819), (0.04, 0.359), (0.05, 0.208), (0.06, 0.110), (0.08, 0.025)

3. $(P_a)_{\text{I}} = P$ (2 or less)
$(P_a)_{\text{II}} = P(3)_{\text{I}}\, P(3 \text{ or less})_{\text{II}} + P(4)_{\text{I}}\, P(2 \text{ or less})_{\text{II}} + P(5)_{\text{I}}\, P(1 \text{ or less})_{\text{II}}$
$(P_a)_{\text{both}} = (P_a)_{\text{I}} + (P_a)_{\text{II}}$

5. (p, ASN) pairs are (0, 125), (0.01, 140), (0.02, 169), (0.03, 174), (0.04, 165), (0.05, 150), (0.06, 139)

7. (p, ATI) pairs are (0, 80), (0.00125, 120), (0.01, 311), (0.02,415), (0.03, 462), (0.04, 483)

9. (100p, AOQ) pairs are (1, 0.972), (2, 0.638), (4, 1.436), (5, 1.040), (6, 0.660), (8, 0.200); AOQL ≈ 1.7%

11. 1, 44; 5, 327; 8, 587

13. 2, 82; 6, 162; 14, 310

15. 3, 195

17. 4, 266

19. 5, 175

21. 0.69

23. (a) *Ac* but *N* in future
(b) *Re* and *N* in future
(c) *Ac* and *R* continues

27. (a) $n = 70$; $Ac = 0$, $Re = 1$
(b) $n = 50$; (#, 2), (#, 2), (0, 2), (0, 3), (1, 3), (1, 3), (2, 3)

29. *T*, *T*

31. No

Chapter 7

1. 28, 0, 62, 4, LQL = 10.0%

3. 130, 4, 260, 19

5. $(P_a)_{\text{I}} = (P_0)_{\text{I}}$
$(P_a)_{\text{II}} + (P_1)_{\text{I}} (P_{3 \text{ or less}})_{\text{II}} + (P_2)_{\text{I}} (P_{2 \text{ or less}})_{\text{II}} + (P_3)_{\text{I}} (P_{1 \text{ or less}})_{\text{II}} + (P_4)_{\text{I}} (P_0)_{\text{II}}$
$(P_a)_{\text{both}} = (P_a)_{\text{I}} + (P_a)_{\text{II}}$

7. 85, 1

9. (p, P_a) pairs are (0.05, 0.908), (0.10, 0.738), (0.15, 0.574), (0.20, 0.438), (0.25, 0.329)

11. $d_a = -2.43 + 0.12n$, $d_r = 3.12 + 0.12n$

13. 15, 25, 32

15. (f, i) pairs are ($\frac{1}{3}$, 321), ($\frac{1}{5}$, 498), ($\frac{1}{25}$, 1147)

19. 303

21. Type 1, *Ac* lot

23. $8.21\% < 9.80\%$, *Ac* lot

25. $1.75\% > 1.30\%$, *Re* lot

Chapter 8

1. 0.78

3. 0.06 difference

5. 0.019

7. (θ, P_a) pairs are (2000, 0.993), (1000, 0.909), (800, 0.832), (600, 0.642), (400, 0.301), (200, 0.009)

9. 80, 20, 160

11. 39, 8, 300

13. 12, 2, 94

INDEX